Paul Cooke is Professor of German Cultural Studies at the University of Leeds, UK.

Chris Homewood is a Lecturer in German and World Cinema at the University of Leeds, UK.

TAURIS
WORLD
CINEMA
SERIES

Series Editor: Lúcia Nagib, Professor of World Cinemas, University of Leeds

Advisory Board: Laura Mulvey (UK), Donald Richie (Japan), Robert Stam (USA), Ismail Xavier (Brazil)

The aim of the **Tauris World Cinema Series** is to reveal and celebrate the richness and complexity of film art across the globe, exploring a wide variety of cinemas set within their own cultures and as they interconnect in a global context.

The books in the series will represent innovative scholarship, in tune with the multicultural character of contemporary audiences, and they will draw upon an international authorship, comprising academics, film writers and journalists.

Prominent strands will include **World Film Theory**, offering new theoretical approaches and re-assessments of major movements, filmmakers, genres, technologies and stars; **New Cinemas**, focusing on recent film revivals in different parts of the world; and **new translations** into English of international milestones of film theory and criticism.

Books in the series include:

Theorizing World Cinema
Edited by Lúcia Nagib, Chris Perriam and Rajinder Dudrah

East Asian Cinemas: Exploring Transnational Connections on Film
Edited by Leon Hunt and Leung Wing-Fai

Lebanese Cinema: Imagining the Civil War and Beyond
By Lina Khatib

Brazil on Screen: Cinema Novo, New Cinema, Utopia
By Lúcia Nagib

Contemporary New Zealand Cinema
Edited by Ian Conrich and Stuart Murray

New Turkish Cinema: Belonging, Identity and Memory
By Asuman Suner

New Directions in German Cinema
Edited by Paul Cooke and Chris Homewood

New Argentine Cinema:
By Jens Andermann

Queries, ideas and submissions to:
Series Editor: Professor Lúcia Nagib – l.nagib@leeds.ac.uk
Cinema Editor at I.B.Tauris, Philippa Brewster – philippabrewster@gmail.com

New Directions in
German Cinema

Edited by Paul Cooke and Chris Homewood

I.B. TAURIS
LONDON · NEW YORK

Published in 2011 by I.B.Tauris & Co. Ltd
6 Salem Road, London W2 4BU
175 Fifth Avenue, New York NY 10010
www.ibtauris.com

Distributed in the United States and Canada Exclusively by Palgrave
Macmillan, 175 Fifth Avenue, New York NY 10010

ISBN PB: 978 1 84885 907 4
ISBN HB: 978 1 84885 908 1

A full CIP record for this book is available from the British Library
A full CIP record for this book is available from the Library of Congress
Library of Congress catalog card: available

Typeset in Stone Serif by Dexter Haven Associates Ltd, London
Printed and bound in Great Britain by TJ International, Padstow, Cornwall

CONTENTS

LIST OF ILLUSTRATIONS

All images taken from the DVD release of the film, except Figures 13.1 and 13.2 which are courtesy of Wüste Film © WÜSTE Film, Kerstin Stelter.

CONTRIBUTORS

Marco Abel is Associate Professor of English and Film Studies at the University of Nebraska, where he teaches film history, film theory and continental philosophy. The author of *Violent Affect: Literature, cinema, and critique after representation* (University of Nebraska Press, 2007), he currently focuses on contemporary German cinema, specifically the cinema of the 'Berlin School'. His book-project-in-progress on the subject, *The Berlin School: Toward a minor cinema*, is under contract with Camden House. Some of his recent publications on German cinema – critical essays on and interviews with directors such as Christian Petzold, Oskar Roehler, Dominik Graf, Christoph Hochhäusler, Andreas Dresen, the Berlin School and the filmmakers of the *Kölner Gruppe* (Cologne Group) – have appeared in *Quarterly Review of Film and Video*, *Cineaste*, *New German Critique* and *Senses of Cinema*.

Daniela Berghahn is Reader in Film Studies in the Media Arts Department at Royal Holloway, University of London. She is the author of *Hollywood Behind the Wall: The cinema of East Germany* (Manchester University Press, 2005) and co-editor of *Unity and Diversity in the New Europe* (2000) and *Millennial Essays on Film and Other German Studies* (2002). She led the international Research Network 'Migrant and Diasporic Cinema in Contemporary Europe' which was funded by the Arts and Humanities Research Council and resulted in two edited volumes, *European Cinema in Motion: Migrant and diasporic film in contemporary Europe* (with Claudia Sternberg, Palgrave, 2010) and a special issue of *New Cinemas*, 'Turkish German Dialogues on Screen' (2009). She currently holds an AHRC Research Fellowship for a project on The Diasporic Family in Cinema and is writing a monograph entitled *Far-flung Families in Film* (Edinburgh University Press).

David Clarke is Senior Lecturer in German at the University of Bath. He studied at the Universities of Leeds, London and Swansea and has taught at the Johannes Gutenberg University in Mainz and Nottingham Trent University. His main research interests are East German literature,

German film and contemporary German literature. He is author of the monograph *'Diese merkwürdige Kleinigkeit einer Vision': Christoph Hein's social critique in transition* (Rodopi, 2002). He has edited *German Cinema since Unification* (Continuum, 2006), with Bill Niven, *Christoph Hein* (University of Wales Press, 2000), with Arne De Winde, *Reinhard Jirgl: Perspektiven, lesarten, kontexte* (Rodopi, 2007) and, with Renate Rechtien, *The Politics of Place in Post-War Germany* (Edwin Mellen, 2009).

Paul Cooke is Professor of German Cultural Studies at the University of Leeds. He is the author of *Speaking the Taboo: A study of the work of Wolfgang Hilbig* (Rodopi, 2000), the 'Pocket Essential' *on German Expressionist Films* (Pocket Essential Press, 2002), and *Representing East Germany: From colonization to nostalgia* (Berg, 2005). His edited books include *World Cinema's 'Dialogues' with Hollywood* (Palgrave, 2007), with Stuart Taberner, *German Culture, Politics and Literature into the Twenty-First Century: Beyond normalization* (Camden House, 2006) and with Marc Silberman, *Screening War: Perspectives on German suffering* (Camden House, 2010). He is currently writing a monograph for Manchester University Press on contemporary German cinema.

John E. Davidson is Associate Professor of Germanic Languages and Literatures and Director of Film Studies at Ohio State University. His research interests cover German film and visual culture, post-Enlightenment literature, and contemporary critical theories. He has published articles on the Sudanese novelist Tayeb Salih, New German Cinema, black humour, Uwe Johnson, representations of the radical Right, post-Wall cinema, and Wolfgang Liebeneiner, as well as the monograph *Deterritorializing the New German Cinema* (University of Minnesota Press, 1999). He co-edited with Sabine Hake *Take Two: German cinema of the fifties* (Berghahn, 2007), and has just completed a book manuscript on 'Ottomar Domnick: Father of the Other German Cinema'. His next projects will be a study of discourses of automobility in German film and serving as Editor-in-Chief of the *Journal of Short Film*.

Owen Evans is Senior Lecturer in the Department of Media at Edge Hill University. He has published on German literature and culture, especially GDR literature, with a monograph on Günter de Bruyn, *Ein Training im Ich-Sagen: Personal authenticity in the prose work of Günter de Bruyn* (Peter Lang, 1996), and articles on Christoph Hein and Uwe Saeger among others. His last monograph, *Mapping the Contours of Oppression: Subjectivity, truth and fiction in recent German autobiographical treatments of totalitarianism* was published by Rodopi in 2006. He has also published on European cinema, with articles on topics such as *Lola rennt, Das Leben der Anderen* and the role of the film festival in Europe. His current major research project is a study of German cinema since 2000. He is also involved in an AHRC network, which looks at the cultural reconstruction of memories of the GDR since 1989. He is co-founding director of the European Cinema Research Forum (ECRF), as well as co-founding editor of the international journals *Studies in European Cinema* and the new *Journal of Popular European Culture*.

Jaimey Fisher is Associate Professor of German and Director of Film Studies at the University of California, Davis. He is the author of *Disciplining Germany: Youth, reeducation, and reconstruction after the Second World War* (Wayne State University Press, 2007) and is co-editor, with Peter Uwe Hohendahl, of *Critical Theory: Current state and future prospects* (Berghahn, 2001), with Brad Prager of *Collapse of the Conventional: German film and its politics at the turn of the twenty-first century* (Wayne State University Press, 2010) and with Barbara Mennel of *Spatial Turns: Space, place, and mobility in German literary and visual culture* (Editions Rodopi B.V., 2010). He has published articles in *Iris*, *New German Critique*, *Genre*, *German Quarterly* and *Germanic Review* and his current project analyses war films from the 1910s to the 1950s.

Christine Haase is Associate Professor of German Literature, Film and Culture at the University of Georgia in Athens. She primarily works on visual representations of the Holocaust and the Third Reich and on a variety of historical and thematic aspects of German national cinema. Her most recent book is a study of the interrelations between German and Hollywood filmmaking entitled *When Heimat Meets Hollywood: German filmmakers and America 1985–2005* (Camden House, 2007). She is currently working on her next book project, an inquiry into the relationship of fine arts and cinematic movements in Germany.

Nick Hodgin is a cultural historian and has taught German and Film Studies at the Universities of Sheffield, Liverpool and Manchester. He is the author of *Screening the East: Heimat, memory and nostalgia in German film since 1989* (Berghahn, 2011) and has co-edited with Caroline Pearce *The GDR Remembered: Representations of the East German state since 1989* (Camden House, 2011). He is currently at Sheffield conducting research on East German visual culture and on world cinema.

Chris Homewood is Lecturer in German and World Cinema at the University of Leeds. He has published several articles on the representation of urban terrorism in German-language film, the most recent of which include 'Making invisible memory visible: communicative memory and taboo in Andres Veiel's *Black Box BRD* (2001)', in Gerrit-Jan Berendse and Ingo Cornils (eds), *Baader-Meinhof Returns: History and cultural memory of German left-wing terrorism* (Rodopi, 2008) and 'Have the best ideas stood the test of time? Negotiating the legacy of '1968' in *The Edukators*', in Ingo Cornils and Sarah Waters (eds), *Memories of 1968: International perspectives* (Peter Lang, 2010). He is currently completing his first monograph, *From Baader to Prada: Representing the RAF on screen.*

Alasdair King is Senior Lecturer in German and Film Studies and Chair of Film Studies at Queen Mary, University of London. His current research interests cover German cinema (contemporary and historical case studies), contemporary European cinema, film and philosophy, film and cultural geography and film aesthetics. He is the author of *Hans Magnus Enzensberger: Writing, media, democracy* (Peter Lang, 2007) and has written articles on Christian Petzold and film noir, time-images in Edgar Reitz's *Heimat*, Enzensberger and film, Enzensberger's *Titanic*, spatial politics and the *Heimatfilm*, and landscape and ideology in National Socialist cinema. He is currently working on the films of Christian Petzold and on Edgar Reitz's *Heimat* trilogy.

Laura G. McGee is Associate Professor of German at Western Kentucky University, where she teaches courses in German language, literature, culture and film. In her research she has focused on films by graduates of the Konrad Wolf Film & Television University (HFF) in Potsdam-Babelsberg. Her publications on films by the last generation of directors educated in the GDR, on approaches to teaching film, and on the cinema of Andreas Dresen have appeared in journals such as *German Studies Review, Film History, German as a Foreign Language*, and *Colloquia Germanica.*

Rachel Palfreyman is Lecturer in German Studies at the University of Nottingham. She is the author of *Edgar Reitz's Heimat: Histories, traditions, fictions* (Peter Lang, 2000), and, with Elizabeth Boa, of *Heimat – A German Dream: Regional loyalties and national identity in German culture 1890–1990* (Oxford University Press, 2000). She has published widely on German cinema from Weimar to the present.

Brad Prager is Associate Professor of German and Film Studies at the University of Missouri. He specialises in contemporary German cinema, Holocaust studies, and the art and literature of the German Romantics. He has authored two monographs: *Aesthetic Vision and German Romanticism: Writing images* (Camden House, 2007) and *The Cinema of Werner Herzog: Aesthetic ecstasy and truth* (Wallflower Press, 2007). He has also recently edited, with David Bathrick and Michael D. Richardson, *Visualising the Holocaust: Documents, aesthetics, memory* (Camden House, 2008) and *The Collapse of the Conventional: German film and its politics at the turn of the twenty-first century* with Jaimey Fisher (Wayne State University Press, 2010).

Introduction

Beyond the cinema of consensus? New directions in German cinema since 2000

Paul Cooke and Chris Homewood

Is post-New German Cinema simply to be situated within an unchartable (*unübersichtlich*) landscape, a site without signposts, a post-histoire locus where all is familiar, foregone and forgettable?

Eric Rentschler (2000: 260)

The first decade of the new millennium has been a good one for German cinema, particularly in terms of its international visibility. In 2002, Caroline Link's *Nowhere in Africa* (*Nirgendwo in Afrika*, 2001) won the Oscar for the best foreign-language film, a feat not achieved by a German film since Volker Schlöndorff's *The Tin Drum* (*Die Blechtrommel*, 1979). This was followed by further wins in 2006 and 2007 for Florian Henckel von Donnersmarck's GDR conspiracy thriller *The Lives of Others* (*Das Leben der Anderen*, 2006) and Stefan Ruzowitzky's Austro-German co-production *The Counterfeiters* (*Die Fälscher*, 2007). Oscar nominations for German films are now regular events, from Oliver Hirschbiegel's story of the final days of Hitler, *Downfall* (*Der Untergang*, 2004) to Uli Edel's account of 1970s urban terrorism, *The Baader Meinhof Complex* (*Der Baader Meinhof Komplex*, 2008). To this we might add the nominations for best documentary of Wim Wenders's *Buena Vista Social Club* (1999) and Byambasuren Davaa and Luigi Falorni's *The Story of the Weeping Camel* (*Die Geschichte vom weinenden Kamel*, 2003), or the three wins for German short films, most recently Jochen Alexander Freydank's *Toyland* (*Spielzeugland*, 2007). And, beyond the Oscars, Hans Weingartner's *The Edukators* (*Die fetten Jahre sind vorbei*, 2004) was nominated for the Palme d'Or at Cannes, the first such

1

nomination for 11 years, the same year that Fatih Akin's story of dysfunctional love *Head-On* (*Gegen die Wand*, 2004) won the Berlinale, the first domestic win in nearly two decades.

The following chapters will explore the present state of German cinema, offering detailed examinations of a number of films and filmmakers that have helped shape German film culture since 2000. However, in order to begin our exploration of the German film landscape at the end of the decade, let us return to its start and Eric Rentschler's abidingly pessimistic snapshot of the state of German national cinema taken at the end of the 1990s. In a now seminal formulation, Rentschler identifies the most visible mode of filmmaking at the time as a 'cinema of consensus' that lacked 'oppositional energies and critical voices', a cinema that stood in stark contrast to that of the previous generation, particularly those associated with the New German Cinema. While the likes of Rainer Werner Fassbinder, Wim Wenders, Werner Herzog, Helma Sanders-Brahms and others, who had learned their craft in the turbulence of the late 1960s, produced films that 'interrogated images of the past in the hope of refining memories and catalysing changes', the increasingly star-driven cinema that Rentschler saw dominating domestic production in the 1990s showed 'a marked disinclination towards any serious political reflection or sustained historical retrospection' (2000: 263–64). By the late 1980s and throughout the 1990s, the German films that got the most press largely followed patterns set by the filmmakers of the so-called New German Comedy with a mode of production that marked a reaction to the avant-garde, overtly critical auteurist New German Cinema. Here counter-cultural strategies gave way to a desire to compete commercially, a desire driven by an industry concerned with maintaining its position within an increasingly diverse range of media. Rather than wishing to provoke or scold audiences, young directors such as Doris Dörrie (*Men* [*Männer*], 1985), Roland Emmerich (*Making Contact* [*Joey*], 1984) and Sönke Wortmann (*Maybe...Maybe Not* [*Der bewegte Mann*], 1994) began painstakingly duplicating the fast-paced, action-driven continuity style of the mainstream Hollywood entertainment film. One need only look to the biography of Roland Emmerich to note this marked turn away from the critical perspectives offered by the protest generation of filmmakers. After beginning his career at home with *Making Contact* he has since gone on to join the Hollywood 'A-List' with hits such as *ID4: Independence Day* (1996), *Godzilla* (1998), *The Day After Tomorrow* (2003) and *2012* (2009).

Although, as Christine Haase notes, such films gesture towards social concerns, notably ecological issues, they are ultimately shaped by the paroles of commercial entertainment, not critique (2007: 130). In the apt forum of a documentary short celebrating the original *Star Wars* cycle of films, Emmerich enthusiastically recalls that, as a film student in Germany, it was not Fassbinder or Wenders who provided him with aspirational models of filmmaking but George Lucas and his blockbuster trilogy.[1] This was a shift, moreover, that in turn seemed to reflect a broader trend in German society as a whole in the aftermath of the *Wende* – the German term used to denote the fall of the Berlin Wall and subsequent unification – as the ideological values of the West German 68er generation began to be challenged by the proponents of the much-vaunted German *Spaßgesellschaft* ('fun society') of the mid-1990s. With the world ostensibly now existing in a post-ideological, post-historical phase, where the battles of the Cold War had been won by the forces of Western market capitalism, German society was gripped, its critics charged, by an addiction to amusement, to the next 'kick' to be found amidst the seductive slogans of consumer pop culture (Politycki 1998: 19). Thus films presented 'tableaux of mobile young professionals', preoccupied by 'careers, relationships and lifestyles' (Rentschler 2000: 272). As such, they presented stories that could take place as easily in New York as they could in Munich. However, as filmmakers turned away from social engagement to stories that did not appear to be specifically German in either their form or content, German cinema lost much of the international appeal enjoyed by the New German Cinema. While a few figures, such as Emmerich, found success in Hollywood, those who aped Hollywood from home offered little of interest to international cinema audiences, their work being perceived as somehow still 'too German and yet not German enough' (Rentschler 2000: 275).

In the first decade of the new millennium, the notion of a 'cinema of consensus' remains a key concept in discussions of contemporary German film. At the same time, we see the debate Rentschler's essay began continue to develop as the cinematic landscape has shifted. Of course, as Rentschler discusses at the end of his essay, while the 'cinema of consensus' was dominant, there *were* other voices to be heard, voices that have gradually grown in volume. By the late 1990s the New German Comedy of the previous decade was on the wane. In turn, it was now possible to find evidence of a form of filmmaking that was, once again, discovering an ability more obviously 'to take risks', as the

New German Cinema had before it, and thus to challenge the banal yuppie-lifestyle films that dominated the 1990s, the party of the *Spaßgesellschaft* having now given way to the hangover of a post-9/11 world of global terrorism and economic recession. During the last decade, many of the marginal filmmakers Rentschler mentions in his earlier essay, such as Tom Tykwer, Hans-Christian Schmid and Fatih Akin have moved into the mainstream, producing films that are both aesthetically challenging and offer a more complex critical assessment of the state of the German nation than the earlier comedies. In such films we at times find echoes of the New German Cinema, and indeed the critical legacy of the East German DEFA (Deutsche Film-Aktiengesellschaft) tradition.[2] In the work of Vanessa Jopp (*Forget America* [*Vergiss Amerika*], 2000), Wolfgang Becker (*Good Bye, Lenin!*, 2003), Andreas Dresen (*Grill Point* [*Halbe Treppe*], 2002; *Summer in Berlin* [*Sommer vorm Balkon*], 2005), Michael Schorr (*Schulze Gets the Blues*, 2003; *Schröder's Wonderful World* [*Schröders wunderbare Welt*], 2006), Christian Klandt (*World City* [*Weltstadt*], 2008), all of whom have gained critical acclaim, the legacies of Germany's divided film and media culture helps shape the way these filmmakers explore the continuing economic and cultural asymmetries between the east and west of the country.

Others, most notably Akin (*Head-On*, 2004; *The Edge of Heaven* [*Auf der anderen Seite*], 2007), but also Lars Becker (*Kanak Attack*, 2000), Torsten Wacker (*Super Sex* [*Süperseks*], 2004), Anno Saul (*Kebab Connection*, 2005) and Özgür Yildirim (*Chiko*, 2008) examine the place of the Turkish diaspora within the Berlin Republic. Here we find one particularly obvious example of the ways in which German film must be seen increasingly within a transnational rather than national context, both with regard to the manner in which films are produced and the stories they choose to tell. The 'transnational turn' in German filmmaking is, moreover, a challenge to all the country's filmmakers, whatever their social or ethnic background, provoking them to reflect upon Germany's place in the world as well as contemporary constructions of Germanness. In this regard, one might mention Dani Levy's investigation of contemporary German-Jewish identity, *Go for Zucker* (*Alles auf Zucker*, 2004), Angelina Maccarone's examination of a gay asylum seeker struggling with her sexual, gender and ethnic identity in Germany, *Unveiled* (*Fremde Haut*, 2005), or Hans-Christian Schmid's exploration of German–Polish relations *Distant Lights* (*Lichter*, 2003). Within this context, we also find somewhat curiously perhaps a rediscovery of that most maligned of German domestic genres, the *Heimatfilm* ('homeland film'), a genre that reached its zenith in the 1950s when a string of films presented images of the nation as a chocolate-box rural idyll. In recent years we have seen the genre updated, developed and at times challenged in the ongoing work of Edgar Reitz (*Heimat 3*, 2004) – whose roots can be traced back to the New German Cinema and its critical reinterpretation of the tradition – as well as in work by younger filmmakers such as Marcus H. Rosenmüller (*Grave Decisions* [*Wer früher stirbt ist länger tod*], 2006) or Hans Steinbichler (*Hierankl*, 2003) who take an at times ironic look at the continuing power of the local in the face of the transnational and ultimately the global. Steinbichler's critical engagement with the morality of the 68er generation in his films also points the way to the renewed interrogation of Germany's past we find in the work of many younger filmmakers, be that Robert Thalheim's investigation of the tensions between global economics and the memorialisation of the Holocaust in *And Along Come Tourists* (*Am Ende kommen Touristen*, 2007), those films mentioned above that examine the continuing ramifications of unification in the former GDR, or the numerous films that explore the legacies of 1970s West German terrorism such as Christian Petzold's, *The State I Am In* (*Die innere Sicherheit*, 2000), Weingartner's *The Edukators* (2004) or, perhaps more obliquely, Marcus Mittermeier's, *Quiet as a Mouse* (*Muxmäuschenstill*, 2004).

Along with social critique, contemporary film also evidences a far greater degree of aesthetic experimentation than the New German Comedies of the 1990s. In this regard, Tom Tykwer's surprise international hit *Run Lola Run* (*Lola rennt*, 1998) deserves special mention. On the face of it, Tykwer's American-styled, techno-fuelled romp through Berlin as Lola races to secure the money necessary to save her otherwise doomed boyfriend can be categorised as part of the trend away from political critique to a concern with relationships and lifestyle discussed above. This was a film for the globalised generation, for whom US-based pop culture is 'no longer experienced as foreign' (Rentschler 2000: 272). A film for the 'joy stick generation', as Nick James puts it, *Run Lola Run's* 'clock-driven, goal oriented narrative, not dissimilar in concept to a computer game [...] was itself thought to be as much a symbol of the Hollywoodising of German culture as any kind of breakout' (James 2006: 26). That said, *Run Lola Run* was also clearly different in tone to the comedies of the 1990s. As Margit Sinka notes, for some critics, if nothing else 'the relief at not having to comment on yet another specimen of the Cola Light, middle-class relationship comedies that had proliferated in recent years was palpable' (Sinka 2000). Moreover, although the film's aesthetic veneer might speak the culturally amorphous language of the *Spaßgesellschaft*, the sheer variety of filmic techniques deployed by Tykwer (from the mix of live-action and animation, the extra-diegetic use of music to propel the narrative forward and, not least, the foray into computer-game territory) led numerous commentators to suggest that the director 'had not only created something new but had expanded the possibilities of the filmic medium itself' (Sinka 2000).

In the last decade Tykwer has continued to explore the visual potential of the cinema screen with films such as *Heaven* (2002) and *Perfume: The Story of a Murderer* (2006), albeit to a generally far more mixed reception. In a similar vein, Oskar Roehler has undertaken a self-conscious reinterpretation of Fassbinder's melodrama (*No Place to Go* [*Die Unberührbare*], 2000; *Agnes and his Brother* [*Agnes und seine Brüder*], 2004), and in so doing become one of a number of filmmakers, along with the likes of Akin, Petzold, or the now deceased *enfant terrible* of post-Wall German film and theatre Christoph Schlingensief, to be viewed, more or less successfully, as having inherited Fassbinder's mantel through their ability to create aesthetically challenging cinema that can also indulge audiences' desire for popular genres. At the same time, we find filmmakers looking more broadly at how aesthetic experimentation in the tradition of the New German Cinema can go hand in hand with the kind of social critique it offered. Those filmmakers categorised as part of the so-called Berlin School, for example, constitute, in Marco Abel's words, 'the first significant (collective) attempt at advancing the aesthetics of cinema within German narrative filmmaking since the New German Cinema' (2008). Coined at the start of the decade, the term 'Berlin School' originally referred to three graduates of the Deutsche Film und Fernsehakademie Berlin: Angela Schanelec (*Mein langsames Leben* [*Passing Summer*], 2001; *Marseille*, 2004), Thomas Arslan (*A Fine Day* [*Der schöne Tag*], 2001) and Petzold (*The State I Am In*, 2000; *Yella*, 2007) (Worthmann 2001). However, as Abel also notes 'the Berlin School label is somewhat misleading when its scope is widened to a second generation of filmmakers' (2008) which includes graduates of the Hochschule für bildende Künste, Hamburg: Ulrich Köhler (*Bungalow*, 2002; *Windows on Monday* [*Montag kommen die Fenster*], 2006) and Henner Winckler (*School Trip* [*Klassenfahrt*], 2002); graduates of the Hochschule für Fernsehen und Film in Munich: Benjamin Heisenberg (*Sleeper* [*Schläfer*], 2005; *The Robber* [*Der Räuber*], 2010) and Maren Ade (*The Forest for the Trees* [*Der Wald vor lauter Bäumen*], 2003; *Everyone Else* [*Alle Anderen*], 2009); a graduate of HFF 'Konrad Wolf', Potsdam-Babelsberg: Maria Speth (*Madonnas* [*Madonnen*], 2007); as well as Valeska Grisebach, a graduate of the Viennese film school, best known for her critically acclaimed *Longing* (*Sehnsucht*, 2006), and Aysum Bademsoy, who studied theatre at Berlin's Freie Universität (*On the Outskirts* [*Am Rand der Städte*], 2006). In the work of this generation, we find a rediscovery of a Bazinian notion of realism with its emphasis on long takes and deep focus. It is perhaps no wonder, therefore, that many of these films have had their greatest success in France, where they have been feted as a 'Nouvelle Vague Allemande' (d'Ovres 2008).

At the same time, one is also reminded of the kind of slow-paced 'slacker' aesthetic to be found in contemporary American independent filmmaking, most notably in the work of the term's inventor Richard Linklater (*Slacker*, 1990) (Stone 2007). Indeed, the influence of Linklater can be felt not only on the Berlin School. Weingartner, for example, clearly learned a good deal about production techniques from his time as an assistant and extra on Linklater's 1995 film *Before Sunrise*. The connection with Linklater, moreover, highlights the way these filmmakers not only challenge the straightforward mainstream aesthetics of much of the previous generation, but also this generation's production context, as the New German Cinema had in the 1970s and Linklater, along with his Austin colleagues, did in the 1980s and 1990s. At times this challenge comes out of necessity. Many of these filmmakers have been unable to access large amounts of the public funding that still fuels the German industry due to their lack of a track record of success in the market. However, with regard to the Berlin School in particular, it also points to their sense of filmmaking as a collective endeavour, alluded to by Abel above, with directors and crews working on each other's projects, commenting on each other's scripts and using their 'house' magazine *Revolver* to publicise each other's work.[3] Thus, their work ethic, as well as the topics and aesthetics they choose to explore, questions the type of vapid individualism we see portrayed in the comedies of the 1990s, the vacuous society of this earlier decade being replaced with slow-paced, evacuated frames providing perhaps critique, perhaps a straightforward declaration of the emptiness of life after the 'end of history' which the fall of the Berlin Wall famously seemed to usher in (Fukuyama 1992).

Finally, we might remember that although the New German Comedy dominated domestic cinema in the 1990s, it would be unfair to say that the legacy of the New German Cinema was completely lost. A number of its directors, including Margarethe von Trotta, Sanders-Brahms and Schlöndorff, continued making films, although in some cases such filmmakers seemed to have lost their critical edge. Von Trotta's *The Promise* (*Das Versprechen*, 1995), for example, tells the story of a young couple separated by the building of the Berlin Wall and thus forced to grow up in two different states. Having endured great hardships, the couple are finally reunited on the night of 9 November 1989 as the Wall first opens, thereby providing a quintessential image of social 'consensus' in the unified state. As Sabine Hake puts it, the film 'presents the post-war division as the story of two young lovers divided by ideology but meant to be united; the happy ending for the nation comes with the post-ideological identity of a unified Germany' (Hake 2002: 189). The cathartic outcome of *The Promise* is a far cry from von Trotta's earlier films, such as *Marianne and Juliane* (*Die bleierne Zeit*, 1981) which challenged the hegemonic consensus surrounding the turn to terror by a radicalised youth (see Homewood 2006: 121–35). In the last decade, von Trotta has continued in a similar vein. However, she is not the only voice to be heard from those that remain of the New German Cinema. There are others that have been more adept at finding ways of using film and other visual media as a tool for critique. Be it the cinematic vistas of Wim Wenders, the critical documentaries of Werner Herzog, or the television interventions of Alexander Kluge, they all, in very different ways, continue to explore the possibilities of the screen in all its forms as a medium that can force the spectator to look at the world with new eyes, thereby challenging the role of the mainstream media as fora of consensus construction.

If some of the marginal voices of the 1990s have become more mainstream, and echoes of the New German Cinema's critique continue to reverberate, Rentschler's charge of 'consensus' nonetheless still holds in the following decade for 'the equally emphatic culture of commemoration and retrospection' that, he notes, now dominates the industry in the form of 'New German heritage films', films that have, for better or worse, been central to the industry's renewed international impact (Rentschler 2002: 4). Within all these films one finds narratives that are, on the face of it at the very least, highly consensual, generally intent, their critics suggest, upon drawing a line under the past. As we can see from the aforementioned list of the Oscar nominations, National Socialism remains a key focus for heritage filmmakers. And the Oscar nominations are merely the tip of a very large iceberg. In films such as Max Färberböck's *Aimée and Jaguar* (1999), Margarethe von Trotta's *Rosenstrasse* (2003), Volker Schlöndorff's *The Ninth Day* (*Der Neunte Tag*, 2004), Sönke Wortmann's *The Miracle of Bern* (*Das Wunder von Bern*, 2003), or Dennis Gansel's *Before the Fall* (*NaPolA: Elite für den Führer*, 2004), we find German filmmakers moving ever further away from the avant-garde, rough edged and self-reflexive sensibilities of the New German Cinema to produce slick, straightforwardly melodramatic, identificatory narratives that follow international genre rules and resonate with mainstream international film audiences. *Downfall*, for example, was sold around the world with great success as 'one of the best war movies ever made', the ostensible authenticity of the German-speaking cast giving the director and his producer Bernd Eichinger a huge market advantage over British and US depictions of the same story (Hansen 2004). Thus, in contradistinction to the failure abroad of German films in the 1990s, it would seem that today's filmmakers have at last found a way to be both German *and* international (Cooke 2006).

If we see the German heritage film as an updated version of the 'cinema of consensus', then for the likes of Hirschbiegel and Eichinger, of course, such cinematic consensus is hardly to be viewed as a weakness of contemporary German filmmaking. This is a point expressed particularly forcefully by Günter Rohrbach, President of the German Film Academy. In a vitriolic diatribe published in *Der Spiegel*, Rohrbach denounces the main German feuilletonists as 'autistic', their invariable condemnation of mainstream German cinema revealing them to be out of touch with the cinemagoing public. He questions the pejorative, patronising implications of the term 'consensus film' as it is used by numerous critics in the German press. Instead, he celebrates the term and the role such film has played in the rediscovery of mainstream domestic cinema by German audiences, questioning the purpose of these critics who seem to approach popular film with a preconceived resentment, unable to see any potential artistic merit in such films, however this might be defined (Rohrbach 2007).

Rohrbach's attack can be seen as part of a wider revaluation of German popular film culture not only by filmmakers and the media but also by the academy. As Tim Bergfelder has pointed out, while German film production since the Second World War has been dominated by mainstream entertainment films, scholars have tended to focus on the work of a small number of more esoteric filmmakers (2005). Through the work of Bergfelder and others this has shifted in recent years, as scholars have starting to re-evaluate the German popular film tradition.[4] With regard to the popular history film, specifically, commentators have begun to argue for the value of the emotional, affective power of mainstream cinema to produce what Alison Landsberg has termed 'prosthetic memory', allowing spectators to 'suture' themselves 'into pasts they have not lived', thereby offering them a 'visceral' empathetic experience of history (2004: 14). For Landsberg, it is precisely the popular film with transnational mass appeal that is particularly well placed to achieve this. She rejects the notion that a mainstream 'consensual' aesthetic must necessarily produce a conservative political message. Working at the interface of 'public' history and 'private' individual memory, such films can, in her view, complicate and problematise both, allowing the spectator to 'inhabit other people's memories *as* other people's memories and thereby respecting and recognizing difference' (2004: 24, emphasis in original). Of crucial importance in relation to the German context is, once again, the generational shift that has taken place.[5] As already discussed, the accusatory glare of the New German Cinema is now giving way to the perspective of a younger generation of artists and, more importantly, audiences who have a less fraught relationship with the past and who are hungry for knowledge. Consequently, for this new generation, the recent wave of history films with their personalised melodramatic accounts of past lives provides, it would seem, a far more immediate and accessible *experience* of the past than is to be found in earlier films.[6]

The immediacy of experience offered by these films can be seen as a particularly obvious example of what has been identified by Martin Walser and others as a new *'feeling* for History' (emphasis added) at work in the representation of German history across society, marking a new phase in the process of coming to terms with the past (quoted in von Moltke 2007: 17). For their supporters, such films are a 'symbol of emancipation', as Eckhard Fuhr puts it, writing in *Die Welt* about *Downfall*. For Fuhr, 'the Germans have their history, but that history doesn't have them by the throat any more'. This distance from the past in turn allows filmmakers at last 'to look Hitler in the eyes' and thereby effect a final 'reconciliation with the "perpetrator generation"' (2004a).

However, far from marking a moment when the past can finally be put to rest, perhaps such films actually at last mark the beginning of a genuine process of coming to terms with the nation's history. Thomas Elsaesser, for example, hints at this in his discussion of the presentation of history in the New German Cinema. Drawing on Freud's essay 'Mourning and Melancholia' ('Trauer und Melancholie', 1917) and its analysis of 'parapraxis', Elsaesser suggests that the world reflected in much of the New German Cinema was caught in an ultimately self-destructive loop of melancholic repetition, in which the films' protagonists were invariably able only to perform the failure of the nation to mourn its past, a process of mourning which is necessary for a true comprehension of the nation's guilt and which in turn could bring about the population's final redemption (2002: 182–91). For a real process of working through the past to begin, such 'performed failure' must give way to a more direct, emotional response to the past that can mourn the loss of both the 'right' and 'wrong' people, as Elsaesser puts it, a response that we see reflected perhaps in this new phase of filmmaking. On the one hand, such an emotional response might well lead to a new process of reflection. As Johannes von Moltke suggests in his analysis of *Downfall*, it is, for example, surely impossible to watch Bruno Ganz's portrayal of Hitler in a vacuum. The very fact that we, as spectators, are at times put in a position during the film where we are asked to sympathise with Hitler's point of view does not mean that we can forget his crimes. Instead, it potentially allows us to reflect anew on the nature of these crimes and the ways they have been, and can be, represented (von Moltke, 2007: 42). On the other hand, following Elsaesser, might the point of this new phase actually be to move away from critical reflection towards the straightforward sentimental expression of the pain of the past?

Thus, we are left with the question, does the affective power of these films, and the emotions they evoke in the spectator, become a means of troubling the political consensus of their diegesis, suggesting that they do, in fact, have the ability to 'refin[e] memories and catalys[e] changes', to return once more to Rentschler's critique of post-Wall German film? (2000: 263–64). Moreover, does their mass appeal, a result of their indulgence of the kind of aesthetic consensus many critics also lament, with the potential to reach a far wider audience than most of the films of the New German Cinema, make them even better placed to achieve this end? Speaking of Wolfgang Becker's international hit *Good Bye, Lenin!* (2003), which tackles the legacy of the GDR and immediate consequences of German unification, Tykwer suggests that the film 'was an unbelievable smash hit not just because it was a good comedy but because there was something that deeply moved people about the historical situation' (quoted in Tykwer 2006: 30). Is it the case that these German filmmakers, along with the likes of Akin and Roehler discussed above, have now found a way to fuse art and commercial concerns, to 'mediate between the personal and the popular, the radical and the accessible, the alternative and the mainstream' which, at the start of the decade, Rentschler saw as a hope that had died with Fassbinder (2000: 265)? Or, do they perhaps suggest that the process for which the films of the New German Cinema were a catalyst has simply entered a less reflective, more sentimental, but nonetheless equally necessary phase, where a genuine process of historical reappraisal can, at last, begin?

The impact of heritage films leads us finally to the role of the audience for German cinema and the question of film consumption, issues that further problematise the concept of national German cinema over and above the 'transnational turn' mentioned above. For whom are German films now made? The budgets spent on films such as *Downfall* or *The Baader Meinhof Complex*, which could never be amortised domestically, suggest that their primary audience is international. In the films of the Berlin School, on the other hand, often supported by *The Little Television Play* (*Das kleine Fernsehspiel*) of ZDF, Germany's second television channel, we witness the continuation of the *Autorenkino* tradition of filmmakers making the films they want to make as opposed to ones that will sell. In both cases, how does the context of their exhibition impact upon their form? How did the likes of Eichinger negotiate a media world that is now even more diverse than it was in the 1990s? Has this diversity led, in some respects ironically, even more forcefully to the type of homogeneity identified by Rentschler? What has been the impact of the digital explosion and the demand this has created for ever more content? How does the kind of interactivity offered by 'Web 2.0' technology, which allows consumers to manipulate footage to create their own 'mash up' versions of familiar film texts that can be shared around the globe in seconds, challenge the concept of German film as a national cultural product controlled by major companies? Moreover, do the new film texts produced, as well as a whole host of other web phenomena, from interactive fanzines to Twitter, provide further evidence of the ability of consumers to undermine or emphasise the politics of any ostensibly consensual film?

This volume is the result of a project developed by the Centre for World Cinemas and German Studies colleagues in the School of Modern Languages and Cultures at the University of Leeds, which brought together an international group of scholars for a workshop in 2009 to discuss recent trends in German filmmaking. In all but one of the chapters, authors offer a detailed examination of an individual film, which has been chosen as a case study of one or more of the trends outlined above. All of the films under discussion have had an international release and in many cases will be well known to international audiences. Moreover, all are available on DVD with English subtitles. The one exception to the single-film format, but not to the question of availability, is John E. Davidson's examination of Alexander Kluge's 'minutefilms', brought together for the first time as opening shorts on the Zweitausendeins edition of his collected cinema films (2007). Kluge has been a key theorist and practitioner of German filmmaking since the 1960s. Within the changing consumption context of visual images described above, Kluge gave up producing films for cinema in the 1980s at a time of falling audiences and the growing domination of television in the wake of its deregulation in the Federal Republic, a deregulation which saw a growth in private television channels that has continued to accelerate in the digital age. For the last three decades, Kluge has seen television, and more recently DVD, as better media than cinema for his exploration of film as a tool of political engagement. Through an examination of competing conceptualisations of time in his work, evoked particularly clearly in his continual recourse to the image of 'the elephant', Davidson highlights the ways in which Kluge challenges straightforward notions of chronological time to create filmic spaces that open up the representation of time to the possibilities of imagination. In so doing, he forces the spectator to reconsider their own understanding of time and, more specifically, their relationship to German history.

It is the reconsideration of history to which we then turn in more detail in several of the following chapters as we discuss the dominant place of heritage cinema in Germany today, exploring if any such films allow the potential for a more differentiated, critical engagement with the past than the concept of 'consensus' might suggest. In Chapters 2–4 we examine the continued importance of the Nazi past within the nation's cinematic landscape. Christine Haase (Chapter 2) uses her analysis of Hirschbiegel's *Downfall* to discuss the utility of the term heritage film itself, first used within the context of British 1980s costume dramas, for German films of the new millennium. Developing the work of Lutz Koepnick, Haase looks at how the concept of heritage intersects with debates on cinematic realism and the ethics of representation when it comes to the crimes of National Socialism. If, as in Haase's view, Hirschbiegel fails to cast new light on the end of the Third Reich in his quest for a hyper-authentic portrayal of this moment in history and, specifically, of the 'human' side of Hitler, Owen Evans (Chapter 3) suggests that this is precisely the achievement of Marc Rothemund's *Sophie Scholl: The Final Days* (*Sophie Scholl: Die letzten Tage*, 2005). Based on the transcripts of Scholl's interrogation after her arrest, Evans examines the multiple ways Rothemund uses our greater historical understanding of events since the opening of GDR archives post-unification to allow us to get nearer to Scholl as a person than previous versions of the story, to humanise the myth and thus to come to a more profound understanding of her motivations for, and achievements in, resisting the Nazi regime. In contrast, Brad Prager's analysis of *The Counterfeiters* (Chapter 4) focuses on the role of fabrication in Stefan Ruzowitzky's account of Operation Bernhard, the plan to flood the US and UK economy with false currency produced by Jewish inmates of the Sachsenhausen concentration camp during the War. Prager extends the concept of counterfeiting to the very narrative strategy employed by Ruzowitzky who, on the one hand, was forced to fictionalise elements of the story out of deference to Holocaust survivors, but on the other uses the imaginative possibilities of film – albeit in a radically different fashion to Kluge – to explore the limits of representation when it comes to the contemporary 'genre' of the Holocaust movie. This is then placed within the context of the 'transnational turn' discussed above, the film being a high-profile German–Austrian co-production.

Chapters 5–8 remain with the question of history, moving to the postwar period and the legacies of German division as they are played out within the framework of the heritage genre, broadly defined. Nick Hodgin (Chapter 5) points to the transnational consumption context of Becker's, *Good Bye, Lenin!*, examining the film's potential as a pedagogical tool for audiences both at home and abroad, a potential that allows the film to escape a dismissive definition as a consensus film. In so doing, he suggests ways in which the film's depiction of *Ostalgie* – the much-discussed phenomenon of popular nostalgia for aspects of East German life, most clearly visible in a contemporary fascination with GDR material culture – opens up spaces for a more critical engagement with the place of the East German past in today's Berlin Republic. Paul Cooke (Chapter 6) identifies a similar potential in Florian Henckel von Donnersmarck's self-declared consensus film, *The Lives of Others*, which Cooke seeks to reposition within the critical debate it generated. He rejects the claim that the film is a 'corrective' to the type of *Ostalgie* one finds in films such as *Good Bye, Lenin!*, as many of those commentators who defended *The Lives of Others* claimed. Indeed, he suggests the film exhibits a far less reflective approach to contemporary *Ostalgie* than Becker's film, if anything offering the type of fetishisation of the past one finds in *Downfall*. At the same time, he argues that the construction of the Stasi within the film nonetheless might offer a more ambiguous engagement with GDR historiography than many of its detractors suggest. In Chapters 7 and 8 we turn to the history of the Federal Republic. Chris Homewood (Chapter 7) examines Uli Edel's *The Baader Meinhof Complex* within the broader rediscovery of German urban terrorism as a topos for the nation's filmmakers. This he compares with its earlier representation by the filmmakers of the New German Cinema. In so doing, he looks at the ways in which the film plays to the pop sensibilities of the children of the *Spaßgesellschaft*, and its consumption of the images of the past, Landsberg's 'prosthetic memory' repackaged as a form of 'terrorist chic', while highlighting the manner in which the film seems to reinstate the type of 'black and white' analyses of the period that dominated the television and newspaper media in the 1970s, but which other filmmakers had long since striven to deconstruct. David Clarke similarly looks at the representation of the 1970s Federal Republic in his examination of Hans-Christian Schmid's *Requiem*, the latest film version of the tragic story of Anneliese Michel, a young student convinced she had been possessed by the devil. Schmid, singled out by Rentschler as a notable exception within the landscape of consensus cinema, provides a counterpoint to the commodification of the past offered by Edel and other proponents of heritage cinema. In his analysis of the film, Clarke discusses the ways in which Schmid engages critically with the Heimat tradition. However, unlike filmmakers such as Marcus H. Rosenmüller mentioned above, who have of late similarly rediscovered the genre of the *Heimatfilm*, Schmid challenges both the cosy construction of Germany as rural idyll, to be found in the films of the 1950s, as well as the critical reinterpretation of the *Heimatfilm* in the 1960s and 1970s by the New German Cinema, his film, Clarke suggests, exploding the very myth of Heimat itself.

In many of the films that explore Germany's problematic past we clearly learn as much, if not more, about the moment of their construction as of the time they represent. In the next four chapters this becomes the explicit focus, as we explore the work of a number of filmmakers who have moved from the margins at the start of the decade to the mainstream by its end, bringing with them a more critical view of German society and its place in the world than can be identified in much of mainstream 1990s cinema. Moreover, we look at some new innovative filmmakers that are themselves on the margins today, examining how they reinterpret and reconfigure the legacy of the New German Cinema and its project of critique through both the form and content of their work. Rachel Palfreyman (Chapter 9) continues the volume's interrogation of the relationship between the nation's troubled past and its present from the perspective of contemporary society along with the discussion of the aesthetic strategies of the *Heimatfilm* begun by Clarke. Palfreyman explores the ways in which Weingartner's *The Edukators* uses a rural Heimat idyll as the location for his encounter between the 'slacker' generation of today's youth and the 68er generation which has now put its days of rebellion behind it, an encounter she reads through the prism of Guy Debord's *Society of the Spectacle* (1967), Debord's critique of rampant consumerism speaking to the carnivalesque protests orchestrated by the young activists in the film. Jaimey Fisher (Chapter 10) similarly explores the legacy of the 68er generation on contemporary film, here with specific reference to the New German Cinema. Through an analysis of Petzold's *Yella*, the final part of his *Ghost Trilogy*, Fisher discusses the ways in which this founding member of the Berlin School reformulates the language of genre cinema in order to present his critique of a post-unification German society in the grip of late capitalism, Petzold's self-reflexive engagement with the horror film operating in a similar fashion to Fassbinder's reworking of Sirkian melodrama.

Marco Abel (Chapter 11) turns to a 'second generation' member of the Berlin School's, placing Valeska Grisebach's *Longing* within the context of the school's broader political use of realism as an aesthetic approach to create a counter-cinema to what he defines as the 'state films' endorsed by the likes of Rohrbach. Here, Abel examines the painterly quality of Grisebach's approach, which forces the spectator to look anew and thus reappraise the everyday world of the East German province she presents in her film, an aesthetic that foregrounds the affective rather than representational qualities of film as a medium.

The question of realism is also central to the work of Andreas Dresen, one of the last filmmakers to be trained at the GDR's state film school, although, as Laura G. McGee (Chapter 12) notes, Dresen's approach to cinematic form is far removed from the work of the Berlin School, having more in common with the 'type of fly on the wall documentary' aesthetic one finds in the work of those artists associated with the Dogme 95 Manifesto. In her analysis of *Cloud 9* (*Wolke 9*, 2008), McGee explores Dresen's representation of sexual desire among the over-sixties in a film that challenges what continues to be a taboo topic within contemporary culture while also pointing to a broader demographic shift within cinema audiences, a shift which demands that the topics chosen by filmmakers increasingly reflect the reality of an aging population. Chapter 13 returns to the role of genre in contemporary film in Daniela Berghahn's examination of Fatih Akin's *Head-On*. Highlighting the interconnected nexus of traditions at play in his film, Berghahn explores Akin's position as a star transnational filmmaker, the 'diasporic optic' of this German-Turkish artist both speaking to and resisting the potentially homogenising forces of globalisation. In so doing, Berghahn offers a further example of the legacy of Fassbinder in contemporary German cinema while at the same time, pointing to important shifts away from the national paradigm of film production that dominated the period of the New German Cinema.

Finally, we return to both the question of the changing contemporary media world and the continuing role of the New German Cinema generation itself in Alasdair King's study of *Heimat 3* (2004) by Edgar Reitz. Reitz, like Kluge, was one of the original signatories of the Oberhausen Manifesto (1962), a foundational document of what would later be termed the New German Cinema. In this third instalment of his *Heimat* epic, Reitz would seem to offer a stark contrast to the view of contemporary Germany found in the work of Akin, focusing on an image of Germanness that seems to elide the hybrid, multicultural nature of so much identity formation in today's Berlin Republic. In so doing, Reitz would also seem to recuperate the image of Heimat called into question by Schmid's *Requiem*. Thus, it might seem that this 'founding member' of the New German Cinema ironically offers one of the most quintessentially consensual images of contemporary Germany to be found among the films examined here. However, as King suggests, the conservative impulse that has been identified throughout Reitz's work must be balanced against his own deconstruction of the Heimat tradition which, in a very different manner to Schmid, nonetheless still challenges the notion of Heimat itself. Specifically, Reitz calls into question the value of conceptualising Heimat in contemporary Germany as a spatial term rooted in the specific geography of the German province. Instead, Heimat is constructed as the product of what King defines – following Nick Couldry and Anna McCarthy – as the nation's changing 'mediaspaces' (2004: 1), in which imagined communities come together fleetingly through their collective identification with mediated images rather than through the collective ownership of physical space. As a result, in its presentation of the transitory nature of such imagined communities, the film ultimately does reflect, albeit in a manner far removed from Akin's work, the changing nature of contemporary Germany within a globalised world, in which populations are on the move and images circulate transnationally.

We cannot hope to cover all aspects of a film culture that currently produces well over two hundred features a year in a single collection. We do not, for example, discuss the comedies of Michael 'Bully' Herbig (*The Shoe of Manitu* [*Der Schuh des Manitu*], 2001) *Dreamship Surprise: Period 1* [(*T)Raumschiff Surprise – Periode 1*], 2004) that have been hugely successful domestically, or in any detail the work of those filmmakers, such as Emmerich or Mennan Yapo, currently making their mark in Hollywood. Nor do we examine the role of Eastern Europe in the changing transnational context of German film production, found in films such as Schmid's *Distant Light* or Lars Büchel's road movie *Peas at 5.30* (*Erbsen auf halb 6*, 2004). Nonetheless, the films we do examine allow us to begin the process of recharting the landscape of German cinema that seemed 'unchartable' in the 1990s, highlighting the variety of ways in which German cinema continues to confirm and question definitions of 'consensus'.

Notes

1 See *The Force is With Them: The Legacy of 'Star Wars'* (no credited director, USA, 2004), available on the 'bonus material' disc included as part of the 2004 Fox Home Entertainment DVD release of Lucas's *Star Wars Trilogy*.

2 Throughout this volume we have adopted the convention of using 'East German' as a synonym for the GDR and 'east German' to refer to the region within the unified state.
3 See the journal website, http://www.revolver-film.de/.
4 See, for example, Rentschler 1996, Koepnick 2002b, Halle and McCarthy 2003, von Moltke 2005.
5 For further discussion see Daniela Berghahn 2006b: 294–308, in particular 296.
6 For an overview of the ways in which popular films have engaged with historical representation see Landy 1997, Toplin 2002, Rosenstone 2006.

Chapter 1

'A kind of species memory': the time of the elephants in the space of Alexander Kluge's cinematic principle

John E. Davidson

Since I have to decide by 4p.m. which side of the civil war I will put myself on, I have just taken up the study of philosophy.

Willi Tobler

MAKING TIME IN SPACE

Alexander Kluge's time is not like everyone else's: it is made rather than spent. In the colloquial sense, Kluge 'makes time' for things that fall outside our normal experience (*Erlebnis*) in order to give a sense of the illusive complexity of experience (*Erfahrung*) that seeks expression in what he understands to be art. In a more abstract sense, within given temporal forms – say the length of a feature film or the 24-minute duration of his 'cultural window' television shows – he produces gestures to different modes of time that spring out of the limits we use to organise experience. Both deadly earnest and yet not serious, the epigraph above gives one example of the inherent tensions between different times that Kluge makes palpable. It is taken from the middle of *Willi Tobler and the Decline of the Sixth Fleet* (*Willi Tobler und der Untergang der 6. Flotte*, 1972), a science-fiction fantasy that displaces one particular instance of coming to terms with the past – namely with the myriad historical elements of Stalingrad – into the outer space of some 'future'. This illustrates that Kluge does not make time without a spatial context, be it a metaphorical space, the universe itself, or a particular place of interaction with images: for Kluge the cinema exists before celluloid and after the digital, and comprises the fantasy space to make time. His post-New German Cinema work answers the rhetorical questions once posed by Eric Rentschler, which serve as the epigraph to this volume with both a resounding 'yes' and 'no'. Yes, the new direction in post-Wall cinema leads through spaces that are yet uncharted, where the signposts signify differently. But no, this is not a 'post-histoire locus where all is familiar, forgone and forgettable'; rather, it is a space where time is made available to fantasy production.

The opening of *The Indomitable Leni Peickert* (*Die unbezähmbare Leni Peickert*, 1970) produces a different time sequence from the one gestured to by Willi Tobler, one that works literally 'in the viewer's head', a reference point Kluge has used for as long as anyone can remember:

> [Medium shot of a woman, Leni Peickert, sitting, who speaks.]
> My father had a favourite idea: Elephants' Graveyard. The elephants are led into the arena. Then they stand there…do this [She swings upper body lightly back and forth]. The lights go out and the elephants are led out, quietly. [Cut to close up of one side of an elephant's face, which shakes some.] Then come the elephant trainers [cut to baby elephant moving out and in toward the camera] and scatter bones around the arena. The lights go up again…
> [Cut to drawing of a pre-historic creature.]

The previous generation's circus performer wanted to generate a number to entertain the audience through the 'elephants' graveyard', a trick that would compress the time moving from that of a living being to its skeletal remains into a few seconds through a trick of light and dark. It is significant that the film viewer does not see that idea realised, but rather hears it as a meta-filmic story: the description of an attempt to integrate the dialectical thought affected by montage into real-time experience. The actual deployment of montage – the clips of the elephants and then the drawing of the now extinct dinosaur – produces a heightened experience of the time of living species that necessarily has no relation to the actual lived time of the spectators and, yet, determines them nonetheless.

These opening examples touch on a number of elements central to Kluge's film work – time, an invocation of dialectical thought, humour, production rather than consumption, film form and questions of space, and, well, elephants. Leni Peickert's story parallels the one that her brother, Manfred, tells near the beginning of *Artists Under the Big Top: Perplexed* (*Die Artisten in der Zirkuskuppel: Ratlos*, 1968). He wondered if he could attach elephants to the rigging and have them fly around the arena above the crowd; you could, the manager responds, but I don't know if the construction would hold. To the repeated objection that the idea seemed too irrational, Manfred reports having replied that it would produce a strong effect and elicit a powerful emotion. Ever mindful of the dialectic of 'powerful emotions' in the circus of the cinema, Kluge again refrains from staging this trick. Nonetheless, the *Artists Under the Big Top* goes on to establish the elephant as a prime visual element in Kluge's treatment of the (German) bourgeoisie. This treatment combines images, textual titles and/or cultural associations, and commentary in a mode that might be thought of as emblematic.[1] The present chapter will trace out the interrelation that such elements continue to have in the era since Kluge stopped producing for the cinema in the late 1980s. As the number of television shows, interviews, literary works and collaborative projects has increased exponentially since that time, I limit myself here to material from the 'Extras' that appear on the box set of his collected cinema films (*Sämtliche Kinofilme*) released in 2007,[2] and begin with a couple of sets of questions. The first set arises because the director claims that the 'artist film' shows the absolute impossibility of an artistic work to handle Auschwitz and also advances the Brechtian aesthetic well beyond Brecht. In *Reform Circus* (*Reformzirkus*, SK4, 1970), the record of a debate Kluge (up)stages with members of the television industry where these comments about Auschwitz appear, he makes clear that film is vital to moving his Brechtian critical aesthetic forward; why, then, include material made for a different medium in this collection of complete cinema films? To what extent can the television work since the mid-1980s be said to be a continuation of the earlier cinematic work? The second set of questions pursues the extent to which the fall of the Wall and the unification of Germany – the understandably seminal events that are used to delimit the backward view of this anthology in search of 'new directions' – really mark a new beginning in Kluge's work? Is the same normative narrative of Germany's return to 'unexceptional' status that is implicit in so much of what Rentschler famously calls the cinema of consensus (2000) and the celebratory secondary work about it staked out in Kluge?

In regard to the second set of questions, my premise is that because Kluge can be seen as the 'last modernist', and because he is an author in the tradition of historical materialism (see Lutze 1998), Kluge has theoretical stakes in 'time' more than 'space', and thus historical events such as the *Wende* will not be without impact in his work. But, beginning with the lecture that he gave in the most immediate proximity to the fall of the Wall, we will see that the contemporary moment of history is a present like many others that threatens to overrun any other experience of time. The purpose in his production since then remains one of making the present into a space in which experience and expression are freed from *chronos* (chronological history) for *kairos* (the time of the creative imagination), as Richard Langston's brilliant treatment of his 'works of art of time' makes clear (2008: especially 195–96). After establishing the director's sense of the global moment at the *Wende*, this essay probes the power of his different kinds of histories.[3] By examining the role of two seemingly disparate elements – 'space' and elephants – I hope to show that for Kluge a new sense of time cannot be experienced without spatial constructions that bind momentarily and yet evoke freedom. If the 'cliché' of an elephant's memory nonetheless involves the construction of a 'species-memory' (*Gattungsgedächtnis*), then these figures may be key to a larger project contributing to a freeing up of what might be called the 'species memory' of humans for their 'preserved elephant dreams' ('Eingemachte Elefantenwünsche', Kluge 1980: 304).[4] It is not so much that elephants symbolise humans in his newer works but rather that they are related to humans as 'pachydermata', the scientifically obsolete order of mammals that once linked the 'thick-skinned' creatures. Discontinued because it is polyphylectic (containing many species that bear no immediate ancestor in common) and, hence, being categorically untenable as a zoological designation, 'pachydermata' employs precisely the polyvalent conceptual space that Kluge feels can open up experience and expression across time.

THE WENDE FOR KLUGE

In 1989 Alexander Kluge received the Lessing Prize of the Free and Hanseatic City of Hamburg. Extended every four years, the award honours figures 'who in the tradition of Lessing have an allegiance to the maxims of enlightenment and bring this to expression through their work'.[5] Clearly the choice of Kluge was an appropriate one, perhaps even long overdue at the time, but this belatedness becomes fortuitous for my present purpose of setting Kluge in a post-Wall context. The ceremony to bestow his prize took place on 25 September 1990, a short week before the first German Unity Day. Between the announcement of his award and his acceptance speech, Kluge witnessed the opening of the inner-German border to new hopes, and the closing down of those hopes through the elections of March 1990 and the accompanying monetary reforms. These circumstances are not lost on Jürgen Habermas, who in his laudatio envisions Kluge standing in a window: 'like already in 1969. Like already in 1977, so too since November '89, September '90 at his telescope, watching troop movements. Straining to observe the happy counterpart to Stalingrad – forty-five years after the end of the fighting now something like the end of the war' (1991: 8). Habermas imagines the film that Kluge might write for this, under the title 'German National Theatre' ('Deutsches Nationaltheater') documenting 'attempts at orientation' ('Versuche an Orientierung'). Habermas talks of Kluge opening windows through the techniques of his interviews (which in 1990 had just begun), windows allowing a two-way perspective – out onto the circumstances and back onto the speaking subject – establishing a constellation that simultaneously contextualises and estranges his theme.

Unwittingly, perhaps, Habermas's evocation of the window and the telescope links back to the time of Alberti, Descartes and Kepler, when the development of the window, both as an architectural feature and a perspectival metaphor in art, coincided with the changes in lensing that allowed the human gaze to turn to the heavens. Prevalent tropes in film discourses that arise from mechanisms shaping vision – like windows, frames and screens – are rooted in a sense of experiencing reality 'virtually' that goes back into the early days of the scientific revolution. Anne Friedberg recently examined the roots of the cinema screen in this tradition in philosophy, optics and architecture in a manner relevant to Kluge's enterprise:

> Like the window, the screen is at once a surface and a frame – a reflective plane onto which an image is cast and a frame that limits its view. The screen is a component piece of architecture, rendering a wall permeable to ventilation in new ways: a 'virtual window' that changes the materiality of built space, adding new apertures that dramatically alter our conception of space and (even more radically) of time. (2006: 1)

Friedberg maintains that the single frame has dominated our sense of perspective since the advent of cinema, and questions the extent to which contemporary digital technologies dislodge that dominance.

Kluge has consistently put these two tendencies of framing through monocular perspective and a straining out towards the cosmos in proximity to one another, in part to break up the strictures of another association with the late Renaissance: the turn inward to the 'individual' as the motive force in the human universe. 'Chance, lucky breaks, the unique instance, [in short] everything that does not result from one's choice is, [...] contrary to the rules of our traditional understanding of experience, *the free surface of connections*, the beginning for a new sense of proximity. Here lie the *new* stories' (Kluge 1984: 650, emphasis in original). From the beginning, his literary and filmic strategy has set *Gegengeschichten* ('counter-stories' or 'counter-histories' [1984: 642]) against codified forms, establishing what Kluge calls fields for 'orientation' that are neither determined by the chimera of individual free will nor deterministic in their own right (2000a: I.7). Self-reflective devices, like frames within frames, multiply divided screens, and the inclusion of various media have long been part of his counter-stories, but his challenge to the single frame of perspective does not simply oppose stories to one another or add up frames. Since the move to television and the unification of Germany, the gesture of these devices has increasingly been aimed at a 'cinematic principle' that is not limited to the screen, as the foreword to his recent collection of *Stories from the Cinema* (*Geschichten vom Kino*, 2007) sets out: 'I want to make clear that I'm interested in the "cinematic principle" in these 120 years [of film history]. I hold "cinema" to be immortal and older than the art of film. It rests on our public communication to one another of something that "moves us internally"' (Kluge 2007: 7).

The first four pieces in that collection have to do either with cameras recreating the glory of celestial bodies on film or with camera-obscura effects of light entering through windows in various empty spaces. One in particular catches my attention, detailing the attempts by Edison's crew to develop a 'solar-camera Jupiter' that made a projection of the sun's glory. It also mentions a film entitled the *View of the Sun from a Distance on the Other Side of Neptune* by Edwin S. Porter, which simulated space effects with a back-lit blanket riddled with various-sized holes. The fake setting of Porter's film, the reader is told, was ultimately much more successful at the box office than Edison's 'real' – and very expensive – solar cinema (Kluge 2007: 17); however, inauthenticity is not a drawback for the narrative voice, because 'one could watch the film many times, as the spectator was moved by so many thoughts in which he imagined living at such a distance and yet still being able to observe the star of his home' (Kluge 2007: 18). The moment of imagination is not excluded from 'real' images, of course, as the fascination with a 'light shower' or with unobserved or unrecognised aesthetic effects of light on water (2007: 19) in these opening literary vignettes make visible. These all might be pieces in the free surface of connections that in the cinematic cosmos serve as raw material for the labour of individual fantasy production of emotion, of that which remains 'inexhausted' ('unverbraucht').[6]

Fantasy is that part of the imaginative power which links all humans (*Vorstellungsvermögen*), that falls outside the direct support of capitalist work processes (Kluge 1975: 242). However, like all the drives of humans, fantasy delivers itself as 'unpaid labour' to society even as it serves a kind of 'buffer' function from it (1975: 244). Labour, then, has always produced two things: surplus value (of whatever type) and fantasy creations. In seeking to free up the latter from proscribed forms, Kluge continues to employ a vocabulary that may seem to some readers quaintly archaic at best. But, as he rightly contends, one should resist the elimination of specific signs until their corresponding referents – whatever the gap between them – have ceased to exist. One such term is 'proletarian', not linked solely to the traditional notion of the working class under industrial capitalism (although that, too, has not ceased to exist, despite the prohibition on the discourse of 'class warfare' within the political context in which this essay is written) but also to the labour of fantasy production that is as close to a universal as one can have. The reclamation of pachydermata that the present essay traces out is not unrelated to this more overtly political evocation of bodies that labour.

Kluge's own productions have always favoured associations with modernism: production over consumption, non-identical collectivity over individuality rooted in identity politics, time over space. But he favours the former of these dyads through a revaluation of the latter through the media. Already with 1972's *Public Sphere and Experience*, Kluge and Oskar Negt sketched out the progress of the consciousness industry, which had shifted from creating a *bourgeois* public sphere to new *production* public spheres (cited here in Negt and Kluge 1997: 228), providing forms for the understanding of emotional life in a manner that eradicated the 'proletariat'. The increasingly privatised modes of distributing and redistributing cultural goods have seemingly democratised the exchange of information, the coalescing of new groups linked by mutual interest – in some cases political interest – and the creation of individual expressions. The age of hand-held technical gadgetry seems to put the means of expression in the hands of consumers and seems to widen the site of individual expression infinitely. But, expression in these pre-formed modes is a kind of second-order consumption rather than an autonomous production. The new forms for making one's experience public have also become a means for mediating whether one even *has* experience: the blog, the webcam, the tweet all verify experience through the fact of something being observed by others and saved in pre-given file form. The ubiquitous invitation to participate as if freely in the cultural domain has replaced the coercion of the dictatorial party in the post-Wall age, but without effecting a significant change in those who profit from the production spheres of publicity. The replacement of fact by opinion, which Hannah Arendt in 1950 pinpointed as a core support of fascism, has expanded exponentially (1993), and the production of fantasy as a kind of ideological buffer in the present has become increasingly standardised.

So, if Kluge still seeks to facilitate an oppositional 'production public sphere' that favours a collective over (bourgeois) individuality, an anachronistic utopian project from the present conjuncture, he does so through a sense of the individual that has been unmoored from its traditional notion of agency. Returning to the Lessing Prize speech makes the importance of this clear. Neither the obligatory gestures to Lessing's democratic dramaturgy nor the consideration of the gravity of the contemporary historical moment that Habermas performs are absent from Kluge's speech, but he views them in a framework of difference to Lessing. One significant difference is that one can no longer identify social conflicts with individual people, as was the case in Lessing's classic drama (Kluge 1991: 20). Another is the 'geopolitical' nature of today's conflicts. Referring to Lessing's *Nathan the Wise* (1779), Kluge notes that the temporal and geographical displacement Lessing enacts in the setting of that dramatic poem was much less out of place for the twelfth or even the eighteenth century than it would be today (1991: 20). To imagine this ring parable in the contemporary Middle East, Kluge explains, brings semi-autonomous structures into play, such as 'Iraq as a system', 'heavily armed Israel' and 'the construction-UNO' (Kluge 1991: 21). He maintains that systematic conflicts have arisen, which tend to make the active people (even people like Saddam Hussein or George H.W. Bush) secondary to ongoing events, despite their appearance on the world's stage to act as if they are in charge of them (1991: 21). Unlike Lessing, we can no longer even pretend that we could enlighten humanity if we could only enlighten its reigning nobles (1991: 20).

One piece from his *Primetime Late Edition* (*Primetime Spätausgabe*) series, entitled *Space Flight as Inner Experience* (*Raumfahrt als inneres Erlebnis*, SK4, 1999), among the productions from his Developmental Television Production Company (DTPC) that have been included on the complete cinema-films collection, illustrates the point wonderfully. Peter Berling plays a Russian Lt General who, in the post-Soviet era, oversees space launches to the Mir station from his bunker at some remove from the actual launch pad: though the countdown continues, the bunker has experienced a power outage.[7] Sitting behind a meagre row of candles, the Lt General is being interviewed by a man off camera (Kluge), and the unscripted back and forth reveals the man in charge to have no real impact on the events he claims to be responsible for: 'It's all fully automated,' he says, 'though I have this thing here [points to microphone], I've really nothing to say about it.' The Russian embodies one of the telltale signs of the modernity that Kluge clings to: the simultaneous elevation of the individual to sovereign status and defusing of individual sovereignty in the given instant of the political structure. Most especially with the advent of the twentieth-century's technological systems, we are increasingly confronted with situations in which 'absolutely no human relationship arises' between individuals and the systems that determine and/or threaten their existence. Nevertheless, what he does have something to say about is the music that he claims pipes down from the ship and that the stars themselves make. The inner experience evoked by space flight provides the impulse for individual expression that, while not escaping the proscribed forms of presentation, makes palpable a Blochian utopian moment. As if to manifest that moment, Lt General Pugatschow's articulation of star-singing is followed by an exaggerated eyeline match to a window and then a series of telescope images accompanied by what can only be described as eerily spacey sounds; here, however, much like in Kluge's 'nature interludes [...] prospects that initially seem beautiful quickly become kitschy' (Rentschler 2008: 10). What seems at first sublime morphs into cliché as the star-singing flits away with the introduction of a romantic score, forcing the spectator to recoil from identificatory consumption.

The labour of fantasy production cannot create a final utopian form in the media, for there it inevitably slides into kitsch. Still, the cinema remains the privileged site of this labour, often by employing the gesture of displacing familiar times into other spaces. If the current geopolitical integration makes Lessing's 'orient' seem a misguided stage for such production in the present, Kluge's consistent deployments to space displace it into the 'future'. As is so often the case in his work, 'space' is both a blunt concretisation of a metaphor and the dialectical decontextualisation of the realm of human emotions in the service of fostering new forms for expressing those feelings freely. Both Willi Tobler's galactic philosophical study and Lt General Pugatschow's celestial music gesture back from space in that direction for a minute, without claiming to last. For Kluge, these kinds of minutes are where the past and the future combat the tyranny of an all-encompassing present that puts blinkers on our fantasy. This is one way in which he feels that his television work poses quite literal challenges to the chronological history of film: 'film history began with films that never lasted more than a minute. Today the classical forms from film history come at us from the future. Cinema is a phoenix.' As we will see, it is a phoenix arising to very complex relationships with the frame of the screen.

PEAKS OF THE PAST AGAINST THE PRESENT: THE MINUTEFILM

The complete cinema-films collection contains a number of 'minutefilms' (*Minutenfilme*), in several of which space is both a literal setting and a decontextualising juxtaposition. These (roughly) sixty-second productions appear on most discs, open on insertion, and begin playing before the main menu is presented. Some of them appear more than once, in *16 Minutefilms* (*16 Minutenfilme*, SK14) and, in some cases, in the *Serpentine Gallery Program* (2006) which has a set of (six) minutefilms made between 1995 and 2005 as its first exhibit. *Five Hours of* Parsifal *in 90 Seconds* (*Fünf Stunden* Parsifal *in 90 Sekunden*, SK3) lives up to its title, showing Einar Schleef's stylised production with the Berliner Ensemble in astronomically fast motion.[8] About ten seconds into the piece, the stage is set adrift against a cosmos of pinpricks of light, reminiscent of Porter's

29

pioneering space-scape. The stage is placed in an imaginary building schematic that looks like a space station.

This visual correlation, accompanied by the compression of the duration of the opera, elicit a number of associative decontextualisations. The grand staging of the emotion-making machine that was the opera of the nineteenth century (and the cinema of the twentieth) is conceptually dwarfed by space. The synthetic *Gesamtkunstwerk* becomes small, frantic and laughable in its futility to signify at this scale. The extreme duration of the performance – itself evoking the 'eternal' – is accelerated to cartoon-like motion and set against the 'duration' of the universe in a way that highlights its ephemeral nature as a human product. This is already highlighted in the title, but the minutefilm by its very nature refuses the grand gesture of the critical juxtaposition it enacts, for each laying bare of the opera here is simultaneously a laying bare of the 'ninety seconds' that try to contain it. Space and time are not better mastered by a superior (filmic) position of criticism over and against operatic emotional machinery; ultimately, the viewer is brought back around to a position of wonder at the attempt, even if – or perhaps precisely because – the mode of expression fails to provide a form for contemporary expression. Indeed, the form that is broken through here is more televisual than operatic, for the undeniable factualness of this television documentation denies itself through the cinematic principle of showing something that moves us internally to others.

As Paul Cooke and Chris Homewood note in the introduction to this volume, one manner in which the seemingly new directions in post-Wall cinema are not really so new is found in the support of an auteurist tradition established through the *Little Television Play* (*Kleines Fernsehspiel*). Instead of simply accepting that the products of

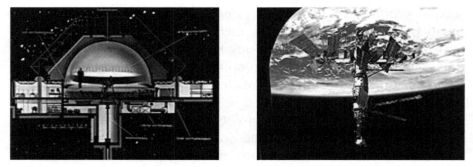

Figure 1.1: Perspectives on the *Gesamtkunstwerk*.

this well-established format are new, Kluge literally creates little plays with the televisual form. Through his DTPC and other ventures, one of the seminal figures in establishing the conditions of possibility for the TV–film interaction as far back as the late 1960s continually explores newer directions by challenging TV's forms, along with its place in reunified Germany. The importance of this cinematic confrontation with (or in) television is foregrounded in the minutefilm that opens the *Sämtliche Kinofilme* collection, *To Vertov* (*An Vertov*, SK1). An accelerated montage of black-and-white images plays upon a round, white television standing on its own short pedestal in the middle of an unidentified white space, which is otherwise unpopulated. The whiteness of the area, as well as the shade and shape of the television, generate a look that is anachronistically futuristic, which poses the question of the relation of the two media ('genre', '*Gattungen*' might be a better term) not in terms of chronological progression but in interrelated folds of temporal possibilities. Simultaneously evoking the beginnings of joyfully dialectical montage cinema, the image bank depicting the space age which arose with the advent of the televisual age in the 1960s, and the anxieties about the threat posed by television to cinema, *To Vertov* juxtaposes the flow of film images with the space-age stasis of the televisual, a point of conflict that is then dislodged and reworked.

Though Kluge does not do so explicitly, it is useful to see pieces such as *Five Hours of* Parsifal *in 90 Seconds* and *To Vertov* – films that highlight the juxtaposition of two primary elements in type, graphic form and pace – in terms of Eisenstein's montage within a single frame enacting conflicts of tempo and conflicts between an event and its temporal nature (Eisenstein 1977: 50). There is, of course, montage between frames as well, both in Vertov's original material and in Kluge's recontextualisation of it, but the latter adds the question of forms to the collision of images. The film goes full screen with the original material at times, plays with alternating negative and normal prints, and moves from urban modernity at its birth to a birth into modernity. Near the end, images from a delivery room reduce labour and birth to a matter of seconds. Returning to the television-window view in the final moments, *To Vertov* continues the negative images but then ends on a normal presentation of the baby to the cameras. If, as Brecht claimed, there was a point when showing a birth was an act of resistance, *To Vertov* again takes the Brechtian moment further into the critical interaction with the media that will give the newborn the images which will infuse its imaginative power (*Vorstellungsvermögen*). The thematic of conflict among various types of time – historical, biological, corporeal, medial and so on – springs from the montage of this ending as well, which concretises the cinematic principle. Showing each other things that move us is key to a critical contestation with the forms that frame such showing, and is at the heart of this piece dedicated to one of the fathers of film.

Using television as a window/screen/frame has broad self-reflective application in the minutefilms. The opening shots of both *100 Years of the German Rhine in 60 Seconds* (*100 Jahre Deutscher Rhein in 60 Sekunden*, SK14) and *Learning Processes with a Deadly Outcome: War and Theater* (*Lernprozesse mit tödlichem Ausgang*, SK5) contain old or damaged televisions as the frame for moving images. In each case, when the frame falls away the montages of images begins to take on a dangerous trajectory that would not be noticed without further interventions in the montage. In the former, for example, a long, high-angle shot of boats and fireworks bursting in a night-time centennial celebration, shown in fast motion, creates an aestheticised view of lights and movement. However, the insertion of a schematic drawing imagining a parabolic rocket-flight coming down on 'earth' provides the other arch not seen here, the link to bomb technology that is the hidden side to this nationalistic celebration hidden by its effusive visual power. In *Learning Processes* the opening shot simulates a large aquarium, holding icons of tragedies – the sunken *Titanic* and an operatic performance running on a broken television. The next shots show the TV set – still running the cultural programming – broken on a street evoking a post-battle, if not post-apocalyptic, scene. From the frame of the television the film cuts to the frame of a window in a ship, which first seems split in three projection frames, showing the sea and two different sizes and angles on an action film. The same window frame then looks out on Kluge's 'stars' backdrop with an obviously fake 'science fiction' space capsule flaming past. The final segment cuts from this space portal to a human in a spacesuit, the man's face through the visor looking rather like the television in *To Vertov*. He turns to look (as if out of a window) at an animated scene of what might be a space station projected behind him. Many of these are recycled images from earlier films, but their reordering here creates a time compression running from curious beginnings to disaster and beyond, something like the trajectory of Kubrick's *2001: A Space Odyssey* (1968) without the grandeur, beautiful yet blinding. Important, too, is the different gesture to the 'dawn of time' for humans: in Kluge's minute it is not the invention of the tool that drives humanity inevitably up and away from our planet and towards our end, but the dialectic of mankind's production of fantasy and the modes of its expression.

Evocations of the different time registers, pre- to post-historic, set the stage from the very outset of the minutefilm that gives the box set's 'Film Album' its name (Kluge and Weinmann 2007b). *Neon Lights of the Sky* (*Neonröhren des Himmels*) refers literally to the northern lights and figuratively to films – especially cinematic forms like the minutefilm.[9] The opening shot shows mastodons drawn into a snow-scape set against mountains in the distance, above which a superscript reads '60,000 Years BC'. There are a full range of Peircean signs gesturing to the 'pre-historic' in this opening: the iconic elephantine figures of the mastodons; the symbolic linguistic signs orienting us to a turning point used to mark human history; and the indexical trace of the pre-filmic form itself. The next shot seemingly jumps further into the scene and forward in time: a much closer film image of a mountain ridge with human structures at its base. Though these two images have conflicting qualities of brightness, they are bridged not just by the mountains and snow, but by a milky veil of light through which points of stars glimmer – what we might by this point consider one of Kluge's signature backdrops. A single tube of light seems to come down from the heavens to light the scene. The exact time of the space illuminated this way remains unclear, except that it belongs to the age after humans appear; their conspicuous absence, however, leaves open the question of whose fantasy production might be sparked by such wonder (in this case shown *without* a reflective frame, although the light in the window gestures to possibilities).

The parallel to the cinema itself seems strong if one considers the visual makeup of another short piece in the collection, which takes place entirely within the frame of film-theatre space. Because of the shot composition, scale and duration, the generation of the image through the light beam coming in from screen left seems as much at stake in *He Doesn't Hear* (*Er hört nicht* in SK15) as the accident that it chronicles. A couple drives in a car, the woman speaking earnestly to the man. He neither listens to her nor hears the locomotive coming up alongside: they are clearly headed for disaster. But the soundtrack's tango gestures to the comedy of the near-miss rooted in miscommunication and a stereotypical gender dynamic, and so the viewer feels confident that all will be well. Unexpectedly, there is no happy ending here, as the car turns in front of the train and is smashed to pieces: another learning process with a deadly outcome.

If *He Doesn't Hear* plays upon the viewer's pre-learned conventions – the soundtrack and the comedic set-up – to carry this set-up through to a surprising extinction of these people, it is all the more 'natural' to think of *Neon Lights of the Sky* as gesturing to a progression from the pre-human to the human age (and perhaps beyond), one that involves the chronological disappearance of species. However, one might take a different tack by seeing it as an emblematic exploration of the 'contradictory product' (*'gespaltenes Produkt'*) that is fantasy within the present concept of work according to Marx (Kluge 1975: 242). The only 'living' creatures in the film's opening shot do not provide the labour that will create the dwellings the viewer sees in the rest of the film, but perhaps they may be seen as the fantasy producers of the sublime imagery of lights in space that play above those dwellings. The dialectical quality of wish-projections would seem to back up this wilfully blunt reading of the split nature of fantasy in labour: since one's desires cannot come into real being in the space where one is, it is logical that the mastodons disappear from view. It is perhaps worth remembering at this point that the term Kluge evokes for imaginative power is most often associated with a spatial sense in German that is not limited to humans: 'spatial visualisation capacity' (*'räumliches Vorstellungsvermögen'*) is the ability of (some) living creatures to think and see mental images in three dimensions, and so there is no reason why Kluge's continual play with the power of imagination should be limited to humans. This reading puts us in mind of T.W. Adorno's description of the openness of the essay-form: 'It resists the idea of the masterpiece, an idea which itself reflects the idea of creation and totality. Its form complies with the critical idea that the human being is not a creator and that nothing human is a creation' (1977: 17). The difference here is that it is not the creative process but the human itself that playfully and critically comes back into focus even as the compression of the minutefilm seems to displace it. In this sense, the visual association of mastodons with elephants brings to mind the trope of the elephant's memory, but figures it differently: on the one hand, those extinct creatures are now but a 'memory' that none of us really have and thus are only available through the social mediation of the imagination (like the image of the chair in the head of Marx's handworker [Kluge 1975:

242]); on the other, this minutefilm is a kind of projection *forward* of their memory in the form of the imagery, of fantasy and desire, rather than a looking back.

A Kind of Species Memory

The tension between notions of memory and fantasy in the context of elephants has been a longstanding one for Kluge, as the brief discussion of *Artists Under the Big Top: Perplexed* above indicates. One vignette included in the print materials that accompany the film *The Patriot* (*Die Patriotin*, 1979) plays out the potential importing of this constellation for this artist. 'Preserved Elephant Dreams' ('Eingemachte Elefantenwünsche', Kluge 1980: 304–8) is the tale of a publisher seeking out an author who is rumoured to have a manuscript of some 1800 pages that might well be the next great thing. Instead of producing the bulk of the tome entitled 'Preserved Elephant Dreams', the author hands over only five different concepts for the first chapter, all of which centre around mundane situations involving a woman and man. After looking at three, the publisher asks about the rest of the tragic material, about its larger contextualisation. The author replies that he always has to begin anew, and that he has no intention of taking one of these concepts to fruition. After some attempts to get at why this might be, the publisher takes a different tack: 'How did you come to the name?' 'I'm playing on the notions of elephants' memory.' 'But you know that is just a cliché.' 'Yes. In addition to that, I assume the elephant's memory is handed down, a kind of species memory.' Once these situations get put into that clichéd cultural memory, wishes get preserved – canned – which is why the writer claims that his will be constantly started but never finished or published. The minutefilms are, in essence, such beginnings.[10]

If 'Preserved Elephant Dreams' expounds on the playful relationship of humans in the bourgeois age and the largest of land mammals in his early films – a relationship marked by innate desires for life and artificially constructed memory that retard them – then the complicated short *Execution of an Elephant* (*Hinrichtung eines Elefanten*, SK3, 2007) develops the darker side of the parallel, the self-destructive pleasure rooted in the projection of the elephant as an anthropocentric other. The film spends much of its time with Edison's *Electrocution of an Elephant* (1903), the documentation of the death of a captive animal that had killed its keepers. Alternating between spoken commentary accompanied by words on the screen and manipulations of the original film, Kluge focuses on the willing submission of the murderous beast to its new keepers' murderous intentions, which strike the viewer as astounding now as it was then. The information that Edison's original one-minute film became a box-office attraction is made even more disturbing by the insertion of images from Edison and Porter's filmic recreation of the electrocution of President McKinley's assassin.

Kluge's film then carries this theme of elephants, humans, entertainment and death into a more contemporary time frame. After a sequence of images stretching from the sixteenth century onward showing humans hurting elephants, elephants (potentially) threatening humans, and the surrealistic morphing of elephant features to an 'American Gothic' configuration, the focus shifts to contemporary scenes of elephant races at the Hoppegarten field in Berlin. The thin strand of wire separating the enormous animals from the insignificantly sized humans watching them perform somehow indicates the near inescapability of disaster in this oddly symbiotic relationship of entertainment. The film's final segment is then introduced with documentary footage showing the birth of an elephant calf. We learn that this is Komali being born into captivity at the Zurich zoo, who before becoming full-grown killed an attendant and was put to sleep.

Figure 1.2: Descent of the Pachydermata.

In an interview with Kluge (asking questions off camera), the head of the zoo speaks of the painlessness of the process, the trouble it caused the staff, and whether the other elephants have memories of Komali. Of course these beasts cannot think so abstractly as to miss the little one when it is not there, he avers. As the screen goes black and the credits flash, his voice continues as if to remind the viewer of the difficulty of memory once visual presence is removed, even as the voice of cultural expertise continues to shape what we know. Of course, visual presence guarantees neither empathy nor productive memory, as the shots of the 'killer' Komali made clear, for it was only through the film's commentary that we 'know' her that way.

What is both new and old in the direction of Kluge's post-Wall production is encapsulated here: the attempt to generate forms that will free fantasy production and spur a kind of 'species-memory' among the pachydermata. He expands his work in the cinematic principle to include and interrogate the televisual medium as arbiter of a present that threatens to block out other times and spaces. Both the authority of experts' voices and the image forms that society establishes seem immediate to the viewer until they become the focus of such an essayistic lens that reveals their mediating functions. That mediation impedes us in the project of remembering others when they are no longer there, whether we have known them or not. If the post-Wall cinema of consensus morphs seamlessly into the recent imitations of heritage cinema, then Kluge's elephants re-enliven a sentiment often attributed to Adorno: 'Auschwitz begins where someone stands in a stockyard and thinks, they're just animals.' A different kind of species-memory arises in the times of the pachedermata, when the unpaid labour of fantasy has a space of its own in which futures and pasts have a chance against the insistence of the present.

NOTES

1 Hyun Soo Cheon explores the parallel between Kluge's literary production and the three-part structure of the baroque emblem as a prototypically modern form, positing that his work should be considered properly *inter*medial rather than multimedial. Peter Bürger initially made the connection between a modernist avant-garde and the decontextualising of the baroque emblem in 1972.

2   Kluge and Weinmann 2007a. Items from this collection will be cited in the text with 'SK' then the disc number. Except in the case of the minutefilms discussed later in this essay, dates will refer to original release or broadcast years. The minutefilms are often credited only within a range of years.

3   Johannes von Moltke places his call for a more rigorous engagement with the 'feeling for history' under the sign of Kluge with an epigram, but does not pursue the connection further in that context (2007).

4   In an extended treatment of Kluge's earlier literary/textual strategies as a kind of hypertext before the fact, Georg Stanitzek peppers his text with images of elephants from Kluge's works as illustrative, if at times unexplained, examples (1998).

5   City of Hamburg Press Archive: http://www.hamburg.de/pressearchiv-fhh /2025392/2009-12-17-bksm-lessingpreis.html.

6   Eric Rentschler points specifically to 'The cinema as cosmos' in this collection, a text that 'speculates "that the images of all previous ages stream past and through us"' (2008: 2). Rentschler moves immediately afterward to align Kluge with the 'systematic indeterminacy' of the Frankfurt School à la Adorno, but that story's concern with the reception of pictures from the 'totality' of time/space seems to have a distinctly Bergsonian stress. Indeed, Kluge seems to have been at work on cinematic memory long before Deleuze's re-animation of Bergson. Haro Müller distinguishes Kluge's (literary) method from Bergson's 'asymmetrically placed' dichotomy of time by claiming Kluge as a guardian of difference between the past and present, as well as the future and the present (Müller and Mieszkowski 1996: 529); however, a closer examination based on film work and images might reveal a more complex relation. Heide Schlüpmann has noted a similarity between Kluge's early theoretical writing and Bergson, but remains critical of the traces of vitalist 'life philosophy' ('*Lebensphilosophie*') one detects there (Schlüpmann and Daniel 1988).

7   *Space Flight as Inner Experience* (SK4, 1999) appears in the 'Facts & Fakes' series that often features Peter Berling. The relatively unscripted dialogue described below is typical for this series (see Kluge 2000b).

8   Kluge's engagement with opera is well documented, and there is no space here to pursue it more fully. A solid summary of his opera projects in the context of his fellow New German Cinema directors can be found in Farmer 2003.

9   Because of the way the light appears in this film, I prefer the literal translation of 'Heavenly Neontubes' for this piece.

10 The opening image of *Learning Processes with a Deadly Outcome: War and Theater* encapsulates that dilemma inside a watery container – a kind of palimpsest of the infinitely repeated process of preserving/canning those wishes.

Chapter 2

Downfall (2004): Hitler in the new millennium and the (ab)uses of history

Christine Haase

In the influential 2000 article that gives this volume its starting point, film scholar Eric Rentschler traced a significant change in German film back to the early 1980s. According to him, 'there is a marked divide between the New German Cinema and its successor', what he termed the 'cinema of consensus', which began to manifest itself in the early 1980s but really came into its own after the fall of the Berlin Wall in 1989 (Rentschler 2000: 264). This change is characterised by a shift from the model of the *Autorenkino* to the Hollywood model of popular and star-based entertainment cinema. As a number of scholars have argued, the post-1989 filmscape thus closely resembles the post-1945 cinematic scene in Germany: both periods are characterised by a surge of easygoing and escapist movies filled with stars, beauty, love and mostly happy endings, presumably taking people's minds off a difficult past, a problematic present and an uncertain future. What audiences looked for during the 1950s as well as the 1990s were arguably 'less complicated narratives of Germanness' in the wake of seismic national changes (Hake 2002: 180).[1]

However, this cinematic trend was countered by many younger and upcoming directors, especially towards the end of the 1990s and into the 2000s. These filmmakers, such as Christian Petzold, Andreas Dresen, Hans-Christian Schmid, Sylke Enders and Fatih Akin, to name just a few, typically told more serious and thought-provoking stories, often taking on uncomfortable contemporary social and political realities of reunified Germany. The comparison between the 1950s and the 1990s thus arguably extends even further to similarities between developments during the 1960s and the 2000s: critical voices of a younger generation, who, tired of the escapist cinematic entertainment fare of the 1950s, produced what became known as the New German Cinema, are echoed by directors of a similar ilk during the late 1990s and the 2000s and their oppositional reactions to the consensus cinema.

However, a third trend has also emerged over roughly the past two decades, which in certain ways straddles the fence between the two modes described above: the serious yet mostly conventional and populist genre cinema of the 'German heritage film' that primarily deals with the difficult past of the Third Reich. As Rentschler observes, 'the frenetic pursuit of a fun culture (*Spasskultur*) with its comedies about errant yuppies and enterprising trendsetters gave way during the late 1990s to an equally emphatic culture of commemoration and retrospection' (Rentschler 2002: 3). German heritage film, a critical concept introduced into German film studies by film scholar Lutz Koepnick and based on the concept of British heritage cinema, typically narrates the difficult past of the Third Reich in a manner illustrated by productions such as *The Harmonists* (*Comedian Harmonists*, Joseph Vilsmaier, 1997), *Aimée and Jaguar* (*Aimée und Jaguar*, Max Färberböck, 1999), the Academy Award-winning *Nowhere in Africa* (*Nirgendwo in Afrika*, Caroline Link, 2001), *Rosenstrasse* (*Rosenstraße*, Margarethe von Trotta, 2003) and, last but not least, *Downfall* (*Der Untergang*, Oliver Hirschbiegel, 2004).[2] Heritage films, according to Koepnick, often upend and trivialise the accounts of history the New German Cinema offered while giving audiences 'sweeping historical melodramas that reproduce the national past, including that of the Nazi period, as a source of nostalgic pleasures and positive identifications' (Koepnick 2004: 192). With regard to the cinema of consensus, Rentschler argues that in following visions of reconfiguring German national cinema such films tried to link themselves with the Ufa (Universum Film AG) tradition of looking for 'ways of saying "we" in its address to German audiences' (Rentschler 2000: 275). Bringing these two arguments together, Johannes von Moltke has suggested that, 'in its similar effort to provide Germany with a "chimera of national normalcy" (Koepnick 2004), heritage cinema poses a further variant of this development' (von Moltke 2002: 100). And Koepnick's characterisation of the heritage film as 'easy to digest' (Koepnick 2004: 197) and as envisioning history, 'including its violent struggles and repressions, from a consensus-oriented perspective, one that can gratify diverse audiences and offer something to everyone' (Koepnick

2002b: 87), again reiterates the close links between heritage film and the cinema of consensus, arguably making the former a subcategory of the latter.[3] Thus, while critical and idiosyncratic voices have regained a lot of strength in German film since the 1990s and have once again turned it into something more than 'a site of mass diversion' (Rentschler 2000: 264), consensus cinema lives on, frequently in the form of heritage film. This chapter investigates the continuing public fascination with the Third Reich as evinced by the popularity of Nazi-period heritage cinema and the constantly evolving role of Germany's past for the present by analysing Hirschbiegel's 2004 production *Downfall*, in particular its representational strategies and goals, within the context of post-Wall and new-millennium Germany.

THE QUESTIONS

The guy is a catastrophe; that is no reason not to find him interesting as a character and a life.

Thomas Mann, *Bruder Hitler*, 1938

It is indecent to write the biography of a mass murderer.

Golo Mann

Thomas Elsaesser wrote of the Holocaust that it is an event 'that defies representation and yet demands it with equal finality' (1996: 147). One of the questions a film like *Downfall* raises is whether something similar holds true for the highest-ranking creators and perpetrators of the Second World War and the *Shoah*. *Downfall* depicts the last 12 days of the Nazi regime in 1945 and focuses on Hitler and his inner circle spending the last days of the Third Reich in the often surreal atmosphere of the bunker below the Reich's chancellery while the Red Army is moving in on the city above. But is there a need for fictionalised representations, renditions, artistic approximations of the *'Führer'* and his closest collaborators, and, if so, how might one best approach them? What do we gain from depicting a personal Hitler; which insights does this afford us? And within this context *Downfall* raises yet another important question: if a heritage film does not involve a reimagining of private German–Jewish relations that transcend the traumatic history of the *Shoah* in reconciliatory fantasies – which, according to Koepnick, is one of the mode's main narrative

41

and ideological strategies – what replaces it (Koepnick 2002a; 2004)? What is the impetus behind films narrating the lives of perpetrators without (or barely) giving voice to the victims? Is it primarily to get over our history and on with reunified life by finding 'reconciliation with the perpetrator generation' as scholars, in condemnation as well as approval, have argued, and thus to draw a line under our past (Fuhr 2004a)?[4]

According to Sabine Hake, *Downfall* approaches 'the German question from a post-national perspective, from which National Socialism can be reduced to questions of identity' and can thus become, at last, a consumable vehicle of (albeit negative) identification and cinematic storytelling, ultimately enabling the 'liberation of the present from the burden of the past' (2007: 189–90). Along similar lines, Johannes von Moltke has suggested that many of Germany's recent cultural productions 'supplied a stream of historical representations characterised by strong affect and emotion', and he views *Downfall* as an expression of such a 'distinctly new feeling for history' (2007: 18, 17). He observes that the texts in question 'generate empathy with victimized Germans, if not with German perpetrators, only by violently repudiating earlier forms of historical representation and emotional cathexis'. They thus signal an 'ineluctable shift from one regime of representation to the next, the overwriting of "1968" by "1989"' (2007: 20). In other words, *Downfall*'s overall project arguably can be understood as being two-pronged: on the one hand, and in line with Koepnick's heritage model, the film rebuffs the generation of directors responsible for the New German Cinema and their attempts to shed light on their nation's recent history and its perpetrators, thereby overcoming 'cinematically the guilt and shame propagated by the 1968 generation, and all in the name of restoring a sense of national self-confidence' (Bathrick 2007: 12). On the other hand, while von Moltke acknowledges the possibility that 'cultural texts can be productive precisely through their emotional appeal', he argues *Downfall* provides a cautionary example of an emotionalised, apolitical representation of the Third Reich 'where that appeal bathes the atrocities of historical perpetrators in the revisionist light of compassion', thereby making the emotional appeal 'fundamentally misplaced' (2007: 42). The film achieves both – the dethroning of a particular cinematic approach to German history and the introduction of a new emotionality into the discourse on the nation's past – by enlisting a staunch realism as its mode of representation, thereby raising some fundamental and problematic issues.[5]

Many of the initial reviews and debates addressing the 2004 release of *Downfall* scrutinised moral, ethical, political and historical implications of the production, while the film's narrative and aesthetic constructions were analysed to a lesser extent. Most critics who did address the latter, though, seemed to focus on the same aspects: they discussed the work's mode of representation – its realism, its striving for authenticity and painstaking verisimilitude of plotlines, sets and performances. This realist mode and the question of whether or not it is appropriate for the subject matter at hand appeared to be at the heart of most of the reviewers' disagreements. Many critics praised the film for it while others attacked it on the same grounds. They thus echoed a longstanding debate concerning the central and controversial question of representational mode and the role of realism in regard to renderings of the Holocaust and the Nazi regime, with opinions ranging from the contention that realism is the only possible mode, to it being the most inadequate and inappropriate. These contradictory convictions manifest themselves in writings by Elie Wiesel or Peter Weiss's *The Investigation* (*Die Ermittlung*, 1965) at the realist end of the spectrum, to George Tabori's grotesque play *The Cannibals* (*Die Kannibalen*, 1974) or Polish artist Zbigniew Libera's

Figure 2.1: Hitler as human – shedding a tear.

controversial Lego concentration camps at the other. In light of these dichotomous approaches and their implications, the following analysis of *Downfall*'s realism and of what is at stake in the 'realism controversy' in which the film, unwittingly or not, partakes, remains central to the discussion and understanding of the production and to the (often harsh) criticism levelled against it.

THE PRODUCTION

From the start, *Downfall* proved to be a media event in every sense of the word. A high-profile, much-hyped and much-talked-about film that involved everything and everyone that would guarantee the German public's full attention: at about €13.5 million, it had one of the highest budgets of any German production to date; it was directed by Oliver Hirschbiegel, a filmmaker well known for his 2001 film *The Experiment* (*Das Experiment*); and, more importantly, it was written and produced by one of the most powerful figures in the German film industry, Bernd Eichinger, well known for *Die unendliche Geschichte/The Neverending Story* (Wolfgang Petersen, 1984) and, more recently, *The Baader Meinhof Complex* (*Der Baader Meinhof Komplex*, Uli Edel, 2008). *Downfall* featured a veritable who's who of German-speaking A-list actors, among them the likes of Bruno Ganz as Adolf Hitler, Corinna Harfouch as Magda Goebbels, Juliane Köhler as Eva Braun and Heino Ferch as Albert Speer. The script was based on well-known German historian Joachim Fest's 2002 book *Inside Hitler's Bunker: The last days of the Third Reich* (*Der Untergang: Hitler und das Ende des Dritten Reiches*).[6] In addition, the narrative drew on the memoirs of one of Hitler's last personal secretaries, Traudl Junge, who in 2002 had gained fame through a successful and critically acclaimed documentary about her involvement with the Nazi regime: *Blind Spot: Hitler's Secretary* (*Im toten Winkel: Hitlers Sekretärin*, André Heller and Othmar Schmiderer, 2002). And last but certainly not least, it was a film not only about the Third Reich but about Adolf Hitler himself, thus offering the voyeuristically enticing prospect of observing the last days of his and the German Reich's existence, made even more alluring by the 'added authenticity' provided by 'its German-speaking cast' (Cooke 2007a: 251). The finished product, accordingly, proved highly successful, nationally and internationally, albeit in Germany – as so often happens – more at the box office than with the critics: on its opening weekend, almost half a million spectators saw the film, a figure which rose to four and a half million by the end of its theatrical run, making it one of the most successful German releases ever. It won the 2004 Bambi Award for Best German Film as well as the 2005 Audience Award at the Bavarian Film Awards, and it garnered a nomination in the category Best Foreign Language Film at the 2005 Academy Awards in Los Angeles.

THE HISTORY OF HITLER-FILMS

During the first five postwar decades relatively few attempts were made to produce narrative fiction films with a well-known leading Nazi figure at its centre.[7] The hesitation to make such films was presumably rooted in a variety of considerations. There was a fear that by personalising and psychologising Hitler – or other Nazi figures of prominent stature – one starts to explain them as people, and hence begins to explain away and to relativise the ultimate evil inherent in their ideology and actions. Another objection raised in this regard concerned the potential glamorisation of Nazism due to the – like it or not – awe-inspiring and seductive nature of vastly powerful figures in general, magnified even more by the self-aggrandising ways in which the Nazi regime imagined and staged itself as heroic, omnipotent and, in every sense of the word, spectacular.[8] And, finally, fundamental questions remained (and remain) about how to represent such destruction, terror and malice, and how to render figures that have become global emblems of evil in a meaningfully complex way. Even so, *Downfall*'s claim to be a groundbreaking endeavour and 'a unique project in the history of German film' is misleading at best, in spite of the proclamations of its makers (Conrad 2004).[9] There are cinematic predecessors dealing with the same or a similar topic: the first deserving of mention remains, of course, Charlie Chaplin's brilliantly insightful *The Great Dictator* (1940). *Hitler: the Last Ten Days* (Ennio De Concini, 1973) was an Italian–British co-production with Sir Alec Guinness in the lead; Anthony Hopkins portrayed the dictator in the US production *The Bunker* (George Schaefer, 1981); and, more recently, Russian director Aleksandr Sokurow attempted to close in on the person of Hitler in *Moloch* (1999).[10]

The first and only fictional German-language film before *Downfall* to focus on the person of Adolf Hitler was G.W. Pabst's *The Last Ten Days* (*Der letzte Akt*, 1955).[11] This Austrian production, co-written by

Erich-Maria Remarque, played successfully in dozens of countries but flopped in West Germany and was never even released in East Germany. Aptly reflecting a nation in denial about its most recent past and in search of absolution, earlier German non-documentary representations of the Third Reich mostly featured the sufferings and sacrifices of 'ordinary' non-Jewish Germans,[12] but later also increasingly focused on the victims of Nazi persecution and the *Shoah*.[13] Over the past decade, however, no doubt due to the greater historical distance, generational changes, and the expanding exploration of the 'genre' of Hitler films, the taboo of putting a human face onto those most responsible seems to have waned rapidly, nationally and internationally. Since 2002, four feature films have been produced in addition to *Downfall* centring, with one exception, on various aspects and periods of the dictator's life, trying to trace 'the human' in the man. In 2002, an international co-production entitled *Max* (Menno Meyjes, 2002) premiered with John Cusack playing Jewish art dealer Max Rothman, who befriends Hitler, portrayed by Noah Taylor, in post-World War One Munich. Next, *Hitler: the Rise*

Figure 2.2: Uncle Hitler – Hitler and the Goebbels children.

of Evil (Christian Duguay, 2003) aired, a US–Canadian television production with an impressive cast, including Robert Carlyle as Hitler, Stockard Channing as his mother Klara, and Peter O'Toole as president Paul von Hindenburg. This film profiled Hitler's life as a child and his rise through the ranks of the NSDAP (National Socialist German Workers' Party) in the wake of the First World War. In 2005, the British ITV production *Uncle Adolf* (Nicholas Renton), featuring Ken Stott in the lead, focused on Hitler's life from 1929 to 1945 and his relationships with women: his ill-fated attachment to his niece Geli Raubal from 1928 until her suicide in 1931 and his later involvement with Eva Braun. The latest addition to the list is the German film *My Fuhrer: The Truly Truest Truth About Adolf Hitler* (*Mein Führer: Die wirklich wahrste Wahrheit über Adolf Hitler*, Dani Levy, 2007), an absurd satire largely slated by critics and audiences in spite of featuring cult musician/comedian/actor Helge Schneider, and the only one of the recent productions not to attempt a sombre and authentic period recreation. All other films mentioned above employed a realist mode of representation in their portrayal of cinematically neglected aspects of Hitler's earlier years and personal development in an effort to uncover something about the making of a mass murderer.

THE PROJECT, THE CRITICS AND THE REALISM DEBATE

When asked about the intentions of his project, *Downfall*'s producer-writer Eichinger stated that he viewed those last 12 days as a kind of

> time-lapse which shows precisely what has been happening throughout the entire twelve years of the Hitler regime. This was the trigger for the dramaturgic approach. With my script, I tried to say something about the whole of the regime, but condensed within a timeframe that is manageable. (Eichinger 2004b)

This statement repeats in a way what the production itself purports to do: it presents itself as a magnifying glass for the Third Reich, the implication being that the film makes things visible that were previously unseen. Its purpose, according to the people involved in its making – and in contrast to other recent productions – was not necessarily to trace the genesis and developmental trajectories of a dictator and mass murderer, but to investigate Hitler's powers of persuasion and manipulation, his charisma, and the people's dedication to him until the bitter end by looking closely at that very end. And while some German reviewers found just the opposite to be true – 'In all the smoke and furore of the downfall, the pivotal question remains unasked and unanswered: why could a person as unpleasant as Hitler attract so much love, following, and fearful obedience until the very end' (Seibt 2004) – *Downfall*, according to Eichinger, was on the one hand an attempt better to understand the 'mass hysteria and mass insanity' inspired by the Nazi regime and its leader, on the other motivated by the conviction that it was 'about time that we ourselves tell our history (*Geschichte*) with the means that are at our disposal, and that we muster the courage also to finally get the main actors in this history up on screen' (Eichinger 2004b). However, the reasons as to why and to what end this should be desirable or necessary – other than to outrun the international competition and the Spielbergs of this world – Eichinger seems to deem self-evident and neglects to explain. Yet, implicitly, he seems to operate under the assumption that, to paraphrase a German critic, once the Germans have a hold of their history, it won't have them by the throat any longer (Fuhr 2004a).

The way in which *Downfall*'s makers tackle their objective, and their answer to any representational challenges, is a stringent and unwavering belief in a realist mode of representation, the attempt of an authentic recreation of what it, what *he*, was like. After a brief introductory scene set in 1942, *Downfall*'s main narrative resumes on 20 April 1945, Hitler's last birthday, and ends on 2 May, the day Berlin surrendered to the Russian forces, the dictator having already committed suicide two days earlier. The film is partly told from the point of view of an omniscient narrator, and a few times seems to be informed by Hitler's point of view. Mostly, however, it is filtered through the eyes of 22-year-old Traudl Junge, played by Alexandra Maria Lara, who served as one of Hitler's personal secretaries from 1943 until his suicide. *Downfall* opens and closes with statements by Junge, poignantly reflecting on questions of personal responsibility and guilt, both taken from the documentary *Blind Spot*. In the beginning, only her off-screen voice can be heard, but after the credits have rolled, the final scene from *Blind Spot* is shown, thereby also making it the final scene of *Downfall*. Traudl Junge's voice, hence, establishes an authentic and 'real' narrative frame that brackets the fictional rendition of the events. One critic speculated that by using *Blind Spot* the makers of *Downfall* pointed to their own ambitions of 'reaching the high level of reflection Traudl Junge has achieved', while in fact admitting that by doing so they believe this to be unattainable, 'since otherwise they would not have to quote her' (Schweizerhof 2004). One might argue, too, that by establishing a connection between both productions the film's makers were attempting to reiterate similarities of intent between the two projects. But whatever their intentions may have been, the overall effect is also one of equating the two films' relationship to reality. As a German critic argued, 'with this [Junge's] voice which is not its own, the film already claims the conflation of historical event and fictional representation' (Knörer 2004). The narrative frame, hence, encapsulates many of the film's predicaments, which stem from its unequivocal belief in the possibility of a realist representation of its subject. By privileging Junge's voice through granting her the first and final words in the film, and by moving without rupture and without self-reflexivity between the documentary and the fictional rendition, *Downfall*'s makers subsume their own work under a meta-narrative of reality and authenticity that the other film establishes. The reference to *Blind Spot* thus intimates a correlation with the real on the part of *Downfall* that is false and problematic.

Even so, *Downfall*'s perceived authenticity and realism were the reasons not just for most of the criticism but also for a lot of the praise the film received. In the foreign press, mainly in America and the UK, reaction to the film was generally positive. Still, some articles pointed out the potential dangers of portraying Hitler in a human, i.e. sympathetic, way. Stanley Kauffmann's review in *The New Republic* spoke of a film 'well wrought' but 'troubling', because it is cast and executed so perfectly that, ultimately, '*Downfall*, apparently faithful to the facts, evokes – torments us with – a discomfiting species of sympathy or admiration' (2005). The *New York Times* – echoing some German reviewers and their objections – criticised a different aspect of the overall project: 'It is fascinating without being especially illuminating, and it holds your attention for its very long running time without delivering much dramatic or emotional satisfaction in the end' (Scott 2005), a notion also shared by *Entertainment Weekly*: '[The film's] portrayal stops short of revelation. Once you witness Hitler's denial, the film has little more to say about him' (Gleiberman 2005). Yet, other leading US critics called the film 'one of the best war movies ever made' (Hansen 2004), 'spellbinding' (Ansen 2005), 'riveting' (Sterritt 2005) and 'thoughtful entertainment' (Elley 2005).

Famous British historian and Hitler biographer Ian Kershaw stated that of all the screen portrayals of Hitler this is the only one which to him is 'compelling'. And even if he conceded that 'seeing Hitler on the verge of suicide cannot help in understanding Hitler the phenomenon', his final verdict ran: 'As a production, it is a triumph – a marvellous historical drama' (Kershaw 2004). The *Sunday Times* called *Downfall* a 'towering performance' and Ganz's Hitler 'daringly shaded in' (Rees 2005), William Boyd wrote in the *Guardian* of a 'mesmerising' and 'riveting' achievement and a 'brilliantly pitched performance' (Boyd 2005).

As already intimated, German critics, on the other hand, were often underwhelmed, if not contemptuous or infuriated: *Spiegel.de* deemed it 'banal', the *Tagesspiegel* 'strangely empty', and *Die Zeit* 'rather pointless altogether'. Wim Wenders famously published a scathing critique – also in *Die Zeit* – which focused primarily on the perceived lack of attitude and position of the film. For Wenders, *Downfall's* ultimate failure is what he sees as a *Verharmlosung*, that is a palliation of the events it portrays, and its refusal to show the deaths of Hitler, Braun and the Goebbels family: 'Why not show that the pig is finally dead' (Wenders 2004). One reviewer – encapsulating a key point of critical discontent – accused the film of 'cowardice and lack of imagination which, of course, passes itself off as historical accuracy' (Knörer 2004). Similarly, many critics attacked the film's slavish attempts at recreating history and its obsessive urge for authenticity, which, arguably, divests the work of the potential for a productive and illuminating artistic confrontation with its subject. Therefore, *Downfall* was ultimately deemed by many a 'mere illustration of facts that are known well enough' (Schlömer 2004), and seen as unable and/or unwilling to provide any new answers or explanations to the old questions of why and how. And for some critics, German and otherwise, such as David Denby of the *New Yorker*, *Downfall's* narrative and aesthetic approaches resulted in something far more problematical than a lack of illumination or an uninspired recounting of events. To them, the film's unquestioning adherence to a realist mode of representation is not only an aesthetically but also an ethically troublesome choice: 'at times one longs for a coldly malicious ironist like Brecht or Fassbinder to come in and take over. The attempt to re-create Hitler in realistic terms has always been morally and imaginatively questionable – a compromise with the unspeakable that borders on complicity with it' (Denby 2005).

So, on the one hand, the film was hailed for its authenticity, its historical and emotional accuracy, and its compelling performances, on the other, it was condemned for its naive belief in an unwaveringly realist mode of representation that 'lets the facts speak for themselves', and, thus, ostensibly eschews any need for further commentary and artistic interpretation or intervention. The discussions surrounding *Downfall* thus echo and continue longstanding debates surrounding the representation of the Holocaust and the Third Reich. To elucidate these opposing views and the realist approach and its implications, the following discussion will draw on the theoretical framework and terminology used by literary scholar Michael Rothberg in a study on Holocaust representation. It should go without saying that by doing so I do not mean to equate the events and sufferings depicted in *Downfall* with those in the concentration camps and the sufferings of the people persecuted by the Nazi regime. However, evil of this nature is a coin with two sides: perpetrators and victims. Hence, it does – whether committed or suffered, whether on the side of its conception and execution or of its effects and consequences – pose, to my mind, similar representational challenges, which result in similar representational demands.

Rothberg, in his 2000 book *Traumatic Realism: The demands of Holocaust representation*, tenders a set of helpful terms and concepts for the analysis of these challenges and demands. He delineates two fundamentally different ways of approaching the Holocaust, 'two almost incommensurable visions' (5), namely what he terms 'realist' and 'antirealist'. By 'realist' Rothberg means 'both an epistemological claim that the Holocaust is knowable and a representational claim that this knowledge can be translated into a familiar mimetic universe'. 'Antirealist' for him denotes 'both a claim that the Holocaust is not knowable or would be knowable only under radically new regimes of knowledge and that it cannot be captured in traditional representational schemata' (3–4). Similar claims could be made for Hitler and other 'unfathomably' evil criminals, whose acts, motivations and reasoning lie far beyond the grasp of any normal human frame of reference and understanding. An obvious difference, however, lies in the desirability of and rationale for rendering the representational object in question knowable: while this may involve the creation of understanding and compassion as well as the prevention of recurrence and the perpetuation of memory in the case of the Holocaust, the reasons for making Hitler *et al.*

knowable may be less compelling and clear-cut. As Golo Mann stated in stark contrast to Eichinger's and Fest's approach, 'It is indecent to write the biography of a mass murderer. How he spent his evenings, which music he liked, whether he preferred Bordeaux to Champagne, all that is of no interest, all that doesn't belong here.'[14] Once again, the lines seem to be drawn between the realists and antirealists. And yet another important element in this analysis shared by the events of the Holocaust as well as the lives of its creators corresponds to this conceptual opposition. This element is what Hannah Arendt famously termed 'the banality of evil',[15] and what Rothberg describes as the 'split between the ordinary and the extraordinary' which, he argues, aligns itself with 'realist' and 'antirealist' critical modes (2000: 6). According to Rothberg, the

> coexistence of such contrasting approaches [...] indicates something about the nature of the events at issue. As I argue [...] the split between the ordinary and the extraordinary found in scholarship reflects essential characteristics of the Nazi genocide itself. [...] I would term *traumatic* the peculiar combination of ordinary and extreme elements. [...] While the traumatic combination of the extreme and the everyday blocks traditional claims to synthetic knowledge, attentiveness to its structure can also lead to new forms of knowledge beyond the realist and antirealist positions. (2000: 6–7)

Rothberg clearly questions the privileging of one mode of representation over the other, which is usually a choice that is accounted for on moral and aesthetic grounds. To Rothberg, however, the pitting of realism and antirealism against one another is a false dichotomy, misleadingly claimed to be about ethical and artistic integrity, because the two *really* reflect different sides of the *same* reality.

Missed Opportunities

Viewed in light of these hypotheses, *Downfall* suffers from limitations that stem not so much from what *is* shown in the film, but rather from what is *not*, paralleling the film's problematic and much criticised *lack* of a standpoint and of any analysis, which Eichinger and Hirschbiegel proudly declared to be fully intentional: 'There is no moral. [...] What we are trying to do is – as much as we possibly can – to present the facts, to tell history. And not to interpret history.'[16] Hence one German critic's astute observation: 'It is not naturalism in and of itself that leads *Downfall* to its ruin, it is rather the denial of the artificiality of this naturalism' (Knörer 2004). If the realist and antirealist approaches reflect two sides of the same events, *Downfall,* by repudiating the possibility of an alternative approach, also repudiates part of the reality of the history it relates. Therein lies its problem. The film's principal shortcoming is its failure to acknowledge the existence of any representational dilemma, because by denying this it also denies something about the fundamental nature of the events it reflects, which, in turn, resonates with what David Denby termed 'complicity' with the 'unspeakable' (2005). In its unquestioned and unreflective realist approach, *Downfall* conceptually simplifies and streamlines a complex and largely inconceivable reality. It thus implies the existence of a logic, order and reason that belies the nature of the Nazi regime and its atrocities. Film scholar Gertrud Koch contended that 'the discrepancy between a single individual and a totalitarian expansion of power to the point of complete destruction is grotesque in and of itself'. Hence, 'all Hitler-films are, in one way or another, farcical. Their quality is reflected in whether or not they understand at least that much about Hitler' (2004). *Downfall*, in its devotion and addiction to realism and authenticity, fails this test. The film reconstructs the history of the Third Reich and the Holocaust as a cruel and crazed but linear and readable story emanating from Adolf Hitler as its centre. In doing so, it not only unduly simplifies, it also falls back on the old revisionist model of primarily implicating a small group of fanatic madmen, thus tracing the existence and crimes of Nazi Germany to one rather confined – and largely uniformed – field of force. In other words, the film does not succeed in pointing to 'the continuities of fascism with Germany's social structure throughout most of its modern history' (Elsaesser 1996: 158), which would prevent the simplistic if not reactionary personalisation of Nazism in its best-known representative Adolf Hitler. It thus also ultimately presents an image of not only ordinary Germans, but even of many of those who are 'convinced followers of National Socialism' not as 'perpetrators complicit with a barbaric regime but rather as having been duped by it and consequently [...] as its victims' (Cooke 2007a: 253). To be sure, by introducing and ending *Downfall* with Junge, and by maintaining her as its main focal point, the film does touch on key questions about the Third Reich: questions of individual and systemic guilt and responsibility, questions about the entanglement between the private, 'inner' lives of Germans during the reign of the Nazis and their public 'outer' national doings, and the implications of the daily reality of Nazism and, hence, its normality. Ultimately, however, it fails to move beyond the asking and never probes these questions.

By complicating the issue of representation, *Downfall* could simultaneously have investigated the complications of history itself. In such a searching, self-reflexive approach, and by complementing and thematising its realist elements, the film could have addressed the questions to which it alludes, and it could have attempted an answer to Rothberg's call to move beyond the traditional divide between the realist and the antirealist approach. In the process, it might have offered new and more insightful perspectives, and it is in this sense that, while *Downfall* is half a cinematic achievement (in its performances, cinematography, production design), it is also half a missed opportunity.

NOTES

NB: This chapter is based on my initial investigation of the film *Der Untergang* (*Downfall*) published in 2006 as 'Ready for his close-up? Representing Hitler in *Der Untergang/Downfall, 2004*', *Studies in European Cinema* 3/3, pp. 189–99, comprehensively revised, updated and expanded for the context of this anthology.

1 German cinema during the fifties was dominated by the *Heimatfilm* as well as the *Schlagerfilm* musical comedies, historical films and period romances such as the *Sissi* series.
2 See Koepnick, 2002a and 2004.
3 While many scholars have referenced Koepnick and his analyses, the utilisation of the heritage concept for a German context has also met with criticism. Sabine Hake, in a 2007 essay on *Downfall*, questions the efficacy of the concept 'heritage film' in a German context, and, pointing out a number of differences between British and German heritage films, voices doubts about the usefulness of applying the term to a 'rather limited and blurry group of films' (202, my translation). Certainly, it is a much debated concept also in the context of British cinema studies, largely because the films under discussion share only loosely connected tropes or iconographical elements and because they seem to collapse so easily into adjacent genres, such as the war film, the costume film, or the historical film. Nonetheless, heritage has established itself as a highly productive critical category in British

and other national film studies, and the significant similarities and overlap between the relevant British and German productions to my mind more than warrant the use of the term as a critical concept and heuristic tool.

4 This and all following translations from German into English are mine, unless otherwise stated.

5 Other points of criticism in regard to *Downfall* include the film's renewed staging of non-Jewish German victimhood harking back to narrative constructions popular during the late 1940s and 1950s, its occupying questionable positions of post-memory and post-ideology, its reductions of history to media event and event cinema, the manipulation and commodification of star texts and celebrity personas/identities in Third Reich films, and more. For studies addressing these and similar issues see, for example, Cooke 2004, Hake 2007 and Bischoff 2005.

6 In 1973, Fest also published the first comprehensive Hitler biography in German.

7 One notable exception with regard to German cinema is Theodor Kotulla's excellent 1977 film *Excerpts from a German Life* (*Aus einem deutschen Leben*, alternative English title *Death is my Trade*) about the life of Rudolf Höss, commandant of Auschwitz-Birkenau.

8 For an insightful discussion of these aspects of Nazism and its aesthetically and erotically charged powers see Susan Sontag's seminal 1975 essay 'Fascinating Fascism'.

9 Also see Eichinger 2004a, 'Daher kommen wir: Der Regisseur Oliver Hirschbiegel über seinen Film *Der Untergang*', interview with Anke Westphal, *Berliner Zeitung*, 11 September 2004.

10 For a comprehensive list of 'Hitler-films' until 2000 see Mitchell 2002.

11 There are two other – much discussed and controversial – German films centring on the figure of Hitler: Hans-Jürgen Syberberg's seven-hour epic *Hitler: A Film from Germany* (*Hitler, ein Film aus Deutschland*, 1977, and Christoph Schlingensief's *100 Years of Adolf Hitler* (*100 Jahre Adolf Hitler – die letzte Stunde im Führerbunker*, 1989), but neither qualifies as the type of narrative feature film with which this article is concerned.

12 Examples in this category – even though they may widely differ in approach and thematics – include Wolfgang Staudte's *Murderers Are Among Us* (*Die Mörder sind unter uns*, 1946), Helmut Käutner's *The Devil's General* (*Des Teufels General*, 1955), Frank Wisbar's *Dogs, Do You Want to Live Forever* (*Hunde, wollt ihr ewig leben*, 1958), Bernhard Wicki's *The Bridge* (*Die Brücke*, 1959), Fritz Umgelter's TV mini-series *As Far as Feet Will Carry* (*So weit die Füße tragen*, 1959), Konrad Wolf's *I Was Nineteen* (*Ich war neunzehn*, 1967), Helma Sanders-Brahms's *Germany, Pale Mother* (*Deutschland, bleiche Mutter*, 1979), Wolfgang Petersen's *The Boat* (*Das Boot*, 1981) and Michael Verhoeven's *The White Rose* (*Die Weiße Rose*, 1982).

13 German films investigating these aspects of the Third Reich only, and at first very intermittently, began to appear about twenty years after the end of the Second World War. Examples include Egon Monk's *One Day-Report from a German Concentration Camp 1939* (*Ein Tag-Bericht aus einem deutschen Konzentrationslager 1939*, 1965), Frank Beyer's *Jacob, the Liar* (*Jakob der Lügner*, 1974), Peter Lilienthal's *David*, 1979, Agnieszka Holland's *Europa, Europa* (*Hitlerjunge Salomon*, 1989), Michael Verhoeven's *My Mother's Courage* (*Mutters Courage*, 1995), Joseph Vilsmaier's *The Harmonists* (*Comedian Harmonists*, 1997) and Max Färberböck's *Aimée und Jaguar* (1999).

14 Remark by Golo Mann about Sebastian Haffner's *The Meaning of Hitler* (first published in German as *Anmerkungen zu Hitler*, but also aimed at Joachim Fest's Hitler biography, for which Mann felt an ambivalent admiration. As quoted in Seibt 2004.

15 Subtitle of Hannah Arendt's famous 1963 study *Eichmann in Jerusalem: A report on the banality of evil*.

16 See NDR Interview with Bernd Eichinger, 'Hitlers letzte Tage als Kinofilm', as quoted in: Cooke 2007a.

Chapter 3

'Wonderfully courageous'? The human face of a legend in
Sophie Scholl: The Final Days (2005)

Owen Evans

Writing about the 'astoundingly large proportion of government-sponsored films' about the Third Reich produced in West Germany between 1975 and 1985, Anton Kaes remarked that the 'numbers were impressive, but from an aesthetic point of view most of these films mean very little: they recycle images of images' (1992: 22). The last ten years have seen a renewed wave of films looking at the Nazi past in the context of a pan-German *Vergangenheitsbewältigung* ('coming to terms with the past') following unification.[1] But is there a sense that Kaes's observation about images merely being recycled is even more apposite today, a generation later? Certainly, when one considers the mixed reception accorded *Downfall* (*Der Untergang*, Oliver Hirschbiegel, 2004), it is self-evident that Germany remains 'a country on which the past weighs heavily' (Kaes 1992: 35), and this burden is exacerbated by the weight of expectation that emanates from both within and outside Germany. Did that film add anything new to the speculation surrounding the occurrences in the Führer's bunker as the Third Reich crumbled? These issues have been debated elsewhere in this volume, and doubtless will continue to rage on in debates for some time to come.[2]

But what of Marc Rothemund's *Sophie Scholl: The Final Days* (*Sophie Scholl: Die letzten Tage*, 2005)? In view of earlier films by Michael Verhoeven and Percy Adlon, could Rothemund do anything other than recycle images of one of postwar Germany's most potent legends? As this chapter will elucidate, Rothemund's film, while not swerving too far away from the earlier hagiographies, simultaneously makes a concerted effort to bring Sophie Scholl closer to us, emphasising her ordinary qualities, her human nature, characteristics which have perhaps been lost in earlier representations of the legend. In this regard, the film reflects very clearly the new feeling for history that the introduction to this volume has already highlighted as a distinct trend in German cinema since 2000. Moreover, in its endeavours to humanise the figure of Scholl, Rothemund's film bears testament to an unflinching willingness to confront the weight of history. In so doing, the truly remarkable qualities of *all* members of the *Weiße Rose* (White Rose) resistance group, and not just Sophie Scholl, are very much to the fore. Not just in terms of its aesthetics, but its more comprehensive handling of the events surrounding the execution of Sophie Scholl than its predecessors, *Sophie Scholl: The Final Days* succeeds in creating new, more powerful, images.

Kaes explored the return of history as film by focusing on some of the key film texts of the postwar period and their engagement with National Socialism. In conclusion, however, he sounded somewhat uncertain about how this problematic past would be represented in the future:

> A memory preserved in filmed images does not vanish, but the sheer mass of historical images transmitted by today's media weakens the link between public memory and personal experience. The past is in danger of becoming a rapidly expanding collection of images, easily retrievable but isolated from time and space, available in an eternal present by pushing a button on the remote control. History thus returns forever – as film. Innumerable Westerns have made the Wild West a movie myth. As the Hitler era slowly passes from the realm of experience and personal memory into the realm of images, will it also become a mere movie myth? (1992: 198)

What especially seemed to trouble Kaes is the way in which the representation of history might become contingent upon generic demands, and thus distorted for the sake of entertaining an audience.

It is certainly striking how internationally successful those German films tend to be which represent the totalitarian past, often garnering broadly more positive receptions abroad than at home. *Downfall* and *The Lives of Others* (*Das Leben der Anderen*, Florian Henckel von Donnersmarck, 2006) are two significant cases in point, where international audiences and critics largely, and perhaps understandably, ignore apparent historical inaccuracies or distortions in their praise.[3] One might even go so far as to say that films such as these are seen internationally to comprise a specific genre that proves very attractive to cinemagoers: the German totalitarian thriller, we could perhaps call it. If one reflects upon the enduring attraction of German villains in the movies, perhaps best exemplified by Major Strasser (Conrad Veidt) in *Casablanca* (Michael Curtiz, 1942), one might see these more recent examples as the continuation of a line extending a long way back in film history. In this regard, one can understand Kaes's unease, since such movie myths have always been popular and eagerly consumed as entertainment first and foremost, with historical fact dissolving into fiction for the sake of a good yarn. Picking up the baton from Kaes, Randall Halle has observed a pronounced trend in the 1990s towards film productions in which 'historical representation becomes explicitly commodified to achieve broad circulation' (2008: 96). In the German context, he identifies this tendency in particular as having created a 'Hitler Boom'(2008: 112), in which he includes *Sophie Scholl: The Final Days*. So where does Rothemund's film fit into this debate? How should we define it generically? Is it the kind of film that prioritises image over content, entertainment and profitability over historical fact? Unsurprisingly it too was very well received internationally, earning itself various significant prizes and an Oscar nomination. So, is it just another Nazi film of the type Halle disparages?

In the early 1990s, Robert and Carol Reimer posited a new generic category in German cinema, namely the 'Nazi-retro' film, as a means of investigating, as their book's subtitle puts it, 'how German narrative cinema remembers the past'. Drawing inspiration from the French *mode retro*, they assemble a canon of films which they feel fit this new category and in which they argue 'history calls attention to itself by referring beyond its purpose in the narrative structure', thereby puncturing the 'dreamlike quality of the cinematic experience', acting as a 'scream that awakens us from a nightmare'. This foregrounding of history, and specifically the traumatic events of the Third Reich, 'functions like a Brechtian strategy, distancing viewers from the screen in order that they might reflect on what they see and feel' (Reimer and Reimer 1992: 7).

While some of the points they make might hold true for some of their case studies, their attempted taxonomy of Nazi-retro as a genre comes a little unstuck in trying to corral the diverse array of films in their study together. Be that as it may, in their introduction Reimer and Reimer make some assertions that are pertinent for our analysis of

Sophie Scholl: The Final Days and its handling of the historical material at its heart:

> Nazi-retro films in particular tend to distort the past to create dramatic conflict where none may have existed, to romanticise the subject matter and emphasise individual, heroic actions, and to emphasise conventional values: valour, commitment to family, concern for one's neighbour, and love for one's country. [...] By relying on filmic conventions (suspense, stereotyping, sentimentalising) and cinematic themes (war heroism, unbeatable will, courageous resistance), Nazi-retro films open themselves up to the criticism that they trivialise the past and distort the truth. By resorting to formulaic structures and melodramatic narratives, the films create worlds that do not reflect historical truth. (1992: 9)

It is certainly true that Rothemund's film does derive affective power from some of those elements, namely the use of suspense when Hans and Sophie distribute leaflets in the university, and the depiction of virtues such as courageous resistance, and a philanthropic concern for the victims of National Socialism. However, any charge that it distorts history is much harder to substantiate.

The motivation for the film was the discovery of the Gestapo records from Munich, which had ended up with the Stasi via Moscow. With this new material to hand, author Fred Breinersdorfer produced a screenplay which 'rationally, but above all emotionally, wants to make the heroic figure of Sophie Scholl "human" and thus understandable' (Breinersdorfer 2006: 8).[4] The film thus adopts not a Brechtian approach, but rather collates a much clearer picture of Sophie Scholl than hitherto, incorporating information drawn from the literary and bureaucratic documentary sources in order to complement some elements drawn from the earlier films to have explored her role in the fateful events of 1943: *The White Rose* (*Die Weiße Rose*, Michael Verhoeven, 1982) and *Five Last Days* (*Fünf letzte Tage*, Percy Adlon, 1982). In so doing, Rothemund's film is not only *not* recycling images, nor seeking to distort the truth, but is wedded instead to a commitment to convey the most factual account as yet assembled of the fate of Sophie Scholl.

Talking about the inspiration for their film, Rothemund and Breinersdorfer acknowledge the qualities of the earlier films, describing Verhoeven's film as a 'classic of German cinema' (Breinersdorfer and Rothemund 2006: 316). Nevertheless, they explain that they believed 'that Sophie Scholl's biography had not been exhausted either filmically or narratively, as new documents had come to light in the interim, especially the Gestapo transcripts of the interrogations and confessions' (2006: 317). The new information lay behind the decision to focus principally on Sophie, and to relay the events from her point of view; as a consequence she is in every scene until the execution scene, at which point the perspective shifts for the only time.

The narrative perspective of *Sophie Scholl: The Final Days* serves to complement the perspectives of the earlier films. The Reimers describe Verhoeven's film as a 'suspenseful thriller [...] and an informative documentary drama' (1992: 87), and both elements are apparent from the outset. The prologue begins with an extract from the second White Rose leaflet, read by Verhoeven himself, before cutting to photographs of the principal members of the group, indicating when they were executed; tellingly Sophie's photograph is the last in the sequence.[5] The film proper then opens with Sophie's brush with the Gestapo on first arriving at Munich. Based principally on Inge Scholl's account of the activities of her younger siblings, published initially in 1953, the film follows the activities of the group as a whole, not just Sophie, from its inception, documenting with broader strokes the way the resistance network grew, including Hans's first-hand experience of atrocities on the Eastern Front. The film culminates with the arrest of Hans and Sophie, their trial and execution, all of which is condensed into a handful of scenes. By contrast, Adlon's film, which like Verhoeven's casts Lena Stolze as Sophie, covers her last five days but is relayed from the point of view of Else Gebel, her cellmate, and draws heavily on her accounts of her time with Sophie. Given its narrative perspective, Adlon's film concludes with Sophie leaving the cell for the last time, still unaware of her imminent execution. In effect, then, *Sophie Scholl: The Final Days* incorporates elements from both its predecessors, but is able to produce an even more accurate account of the events of those final days by virtue of the wealth of new information now available.[6] One could even see Rothemund's film as a corrective exercise in certain respects. In Verhoeven's film, for instance, it is Hans who fatefully pushes the leaflets off the balcony in the atrium of the university; the Gestapo documents reveal that it was, in fact, Sophie who made the foolhardy decision that led to their arrest.

It is readily apparent, from the bonus material on the German edition of the DVD, as well as the extensive documentary material provided in the published screenplay, that *Sophie Scholl: The Final Days* is the product of a very meticulous attention to detail, which militates against any accusation that the film simply retreads familiar ground. Benefiting from the availability of the Gestapo records, Breinersdorfer was able to draw from an eclectic mix of extant letters, diaries and journals, as well as interviews with some survivors and relatives of the group in constructing the screenplay. Two of the most significant testimonies in the context of Rothemund's film are Annaliese Knoop-Graf, Willi Graf's sister who was also arrested at the same time as Sophie, and Robert Mohr's son.

It is the presence of Mohr, the Gestapo interrogator, a peripheral figure in Verhoeven's film, totally absent from Adlon's film and until recently something of a shadowy character in the history of the White Rose, that gives the film its particular *frisson*. Mohr's interrogation of Sophie lies at the very heart of *Sophie Scholl: The Final Days*. His reports of the interrogation provide a much more detailed picture not only of Sophie's motivation for getting involved in the activities of the White Rose, but also her resilience and grace under pressure. As Ulrich Chaussy observes: 'Whoever looks in great detail at Sophie Scholl's last days [...] discovers, first of all, that she spent more time with, spoke more to and had to compete more with the Gestapo officer Robert Mohr than any other person during the last days of her life' (2006: 141).

For this reason, the discovery of the transcripts, and their interweaving into the screenplay, offers invaluable new insights into Sophie as a person, for whom Mohr clearly had respect despite her 'terrorist' activities. In a communication with Robert Scholl, he wrote: 'I can only reiterate that this young woman [...] maintained a composure, which can only be explained in terms of strength of character, a pronounced brotherly love and a rare, deep religious conviction' (Chaussy 2006: 142).

There is inherent drama in the accounts of Sophie's interrogation by Mohr, which Breinersdorfer carefully transposes into the screenplay, crafting dialogue that is both authentic and gripping in order to meet the demands of an historical film. The impact of the four interrogation scenes is accentuated by the theatricality of the *mise-en-scène*, which appears quite gothic with the dark baroque furnishings in the room, and the cinematography, which is restrained, yet affective. Most of all, it is the performances by Julia Jentsch (Sophie) and Alexander Held (Mohr) which captivate and inject intensity into these exchanges. The initial interrogation, which centres on Sophie's empty suitcase, her claims to not having had anything to do with distributing the leaflets at the university – 'I steer clear of anything political' – and her family background, is based almost exclusively on the transcripts recovered. The scene is marked principally by the use of shot/reverse-shot, with several medium shots of Sophie and Mohr facing each other across the table, emphasising the prisoner's calm and the impression of innocence she conveys. Indeed, Sophie's demeanour reflects the Gestapo man's observation at the university that 'both [Hans and Sophie], but above all the young woman, gave the impression of being completely calm' (Chaussy 2006: 141). The scene ends with the hint from Mohr that Sophie might be released later that day, which simply underlines the innate drama the transcripts contain. The subsequent discovery of the stamps in the siblings' flat leads to the second interrogation, during which Sophie's stance begins to change. Initially, Sophie reiterates her apolitical nature, but that changes as soon as she learns that Hans has confessed. When Mohr's tone becomes more hectoring, challenging her to admit her involvement in producing and distributing leaflets, Sophie responds defiantly: 'Yes, and I'm proud of it.'

The increased number of close-ups deployed, as the potential implications of her involvement become clear, underlines cinemato-graphically the heightening tension of Sophie's position in this second interrogation. What the new information facilitates, therefore, is the opportunity better to understand, and appreciate, Sophie Scholl's remarkable fortitude in the face of injustice and inhumanity, that motivated her to attempt to assume full responsibility with her brother in the ultimately futile endeavour to protect the others involved, and primarily Christoph Probst, whose handwritten draft leaflet about the carnage at Stalingrad was found on Hans Scholl.

It is during the subsequent two encounters with Mohr that we see the remarkable transformation that Sophie has undergone. Having signed the confession at the conclusion of the previous interview, she appears calm and steadfast in her attitude, despite being confronted with an increasingly agitated opponent: 'Damn it, you have to tell the truth here!' Mohr exclaims at one point, furious at Sophie's adherence to her story. Her composure is all the more striking in that by this stage it was evident that the Gestapo knew of the participation of the likes of Christoph Probst, Willi Graf and Alexander Schmorell in the group: 'There is no group,' she insists. She is even unafraid to goad Mohr at times. When he sarcastically remarks: 'If you are to be believed, Fräulein Scholl, then the whole Reich is swarming with apolitical people and followers of the movement,' she retorts,

'Then you have nothing to worry about, Herr Mohr.' For a shy student, such composed defiance in Gestapo custody cannot fail to spark admiration.[7]

But it is during the final interrogation scene that the qualities upon which the legend has justifiably been built come to the fore. Interestingly, as Breinersdorfer reveals on the DVD's commentary track, the bulk of this exchange is based less on the actual transcripts, but collated instead from other extant material such as letters and diaries. In *From Hitler to Heimat*, Anton Kaes quotes Jean-François Lyotard, who argues that history

> Consists of wisps of narratives, stories that one tells, that one hears, that one acts out; the people do not exist as a subject but as a mass of millions of insignificant and serious little stories that sometimes let themselves be collected together to constitute big stories and sometimes disperse into digressive elements. (1992: 84)

One can readily relate Lyotard's observation to Breinersdorfer's construction of the screenplay for *Sophie Scholl: The Final Days*, not least this final dialogue between Mohr and his young antagonist. But Lyotard's assertion of how history is comprised also hints at the contingent nature of such narratives, the need to revise, to test them, and the lacunae that any representation of history necessarily leaves. For any historical account necessarily has to interpret and select, to reduce the 'mass of millions of insignificant and serious little stories' to a narrative that can be engaged with. It is these gaps permeating the history of Sophie Scholl's final days that Breinersdorfer and Rothemund seek to fill by imbuing the legend with a human face. Else Gebel's account of Sophie, after this final meeting with Mohr, conveys the young woman's enthusiasm at having been able to express her views openly and eloquently in a debate between two diametrically opposed worldviews. Thus the film extrapolates the course this discussion might have taken, distilling it down to the clash between *Gewissen* ('conscience') and *Gesetz* ('law').

The dialogue maps the precise contours of these diametrically opposed positions, with Mohr spouting the platitudes of National Socialism – 'The new Europe can only be a National Socialist one' – in response to Sophie's Christian and moral convictions – 'Of course what I am saying has to do with reality, with common decency, morality and God.' As Breinersdorfer maintains on the DVD commentary, from Gebel's account it seems as if Sophie

Figure 3.1: Mohr offers Sophie the 'golden bridge'.

believed that, as well as defending her position and what the White Rose stood for, she could convince Mohr to change his view. Most of all, however, it is the courage with which she challenges his view of the world during their final exchange which highlights those exemplary qualities underpinning the legend: accusing Hitler of being a 'mad man', denouncing antisemitism and the euthanasia programme, and speaking openly of the extermination camps in Eastern Europe. At every juncture, she rejects Mohr's fanaticism – 'Do *you* believe in the final victory, Herr Mohr?' – the film depicting the dynamic shifting dramatically between them over the course of her interrogation. The young woman's composure and conviction appear to rattle the Gestapo man, whose own self-assurance seems badly shaken, reflected by his turning to the window, almost in despair at his antagonist's unwavering self-belief. It is at this point that he offers Sophie a way out, what she calls a 'golden bridge', if she will distance herself in her statement from Hans and the activities of the group. But Sophie rejects his suggestion: 'I would do it all over again, because I don't have the wrong world view; you do. [...] I am still of the opinion that I have done the best for my people, I do not regret it and I will accept the consequences of my actions.'

When Gebel is incredulous at Sophie's decision, the latter replies simply, 'There is no going back.' Symbolically Mohr, whom Breinersdorfer and Rothemund describe on the DVD commentary as cowardly and whose own son described him as having laid the foundations for the Nazi judge Roland Freisler (Chaussy 2006: 148), washes his hands. It is a moment unrecorded in the transcripts, but as a poetic contrivance and a clear allusion to Pontius Pilate, it is a highly effective conclusion to the dramatic exchanges between the two characters, distilling the fundamental difference between them into one symbolic gesture, as well as bringing out the strong religious connotations that underpin the film.

In many ways, the interrogation scenes between Sophie and Mohr help to underpin the legend of the White Rose in general, and their importance as symbols of the resistance to Hitler, as well as the young woman's own admirable significance specifically. Much is made in earlier accounts and representations of Sophie Scholl, such as Michael Verhoeven's film, of a young woman remarkably in control of herself, calm and composed enough to be able to face down Freisler in the courtroom, boldly, and famously, declaring, 'What we have said and written is what so many others think, they just do not dare to voice it out loud.' Mohr, who encountered her one last time just after she had said goodbye to her parents, observed that it was the only occasion he had seen her in tears (Chaussy 2006: 142). The prison guard at Stadelheim prison, where the three executions were carried out in February 1943, described the victims as 'wonderfully courageous' (Scholl 1979: 88), which is why, in defiance of the regulations, they were allowed to share a last cigarette together. As Sophie was led away, 'she went without batting an eyelid. [...] The executioner said that he had never seen anyone die like that' (Scholl 1979: 88). 'The sun is still shining,' she tells Hans in the film, seemingly reconciled to her fate and prepared to die for the idea she believed in. As Christoph Probst avers, 'It was not in vain.'

The primary rationale for *Sophie Scholl: The Final Days* was, however, to salvage a fully rounded picture of this young woman, which her courage in the face of totalitarian terror has arguably tended to obscure. As Inge Scholl remarked of her siblings,

> They didn't do anything superhuman. They defended something simple, stood up for something simple, for the right and freedom of individuals, for individuals' right to develop freely and their right to a free life. They did not sacrifice themselves for any extraordinary idea, pursued no great goals; what they wanted was that people like you and I should be able to live in a humane world. [...] Therein lies, perhaps, their true heroism, stubbornly to defend ordinary, small

and obvious things, when far too much is spoken about great things. (1979: 10–11)

It is this sense of her ordinariness that Rothemund's film seeks to recapture in its depiction of Sophie Scholl, the young woman of whom Knoop-Graf admitted, 'I didn't notice that there was anything special about her.'[8] As the screenplay writer and director put it, 'The task was to develop a film with exciting, emotional scenes, in which Sophie Scholl should grow for us as a person rather than as a "hero"' (Breinersdorfer and Rothemund 2006: 318).

To this end, the decision in *Sophie Scholl: The Final Days* to focus principally on the young woman, and specifically on her last five days, facilitates a much more nuanced portrayal, drawing largely on sources such as letters, diaries and interviews. Thus the film opens with Sophie and Gisela Schertling, Hans's girlfriend, listening to Billie Holiday illegally on the radio, singing along to 'Sugar'. The prevailing impression is of a young woman full of life, prepared to do things she should not, as students are wont to do. As the unexpurgated screenplay makes clear, Sophie loved black American music, which National Socialism condemned as *entartet* ('degenerate'); but more significant still, listening to a *Feindsender* ('enemy broadcaster'), the BBC in this case, could lead to the death penalty.[9] Despite the risks, such behaviour appears typical of most young people, possessed of a potentially rebellious streak, even in such an intimidating environment. Certainly, Sophie's decision to push the leaflets off the balustrade into the atrium at the university, which in hindsight cannot but be viewed as reckless, does nevertheless point to an irreverence, a foolhardiness at odds, perhaps, with Knoop-Graf's characterisation of Sophie as 'serious'.[10] Asked by Mohr why she had tipped the leaflets, she responds, 'Pranks like that are in my nature.' The film thus hints at the ways in which Sophie was, indeed, in so many respects the ordinary young woman her elder sister describes.

To help bring out her ordinary qualities, *Sophie Scholl: The Final Days* presents a picture of a young woman deeply devoted to family and friends.[11] The strong bond with Hans, which Mohr observed, is a *leitmotif*, emerging powerfully in the opening scenes, reinforced by her determination to stand by Hans and the affectionate, and affecting, look she gives her brother in the courtroom and shortly before their execution. Mostly though, it is the scenes in the cell with Else Gebel, relying on the latter's account, where we witness a more human and fragile side to Sophie. It is in these moments that she is granted respite from needing to keep her composure under interrogation, and where we learn more about her dreams, loves, longings and fears. News of Christoph Probst's arrest, for example, causes her to break down, on account of his young family and the implications of his arrest for them, as do thoughts of how her mother will cope with what has happened. Her relationship with her fiancé, Fritz Hartnagel, is also granted space in the narrative, when she agonises over her mistake in listing him as one of the unwitting donors to the group's activities. Asked by Gebel when she had last seen Fritz, Sophie grows wistful at the memory: 'At night we sang and talked of peace. And there weren't any soldiers, pilots or bombs anywhere to be seen. Just the sea, the sky, the wind and our dreams.' Once again, the ordinary young woman reappears, serving to remind us that she is only 21.

In seeking to draw this more human portrait of Sophie, a figure that audiences are invited to identify with, the film makes creative efforts to enhance the factual material, and supplement earlier representations. Randall Halle sees in this approach, which he deems characteristic of the films that comprise the so-called 'Hitler boom', a desire to privilege story over history and 'a move away from commitments to historical accuracy and precision' (2008: 125), and identifies 'a naïve expectation that the past is somehow holistically representable' (2008: 127). In many respects, every historical film could be accused of such naiveté, but does it necessarily invalidate each historical representation that is thus attempted? And is historiography itself not attempting something similar by reducing a complex network of events to a coherent narrative, to a representation of what might have happened, 'a historical subjunctive' (Halle 2008: 126) to facilitate understanding and debate? In his exploration of the nature of historical representations on film, Pierre Sorlin offers his own thoughts on the ways that 'historical films are all fictional':

> By this I mean that even if they are based on records, they have to reconstruct in a purely imaginary way the greater part of what they show. Scenery and costumes similar to those of the period represented can be based on texts and pictures, but the actors alone are responsible for the gestures, expressions and intonations. Most historical films (though not all [...]) combine actual events and completely fictitious individual episodes. [...] Fiction and history react constantly on one

another, and it is impossible to study the second if the first is ignored. (2001: 38)

The master narrative of history is full of lacunae that new information can always help to plug, when such material comes to light, as in the case of *Sophie Scholl: The Final Days*. As a consequence, do not all historians interpret, and manipulate, the extant facts at their disposal in order to assemble a narrative that might serve as the basis for ongoing research and discussion? Can there ever be a definitive version of history? Can one ever fill all the gaps without resorting to some interpretation, to fiction even, as Sorlin intimates?

In its portrait of Sophie Scholl, Rothemund's film attempts its own interpretation of this historical figure from the material available, and does not shy away from attempting to fill some of the gaps that remain. Close-ups of her hands during the early interrogation scenes and the tears she sheds in the toilet intimate to us the anxiety that Sophie must surely have felt in her predicament, even if these moments represent creative interpretation rather than recorded history. On the DVD commentary, Marc Rothemund avers that it was impossible for Sophie to be shown shedding any tears in Michael Verhoeven's film, because his motivation was inherently political, seeking as he was to have the West German *Bundestag* and the *Bundesgerichtshof* (Constitutional Court) annul the Nazi *Volksgerichtshof* judgements on the members of the White Rose, which were still valid at the time his film was released.[12] As a result, even when she is told of her impending execution, in *The White Rose* Sophie appears almost uncannily composed; in contrast, in *Sophie Scholl: The Final Days*, she emits an anguished howl before gathering herself once more to write her last letter to her fiancé.[13]

The other element which plays a significant role in Rothemund's film and is wholly absent from *The White Rose* is the importance of Sophie's faith.[14] Not only is this significant in her exchanges with Mohr, when she explains how her resistance is a matter of conscience, of faith, but it also appears, corroborated by Gebel's account, that it sustained her throughout her imprisonment, as she was often seen and heard to pray. Breinersdorfer and Rothemund assert that it was her faith that enabled her to withstand the pressure she was placed under, and thus they selected prayers from her diary and added them to the film, a 'creative addition' to help bring us closer to the young woman.[15] These extrapolations are complemented by a series of shots

Figure 3.2: Sophie draws on her faith.

where Sophie is shown looking up at the sky, which serves as a visual metaphysical *leitmotif*. She does this upon leaving the apartment with Hans on their way to the university, and again when being led from the courtroom; in her cell, she is often depicted gazing out of the window. But the most potent example is the final one, when she is being led to the guillotine and looks up into the sky, seemingly reconciled to her fate.

The endeavour to humanise Sophie Scholl, to present her as a figure with whom we can more readily identify, gains real impact by virtue of a strong performance from Julia Jentsch, for which she understandably won a Silver Bear at the Berlinale. She is able to convey the full gamut of emotions that the screenplay demands, and the emotional intensity of her performance is especially affecting during her scenes with Alexander Held as Mohr. The transformation in the young woman that inspired the film is believably realised by Jentsch. She manages to reflect Sophie's moral superiority and integrity when Mohr begins to harangue his antagonist or when confronted by Freisler's fanatical tirades, but is equally adept at showing the emotional cracks in her armour, such as when she is confronted by Hans's confession and needs to re-gather her composure in the toilet, or when she learns of Christoph Probst's arrest. But the film also draws attention to the number of errors of judgement the young resisters made, such as Sophie pushing the leaflets off the balustrade, and listing her fiancé in the book of donors, or Hans fatefully taking Christoph Probst's handwritten draft leaflet with him to the university. It is Jentsch's ability to convey these nuances so sensitively, the very facets that were the inspiration for the film, that makes Sophie a figure we can both admire and identify with, but prevents any tendency to hagiography in the film. Her emotional reactions appear authentic, while also having affective potential.[16] Physically, too, she manages to portray Sophie's ordinariness, which in so many ways enhances her potential as an identification figure.[17] As Philip French puts it, 'Jentsch [...] gives a wonderful performance, tough, tender, vulnerable, and illuminated by an inner decency' (2005).

As we have seen, Pierre Sorlin stresses how actors' interpretations of historical figures contribute to the fiction that permeates historical films; but it is a fiction, as in the case of Jentsch's performance, which helps to enlighten and clarify, rather than distort the truth. Sorlin goes on to suggest how it is common for history to be reflected, and inflected, through a single representative figure: 'It is very seldom that a film does not pass from the general to the particular, and arouse interest by concentrating on personal cases; this is one of the most direct forms of the appeal to identification, an appeal which is in fact not specific to the cinema' (2001: 38).

Breinersdorfer and Rothemund are open about their decision to focus solely on Sophie in order to invite the audience to identify with her in the manner Sorlin outlines above: 'The closer the bond, the stronger the identification with her fate, her attitude, her arguments and emotions' (2006: 320).[18] In Jentsch, they found the perfect actor to enhance this connection. Rothemund further justifies the decision to make Sophie central to the film by indicating how her involvement with the group was motivated by her disquiet at the atrocities committed by the Nazis.[19] For the director, the key to her as the ideal identification figure is that she was *told* about these events, as many were; in her case, learning about Hans's experiences on the Russian Front activated her politically, whereas the majority of other people who had heard of such events turned a blind eye.[20] In this regard, her decision to act adds another level to her appeal as the focal point of the film, hinting at a political imperative for screenplay writer and director, in that injustice and inhumanity stimulate agency.[21]

Nevertheless, such a reading of the film finds little support from Randall Halle, who believes in his study of transnational aesthetics in contemporary German cinema that the films of the 'Hitler boom' are characterised by a 'liberal "post-ideological" position that concentrates on the individual perspective' (2008: 126). In general terms he sees history in such films as merely window dressing, which look to entertain rather than enlighten: 'They offer a visual opulence and likewise move to entertain with plot lines that turn from explicit explorations of history to rely on melodrama, love stories, fantasies and even feel-good comedies' (2008: 97–98). One ramification for Halle of this distillation of history into straightforward genre cinema is the way in which the narratives produced 'exclude too much historical complexity' (2008: 113), in order to make the films more attractive to a broader audience, and thus potentially more profitable: 'In general then, transnational historical films break with educational aspirations. In striving for universal spectator appeal, the films tend toward platitudes and clichés' (2008: 126). To support his thesis, Halle offers two case studies that are convincing for the most part, namely *Enemy at the Gates* (Jean-Jacques Annaud, 2001) and *Downfall* (2004). However, his contention that *Sophie Scholl: The Final Days* should be viewed in the same light seems much less compelling.

Halle is disparaging about the new information underpinning Rothemund's film, dismissing it as a 'promotional strateg[y] interested foremost in drawing an audience' (2008: 114). While it would be disingenuous to argue that the film's director and producers were not interested in finding an audience, the attention paid to rendering the story as authentically as possible suggests a commitment to more than merely peddling 'visual opulence'. Rather than an attempt to eschew any engagement with the complexities of history, the film's painstaking efforts to garner as accurate a picture as possible not only of Sophie Scholl, but the group as a whole, is well documented in the extra features on the DVD, as well as the comprehensive book accompanying the film. The interviews with eye witnesses from the time, as well as relatives of the participants, such as Annaliese Knoop-Graf and Willi Mohr, provide fascinating insights, many of which were interpolated directly into the screenplay or informed the general tenor of what is represented. The book is a rich documentary resource, collating detailed essays on the White Rose, biographies of the key historical figures, including Robert Mohr and Roland Freisler, as well as some of the original Gestapo documentation. In this way, *Sophie Scholl: The Final Days* can be seen as the main component of a much more comprehensive documentary enterprise, which militates against any dismissal of the project as an example of 'the commodity orientation of the transnational aesthetic' which 'breaks with the ethical pedagogical goals developed over decades within the national ensemble' (Halle 2008: 115). And given the nature of the discussions between Mohr and Sophie, especially in the final interrogation, it is hard to agree with Halle's contentions that 'we never learn the nature of Sophie Scholl's political convictions' (2008: 114) or that the film provides a 'decontextualised stor[y] of resistance, so that [...] all we can do is identify with the courage on display' (2008: 126).

The people behind the film are very open in their belief that it could appeal beyond the German context and encourage a wide audience to identify with the actions of the young people, but that does not bespeak a naked transnational commodification of the material at its heart.[22] Nor does it betray any post-ideological attitude. Halle believes that the 'post-ideological vision of the [Hitler boom] films deceives the audience', as the '"ideals" motivating the [Second World] war are still very much alive today: nationalism, anti-leftism, racism, anti-Semitism, totalitarian authoritarianism, and so on' (2008: 127). While he is right to draw attention to the ongoing existence of such phenomena, his charge of deception can easily be refuted with regard to *Sophie Scholl: The Final Days*. In their notes about what motivated them, Breinersdorfer and Rothemund suggest that, despite Halle's assertion that 'educating the audience is secondary' (2008: 114), on the contrary, their film had a distinct pedagogical, political thrust to it:

> We live in a time when fascist parties are on the march again in Europe, and in Germany extreme right-wing parties are being elected in parliaments – predominately by young voters. Principally people are complaining that the youth have no role models. Yet at the same time pupils are skipping school in order to demonstrate against the war in Iraq, and colourful flags bearing the word 'Peace' are fluttering from windows and balconies. A film about Sophie Scholl, about the last moments of a young woman so full of life, about the way she grew under increasing pressure, about the consistency of her attitude, is necessary in times like these. (2006: 317)

Their claims are broadly borne out by the film produced. Halle is correct to observe that 'there is no mechanistic relationship between spectatorship and social action' (2008: 128), and it is difficult to demonstrate that the avowed intent of those behind the production of *Sophie Scholl: The Final Days* had the expected impact on the audience. Nevertheless, every care was taken to ensure that those who saw the film were presented with an authentic, emotionally engaging narrative that might, just might, confirm Christoph Probst's belief that the efforts of the White Rose had not been in vain, that their sacrifice would lay the foundations for a better society. In this respect, the film can be seen as a potent example of the new, more emotive approach to history found in German cinema since 2000. And in Sophie Scholl, the film has an affecting heroine whose fate unsettles and provokes, and whose 'legacy is a challenge for succeeding generations, most especially the youth of today' (Welter 2005). As Philip French notes, at its conclusion 'a life is extinguished, but the movie has captured the generous human spirit that animated it' (2005).

NOTES

1 Of course, the legacy of East Germany has also become the subject of many film and television productions, most significantly *The Lives of Others* (*Das Leben der Anderen*, Florian Henckel von Donnersmarck, 2006).
2 See also Haase 2007 for a recent example.
3 For more on the critical reception accorded *The Lives of Others*, see my own 'Redeeming the Demon?: The Legacy of the Stasi in *Das Leben der Anderen*' (2010).
4 All translations from the German are my own.
5 Rothemund's film ends with photographs of the key figures in the White Rose, starting with Sophie, and the judgements passed on all members of the network.
6 As Michael Verhoeven suggests, in an interview on the DVD of *The White Rose*, the surge of interest in, and material on, the Scholl siblings was sparked by his film.
7 See the interview with Knoop-Graf on the DVD, who stresses how shy and insignificant Sophie seemed compared to her older brother.
8 Interview on the DVD.
9 Much more is made in the full screenplay of Sophie's love of jazz and swing music in the opening scene with Gisela Schertling; and later, when recounting to Else Gebel how she met Fritz Hartnagel, she explains that they met at a 'tea dance': 'We put on swing records, although my friend's parents had banned 'nigger music'. Count Basie, Satchmo and above all Billie Holliday!' (Breinersdorfer 2006: 238).
10 Interview on the DVD. Knoop-Graf suggests that Sophie was very much overshadowed by her more extrovert elder brother.

11 Indeed, this devotion also manifested itself in the way Sophie and Hans kept their activities secret from those close to them, which also made it difficult initially to piece the events together.

12 *The White Rose* concludes with a statement by Verhoeven and Mario Krebs in which they quote, with barely concealed incredulity, *inter alia*: 'In the opinion of the Constitutional Court the paragraphs under which the resistance fighters of the White Rose were tried were not part of the Nazi terror system, but were in accordance with the law as it stood at that time.' The German Parliament passed a resolution in January 1985 overturning this decision.

13 It should perhaps be noted here that Verhoeven only devotes around 15 minutes in his film to the events that comprise *Sophie Scholl: The Final Days*.

14 Verhoeven does not show Sophie taking the sacrament from the prison priest at Stadelheim, whereas *Sophie Scholl: The Final Days* devotes an entire scene to this moment.

15 Director's commentary on the DVD.

16 Anthony Lane notes that some reviews complain about the film being a 'cartoon of saintliness, in the case of Sophie' (2006), which seems to disregard the fact that the film makes ample reference to the number of mistakes and errors the young resisters made, and which led to their own downfall, as well as that of others.

17 Interviewed on the DVD, Annaliese Knoop-Graf remarks of her contemporary, 'I didn't find her at all attractive.'

18 There could not be a clearer indication than this that the film has no aspirations to adopt the Brechtian approach that the Reimers identify in their study of the so-called 'Nazi-retro' film.

19 There seems little doubt, though, that one important element of her power as an identification figure resides in her having been a young woman, in an environment that required women to play subservient, maternal roles, as the film makes clear in the interrogation with Mohr. That is not, however, to say that any identification with Sophie is necessarily gendered.

20 When Sophie speaks of the deportation of Jews to the extermination camps, Mohr replies, 'You believe this nonsense? The Jews are emigrating of their own volition.' It is unclear whether he genuinely believes this himself, but at the conclusion of this final interrogation, his conviction seems badly shaken, perhaps suggesting that he is not beyond redemption, despite Breinersdorfer's and Rothemund's critique of Mohr. It may be an unexpected consequence of Held's wonderfully convincing portrayal of the Gestapo man.

21 It is perhaps worth noting here that while Verhoeven's film explores the group as a whole, it ends with the sole focus on Sophie. By contrast, Rothemund's film ends with the emphasis on all three of the young people

executed in February 1943, reasserting Sophie's role in the context of the group as a whole.

22 The book is only available in German, suggestive therefore of a clear national focus within the project. In this way, Rothemund and Breinersdorfer's project might be regarded as a continuation of Michael Verhoeven's endeavours in the 1980s to bring a fuller picture of the White Rose to light, to breathe life into the myths and legends behind schools, squares and streets in Germany that bear the name of the Scholl siblings.

Chapter 4

Music after Mauthausen: re-presenting the Holocaust in Stefan Ruzowitzky's *The Counterfeiters* (2007)

Brad Prager

Based loosely on Adolf Burger's memoir *The Devil's Workshop* (*Des Teufels Werkstatt: Die größte Geldfälscheraktion der Weltgeschichte*, 1983), Stefan Ruzowitzky's film *The Counterfeiters* (*Die Fälscher*, 2007) was widely acclaimed and won the 2007 US Academy Award for Best Foreign Film. Much in Ruzowitzky's work had to be falsified (or counterfeited), partly out of deference to Holocaust survivors such as Salamon Smolianoff, the real historical figure at the story's centre, who was no longer alive to offer his consent. Moreover, much had to be fictionalised owing to the conventions surrounding cinematic representations of the Holocaust, which dictate that it is preferable merely to 'base' such stories on the truth because the truth itself (or the 'truly truest truth', to cite the title of Dani Levy's satirical and self-reflective Hitler film of that same year [*Mein Führer: The Truly Truest Truth About Adolf Hitler* (*Mein Führer – Die wirklich wahrste Wahrheit über Adolf Hitler*)]), about the atrocities endured in the camps is generally taken to be nearly if not entirely unrepresentable.

At the centre of the story on which Ruzowitzky based his film's screenplay are the workings of 'Operation Bernhard', a secret Nazi plot named after SS Major (*Sturmbahnführer*) Bernhard Krüger. Although the film refers to the scheme as Operation Bernhard, Krüger is not mentioned in the film. Some of Ruzowitzky's characters, particularly the Nazis, are composites, and the character Major Friedrich Herzog (Devid Striesow) can be seen to stand in for Krüger. The aim of Operation Bernhard was to wage a campaign against the US and British economies by flooding their respective markets with a surfeit of counterfeit pounds and dollars. The plan has been attributed to Alfred Naujocks, a man said to have started World War Two by orchestrating (or counterfeiting) an attack on a German-operated radio transmitter at the end of August 1939 in order to justify the invasion of Poland to the Germans (as is depicted in the DEFA film *The Gleiwitz Case* [*Der Fall Gleiwitz*, 1961]).[1] Naujocks suggested the scheme to Arthur Nebe, chief of the SS Criminal Police and adaptor of the mobile gas vans that were used to kill large numbers of Jews before the gas chambers were constructed. Nebe and SS Group Leader (*Gruppenführer*) Reinhard Heydrich, who was an avid reader of spy fiction, were particularly enthusiastic about the idea (see Malkin 2006: 5). Ultimately, according to Lawrence Malkin, it was Heinrich Himmler who came to Krüger with orders to carry out the plan. The later stages of the operation, those put into effect in a special clandestine block in the Sachsenhausen concentration camp starting in 1942, were under Krüger's direct administration, and constitute the primary setting of Ruzowitzky's film.

The Counterfeiters has been described as a crime thriller ('*Krimi*') (see Schulz-Ojala 2007), and the director speaks of his main character, who is based on Smolianoff but is named Solly Sorowitsch in the film (and played by Karl Markovics), as 'a film noir character in a Holocaust movie' (Ruzowitzky 2008). The director's comment is revealing insofar as it affirms not only that Holocaust film is a recognisable genre, but that it could be in some way connected to – as either compatible with or distinct from – film noir. Additionally, the sub-genre of the German or German-language Holocaust film makes matters even more complex. Volker Schlöndorff, who directed the similarly themed and similarly debated film *The Ninth Day* (*Der neunte Tag*, 2004), famously noted that the Germans should not simply leave Holocaust filmmaking to Steven Spielberg and the Americans, adding 'it's a challenge you have to meet' (Schlöndorff 2004). Ruzowitzky's film calls these terms to mind not only because the filmmaker is Austrian, but also because he is the director of *Anatomy* (*Anatomie*, 2000), a conventional genre-based horror-thriller about medical students in Heidelberg, which references the legacy of German perpetration (and in particular that of Nazi medicine), as well as *All the Queen's Men* (2001), a comedy-drama (dramedy) about World War Two spies featuring the US television star Matt LeBlanc.[2] *The Counterfeiters'* predominant genre can, however, be most closely identified with the German-language 'heritage film', a label imported from British film studies by Lutz Koepnick, and referring to that familiar wave of high-profile, affirmative and box-office-friendly German films from the end of the last century including *Aimée and Jaguar* (1999), *The Harmonists* (*Comedian Harmonists*, 1997) and *Nowhere in Africa* (*Nirgendwo in Afrika*, 2001) (see Koepnick 2002a). Such films are distinct from the well-known Ismail Merchant and James Ivory productions that are the calling card of the British heritage genre insofar as German heritage films tend to centre on German life during the Second World War. They generally depict the war years in a way that romanticises the history of German-Jewish partnerships and excises the spectre of racist zealotry among all but the most diabolical Nazis.

Though the film shares some thematic overlap with the German heritage films that preceded it and carved out its marketing niche, its connection to such films has less to do with its subject matter – which diverges from them insofar as it aims to depict a predominantly Jewish story and not a story of German-Jewish symbiosis – than with its apparent emphasis on emotionality, or how this period film affects its audience in a manner consistent with expensive, studio-based cinematic melodramas. In an anti-Brechtian proclamation Ruzowitzky praises costume dramas, explaining, 'I like greatly emotive cinema – its pathos, grandiose sets and costumes' (Ruzowitsky 2007). Because the director himself finds emotional filmmaking ('*Gefühlskino*') compelling, and because his film won wide international acclaim, it is little surprise that *The Counterfeiters* has been linked to other successful German melodramas such as *The Lives of Others* (*Das Leben der Anderen*, 2006).[3] All of this generic embedding (that it is a *Krimi*, a Holocaust film with elements of film noir, and a melodramatic German heritage film) suggests a degree of over-determination insofar as genres establish audience expectations. Viewers are meant to know in advance what to expect from genre films. Yet an acknowledgement of *The Counterfeiters'* conformity with expectations becomes complicated once one acknowledges the ambiguities that necessarily attend the interpretation of any cinematic object: images do not always (or ever) mean in singular ways, and films frequently do not produce the meanings their directors and producers intend. Moreover the gaps between sound and image – or in this case between the drama and its accompanying *meloidía* – allow for slippages between the filmic *fabula* and *sujet*, ones that make dogmatic ideological critique, even of consensus-building and affirmative German heritage cinema, difficult. Films, including those that aim to establish national consensus, build upon existing conventions and put the past squarely in the past, always produce a multitude of meanings. As with most historical films, *The Counterfeiters* is more complicated than its generic labels suggest. It aims towards building consensus about the Holocaust, yet it is, at the same time, slippery in terms of what it concludes about that past. The film thus may not function seamlessly as an ideological instrument.

Another initial consideration as to how to approach Ruzowitzky's film concerns its country of origin. As Randall Halle has noted, many of today's transnational – a modifier for which he opts in place of 'postnational' because national boundaries are still a relevant determining factor in film studies – productions have to be understood in multinational contexts (2008: 25). *The Counterfeiters*, although it is Austrian, can also be described as a German-language film, one that features high-profile German actors such as Devid Striesow and August Diehl, and which was co-funded by German companies including Studio Babelsberg (in Potsdam) and ZDF (in Mainz). And although Ruzowitzky is Austrian-born, he is descended from Nazi grandparents and grew up in Germany.[4] Despite the Academy's need for national categorisation, *The Counterfeiters* is only partly an Austrian film. This fact, however, may productively inform interpretations. Austria, like Germany, after all, has its own troubled and complex relationship to Holocaust atrocities. In the terms of Austria's cultural memory, it seems – in relation, for example, to the election of President Kurt Waldheim, a former Wehrmacht intelligence officer – that much of Austria's population has difficulty accepting obvious evidence about their nation's massive collaboration with the Nazis and still today view Austria as foremost among National Socialism's victims.[5]

Concerns about the legacy of Austrian perpetration arise not only in connection with debates around Waldheim or the late xenophobic politician Jörg Haider, but also in connection with discussions surrounding the site of the former concentration camp Mauthausen, a stone quarry near Linz in which hundreds of thousands of prisoners were worked to death, and which constitutes one setting of *The Counterfeiters*. Early Austrian quarrels about how to memorialise the site of the camp included a discussion of whether or not it should be adorned with an enormous illuminated cross (Perz 2002: 155). Subsequent debates centred on the European fascination with 'event culture'. A spectacle called 'Mauthausen 2000', at which Beethoven's *Ninth Symphony* (1823–24) was played in the quarry to commemorate the fifty-fifth anniversary of the camp's liberation set in motion a controversy about the inappropriateness of calling upon the Vienna Philharmonic to play Beethoven – something they had done at Hermann Goering's request in 1938 – in this sacred place. Beethoven's *Ninth*, generally linked with Friedrich Schiller's *Ode to Joy* (*Ode an die Freude*, 1785) to which its final movement is set, has a special history, having been twice played for Hitler on his birthdays in 1937 and 1942 (Buch 2003: 205). Objections to 'Mauthausen 2000' were expressed by Elie Wiesel, who cancelled plans to attend, and by Marta Halpert, the director of the Central European office of the Anti-Defamation League, who found the project distasteful and told the *New York Times*, 'this is the worst sort of event-culture, like taking the Three Tenors to the Baths of Carcalla'. She added, 'You can hear the screams in the quarry. You should not make any other sounds' (Cohen 2000; Morrison 2000). The controversy thus concerned more than merely the choice of the piece, which makes for a complicated objection insofar as Beethoven's work is by no means an explicit endorsement of fascism and has been the official anthem of the European Union since 1985.[6] Simultaneously, although Beethoven is not Wagner, for some he retains an unfortunate metonymic link with German cultural hegemony under the Nazis.

At issue is less Beethoven's *Ninth* than the relationship between silence and sound where Holocaust memorialisation is concerned, and the question of whether one can or must 'still hear the screams in the quarry'. Bertrand Perz compares the playing of Beethoven at Mauthausen unfavourably with a project that resulted in *Chronicles from the Ashes* (*Mauthausen – Vom großen Sterben hören*, 2000), a piece by the jazz keyboardist Joe Zawinul composed specifically for the Mauthausen memorial site and thus untainted by darker cultural legacies (Perz 2006: 256). The chief element of the disputation, therefore, is not whether there may be music after Mauthausen (if one may vary Theodor Adorno's famous formulation),[7] but what uses of music and silence are more or less appropriate to Holocaust memorialisation. It makes sense to weigh the various meanings of sound against those of silence, and *The Counterfeiters* engages in this type of negotiation. The film can be analysed in light of questions similar to those raised by 'Mauthausen 2000' as a reflection on Holocaust memory and on what serves as a proper balm where deep wounds – in this case German and Jewish wounds – are concerned. The film moves between its music and certain sound effects that are calculated to draw attention to the soundtrack's function vis-à-vis violence. The choices made in regard to the film's audio reflect its orientation towards, on the one hand, the questions of collaboration that form *The Counterfeiters'* central theme, and on the other the larger question of whether it is possible to comprehend atrocities endured during the Holocaust. Subsequent to a consideration of such issues – of the film's depiction of the victims' sufferings – the film's choices concerning its music and sounds can be interpreted anew.

Following *The Counterfeiters'* first twenty minutes most of the film is set in Sachsenhausen concentration camp, where the labour associated with Operation Bernhard took place. Mauthausen is, however, briefly depicted in early sequences as the camp to which Sorowitsch is first deported. It plays a key role in portraying the lessons the main character learns in order to survive. At Mauthausen Sorowitsch acquires privileges and opportunities based on his artistic skills. He paints flattering portraits of the guards as a means of acquiring additional food. Through presenting Sorowitsch's management of his predicament, the film speaks to the issue of collaboration. He adopts a false persona and, one might say, plays to Mauthausen's cruel rules. The theme recalls discussions around an incident described in the memoir of Dr Miklos Nyiszli and later explored in Primo Levi's discussion of 'the gray zone' in which a soccer match was played at Auschwitz between members of the SS and the *Sonderkommando* (Levi 1988: 54–55).[8] Levi suggests that the division into two teams on a single playing field was one among many ways in which the SS taunted the *Sonderkommando*, coercing them into performing the part of equals and thereby undercutting the otherwise obvious moral distinction between the group that wilfully coordinated the gassing of Jews and the group of prisoners who were made to incinerate the victims' bodies – to dispose of the evidence – under penalty of death.[9]

Although there is no explicit reference to Levi in Ruzowitzky's film (as there had been in Schlöndorff's *The Ninth Day*, which adapts passages from Levi's *The Drowned and the Saved*, 1986), *The Counterfeiters*, consistent with Levi's position, declines to demonise Sorowitsch for playing a role, and even for the fact that he counterfeited in the service of the Nazis, thereby advancing Germany's war aims.[10] The film thematises the difficulties in assuming high moral ground with respect to the compromised situations depicted in the film. For example, when Major Herzog tries to convince Sorowitsch to cooperate, he encourages him by explaining that Sorowitsch should not engage in deceit because the two of them are now 'on the same side'. Herzog is coercing Sorowitsch, and as such his position is deeply cynical. They are only on the same side insofar as Sorowitsch's fate rests in Herzog's hands. Sorowitsch is admonished to perform his role convincingly, and, as he learned at Mauthausen, it is important to allow one's behaviour to be falsified (or counterfeited) as need be. The issue arises throughout the film, but was already a theme in Adolf Burger's memoir. Burger, for example, recalls playing ping-pong with Squad Leader (*Hauptscharführer*) Werner (a man who resembles the film's diabolical character Holst). Because of the counterfeiters' special privileges – that they were, like the *Sonderkommando*, in the unusual position of having access to diversions such as ping-pong tables and being periodically treated otherwise than as animals – the rules were different; ordinary prisoners would never have been in the position of playing ping-pong against guards. Burger recalls that he beat Werner the first time, but then, realising his mistake, he let Werner win. He credits his survival to this concession.[11]

How does the masquerade in which Sorowitsch is engaged square with his character's noir-ishness? Karl Markovics's performance recalls Humphrey Bogart's in *Casablanca* (1942), and his character is presented as someone who is predisposed to opportunism and self-interest. Ruzowitzky underscores the fact that Sorowitsch was a forger prior to the war. On the eve of his 1936 arrest we see the character express his longstanding interest in forging the dollar. He was an accomplished criminal before the Nazis took hold of him, and his criminality is highlighted to draw attention to his willingness to place his own needs first and thus as a measure of insight into his survival. The noir-ishness may be understood to introduce a gap, or a Brechtian defamiliarisation between the viewer and the protagonist. Given the situation, however – that he is more or less a sympathetic figure who negotiates with Nazis for his life – it is difficult not to identify with him. Sorowitsch's criminality instead offers insight into the film's links with Levi, making explicit what we are meant to conclude concerning the central protagonist's navigation of the grey zone. Levi points out in his discussion of who in the camp was 'drowned' and who was 'saved' that those prone to moral compromise were most likely to survive. He writes, 'The "saved" of the *Lager* were not the best, those predestined to do good, the bearers of a message,' and adds, 'what I had seen and lived through proved the exact contrary. Preferably the worst survived, the selfish, the violent, the insensitive, the collaborators of the "gray zone".' (1988: 82).

To describe Sorowitsch's character as selfish misses the mark; given the context, this term does not fit. Based on his study of oral testimony, Lawrence Langer observes that actual experiences in concentration camps were such that the terms heroism and selfishness do not apply, and that normal reactions in situations such as these, which grossly exceed any conventional moral guidelines, are predicated on one's capacity to improvise. Langer is interested in 'how an individual reacts when situation rather than character controls response', and he notes that in the absence of certain rules, 'one is left vulnerable to desperate gestures that have little connection to the moral assurances we customarily associate with efforts at self-preservation' (1991: 139 and 123). Ruzowitzky, however, opts to present us with a protagonist who was morally pliable before the war began – a forger who sometimes barters for sex. He is not unusually nefarious, beyond engaging in some loan-sharking, yet he is surely inclined to improvise where his survival is concerned. Unlike the priest Henri Kremer in Schlöndorff's *The Ninth Day*, a protagonist who finds high moral ground through self-sacrifice and refuses to compromise, Sorowitsch survives because he has from the outset relinquished any stake in his own sanctification.

Sorowitsch is not wholly insensitive, and is at one point depicted taking pains and risks to acquire tuberculosis medicine on behalf of Kolja (Sebastian Urzendowsky), a young Russian art student he had paternalistically befriended on the way to Sachsenhausen.[12] Sorowitsch is a paradigmatic Levian subject, who here practices an improvisational form of solidarity called 'us-ism'. Levi describes 'us-ism' as 'selfishness extended to the person closest to you', which, he explains, was the only manifestation of generosity and self-sacrifice left to those in the camps (1988: 80). Sorowitsch, however, does not want his response to be mistaken for solidarity. When Burger (played by August Diehl) lauds Sorowitsch for having shared his food with Kolja ('That was solidarity!'), Sorowitsch corrects him ('That was *soup*'). When it comes to toeing a moral line, he is resolutely cynical and would not wish to be seen as an exponent of an ideology, particularly a moralising one.[13]

As much as Herzog serves as a foil for Sorowitsch, the contrast between Sorowitsch and Burger illuminates key distinctions within *The Counterfeiters*' attitude to how these prisoners can understand, identify with and forgive one another. Burger, the character on whose memoir the film is largely based, worked in *Kanada*, the area of

Auschwitz-Birkenau where the stolen possessions of murdered Jewish prisoners were collected and sorted. He is apparently repulsed by the extent to which he and the other forgers are expected to collaborate, and argues for open revolt – an option Sorowitsch, and the film itself, view as untenable. Burger is idealistic and explains to Sorowitsch that he cannot play by the Nazis' rules – that his wife, a victim of the Nazis, used to remind him that printing presses such as the one they are using to abet the Nazis' criminal enterprise were made for printing the truth. Though Sorowitsch is not sympathetic to Burger's past political orientations, his constant pestering strikes a chord. When the two play a game of ping-pong and shots ring out from the other side of the wooden wall, Burger, still agitating for rebellion and trying to awaken Sorowitsch's conscience, provokes him with the words 'Be glad we're standing on this side of the wall.' The film here addresses the heavy burden associated with inhabiting the grey zone. It emphasises both the connections between the prisoners as well as the limits placed on solidarity in the camp, a contradiction that is difficult for even an opportunist such as Sorowitsch to bear.

That the counterfeiters are ultimately all on the same side and share a common predicament is made evident when Sorowitsch is first

Figure 4.1: Soli Sorowitsch reacts dismissively to the accusation that he is a criminal.

shown around the workshop. He is introduced to Dr Viktor Hahn (Tilo Prückner), who, upon noticing the green triangle on Sorowitsch's uniform, is indignant that he should have to work with a criminal. Hahn comments that the only criminals before Sorowitsch's arrival were the ones wearing Nazi uniforms. As Levi would have recognised, in light of the magnitude of the real crime that was taking place – the Holocaust – the distinction between the prisoners is specious. This is not to say that some of the career criminals who became *Kapos* were not vicious, but Sorowitsch is no *Kapo*. The error of labelling Sorowitsch a criminal, given the circumstances, is a shadowy reflection of an error made after the war by Major Krüger himself, who, in a 1958 interview with *American Weekly*, commented that Soli Smolianoff (the real Sorowitsch) was 'the only criminal we ever had in Operation Bernhard' (Krüger 1958: 22). Krüger seems to have forgotten to judge himself alongside everyone else who oversaw the forced labour. A comment of this sort made during the war is evidence of confusion; making it 13 years later is perverse. The character Sorowitsch, by contrast, is depicted as having an intuitive and immediate understanding of the false dichotomy where the prisoners are concerned. Ruzowitzky seems to second his character's dismissal of Hahn's self-righteousness (Sorowitsch replies, 'Kiss my ass!' ['*Leck mich!*']) through his use of *mise-en-scène*: Hahn and Sorowitsch hold their conversation through a superfluous set of bars that serve little more than an ornamental function in the workshop. The film asserts that the inhabitants of this grey zone – Sachsenhausen's barracks 18 and 19 – were all in the same boat, and although the prisoners each managed the situation differently, the terms heroism and selfishness lose their traditional meanings. Ruzowitzky's screenplay presupposes that the moral playing field among these forgers is level and that they can ultimately see eye-to-eye with one another. Whether we can understand them – whether the truth of their experience can be represented adequately, and what purpose such representation serves – remains a separate question.

How the wounds associated with the real story behind *The Counterfeiters* are confronted, and whether one still 'hears the screams', is reflected in the implied distinctions between what the film's characters hear and what the film intends for us to hear. The music on the soundtrack plays a prominent role, repeatedly serving to cover over painful parts of Sorowitsch's experience. The most recurrent *motif* is the tango, performed here by the Argentine harmonica player Victor Hugo Díaz. The music is frequently introduced non-diegetically as memory, and if one makes the working – though by no means absolute – assumption that this non-diegetic music reflects Sorowitsch's subjective state of mind (as opposed to source music's apparent 'objectivity'), then we are being drawn into Sorowitsch's past and made aware that he is returning in thought to a time before the war (Stilwell 2007: 190–91). Although we hear the strains of the tango at the film's beginning (Diaz's 'Mano a Mano' ['Hand to Hand']), the earliest chronological point at which they are heard in the film is 1936, Sorowitsch's last night of freedom before being arrested by Herzog, who was then working with the Criminal Police. The tango appears diegetically when Sorowitsch turns on the record player (the piece is Diaz's 'Volver' ['Return']), quickly becomes non-diegetic as a means of stitching together the ensuing montage, and again – as 'Mano a Mano' – returns non-diegetically as memory later in the film. That the tango permits Sorowitsch to return in his mind to happier times corresponds to how music is employed in the Sachsenhausen barracks. He learns shortly after his arrival that the forgers have the privilege of listening to music, but that the operas they play on their phonograph are meant primarily to overwhelm the horrific sounds that would otherwise seep in through the windows, specifically the cries of pain associated with a cruel ritual during which Sachsenhausen prisoners were made to run through the camp in ill-fitting shoes (Malkin 2006: 84).[14]

Music is thus entangled with the attempt to cover over cosmetically what cannot be covered over; what is repressed will surely return. In both its diegetic and non-diegetic forms, music conceals pain, as in the workshop, where the forgers play music to divert them from their forced labour. The first time Sorowitsch and Burger are shown their work assignments we hear diegetically 'Mein Herr Marquis' (also known as 'Adele's Laughing Song') from Johann Strauss's *Die Fledermaus* (1874). At the centre of *Die Fledermaus* a character is avoiding going to prison, and the song thus not only picks up on one of the film's key themes but echoes the other 'light' songs on the soundtrack, ones borrowed from operettas such as Strauss's *The Merry War* (*Der lustige Krieg*, 1881). This song in particular concerns a masquerade: Adele, the maid, has gone to a ball dressed as an actress and is laughing to disguise the fact that she has been mistaken for what she is – a maid. The 'joke' of being mistaken for a criminal in the midst of a wholly criminal enterprise could likewise serve as the conceit at the centre of an Austrian operetta were it not so tragic.

There are, however, points at which the film offers a contrasting acoustic paradigm, or where it acknowledges the limits of music's ability to paper over wounds. In an early sequence of the film we glimpse Sorowitsch in Monte Carlo immediately following the war, when he has picked up a woman (Dolores Chaplin) at the casino. She is not a professional prostitute, but she seems to be comfortable accepting money in exchange for sex, which, in underscoring the role of exchange in defining human relations, recalls one of the themes of the film. As she notices the number tattooed on Sorowitsch's arm, the noise of waves lapping against the Mediterranean shore becomes suddenly strange. The pleasant sounds, as if one were standing on the beach, now call to mind the experience of drowning. This noise suggests either deep memories that refuse to rise to the surface or Sorowitsch's sense that he had been drowning during his imprisonment. On this point the film is not specific. The 'drowning' may be Sorowitsch's own, insofar as we hear it again upon his arrival at Mauthausen, but it may also be a sound evoked by watching others drown: we also hear it when Sorowitsch realises the 'new' jacket with which the Nazis have furnished him was taken from another Jew, one recently sent to his death.

These sounds return once again at Sachsenhausen in a dramatic sequence in which the sadistic Squad Leader Holst explains to Sorowitsch how worthless he is and then urinates on him. Sorowitsch's anger initially manifests itself as virtual silence. The camera swings, following the bodily motions associated with his fit of rage, and as his own anger subdues the sounds of Nazi laughter and he goes to wash himself off, his footsteps begin to echo thunderously. The ensuing silence is not absolute, but rather, insofar as the noise is meant to reflect what is taking place inside his head, is deafening. The film here alludes to a mode of sublime anger – an experience that exceeds Sorowitsch's ability to generate an acoustic inner representation that would facilitate more than the barest comprehension of what has transpired. A similar profoundly deafening silence is depicted in a subsequent sequence in which Holst executes Kolja, the art student Sorowitsch had struggled to protect. Sorowitsch watches from the bathroom as Holst executes the young prisoner with a single shot to the head. He shakes and shudders, and in its initial moments the musical composition (named 'Kolja executed' on the soundtrack) very fleetingly evokes harmonious play of stringed instruments as though Sorowitsch were struggling to recall the comforting sounds of Argentine tangos but cannot. It is as though he finds himself submerged once more. He then returns to the barracks only to hear Holst giving a perverse eulogy for Kolja, and everything is muted; it is almost as if Sorowitsch himself has been partially deafened by the gunshot.[15] Again, the film gestures towards a sublime screaming, or suggests an inner response so violent and tumultuous that it exceeds representation. Only after Holst walks out can Sorowitsch return to 'normal', which is to say that he can again begin to function as he had done habitually, by recalling the strains of Diaz's 'Mano a Mano'.

Most of the film depicts how Sorowitsch and this group of forgers – who were afforded special treatment, could grow out their hair and were given enough to eat – were separated from the general population of Sachsenhausen. At the film's end, however, once the camp is liberated and the emaciated inmates have stormed the barracks, the forgers, alongside the starved and dazed survivors (a group who, at this point, appear to constitute the filmmaker's principal depiction of the unprivileged or 'real' victims of Sachsenhausen) listen to music on a phonograph. One member of this latter group places a hand on Burger's shoulder, which may be meant to suggest that the two could reach an understanding of one another's experience despite the enormity of the gap between them. Although Burger looks bewildered and wonders what he is to do with the shame that now overshadows his survival – the guilt of having collaborated, however unwillingly, to keep a set of privileges not available to others – the survivor's gesture seems to indicate the possibility of forgiveness.

The song that plays on the phonograph is Beniamino Gigli's rendition of 'Rimpianto' ('Regret'), a serenade by Enrico Toselli. The song is about memory and lost love. Gigli sings,

> Like a golden dream
> it is carved in my heart.
> The memory still of that love
> that no longer exists [...]
> But it was very brief in me
> the sweetness of it truly vanished
> this beautiful golden dream
> leaving sorrow within me.

When Gigli reaches the line 'dark is the future' ('cupo è l'avvenir') and sustains the final syllable (the -ir in 'avvenir'), Ruzowitzky cuts away

89

Figure 4.2: Adolf Burger shares a sympathetic moment with a uniformed survivor of Sachsenhausen.

from the camp to a tight shot of Sorowitsch in a Monte Carlo casino following the war. In that moment it seems that Sorowitsch has decided to be done with his past, to deliberately gamble away every penny of the counterfeit money he had kept. At the onset of the film, when we first encountered Sorowitsch staring at the water, he seemed lonely and may have been considering drowning himself, but later, at the very end of the film and in the company of an attractive woman, he dances on the shore and comfortably professes – in a forger's *double entendre* – that if he needs money he can always make more. His future hardly seems dark, and the tango for two has returned to close the wound and replace Gigli's lonely serenade.

Levi remarks that liberation from the camps was difficult, and that, 'coming out of the darkness, one suffered because of the reacquired consciousness of having been diminished'. He explains that this was, 'not by our will, cowardice or fault, yet nevertheless we had lived for months and years at an animal level' (1988: 75). However, the depiction of Sorowitsch's release gives an indication that his experience could be left behind him. Surely this was the story of a uniquely privileged prisoner (a fact of which Ruzowitzky was well aware)[16] and perhaps for that reason Sorowitsch is depicted as less traumatised. Such subtleties, however, may be lost on audiences. Insofar as he stands for other survivors, his experience, difficult as it was, is presented as something that can in the end be assimilated into his postwar life and made comprehensible to the viewer. The film's status as emotive cinema (*Gefühlskino*) is predicated on the presumption that we can grasp what he has endured.

On the road to Ebensee, the concentration camp near to Mauthausen from which the real forgers of Operation Bernhard were liberated (rather than from Sachsenhausen, as is falsely depicted in the film), some forgery equipment, SS files and a good number of remaining counterfeit pound notes were dumped in the water (at Traunsee and in Lake Toplitz [Toplitzsee] in the Alps). The metal crates eventually became buried treasure, themselves drowned, and exploration for them became tabloid fodder in the years that followed. Lawrence Malkin observes that the 'hands down winners' of the story of Operation Bernhard were the tourist operators around Lake Toplitz, 'who have in recent years turned it into an Austrian Loch Ness, complete with its own website' (2006: 207).

Whether as tourism or as event culture, popular modes of coming to terms with the Holocaust presuppose that there can be some understanding between victims and contemporary observers. This is by and large false currency and is predicated primarily on purchasing reconciliation and papering over collective wounds. Recent films that have reflected on the obstacles in the way of coming to terms with the past include Robert Thalheim's *And Along Come Tourists* (*Am Ende kommen Touristen*, 2007), which was directly concerned with whether a young German, born forty years after the end of the war, could understand anything of the Holocaust past, and whether he owes any debt to the victims. Similarly Rex Bloomstein's documentary film *KZ* (2006) was directed specifically at Austria and cast a critical eye on tourist culture in and around the site of Mauthausen concentration camp. Thalheim's and Bloomstein's films excel at illustrating how the past remains far from having been properly worked through. Whether by accident or by design Ruzowitsky's film engages with the question of representation, specifically in the choices it makes concerning its music and sound. As with a symphony played at the site of Mauthausen's quarry, music can be treated either as a sufficient or an indecent measure of how one memorialises and reflects. *The Counterfeiters* is not without its complexities; it acknowledges the challenges inherent in depicting traumatic experiences and thematises its central protagonist's difficulty processing his sufferings and the sufferings of those around him. However, to judge from the sense of closure its final waterfront tango provides, Ruzowitzsky's film, akin to its heritage film counterparts, inclines towards the affirmative assertion that the case can be closed – or in this instance, that the forger's case can be emptied and discarded – and that the past can be left behind.

NOTES

1 Adolf Burger (2009: 125; 2007: 127) attributes the scheme to Naujocks.
2 On Ruzowitzky's *Anatomy* as a thriller and in relation to its depiction of the past, see Prager 2006: 301–2.
3 On *The Lives of Others* as a melodrama with similarities to German heritage films, see Fisher 2010.
4 Speaking about his Nazi grandparents, Ruzowitzky explains, 'Living in Austria, if you're not completely blocked [off], you are aware that this is part of your history – your family history, your country's history – because the remains are everywhere. My grandparents weren't some huge war criminals, they were just average people fascinated by the Nazi's [sic] ideas' 2008.
5 On how Austrians see themselves as victims, see Perz (2002: 151) and Stuhlpfarrer (2002: 235).
6 On the politics of *Ode to Joy*, see Buch 2003: 209.
7 Adorno raises the question of what constitutes appropriately critical art for the culture that created Auschwitz throughout his postwar writings. The most common reference point is his remark that 'to write poetry after Auschwitz is barbaric' in Adorno 1981: 34. His remarks are commonly misunderstood as an assertion that no art is justifiable after the Holocaust.
8 The reference to the soccer game can be found in Nyiszli 1993: 68.
9 Debarati Sanyal describes the soccer-playing scene as an example of 'coerced mimesis between executioner and victim'. This is, in other words, another example of Jews being forced to play a part at the behest of the Nazis – in this case, for their amusement (Sanyal 2002: 2).
10 On the use of Primo Levi in Schlöndorff's film, see Prager 2010.
11 The story is recounted in Burger 2009: 160; 2007: 163.
12 The figure of Kolja seems to be inspired by Pjotr Sukiennik. See Burger 2009: 178–79; 2007: 180–81. The English version renders his name Sukienik.
13 An inspiration for Sorowitsch's cynical persona may have been the Greek philosopher Diogenes of Sinope (also known as Diogenes the Cynic). A

story is commonly told that when Alexander the Great met Diogenes, who was lying in the sunlight, Alexander asked him if there was anything he could do for him, to which Diogenes simply replied, 'I would have you stand elsewhere than between me and the sun.' Given Sorowitsch's cynicism, the scene in *The Counterfeiters* in which he asks Burger to move out of his sunlight may be taken as a conscious evocation of Diogenes.

14 The description of this ritual can also be found in Burger 2009: 113; 2007: 115.

15 The 'eulogy' has an origin in Burger's memoir. According to Burger, after Senior Squad Leader (*Oberscharführer*) Heizmann shot Sukiennik he told the other prisoners, 'Although he knew he would be shot, he was so brave. He made a deep impression on me' (Burger 2009: 178; 2007: 181).

16 In interview Ruzowitzky explains, 'I would not have dared to make a movie that tries to show the normal life of a concentration-camp inmate because I think that that is not possible. It's not possible because we cannot identify with such a person. We cannot say, "What would I do if I was an inmate in a concentration camp?" because the situation is so extreme and so far away from what we know' (Archibald 2008).

Chapter 5

Aiming to please? Consensus and consciousness-raising in Wolfgang Becker's *Good Bye, Lenin!* (2003)

Nick Hodgin

Released in 2003, Wolfgang Becker's *Good Bye, Lenin!* was soon identified as a pedagogically useful film. Its value was almost immediately recognised by Germany's Federal Agency for Political Education, whose declared aim is to 'promote awareness for democracy and participation in politics'. The agency was quick to produce an accompanying booklet which offered a synopsis and analysis of the film, background information and a series of questions designed for teachers. *Good Bye, Lenin!* has indeed come to be used in secondary education both in Germany and abroad, while Goethe Institutes from Tanzania to Buenos Aires and New York have included it in festivals showcasing German cinema, making use of the film in their language-learning programmes and as a key text for studying German history. The film's importance is not limited to Germany's cultural and political institutions. In Britain and in North America in particular, university modules focusing on German cinema or on German post-unification society often include the film in their syllabi.

It is not surprising that many of those who work in education hope for a text or exhibition or film that manages to incorporate those issues that are considered significant in our understanding of the past, or indeed the present. How best to represent and to engage with what is often described as the Germans' difficult history – i.e. its National Socialist past – has been an uncomfortable and controversial matter for over five decades. After 1989, the challenge of representing the past likewise affected the GDR's past, and debates about appropriateness and responsibility have centred on all manner of representation, from museum exhibition to biographies, novels, historiography, documentary and feature films.

Good Bye, Lenin! was by no means the first film to engage with events of 1989. Several dozen films looking at the collapse of the GDR and the experience of unification had been produced in the interim (Hodgin 2011). These responses to unification and the reassessment of the East German regime were naturally wide-ranging. Where some directors saw the conjoining of the two German states as an encounter rich with comic potential, others focused on the despair brought by unification, as east German communities struggled to survive in a new and unfamiliar free-market society. The assortment of genres – grotesques, satires, banal comedies, melodramas, thrillers – attests to the different approaches towards thematising post-unification Germany (Cooke 2005; Hodgin 2011). Though some of the films fared reasonably well on the international film-festival circuit, where they were either highlighted as serious reflections of the post-unification condition and/or recognised for their artistic value (Andreas Dresen's *Silent Country* [*Stilles Land*, 1992]; Andreas Kleinert's *Paths in the Night* [*Wege in die Nacht*, 1999]), very few of the films made any impact on German cinema audiences.

Such commercial failure (and critical interest) is not unusual. Many of these narratives offer bleak accounts of east German life. The social anomie evident in these films is the consequence of several interrelated factors: psychological instability as a result of economic fatigue, ideological insecurity and material deterioration. However, these issues are not necessarily attributable only to post-Wall developments. A number of directors outline the challenges facing the east German communities before 1989, albeit with different motives. In *Apple Trees* (*Apfelbäume*, 1992), for example, Helma Sanders-Brahms uses her narrative to sketch out the incompatibility of genuine socialist ideology with the SED (Socialist Union Party) regime. In *Silent Country*, Andreas Dresen gainsays any historical revisionism that attempts to cast the population in the role of dissidents and revolutionary heroes by highlighting the people's innate passivity, albeit with considerable humour. Andreas Kleinert, meanwhile, considers the individual choices that east Germans have had to make since the GDR's collapse, choices that relate to personal responsibility and to private and collective memory in his films *Lost Landscapes* (*Verlorene Landschaft*, 1992) and *Outside Time* (*Neben der Zeit*, 1995). Those films that did succeed were mostly farcical comedies such as Peter Timm's early unification film, *Go Trabi Go* (1991), which follows an east German family's eventful journey through Germany and into Italy. The success of that film might partly be explained by its sympathetic stance towards its protagonists, a family of newly self-liberated east Germans. Timm's film effectively encapsulates many of the preconceptions about the eastern population, relying on and celebrating east German stereotypes (provincial, unsophisticated, inept), as well as offering an equally crude parody of west German stereotypes (opulence, gluttony, egotism).

Neither the serious social-critical films nor the banal crowd pleasers provoked the Federal Agency for Political Education's interest. The only film set in the GDR to have been included on its film list prior to *Good Bye, Lenin!* was the teenage drama *Never Mind the Wall* (*Wie Feuer und Flamme*, Connie Walter, 2001). *Good Bye, Lenin's* impact was profound; the interest in Becker's film went far beyond film journalism. So well received was Becker's film and so significant was its perceived cultural status that 180 politicians duly heeded the invitation extended by the Minister for Culture, Christina Weis, to attend a screening of the film at the former prize GDR cinema on Karl Marx Allee in Berlin. The parliamentary outing was widely covered in the German press, with many journalists focusing in particular on Wolfgang Schäuble's reaction. The former Federal Minister of the Interior, who, with GDR State Secretary Günther Krause, had co-signed the Unification Treaty in 1990, was said to have been moved to tears by the film, though the politician later played down these claims, conceding only that his eyes had 'moistened' (*Der Tagesspiegel* 2005).

THE CINEMA OF CONSENSUS

Before considering the pedagogical appeal of Becker's film, which follows Alex Kerner's (Daniel Brühl) chaotic and convoluted efforts to convince his mother (Katrin Saß), a recovering coma patient who is unaware of recent momentous historical events, that the GDR is unchanged, I would like to assess its significance in the context of post-unification filmmaking and especially in the context of Rentschler's 'cinema of consensus', the impetus for this volume (Rentschler 2000: 260–77). Rentschler's essay is partly an attempt to arrive at a suitable designation for the kind of films that, at the end of a lacklustre decade, he considered typical of the post-Wall period, films which lack a 'convincing paradigm or even useful catch phrases' (2000: 260) suitable for discussing contemporary German cinema. Rentschler is, by his own admission, a devoted fan of New German Cinema, which he admires for its risks and its provocations in theme, content and intent, something that is altogether lacking in those contemporary films under his scrutiny which he categorises as primarily star-driven, 'yuppie comedies of errors', whose narratives offer nothing more than 'pseudo-crises, for they have no depth of despair, no true suffering, no real joy' (2000: 263). Rentschler's is not a lonely voice in criticising such generic fare. While important research has been conducted in reception studies and popular film, film studies, as Ginette Vincendeau notes, has long been dominated by commentators and academics who privilege 'works that are, to various degrees, aesthetically innovative, socially committed, and humanist in outlook' (2000: 56).

New German Cinema is often associated, not entirely accurately, with profundity, and a deep sense of despair. What is understood as New German Cinema is therefore set up in opposition to the newer German cinema along a familiar dialectic, one which Steve Neale previously identified in his assessment of so-called art cinema as a question of 'genre versus personal expression, of [...] trash versus taste, hysteria versus restraint, energy versus decorum and quality' (2002: 103). Such a formulation is, as Neale acknowledges, a simplification, but pertinent to the general view of the films championed by Rentschler and others. Generalisations and assumptions about the previous generation of *auteurs* abound. There is a problem in attempting to define too closely those directors associated with the New German Cinema. While film courses studying postwar German cinema typically embark on a chronology that starts with the Oberhausen Manifesto in 1962 and ends with Fassbinder's death in 1982, often focusing on the canonised few (particularly Herzog, Wenders and Fassbinder), it is important to remember that there was no organised agenda, no distinct political aim or uniform aesthetic programme that brought the directors together, not the filmmakers dubbed the Young German Cinema of the 1960s, nor those associated with the New German Cinema of the 1970s. However dissimilar the results, film scholars have sought to focus on certain points of convergence: the symbolic rejection of *Papas Kino* (Dad's Cinema), formal experimentation (using and abusing Hollywood references), self-reflexivity, and certain ideological impulses that distinguished them from contemporary commercial cinema. These filmmakers were certainly not interested in providing the public with unreconstructed genre films (such as the commercially successful relationship comedies to which Rentschler objects), though their imputed antagonism towards their audiences is, as Thomas Elsaesser has shown, not as clear cut as is sometimes suggested (1989: 2). The directors who comprised this loose film movement were more significant in terms of cultural capital (the kudos of international recognition for example) than they were in terms of revenue, since the films, unlike, the earlier New Wave films in Italy, France and Britain, did not enjoy widespread appeal.

GENERATION X-FILME

Underpinning the notion of a 'cinema of consensus' is a suspicion of the mainstream, of a popular cinema that is typically associated with crass entertainment, star vehicles, the worst kind of genre cinema, one that is formulaic, conservative, predictable – and popular. Published in 2000, Rentschler's article provided an accurate if pessimistic assessment of developments in German cinema in the 1990s. The label could be applied to other national cinemas – certainly the lack of 'serious political reflection or sustained historical retrospection' (2000: 263) is true also of British and North American cinema culture in the same decade. British filmmaking in the 1990s may have enjoyed some critical and commercial success for films that represent important contemporary issues (drugs, unemployment, conflicts within hybrid communities) in (comic) films such as *Trainspotting* (Danny Boyle, 1996), *The Full Monty* (Peter Cattaneo, 1997) and *East is East* (Damien O'Donnell, 1999), but the most successful film of the decade, Roger Michell's *Notting Hill* (1999) is proof that 'upscale urbanites working in a sector of the culture industry' is not a characteristic only of German filmmaking in the 1990s (Rentschler 2000: 262).

Rentschler's analysis corresponded with some directors' and producers' experience and view of the German film industry as moribund and in desperate need of rejuvenation. Wolfgang Becker had previously identified the problems facing German cinema in an interview in 1997.

The majority of people who go to see German films, the average folk, just aren't represented on screen any more. Instead, we get media presenters and advertising characters prancing about, all those hip thirty-year-old professionals with stupid identity crises, who in reality represent a tiny percentage of Germans.[1] (Weingarten 1997: 217)

Becker had already sought to distance himself from this cinema culture by establishing with fellow directors Dani Levy, Tom Tykwer and producer Stefan Arndt, an independent film company, X-Filme Creative Pool in 1994. Inspired by United Artists, the production company founded in 1919 by Hollywood stars and directors seeking some autonomy from the contractual straitjacket imposed by Hollywood studios, they hoped to foster a new type of filmmaking in Germany, specifically, as the website makes clear, to 'create a platform for diversity [sic] ideas, with the aim of producing challenging (audience) films' (2010).

Though in parenthesis, the inclusion of the word audience is significant to understanding of the company's approach. The new-wave *auteurs* may have also wanted to 'win new audiences', but in truth these were to be found primarily in the art houses, even when directors produced films that borrowed, referenced or recycled popular genres (Elsaesser 1989: 2). While the films produced under the auspices of X-Filme in general lack the 'distinctive aesthetics' of the New German Cinema, one might argue, in the case of some of the titles, that they are at least reminiscent of the earlier films' tendency 'to be read as nationally representative' and demonstrate, in varying degrees, a commitment 'to themes of national import' (Gallagher 2009: 39). Scholars such as Sabine Hake argue that X-Filme 'has produced the most innovative films of the 1990s and early 2000s' (2002: 195). Certainly the recent addition of Michael Haneke's *White Ribbon* (*Das Weiße Band*, 2009) to its portfolio is evidence of a continued interest in more challenging films (although Haneke is now as much the cover star as the *bête noire* he once was). X-Filme can, then, boast an impressive number of inventive, sometimes original films, many of which have won industry and festival prizes, but it has also produced numerous films which, while well enough received, hardly count as original in either form or content. This willingness to produce popular genre films distinguishes them from some of the previous generation of filmmakers, such as Straub and Huillet, whose uncompromising commitment to their artistic vision (evident in their difficult and rarely seen work) reminds Barton Byg of Brecht and Adorno's belief that the 'artist must try only to make the best art possible; to make things less well than one could so as to be popular leads nowhere, politically or aesthetically'. Byg rightly acknowledges that this 'seems more eccentric in the 1990s than it did in the 1960s' (1995: 8).

Despite the difference in quality of its output, X-Filme has maintained its reputation as a brand of quality. This is in part due to the 'distinctly contemporary sensibility' that shapes many of its films (Hake 2002: 195). The success of some titles, notably Tom Tykwer's *Run Lola Run* (*Lola rennt*, 1998), the company's first major success (and a significant international hit), is in part attributable to its hip depiction of modern Berlin, and capitalises on the city's modish reputation, its dance-music culture, and hints at the counter-cultural and bohemian lifestyle with which Berlin was long associated and which profile the new, unified Berlin has sought to maintain.

The company's self-assurance, its desire to tell stories, to chronicle contemporary Germany without recourse to either Hollywood conventions and tropes or to those of the New German Cinema, is emblematic of a new-found confidence within the German film industry. Less ideologically opposed to mainstream conventions and popular taste, some of the younger German directors have distanced themselves from the older *auteurs*. Emphasising difference has not necessarily been mutual: Wim Wenders, admittedly among the most commercially minded directors associated with New German Cinema, has identified common aspirations:

> There is a new generation about in Germany which has succeeded in reaching an audience in a way that is quite different to anything my generation – Herzog, Fassbinder and a couple of others – ever managed. I think it's great that a misunderstanding between the Germans and their history has finally been undone. I think Dani Levy, Wolfgang Becker und Tom Tykwer, who founded X-Filme, are great. Their idea isn't very different to ours back then with the Filmverlag der Autoren. (Jekubzik, no date)

Good Bye, Lenin!: Authenticity and Artifice

Good Bye, Lenin! is evidence of German directors' newfound confidence to narrate their own history. But although the history in question – the collapse of the East German state and subsequent unification – is the subject of continuing controversy, knowledge of the contentious post-unification debates was not crucial to the film's reception. Foreign commentators tended to focus on the film's tender-tragic qualities, seeing the historical context more as a backdrop to a touching mother–son relationship; few felt the need to adumbrate post-unification concerns. This was less the case in Germany, where critics and audiences were naturally more familiar with the film's specific political and historical circumstances. When asked about his tearful response, Schäuble later explained that the film had prompted memories of his time in office, but also added that 'I'm beyond being able to see anything good about the GDR but I can empathise with how difficult it must be to have lost this Heimat together with all its ideology' (*Der Tagesspiegel* 2005). Such empathetic analysis distinguishes Schäuble from others on the right who have spent the years since unification decrying those who fail to see the East German state as anything other than a totalitarian regime ruthlessly managed by the SED.

Schäuble acknowledges an important issue, namely the keen sense of loss felt by many east Germans. This loss is manifold: for some, it is ideological in nature and refers directly to the GDR's collapse and the wider defeat of Communism. For others, loss refers to the disappearance of certain values associated with life in the GDR and felt to be lacking in modern, post-capitalist society. Community, camaraderie, utopian aspirations were integral to the GDR's self-definition. A great number of its citizens may have been sceptical of the values as championed by the SED, but post-unification biographies, autobiographies, website forums and questionnaires suggest that many east Germans, including those with no first-hand experience of the state, often choose to remember the GDR in terms of certain principles or individual experiences rather than in terms of the regime's mismanagement or systematic abuses. Such selective memory of the socialist past has led to accusations and counter-accusations over the years. While some regard the east Germans' much-discussed nostalgia for the GDR (*Ostalgie*) as morally indefensible, others view it as a means of safeguarding memories against history, of maintaining a connection with a private past without reference to the former state's increasingly public past.

The *Ostalgie* trend initially came as a shock to many, who failed to understand certain extenuating factors (a reaction that was not limited to those in the west). Not least among these factors was the irony that characterised many *Ostalgie* events, a perspective that rarely travels well between generations and even less so across cultures. Irony creates a discursive context for a specific audience – in this case the east German community. Using Linda Hutcheon's framework for considering irony (1994: 89–115), we can see how, initiated in particular rhetorical forms and other strategies of communication, the east Germans may be able to register certain codes that others, i.e. the west Germans, would not. To some degree, the irony that informed *Ostalgie* continued a tradition of irreverence that had existed in the GDR. But while irony may be therapeutic and facilitate critical reflection, it also risks alienating some people and of being misunderstood.

The assessment of *Ostalgie* certainly differed. Its critics (in both east and west) criticised it as a tasteless and irresponsible celebration of the GDR, an evaluation that corresponds with what Svetlana Boym terms 'restorative nostalgia', a 'psychotic substitution of actual experiences with a dark conspiratorial vision: the creation of a delusionary homeland' (2001: 43). Others regarded it as a counter-narrative, one that reconnected east Germans with aspects of their past that would otherwise be subsumed by official histories of the SED state. *Ostalgie* was even accorded a counter-cultural profile: celebrating the GDR's often unremarkable products (whether groceries, packaging, technological hardware or East German bands) was seen as a simultaneous celebration of the local over the global, though this critical edge has since been blunted by commercial exploitation and popular interest (Cooke 2005; Hodgin and Pearce 2011).

By the time *Good Bye, Lenin!* was released, several so-called *Ostalgie* films had been made. The most significant of these (in terms of its cultural resonance rather than its filmic merits) was undoubtedly Leander Haußmann's *Sun Alley* (*Sonnenallee*, 1999). Though typically discussed in the context of *Ostalgie*, the film's success did not rely exclusively on the fashionable postmodern celebration of GDR styles and features. Its appeal rested also on certain generic pleasures. Like other coming-of-age films, it offered generational conflict, affairs of the heart, pop culture and standard teenage concerns. These generic features ought perhaps to have ensured universal appeal, but the many GDR details, abundant in-jokes and irreverence towards, and subversion of, official histories meant that though the film was a considerable success, it was better received by those equipped with the necessary cultural knowledge, i.e. the east Germans, even if their memories were subtly lampooned. Beyond Germany its appeal was even more limited.

Together with the scriptwriter and author, Thomas Brussig, Haußmann sought to challenge those historical accounts that disregard individual experience while simultaneously emphasising the artificiality of their representation (wobbly sets, theatrical *mise-en-scène*, and a range of anachronistic details) (Cooke 2005: 111–19; Hodgin 2011: 161–64). This approach offered (eastern) audiences a mostly affirmative reconnection with their past (when the realities of the dictatorship are acknowledged, these are mostly humorised) but could also be seen as a subtle critique of *Ostalgie* and the constructedness of memory, though this critical perspective did not register with many reviewers.

Where the directors of films such as *Sun Alley* and *Heroes Like Us* (*Helden wie Wir*, Sebastian Peterson, 1999) point to the parodic and satirical aspects in their GDR narratives, Becker and scriptwriter Bernd Lichtenberg were keen to emphasise the authenticity of their co-scripted film, *Good Bye, Lenin!*. In the film *That's Exactly How it Was* (*Genauo So War's*, Elena Bromund, 2002), included in the deluxe three-disc DVD edition, Lichtenberg, for example, discusses his extensive research of East German media culture, and recounts his own visits to East Berlin. Becker, meanwhile, details the lengths to which the production team went in order to recreate the GDR for the film (*Good Bye, Lenin! Deluxe*, Warner Home Video, 2003). Great care was taken to recover or reproduce original features, costumes, locations in order to capture not just the look of the GDR but also how it felt to live there. Conscious of the new fashionable interest in and nostalgia for East German design, Becker stresses that they were keen to avoid glamorising the state. The clothes, for example, were not to resemble the retro outfits which were then being sold at German clothing retailers or to signify GDR chic (a point that is underlined when the protagonists look appalled at having to wear old outfits).

Ensuring the film's authenticity and accuracy was not always easily accomplished: it was especially difficult when restaging the 1989 demonstrations at which Alex is arrested and his mother, a chance witness, suffers a heart attack. The demonstrations that autumn were wholly unexpected; consequently, there was little footage from which to draw. The scant (and poor quality) footage the production team did find was therefore carefully re-enacted, so convincingly according to Becker, that people watching the filming became upset when they saw the security forces' (staged) rough treatment of the protesters. The importance the filmmakers attach to authenticity and accuracy is symptomatic of post-unification discourse. Yet the emphasis on authenticity may seem incongruous given the film's ironic perspective and the artificially recreated GDR that is central to the protagonist's efforts.

Should *Good Bye, Lenin!* be more accurately read as counter-historical narrative? It does after all focus on a contrived counter-history: Alex inverts various historical truths in an effort to protect his frail mother from one of the most surprising events of the century. His solution is to act as if it were only his mother who had suffered a collapse and not the state into which she had invested time and energy, a pretence that involves recreating the GDR in their home. Almost undone by chance encounters, he is forced to improvise explanations in an effort to maintain his illusion. The unexpected sighting of a Coca-Cola advert in East Berlin requires an invented history for the now Socialist beverage; his mother's surprised encounter with west Germans moving into their apartment block necessitates an even more fanciful answer, namely that the GDR has become a refuge for western emigrants seeking a better life.

Such invented history-writing may alternatively be seen as a means of critiquing post-unification revisionists – not just those who may have reimagined their own opposition to the state or minimised their culpability, but also those whose cosy view of the defunct state privileges individual memories over its harsh realities. But *Good Bye, Lenin!* is, as the title suggests, more valedictory in tone than it is condemnatory or celebratory, and this, I would argue, is key to the film's success and goes some way to explaining its perceived value to educators. Unlike so many depictions of East Germany, Becker's film strives to present an ostensibly neutral account of the GDR. His film is not the paean to GDR life that some were seen to be; nor is it an exploration of the regime's abuses and many failings (a stock theme in many documentaries); and it in no way resembles the many dour, feel-bad accounts of post-unification life in the eastern provinces or the grim urban Berlin narratives of recent years. Becker's approach to the GDR is in fact rather diplomatic: it offers evidence that supports a positive view of East Germany while simultaneously reminding audiences of the iniquities and limitations of the SED state. Similarly, it traces developments in the lead up to unification, acknowledging both the excitement of that year, the aspirations and new freedoms, and referencing related frustrations and disappointments.

The opening scene best illustrates Becker's approach. While the young Alex sits transfixed in front of the broadcast of Sigmund Jähn's historic 1978 space flight, his mother is questioned by Stasi officers about her husband's alleged *Republikflucht* ('flight from the republic'). Thus Becker's film begins by acknowledging the best and the worst of the GDR. In the context of the film, the GDR's space mission is significant for several reasons. It introduces (western) audiences to Jähn, the perennially popular cosmonaut, whose look-alike will subsequently feature in Alex's charade. A genial figure, the real-life Jähn quickly became a folk hero, whose appeal the SED recognised and exploited for propagandistic purposes. Unlike the men and women routinely selected and promoted by the regime as champions of Socialism, the cosmonaut was a genuine hero for many East Germans and his reputation remains intact today. His space mission was one of the GDR's greatest accomplishments, an achievement with significant public interest. Such a triumph was naturally used to signal the GDR's advances in science and technology, to demonstrate the success of its alliance with the USSR, and also counted as a symbolic victory over their western neighbours (the west German Ulf Merbold would not leave the earth's atmosphere until the following decade). Ronald Hirte (2002: 165) suggests that people were won over by the cosmonaut and not by the propaganda machine that accompanied him; the pride in his achievement should not, then, be conflated with pride in the SED state.

Alex's interest in space travel and in Jähn serves as a motif throughout: the look-alike will later be inducted as the new General Secretary in Alex's reimagined GDR, and his mother's ashes will be sent into orbit in a homemade rocket. An early sequence shows original footage of Jähn's PR tour of the GDR intercut with authentically rendered images of the young Alex enjoying the GDR's space museum. Where the son is fascinated by space flight (anticipating a utopianism that will later manifest itself in his idealised recreation of the GDR), his mother, following a breakdown triggered by her husband's escape to the west, displays a ground-level commitment to Socialism, becoming, as Alex's voiceover tells us, a 'a passionate activist taking a stand for the simple needs of the population and against the small injustices in life'. Addressing these small injustices does not approximate to clear ideological opposition, but her disinterested commitment to Socialism does set her apart from the Party elite and their corrupted version of the same ideology – a difference that is most apparent when she collapses after seeing the regime's henchmen brutally mistreating her son and fellow protesters in the 1989 demonstrations. Becker's depiction of this benign Socialist mollifies those on the left who have spent the years since 1989 attempting to wrest Socialism from its association with its notorious Eastern Bloc practitioners. The point is emphasised when she explains that she has no interest in meeting 'the party bigwigs', but is keen to see Gorbachev, whose notion of 'socialism as genuine humanism' she embodies (Gorbachev and Ikeda 2005: 118). This generous view of Socialism is not as provocative to modern (German) audiences as one might think; rather, it reflects many east Germans' continued belief that Socialism is a sound theory that has not (yet) been properly executed (Peter and Jungholt 2009). Frau Kerner's modest efforts provide an example of a good, untainted Socialism in practice, while the simulated home-movie footage of smiling children wearing the uniforms of various youth organisations, singing socialist anthems and enjoying organised activities accords the Socialist childhood a degree of innocence untypical of post-unification films (but less unusual in post-unification literature).[2] That Alex's mother finally reveals her original plan was for them to leave the GDR with her husband may render her son's deception meaningless but it does not reduce the sincerity of his efforts or negate his idealised GDR.

'Flashes of Memory'

After more than a decade's scrutiny of the East German regime, the fact that many reviled the out-of-touch, dictatorial SED gerontocracy hardly needed to be underlined. Accordingly, Becker keeps direct criticism or analysis of the state to a minimum. The effect of the Stasi's intrusion into people's lives and their brutality (at the demonstrations) is evident but not developed. The tone of Alex's criticism is ironic and dismissive rather than stridently critical and lacks any clear ideological opposition, as is clear when he refers to the Politburo simply as 'the old farts' and 'the world's last great shooting club'.

This ironic distance characterises the voiceover and is used to describe key social and political developments. It does not simply make fun of the GDR's overused phrases, it also de-dramatises those early tumultuous days, and satirises western culture, political and economic developments. The demonstrations that will eventually lead to the

Figure 5.1: Challenging *Ostalgie*?

collapse of Communism, if not the end of history, for example, are described as a 'march for the right to go for walks without the wall getting in their way'; the shift from one economic system to another is acknowledged when his sister abandons Marxist economics in order to work at Burger King, a move Alex describes as 'her first practical experience with monetary circulation', while Rainer, her romantic interest, is introduced as 'class enemy and greasy spoon manager'. Alex's first 'cultural encounters with a new land' is a sarcastic description of his wide-eyed encounters with pornography and exposure to crass materialism and advertising. The blossoming east German landscapes famously imagined by Chancellor Helmut Kohl are, according to the narrator, evidenced by the arrival of western satellite dishes adorning east German balconies.

The ironic commentary accompanies montages of authentic footage and fictional scenes. One sequence includes original iconic televisual images showing crowds chipping away at the Berlin Wall, Kohl's and other politicians' tuneless rendition – or, as Alex notes, 'a classical concert' – of the (west German) anthem, people ransacking Stasi offices, and watchtowers toppling, alongside the director's own symbolic scenes: East German soldiers goosestep for the last time as a convoy of Coca-Cola trucks rumbles eastwards; border guards pose with drunken visitors as Alex stumbles across the once-secure frontier. Other key events such as Honecker's resignation, the currency reform of 1990, (West) Germany's World Cup triumph, are likewise referenced, sometimes only indirectly, through glimpsed television footage or radio broadcasts played in the background. Becker describes these documentary insertions as 'flashes of memory', which were not crucial to the narrative but included to remind audiences of that eventful year and especially to enlighten foreign audiences, whose knowledge of German history was likely to be less detailed. That Becker has these audiences in mind reveals something of a pedagogical approach and distinguishes *Good Bye, Lenin!* from other films of the period, especially *Sun Alley*, whose remembered past was not objective but subjective and whose markers were specifically intended to stimulate eastern audiences' memories (Hodgin 2004: 40).

Though *Good Bye, Lenin!* is ostensibly concerned with a son's increasingly elaborate efforts to protect his mother, the film also seeks to chronicle the social and political changes in 1989–90, the final year of what Hobsbawm famously called the 'short twentieth century'. Stefan Arndt (2003: 138) has explained that X-Filme received a great number of scripts thematising that transitional period, none of which he and his colleagues considered to be '*the* film' – until the arrival of Lichtenberg's outline. The film is a feature film and not intended as a documentary about what Arndt and his colleagues call the 'forgotten year' (most films about the eastern experience are set either in the GDR or take place in the years that follow its collapse; few consider the year in question), but

Figure 5.2: Feeding *Ostalgie*?

the comment is revealing for it acknowledges a desire, evident in literary debates too, to provide the definitive unification account, a label previously attached to *Go Trabi Go* and attached since to Florian Henckel von Donnersmarck's 2006 film *The Lives of Others* (*Das Leben der Anderen*). That the special-edition DVD set also includes not just the usual making-of feature, interviews with the cast and crew but also a 'Spiegel TV' documentary about 1989–90, a collection of East German news broadcasts along with *That's Exactly How it Was*, which provides some insight into the filmmakers' view of the GDR as well as an account of the efforts required to recreate an authentic GDR, is some indication of the educational potential that the production company feels the film offers.

A further possible explanation of the film's success can be found on X-Filme's website on a page titled 'Philosophy', where the national and international success of many of their films is declared to be a validation of the company's commitment to making films that are 'both challenging and accessible' (2010). Is *Good Bye, Lenin!* one of their most prominent triumphs, an example of this ethos? Certainly in terms of its depiction of the GDR, the film takes few risks. Identifying the Stasi as villains and mocking the authorities from the party elite to the border guards, is hardly controversial. The film does not humanise the Stasi in the way von Donnersmarck's film was widely seen to; nor does it flagrantly celebrate East German adolescence, as did *Sun Alley* or the lesser-known *Kleinruppin Forever* (Carsten Fiebeler, 2004) (Hodgin 2011: 171–75). The film's box-office performance undoubtedly benefited from the *Ostalgie* phenomenon (in Germany at least). Alex's quest to retrieve obsolete products and authentic details is, after all, a recurring feature of the film, and one which may indulge an audience's interest in GDR ephemera. Their inclusion both enables and undermines commodity fetishisation. The fact that these objects are ultimately assembled in order to recreate a GDR that Alex prefers but, he acknowledges, never really existed, offers a cautionary warning to those whose celebration of the GDR may, even if only unconsciously, elide the much less desirable realities of East German life.

The opening title sequence of *Good Bye, Lenin!* begins with a montage of picture postcards of East Berlin. These low-resolution images of urban scenes with groups of smiling young East German citizens may imply that the film will offer a nostalgically rendered GDR, but this sequence can also be seen as an attempt to deconstruct that very nostalgia. The postcards are ultimately carefully staged images. The pictorial message they communicate is of an idealised, illusory version of the sunny GDR as a vibrant, modern state populated by bright, young citizens and is in stark contrast to the usual monochromatic representations of the SED state.[3] In contrast to those films whose feel-good nostalgia is connoted by the selection of up-tempo pop songs for their soundtracks, Yann Tiersen's 'Summer 78', the melody with which the film opens, and which is reprised sporadically throughout the film, is mournful in tone.

Importantly, Becker's film also provides explanations for the east Germans' continued attachment to the GDR (beyond Alex's filial devotion). When, for example, Alex's Jähn is finally installed as the new General Secretary he delivers a mock-television address. Reading a speech written by Alex, he acknowledges the state's deficiencies (with a candour that none of the Eastern Bloc's regime heads ever showed):

> We know that our country isn't perfect. But the ideals we believe in continue to inspire people all over the world. We might have lost sight of our goals at times, but we managed to regain our focus. Socialism isn't about walling yourself in. It's about reaching out to others and living with them. It means not only dreaming about a better world but making it happen.

This explanation, which challenges the triumphalists on the right, effectively rescues Socialism from the SED's corrupted version and accords it the aforementioned 'genuine humanism', thus acknowledging and even validating the east Germans' continued affinity for Socialism.

The east Germans' nostalgia for the old days is further rationalised during the television presenter's commentary at the end of the mock broadcast which covers the west Germans' apparent interest in relocating to the east. Spoken over original footage showing east Germans crossing from east to west (atypical images of the crowds moving from left to right which appears to confirm Alex's alternative reality), Denis's analysis may be wholly unrepresentative of the real-life mood in 1989 but would have resonated with many east Germans, whose subsequent post-unification experiences had not been as rewarding or successful as they had hoped and who, in some cases, had begun to reflect on the advantages of the socialist system: 'It's a tough struggle for survival under capitalism. Not everyone wants careerism and spiralling consumption. The rat race isn't for everyone. These people want a different life, they realise there's more to life than cars, VCRs and TV sets.'

AIMING TO PLEASE

Just as it would be impossible to imagine any producer today rushing to finance a film in which witless Germans venture west in their Trabant, so it would have been impossible to imagine Becker's film having been made soon after unification. *Good Bye, Lenin!* is, then, finally less about the GDR past than it is about the present and its relationship to that past.

The filmmaker's approach to recent German history is a necessarily cautious one. Such circumspection would seem to align it with those films that Rentschler believes 'aim to please' (2000: 264). The GDR's failings are acknowledged but so, too, are its achievements. It recognises the state's collapse as a positive development but one that is not without consequence. This is a more sober assessment of unification than had often been the case; unification is celebrated, but without any eastern euphoria or western triumphalism. The film's acknowledgement of east German woes and frustrations (unemployment, the perceived absence of ideology, the loss of community) are more revealing of contemporary frustrations than they are period details. Though a fiction, his account of unification follows chronological fact, the authenticity of which is emphasised through the inclusion of documentary footage and the production's repeated insistence on authenticity and accuracy. Used in education, the film's brief history of a past time has the potential to promote awareness and raise consciousness – the film fills the gaps in knowledge of the GDR that young Germans in particular are known to have, an issue that has generated considerable attention in Germany, where the implications of historical ignorance have long been a cause for concern (*Der Spiegel* 2007). Its significance goes beyond the reliable, albeit brief, historical narrative; it also reflects contemporary German concerns about the east–west relationship and the contested memory landscapes. The desire to please may be one of the hallmarks of the 'cinema of consensus', but to achieve consensus on issues where no such consensus exists is ultimately impossible. A more accurate

111

description may be that the film manages to please some of the people some of the time. In a plural democracy that alone may make the film educationally useful.

Notes

1 With the exception of lines quoted from the film, all translations are those of the author.
2 It is worth noting that the voiceover obscures the final lines of the song 'Unser Heimat' at a point where the tone shifts from the bucolic to the defensive, and underlines the people's ownership and defence of their Heimat (against unspoken western intruders).
3 Should this irony be missed, viewers of the special features available with the DVD can hear a former state photographer explain what was required of him when taking pictures of the GDR.

Chapter 6

Watching the Stasi: authenticity, *Ostalgie* and history in Florian Henckel von Donnersmarck's *The Lives of Others* (2006)

Paul Cooke

Florian Henckel von Donnersmarck's Oscar-winning film *The Lives of Others* (*Das Leben der Anderen*, 2006) was something of a surprise choice by the American Academy of Motion Picture Arts and Sciences for an award. That a German film should be nominated, or indeed win the Oscar for Best Foreign Language Film is, of course, no longer such a rare event. Since unification German films have been a regular feature of the awards ceremony. However, a film that cost only $1.9 million hardly seemed to be in the running when compared with the $19 million spent on Guillermo del Toro's *Pan's Labyrinth* (*El Laberinto del fauno*, 2006) which *was* tipped to win (Bauer 2007). Moreover, this was a film looking at life in the GDR, the common denominator in most other postwar German nominations in this category, and both the previous winners, being an engagement with the legacy of National Socialism.

That said, the film does still examine Germany's problematic history. Set in 1984, it offers the spectator a suitably Orwellian image of the GDR, in which the writer Georg Dreyman (Sebastian Koch) is placed under surveillance by the state's infamous security service, the *Ministerium für Staatssicherheit* (Ministry for State Security, commonly referred to as the MfS or Stasi), on the advice of a corrupt SED party official, Minister Bruno Hempf (Thomas Thieme), who claims to suspect him of dissidence – an accusation which at the start of the narrative is entirely false. During the surveillance operation, the controlling Stasi officer, Captain Gerd Wiesler (Ulrich Mühe), a man initially wholly convinced of the GDR's status as the better of the two postwar German states, and the need of his organisation to protect it against Western counter-revolutionary forces, begins to lose faith in the GDR's draconian understanding of its 'socialist' project. He is drawn, instead, to the humanist artistic worldview to which he is introduced by spying on the writer and his actress partner Christa-Maria Sieland (Martina Gedeck). As a result, rather than relaying to his superiors Dreyman's gradual turn to dissidence, he protects him, producing innocuous reports and even removing an incriminating typewriter from the man's flat which would have provided his Stasi colleagues with evidence that Dreyman was the author of an inflammatory essay published in the West.

Internationally the film was almost uniformly praised for its gripping, beautifully shot narrative which ostensibly gave its audience an authentic and detailed presentation of the oppressive reality of life in the GDR. 'It's hard to believe that this is von Donnersmarck's first feature,' David Ansen declares; 'His storytelling gifts have the novelistic richness of a seasoned master' (Ansen 2007). Peter Bradshaw is similarly effusive in his praise, describing it as an 'intensively crafted liberal tragedy' that provides an effective 'antidote to *Ostalgie*', the much-discussed 'nostalgia for the days of the Berlin Wall' that has, Bradshaw suggests, so gripped the nation of late and is to be found most obviously in the success of Wolfgang Becker's 2003 film *Good Bye, Lenin!*, a film that 'frankly, came close to indulging the shabby communist regime' (2007). In Germany its reception was far more mixed, sparking a major debate. On the one hand, there were those who also saw the film as a corrective to *Ostalgie*, or to the 'Sun-Alley-ization of GDR memory', as Sebastian Handke puts it, here referring to that other key *Ostalgie* film, Leander Haußmann's coming-of-age teen comedy *Sun Alley* (*Sonnenallee*, 1999) (Handke 2006). Indeed, no less an authority on Stasi oppression than Wolf Biermann praised the film for its authentic image of the GDR, a remarkable achievement for a 'debut director who grew up in the West' (Tilmann 2007). For its supporters in Germany, particularly impressive was again the film's quest for authenticity. Thus, it was praised for its painstaking attention to detail. Indeed, it seemed that every aspect of the set was an accurate reconstruction of the period, down to the bugging devices installed in the writer's flat, as Henckel von Donnersmarck was at pains to point out in numerous interviews he gave during the film's theatrical release (Handke 2006; Radow 2007). Its apparent authenticity, moreover, was a major reason behind the level of official endorsement the film received (Handke 2006; Zander

2006). Manfred Wilke, a historical consultant on the film and member of the Federal Enquete Commissions that investigated the nature of the SED dictatorship in the 1990s, could not praise this aspect of the film highly enough (Wilke 2008). For the Federal Agency for Political Education, this same attention to detail made the film an ideal text for teaching schoolchildren about the oppressive reality of life in the East (Falck 2006). And the positive reviews of the numerous film screenings specifically for children would seem to support its decision, the organisers of such events precisely seeing the film as a way for the younger generation to gain a non-*Ostalgie*-tainted view of the GDR (Harmsen 2006; Rössling 2006).

On the other hand, there were those such as Rüdiger Suchsland who condemned the film as 'Disney's GDR-Melo[drama]', a reference to its distribution in Germany by Buena Vista. Suchsland is particularly scathing of both the film's official endorsement and its potential educational value:

> This is one of those films that culture ministers like. A palatable melodrama, from the brown, dusty days of the GDR, seasoned with some sex and art, lots of horrible repression, some dead people, still more heartache, a few cold, evil perpetrators, lots and lots of German victims and a Saul who becomes a Paul. [...Henckel von Donnersmarck] presents the GDR so simplistically, clearly and unambiguously that one doesn't have to think about it much, that one knows where one stands. He divides the past up into small, bite-sized, consumable pieces, into teaching units. School classes will be shown it until they can't stand it any more. (2006b)

Of course the authorities liked the film, Suchsland suggests. Its straightforward melodramatic narrative allowed a clear-cut reading of the past that required no reflection. In this regard, it is no surprise that the film's historical advisor was part of the Enquete Commissions, since Henckel von Donnersmarck seems to construct a similar view of 'Germany's Second Dictatorship' to their findings, namely that the GDR was a period of history under which a line could now be drawn, the problems of the past having found their resolution in the present-day Berlin Republic (Cooke 2005: 27–60).

Others, such as Gerhard Ehrlicher go further, suggesting that the film 'trivialises the misdeeds of the State Security Service' (2006), turning Wiesler into 'a State Security Schindler', as Günter Jenschonnek put it (2006). Interestingly, for its detractors, the question of authenticity plays a similarly crucial role. The historian

Thomas Lindenberger, for example, rejects Wilke's claims of historical accuracy. While he understands that this is a fiction film and not a historical treatise, Henckel von Donnersmarck's explicit claims of authenticity mean, he argues, that the film must be judged not only aesthetically but also as history. In this regard, while the 'bugs' used in the film might well be 'real', its presentation of the workings of the Stasi are not. Instead, he suggests that the Stasi is used as the backdrop for a classic 'exploitation film', designed to attract international audiences (2008). As Anna Funder notes in one of the few critical foreign reviews the film received, the Stasi would never have let a lone individual run an operation like this. Consequently, a single officer betraying the Stasi could never have had such a large impact on an operation, and this is not to mention the fact that there is little or no evidence that such conversions among members of the organisation ever took place (Funder 2007: 18).

For the broader theme of this volume, the attacks on the film are particularly revealing. Repeatedly it is condemned as a 'Konsensfilm' ('consensus film') that is both politically and aesthetically conservative (Körte 2006). As such, it is accused of wilfully misrepresenting the reality of the Stasi's activities, turning the past into an easily digestible melodrama, the worst kind of heritage cinema which makes a 'straight-edged perpetrator into a sensitive good person, then into a hero and finally into a pitiable victim' (Jenschonnek 2006).[1] For its critics, the straightforward narrative undermined any potential the film might have as a useful intervention in debates on how the nation should deal with the historical legacy of the GDR. Returning for the moment to Suchsland's diatribe, it is revealing that he twice cites Fassbinder as a counterpoint to Henckel von Donnersmarck and his supporters in the industry, most notably Günter Rohrbach, President of the German Film Academy. For Suchsland, Fassbinder embodies a far more aesthetically and politically valid German film tradition, one that understands the self-reflexive, critical potential of melodrama, served up here as unreconstructed kitsch (Suchsland 2006b).

As discussed in our introductory chapter to this volume, in response to the views of critics such as Suchsland, Rohrbach himself produced a similarly vitriolic attack in *Der Spiegel*, condemning German feuilletonists as 'autistic' and questioning the pejorative implications of the term 'consensus film'. Henckel von Donnersmarck, for his part, supports Rohrback, taking on those who condemned his film as 'consensual', redefining the term positively:

Those who repeat this verdict presumably want Germany to be lumbered with the kind of mediocrity that has induced so many 'consensus people', from Wilhelm Weiller to Wolfgang Petersen, to flee the country! If 'consensus film' is supposed to mean the same as 'trivial' or even 'bad film', then I want to make a lot more bad and trivial films in my career. What would those critics say of films like *Casablanca* or *Godfather Part II*? They must be the worst films of all time, for absolutely everyone thinks that they are good, and not – as in my case – almost everyone. I wish that *The Lives of Others* was much more of a consensus film! (Rupprecht 2006)

For Henckel von Donnersmarck it is possible to be 'consensual', in the sense of being popular with audiences and aesthetically mainstream, but still to have artistic credibility.

In the rest of this chapter, I wish to explore the ways in which *The Lives of Others* presents the GDR as history. In so doing, however, my aim is less to examine the nature of this representation *per se* than the manner in which it challenges the parameters of the debate outlined above. First, I look at how the film does indeed turn the GDR into a consumable form of heritage past, discussing the ways *The Lives of Others* can in fact be seen to continue aspects of the *Ostalgie* one finds in films such as *Sun Alley* and *Good Bye, Lenin!*, to which it is ostensibly a corrective. However, I then go on to examine its potential to engage critically with contemporary popular discourses on the historical appraisal of the GDR. Specifically, I examine the manner in which the film presents the relationship between Wiesler and his surveillance operation, investigating how this might allow a mainstream 'consensus film' to offer a more complex view of GDR historiography than that identified by the film's detractors.

The Lives of Others as a Corrective to Ostalgie?

Turning firstly to the question of the film as a corrective to *Ostalgie*, how far can *The Lives of Others* be viewed as a departure from the 'Sun-Alley-ization of GDR memory'? Haußmann's 1999 comedy set in the shadow of the Berlin Wall, along with the later *Good Bye, Lenin!*, Becker's humorous account of a young man's attempt to reconstruct the GDR for his sickly, devout communist mother, were seen by many critics at the time as quintessential *Ostalgie* films. Both Haußmann and Becker, it was claimed by some, were intent upon indulging the east German population in its bizarre nostalgic fascination for the past, particularly obvious in its rediscovery of a whole range of East German styles and consumer products (Buch 1999; Stecher 1999). This was a fascination which grew throughout the 1990s, reaching its zenith in the aftermath of Becker's film, and spawning nothing short of a GDR 'craze' in the summer of 2003 (Cooke 2004).

For critics of this trend, including Henckel von Donnersmarck himself, such manifestations of *Ostalgie* were simply an apology for the GDR, intent upon ignoring the true nature of the SED's dictatorship, along with, most importantly, the population's role in supporting it. In an interview for the UK's Radio 4, the director explains how he 'prides himself' that *The Lives of Others* has helped to overcome the *Ostalgiewelle* ('wave of *Ostalgie*') which, he suggests, has dominated popular culture since unification and which is intent upon producing a picture of a 'good old GDR', through which the population can ignore the fact that 'their lives had been spent supporting a dictatorship' (Collins 2007). However, what such a view elides, and what has been ignored in the critical reception of the film, is both the competing, underlying reasons for the mass appeal of *Ostalgie* and the complex critical engagement with the phenomenon we find in these earlier films. As I have discussed elsewhere, *Ostalgie* has not always dominated popular representations of the GDR (Cooke 2005). Rather, it can be viewed, in part at least, as a response to a perceived over-emphasis in the early 1990s on the sort of picture of the GDR to be found in Henckel von Donnersmarck's film, namely, of the former East Germany as a totalitarian 'Stasi state', where all activity was monitored and manipulated by the MfS, and consequently where anything resembling a 'normal' life, as one might understand it in the west, was impossible, a view explored in the many films that have presented the machinations of this organisation since unification, including Volker Schlöndorff's *The Legend of Rita* (*Die Stille nach dem Schuß*, 2000), Connie Walter's *Never Mind the Wall* (*Wie Feuer und Flamme*, 2001) and Christian Klemke and Jan Lorenzen's *The Ministry of State Security: The Daily Routine of an Agency* (*Das Ministerium für Staatssicherheit: Alltag einer Behörde*, 2003). *The Lives of Others* is hardly the first film to have addressed seriously the legacy of the Stasi, as many of its supporters suggest (Stein 2008: 568).

In the immediate aftermath of the *Wende*, German public life was regularly punctuated by scandals about the collaboration of public figures with the MfS which came to light as the miles of Stasi files accumulated in its forty years of existence were gradually worked through; scandals which fuelled the impression that life in the GDR was like living in an Orwellian Big Brother state where, as Jürgen Habermas famously described it, a giant octopus-like organisation stretched its tentacles through the whole of society, leaving no aspect of life free from its influence (Bathrick 1995: 221). One area of life that seemed to have been particularly affected by the Stasi's activities (and of specific interest to this present discussion) was the literary sphere, where it was discovered that numerous 'critical' writers had worked as *Inoffizielle Mitarbeiter* ('unofficial collaborators', commonly referred to as IMs) for the organisation, from Christa Wolf and Heiner Müller, the two best-known GDR writers internationally, to Sascha Anderson and Rainer Schedlinski, key figures in the radical underground artistic scene of the 1980s (Lewis 2003a; Cooke and Plowman 2003). Indeed, such was the level of infiltration that for some commentators it seemed that the whole notion of 'dissident' activity in the GDR was nonsensical, that these so-called 'critical' writers were part of nothing more than a postmodern 'simulation', sponsored by the State Security Service, in which well-placed IMs who could act without fear of state reprisals guided all apparent opposition (Michael 1995: 1638).

However, for many ordinary east Germans, it was clear that this view of life did not correspond to their own experience. Haußmann's film, for example, was a direct response to this perceived overemphasis on the GDR's totalitarian nature and the concomitant sense we find in Henckel von Donnersmarck's comments above that the population at large was complicit in its survival. For Haußmann and others, the result of representing the GDR as a 'Stasi state' was the growing alienation of many ordinary east Germans within the Berlin Republic, due to their conception that the actual experience of everyday life in the GDR was being misrepresented by the mass media in its construction of the population as either complicit with or having been traumatised by the SED regime. At the same time, the film attempts to deconstruct the contemporary fascination with GDR consumer products, calling on the ex-GDR spectator to reflect critically on their relationship to the past, undermining a simplistically rose-tinted view of the period. Initially, it appears that we are presented with an authentic image of the GDR in the 1970s that allows the spectator to celebrate the type of products one now finds in *Ostalgie* shops in Berlin. However, as

Haußmann himself points out, 'when you look more closely, you can see that the film is completely unrealistic. The décor, the street, everything looks constructed' (Maischberger 1999: 22). By deliberately constructing its version of the GDR through the iconography of contemporary *Ostalgie*, the film becomes overcoded, and therefore ironically draws the spectator's attention to its artificiality, and with it the artificiality of seeing such products as a means of recapturing the past.

As already noted, in the critical reception of *The Lives of Others*, much was made by the filmmaker of the authenticity of his set. Every detail had to be 'real' in order to present a perfect re-enactment of the past. 'I wouldn't know how one could make a film look more authentic,' Henckel von Donnersmarck declares (Handke 2006). The result is, indeed, a chillingly authentic-looking set, augmented by cinematographer Hagen Bogdanski's use of a colour palette of grey and brown tones and a decision to record in analogue rather than digital which seems to transport the spectator back to the GDR of the 1980s by replicating the sound and hue of images we see today in old television footage of the time (Anon. 2006). In so doing, as in *Sun Alley*, we are given shots of everyday GDR styles and products, from Trabis to television sets to bottles of Berliner Pilsner, upon which the camera repeatedly dwells, and which allow the audience to indulge its present-day fascination with such items, but without the critical distance that we find in the earlier comedy. Nonetheless, such indulgence would seem to be tempered by the film's focus on the Stasi's mechanics of surveillance and oppression, including a detailed tour of the room from where the surveillance operation against Dreyman is carried out. We are first introduced to the surveillance suite as Wiesler enters it. He walks in, flicks a switch, and the room is lit up in a flash of neon, revealing a GDR chamber of horrors from where the Stasi can both listen to and influence life in the flat below. While we are left in no doubt as to the destructive capabilities of Wiesler in particular and the Stasi in general, the focus on original artefacts often allows the spectator once again to indulge their fascination for German history, rather than critically engage with it. One is reminded of numerous moments in those heritage films that depict Germany's other, even more marketable, difficult past. Oliver Hirschbiegel's film about the last days of Hitler, *Downfall* (*Der Untergang*, 2004), for example, similarly allows audiences to indulge Western society's perennial fascination with Nazi paraphernalia in its detailed visual presentation of the period, offering the spectator a virtual tour of Hitler's bunker.

And this is not the only way in which the film seems to continue, rather than 'correct' the type of *ostalgic* indulgence for which the earlier comedies, in my view, were unfairly criticised. In *Good Bye, Lenin!*, as in *Sun Alley*, we find an ironic engagement with society's present-day celebration of East German material culture. However, in Becker's film we also glimpse a more ideologically-based version of *Ostalgie,* where the filmmaker attempts to recuperate certain elements of the GDR's socialist project, a dimension wholly absent from Haußmann's film. As his illusionary GDR becomes ever more complex, the film's hero Alex (Daniel Brühl) starts to realise that the world he is creating is not the East German state as it actually was, but rather as he would have liked it to be, namely a truly socialist utopia in which the population can live together in harmony without fear, a world in which we might find 'socialism with a human face', the type of society called for by many leading writers and intellectuals in their famous Alexanderplatz demonstration on 4 November 1989. This was a group that had always seen its role as helping to liberalise the GDR and who saw the *Wende* as the moment when this dream could be realised.[2] In the event, of course, the population voted with its feet to reject a reformed socialist state. However, in *Good Bye, Lenin!* this political dream is given expression, allowing the spectator a moment to reflect on what might have been, and to consider the limitations of the materialism of contemporary Western capitalist democracies.

Through its focus on the impact of the Stasi on artistic life in the GDR, *The Lives of Others* similarly revisits the type of liberal worldview propagated by the GDR's writers and intellectuals. The importance of Culture (with a capital 'C') to the GDR, which made it such an attractive society for many of its state-sanctioned artists, is first alluded to early in the film when we are introduced to Hempf. At the party to celebrate the opening of Dreyman's latest play, Hempf hypocritically praises publicly the writer that he has just denounced to the MfS, quoting Stalin's famous maxim that writers were to be the 'engineers of the human soul' who would help lead society on to the socialist utopia (Henckel von Donnersmarck 2007: 31). While, as Dreyman's friend points out at the party, it is rather risqué to quote Stalin at this point in the state's existence, nonetheless it reminds us of the special place artists had in the GDR, and one of the reasons why the SED was so concerned to devote a huge amount of its resources to finding out their every thought. The GDR was a place where, for better or worse, the artist mattered, in contrast with post-unification society, where, once more through the character of Hempf, we are told that this is not the case. Dreyman and Hempf meet again two years after the collapse of the state. The former minister laments Dreyman's inability to write in post-unification Germany: 'But I can understand you Dreyman, honestly. What should one write in this Federal Republic, where there's nothing one can believe in or rebel against' (Henckel von Donnersmarck 2007: 149).

The reason why the state put such an emphasis on the role of the artist is also examined in the film through its central conceit, namely the conversion of Wiesler from convinced Stasi functionary to humanist fifth columnist. From the outset it is clear that he, like Alex's mother, believes fundamentally in the value of the state's socialist project, in contrast to his superior, the opportunist Grubitz (Ulrich Tukur). For Wiesler, it is more a religion than a political ideology. Moreover, Wiesler's faith would seem to exist despite rather than because of his experience in the GDR. He lives alone, excluded from the rest of society, able only to find companionship for a few moments in hiring a prostitute. By observing the everyday activities of Dreyman and Christa-Maria he is given insight into another way of life, of a socialism that also understands human compassion, most obviously through the art to which he is introduced through them. We see how he is moved by reading Brecht's love poem 'Remembering Marie A.', a copy of which he steals from Dreyman's flat. And his conversion becomes complete as he listens to the author play the melancholic 'Sonata for a Good Person', a piece of music given to him by the director of his plays who, having been banned from working by the Party, has just committed suicide. The film cuts between Dreyman, deep in concentration at his piano, and a transfixed Wiesler, who stares into space in the attic surveillance room above, a tear rolling down his cheek, the parallel montage seeming to suggest that the Stasi officer is somehow watching as well as listening to his target. 'Can anyone who has heard this music, really heard it, remain a bad person?' asks Dreyman as he contemplates the power of the music he has just played (Henckel von Donnersmarck 2007: 77). It would appear not, as we begin to see the Stasi officer intervene in the artist's life, not to increase Dreyman's sense of paranoia, as was so often the case during the organisation's *Operative Vorgänge* ('operational procedures' – the euphemism given by the MfS to such surveillance operations), but to support him in his efforts to write and publish an essay in the West that will expose the high level of suicide in the GDR. Thus, the Stasi man joins sides with the artists to help in their project to create a more liberal state. As such, while the film revisits a view of the GDR as a 'Stasi state', where all activity, even that which was supposedly 'dissident', was controlled by the MfS, it also challenges this image, ironically recalling elements of the type of ideological *Ostalgie* we find in *Good Bye, Lenin!* Through his exposure to art, Wiesler, an instrument of state oppression, becomes a liberal maverick intent upon seeing good prevail.

WATCHING THE WATCHERS: THE STASI AS HISTORY

If *The Lives of Others* has more in common with earlier criticisms of the *Ostalgie* films than its supporters suggest, the film would also seem to question some of the views of its detractors, who argue that it has nothing to add to contemporary debates on the historical appraisal of the GDR. As already suggested, the film has, for better or worse, been used as a didactic tool to engage the generation that has grown up since unification about the nature of life in the GDR, the film's use of a mainstream aesthetic allowing it to speak to a far wider audience than would have been achievable for a more esoteric film text. In his discussion of the film, Owen Evans examines the use of melodrama as a tool in the film's widespread appeal, arguing that even within a mode which traditionally relies on the kind of polarised '"Manichean" world-view' Barry Langford identifies in such films, where emotion is prioritised over critical distance, Henckel von Donnersmarck nonetheless provides a degree of psychological depth to his characters which might allow a more nuanced reading of the GDR past than the film's critics allow (Evans 2010: 8).

Central to such a reading is the character of Wiesler. On the one hand, his conversion might be seen as an apology for the crimes of the Stasi, a conversion that sets up the final moment of 'consensus' at the end of the film, when the former officer understands that he has been forgiven by his former victim through the dedication of Dreyman's book to 'HGW XX/7', Wiesler's official title. On the other, the presentation of Wiesler's humanity also recalls the experience of

123

Timothy Garton Ash when he met the Stasi officer tasked with conducting a surveillance operation on him, a meeting that left him with a strong sense that this was a good man, a man of conscience (cited in Evans 2010: 12). Might the film, like Garton Ash's experience, suggest a more problematic, less consensual reading of the Stasi as an organisation that allows it neither to be forgiven nor to be dealt with straightforwardly as yet another monstrous moment of aberration in German history?

The place of the Stasi in GDR society is similarly problematised in the central relationship between Wiesler and his *Operative Vorgang*. *The Lives of Others* is part of a long tradition of films, from Alfred Hitchcock's *Rear Window* (1954) to Tony Scott's *Enemy of the State* (1998), which explores the question of surveillance. Most obviously Henckel von Donnersmarck's film recalls Francis Ford Coppola's *The Conversation* (1974). Coppola's representation of a paranoid corporate America wallowing in the corruption of the tail end of Nixon's administration translates easily to Henkel von Donnersmarck's GDR and helps to explain for some commentators the reason why the film was so successful in the US, where a post-9/11 public could see its own dystopian future reflected in the film's portrayal of a government obsessed with its own 'state security' (Beier 2007).

Echoes of *The Conversation* are most obviously located in the striking similarities in the *mise-en-scène*, particularly in the spartan surveillance room we find in both films. Moreover, in both films we find a protagonist using sound to compensate for the lack of a visual narrative. In so doing, and as has been discussed by generations of critics, these films draw attention to the leap of the imagination which, in the classic Metzian construction of spectatorship based on Lacanian psychoanalysis, is seen to be at the very heart of cinema itself (Metz 2000). Through the process of watching the watcher, such films play to and simultaneously deconstruct the scopophilic impulse of the spectator. In *The Lives of Others*, as in these earlier films, we find a performance of the fantasy of a transcendent, all-seeing, all-powerful spectator as described by Metz, his primary identification between the spectator and the screen here transferred to the secondary level of the diegesis. Crucially for Metz, of course, along with other theorists associated with *Screen* during the 1970s, the power of the spectator is an illusion. Indeed, the very apparatus of film is shown to undermine the processes by which the spectator attempts to give *himself* meaning, presenting the subject position that he constructs (via the

124

film text as 'other') to be a chimera. Thus, we see the male all-seeing I/eye exposed as a fantasy, and replaced by a disempowered, interpolated voyeur, inevitably subjected to the machinations of ideology, be that patriarchy, capitalism or imperialism (Aaron 2007).

That the Lacanian model, now largely out of fashion with film scholars more focused on real audiences than imagined spectators (Jancovich, Faire and Stubbings 2003), might still prove illuminating in a reading of Henckel von Donnersmarck's film is perhaps unsurprising given its title. The use of the plural in *The Lives of Others* is particularly revealing, highlighting the competing 'others' at work in the film. This is a competition which ultimately leads us away from film theory and – more importantly for my examination of the place of the film within the media debate it sparked – back to an examination of the text as a socio-historical representation of the GDR and, in particular, its construction of the relationship between the State Security Service and the rest of the population.

At the outset of the film, Wiesler is constructed as a transcendent all-seeing, all-powerful spectator, a position that is established in a sequence where he first sees the man who is to be the victim of his surveillance operation. He is taken to the theatre by a superior officer to watch the production of one of Dreyman's plays, starring the latter's partner Christa-Maria. Wiesler sits in a box, at a distance from the rest of the audience, able to look beyond the performance itself, which transfixes the rest of the public. In cinematic terms, Wiesler can create his own 'frame', his use of binoculars highlighting his status as the 'master' spectator in the room, to whom we are subsequently sutured in a series of point-of-view shots: of Christa-Maria's performance; of

Figure 6.1: Wiesler mesmerised at the theatre.

Figure 6.2: Dreyman approaches as Wiesler withdraws from the frame.

Dreyman talking to a journalist already under suspicion by the state; of Hempf whispering to his aide, a conversation that perhaps suggests to the astute agent the reason why he has been asked to come to this performance.

Most importantly, and in contrast to these other men, it would seem that Wiesler can see beyond the beauty of Christa-Maria, the woman Dreyman loves and who Hempf, we subsequently learn, is determined to have. Wiesler, at first sight, appears to maintain his distance, always standing at the edge of the main action, silently making notes and never participating actively. When he does decide to intervene it is, initially at least, in order to direct events. He decides, for example, to reveal to Dreyman the Minister's desire for Christa-Maria, ringing the doorbell to Dreyman's flat remotely from his observatory so that the writer comes down just as the woman is getting out of Hempf's car. Within the diegesis, Wiesler once again controls the frame, turning Dreyman into a spectator in his own narrative, dictating the view of the world that he is given.

However, there are in fact indications from the start of the film that Wiesler's objective distance, and with it his spectatorial power, are illusory. Indeed, even during the initial theatre performance there is the suggestion that he, like Hempf and Dreyman, is in reality also transfixed by Christa-Maria's performance. For the briefest of moments Wiesler's point-of-view shots are interrupted by a shot/reverse-shot sequence between himself and Christa-Maria. Just for a second the woman seems to return his gaze, leaving the man momentarily mesmerised and thereby breaking the illusion of his objective distance from events. The Stasi operative's position as a transcendent, detached observer is undermined. Wiesler is drawn into the traditional libidinal economy of mainstream cinematic texts of desiring and objectifying the female 'other' in order to empower his own subject position.[3]

As the narrative progresses and Wiesler increasingly rejects the state's position, desiring ever more the life of the artist he observes, he becomes ever more embroiled in his case. Crucially, however, the more he intervenes, the less he is in control of events, his cool observation turning into a confused emotional stare. When, for example, he hears Dreyman's plea that Christa-Maria should not go to meet Hempf, Wiesler leaves his attic for the street outside, hiding in the shadows to see if Christa-Maria comes out. 'What are you gawping at?' he is asked by a drunk passer-by, a question which makes it clear that Wiesler can no longer stand outside the narrative (Henckel von Donnersmarck 2007: 84). Then, in the final moments of the main story arc, as we watch Christa-Maria commit suicide, unable to live with the guilt of having betrayed her partner – during the course of the narrative she becomes an IM, agreeing to inform on him to the Stasi – Wiesler's impotence is complete. He can only look on as Christa-Maria steps off the pavement into the path of a passing lorry. He rushes to her side, able to touch the blood seeping from her body but unable to give her a final embrace before being jettisoned backwards out of the frame as Dreyman enters and picks her up to let her die in his arms. While Wiesler's observation tactics give the impression of control, he discovers that, like the fantasy of spectatorship itself, this control is ultimately illusory. His narrative has a life of its own, finally expelling him to its periphery, allowing him only to look on, an impotent voyeur. Yet while he has been rejected by the narrative, he is still implicated within it, the blood on his hands from Christa-Maria's body highlighting that he can neither transcend events nor escape his guilt for her death.

In this reading of the relationship between Wiesler and his *Operative Vorgang*, the credibility or otherwise of Wiesler's conversion to the enlightened protector of Dreyman becomes less important than how the place of the 'other' in the construction of the self speaks to contemporary GDR historiography. Like the Metzian spectator, the Stasi was an organisation assured of its own agency, of its ability to steer events and of its unassailable position of authority. However, as we know from what happened in 1989, the organisation was itself ultimately impotent in the face of the mass demonstrations by the GDR population as a whole. At the end of this particular *Operative*

Vorgang, Grubitz knows that his officer has betrayed him and assures the man that he will have his revenge: 'At best, you'll be opening letters in a cellar somewhere for the rest of your career. That's the next twenty-five years' (Henckel von Donnersmarck 2007: 145). Of course, as is revealed in the following sequence, time will run out for the Stasi. The film cuts to an intertitle, 'Four years and eight months later'. We find Wiesler, having been demoted to steaming open the population's mail, listening to the news that the Berlin Wall has fallen. He gets up from his desk and walks away, free from Grubitz's authority. Here Wiesler becomes a representative of the GDR masses who were ultimately themselves able to reverse the Stasi's gaze and challenge state oppression.

The relationship between Wiesler and his *Operative Vorgang*, as well as Wiesler's final relationship with the organisation he has served his whole career, troubles a unidirectional conceptualisation of the power dynamic at work in the film. Henckel von Donnersmarck's engagement with the tradition of the surveillance film perhaps adds little to the discussion on the scopophilic nature of cinema as a medium that we do not find in Hitchcock or Coppola. However, it does potentially allow a reading of the organisation's legacy in post-unification Germany that counters the straightforward presentation of the GDR as a 'Stasi state' the narrative, at first sight, seems to deliver. Moreover, it particularly troubles the place of the Stasi files in popular readings of the GDR. At the end of the film, in which Dreyman discovers the truth about Wiesler – that the man tried to protect him from arrest – we find a further level of inversion in the spectatorial 'self–other' relationship at work between Wiesler and the object of his surveillance. Now the Stasi file acts as 'other' to the writer. By revisiting his past as it is presented in Wiesler's account, he can at last overcome the trauma of Christa-Maria's death and finally 'arrive' in the Federal Republic, a development symbolised in his rediscovery of the ability to write. But, as with the image of Wiesler discussed above, or Wiesler's relationship to Dreyman, the film's presentation of the Stasi file is open to contradictory readings. On the one hand, Dreyman's revisitation of the past allows the type of narrative resolution demanded by mainstream cinema, thereby again laying the film open to the charge of being a reactionary form of consensus cinema. On the other, however, the specific example of its usage here potentially challenges the broader question of historical 'closure' the opening of the Stasi files seems to offer.

The importance of the Stasi archive in contemporary readings of the GDR cannot be underestimated, as already noted in the numerous scandals to which the opening of the files have given rise. Yet through Dreyman's engagement with the files as historical archive, their status as a repository of absolute truth, as the final word on the reality of life in the GDR, as they have been construed either implicitly or explicitly in countless popular readings of the period, is called into question, in the same way as the film calls into question the existence of a straightforward, unidirectional relationship between the Stasi and the GDR population as a whole. The Stasi file is only helpful to Dreyman because it does *not* hold the truth. Like the rest of the archive, Dreyman's file is a written text constructed within a specific socio-political context, by people with their own agenda, abilities and competing desires. Consequently, the file's presentation of events might be shaped by Grubitz's request to Wiesler not to put anything in his reports about the relationship between Christa-Maria and Hempf, or by Wiesler's assistant's only partial knowledge of the 'backstory' to an argument he hears between the lovers in the flat below. Through the film's presentation of the Stasi files as a flawed, incomplete archive of the past, the film once again calls into question the view of those critics who see it as a rejection of earlier *Ostalgie* films, films that were often intent upon troubling a view of the GDR as a one-dimensional, totalitarian 'Stasi state', even as it also seems to indulge in the fetishisation of GDR material culture for which these same films were often attacked. Furthermore, in so doing, *The Lives of Others* would seem to challenge the criticism that, as a 'consensual' cinematic text, it cannot engage critically with contemporary debates on the historical appraisal of the GDR.

NOTES

1 For a fuller discussion of the reception of the film in Germany see Seegers 2008. For a good discussion of the film as part of the German heritage film production trend see Fisher 2010.
2 For an overview of the political role of the writer in the GDR see Emmerich 1996.
3 For a digest of feminist views on spectatorship see Chaudhuri 2006.

Chapter 7

From Baader to Prada: memory and myth in Uli Edel's *The Baader Meinhof Complex* (2008)

Chris Homewood

As a technology able to picture and embody the temporality of the past, cinema has become central to the mediation of memory in modern cultural life.

Paul Grainge (2003: 1)

Uli Edel's Oscar-nominated film *The Baader Meinhof Complex* (2008) is reportedly the most expensive German production to date, with a final cost of circa $20 million. A visually lavish adaptation of journalist Stefan Aust's study of the same name, the film offers a snapshot of the urban terrorism experienced by the Federal Republic of Germany at the hands of the Red Army Faction (RAF), better known to contemporary witnesses as the Baader-Meinhof group. The film focuses on the inception and subsequent 'armed struggle' of the first and most publically recognisable generation of terrorists (led by Andreas Baader, Gudrun Ensslin and Ulrike Meinhof) who viewed the Federal Republic as a thinly veiled continuation of its fascist predecessor, charting the escalation in violence against state institutions and representatives that culminated in the worst political crisis yet faced by the young democracy of the Bonn Republic – the notorious German Autumn of 1977.

Although *The Baader Meinhof Complex* might represent the most technically accomplished cinematic engagement with Germany's legacy of urban terrorism, it is by no means the first. Having read the terrorism of the RAF as a violent reaction to the repressed trauma of National Socialism, the filmmakers of the New German Cinema found themselves working in the immediate aftermath of the German Autumn to elucidate the mysterious links between the terrorist violence of 1977, the post-war response to National Socialism and the perceived authoritarianism of state institutions. Roused into action by the veil of repression which, they felt, threatened to engulf the very recent memory of urban terror, the collective essay film *Germany in Autumn* (*Deutschland im Herbst*, 1978), Margarethe von Trotta's *The German Sisters* (*Die bleierne Zeit*, 1981) and Rainer Werner Fassbinder's *The Third Generation* (*Die dritte Generation*, 1979) offered analysis of left-wing terrorism, its causes and destabilising consequences in a bid to provoke reflection in a nation that was otherwise encouraged to forget (see Homewood 2006).[1] But as Germany entered the new millennium the debate on urban terrorism was reignited, due, in part at least, to the formation of a new coalition government with its roots in the radical ferment of the 1960s. Following revelations in 2001 about the then Foreign Minister Joschka Fischer's activist past, the use of violence as a means of protest returned to the political agenda, as James Skidmore suggests: 'Here they were arguing the same issue that often split them twenty-five years earlier: what kind of action was justifiable in the fight against a system which was, in their view, merely a disguised continuation of German fascism'. (2002: 552) As if having sensed the developments that were to come, a new cluster of terrorism films began appearing in German cinemas around the same time. Films such as Volker Schlöndorff's *The Legend of Rita* (*Die Stille nach dem Schuss*, 2000), Christian Petzold's *The State I Am In* (*Die innere Sicherheit*, 2000), Andres Veiel's *Black Box Germany* (*Black Box BRD*, 2001) and Christopher Roth's *Baader* (2002) re-examine the theme of German terrorism in light of the generational and socio-political shifts which characterise the Berlin Republic.

Curiously, it is also from this changing cultural perspective that a 'new' dimension to the debate on terrorism emerged. While politicians were experiencing political *déjà vu*, young Germans were eagerly seizing upon the terrorist past as the latest lifestyle badge in a bid to aid their attempts at self-determination. The raw material for this impulse was facilitated by the commodification of the RAF at the hands of consumer pop culture. From Andy Warhol-styled pop-art prints of Baader and Meinhof available for sale on e-bay.de to the 'Prada-Meinhof' fashion range, by 1999 the RAF had seemingly become *the* new brand of choice for the so-called 'neon kids' of the

Berlin Republic, who, according to critics such as Matthias Politycki, had become addicted to amusement and instant gratification, which the capricious fads of consumer 'pop' can provide (1998: 19). In 2001 the glossy lifestyle magazine *Max* picked up on the marketing of the terrorist past to the youth, declaring that 'the time is ripe for RAF popstars' (Andreas 2001). In the same year another lifestyle magazine, *Tussi Deluxe*, consolidated this proclamation through a feature on 'terrorist chic', which recreated iconic images of the German Autumn but with fashion models portraying the terrorists. The most potent example of *Tussi Deluxe*'s 'remodelling' of the terrorist past for 'pop' consumption was the recreation of a photograph originally published by *Stern*, which showed Baader's corpse following his alleged suicide in Stammheim prison. The image is recreated down to the last detail, from the pool of blood issuing forth from the exit wound in his skull to the positioning of an extension cord running behind his head, but with the greatest emphasis placed on what he was wearing: an insert shows a close-up of his footwear with an added consumer imperative: 'Andreas Baader's Woolworth-slippers are cult [sic]' (quoted in Drilo 2001).[2] In the pages of *Tussi Deluxe*, the pop commodification of the RAF found its most cohesive expression.

This turn to 'terrorist chic' was at once fuelled by, yet also served to fan anew the flames of a mythologising impulse that had accompanied the RAF since the organisation's inception, marked by the audacious liberation of Baader in 1970. The 'RAF myth' was perpetuated, in part, from within the ranks of the organisation itself: Baader's penchant for stylish getaway cars as well as a youthful impulse towards designer clothes cocooned the RAF's terrorism in a 'hip' shell. In addition, a romanticised socio-political function and the controversial 'murder thesis', which claimed that the Stammheim suicides were in fact state-sanctioned murders, lent the RAF's trajectory a mythic basis. For social historian Wolfgang Kraushaar, the trend towards 'terrorist chic' among Germany's youth is contingent with their 'insatiable, romantically charged longing for adventure', which the dry political reality of the Berlin Republic cannot reflect. Thus, in an increasingly commodified form the RAF myth, which stresses dissident heroism and a star potential highly sought after in today's cult of celebrity, has come to promise what Kraushaar terms an 'ideology of adventure'; an antidote of sorts to the lack of excitement offered by the 'normality' of the republic (2008). However, this uninhibited popularisation and glorification of Baader and his comrades is problematic because it is informed by a very selective process of remembering and forgetting, which threatens to decontextualise and depoliticise the RAF through ignorance of the hard, often uncomfortable historical facts that surrounded the group in favour of what Niels Werber has termed 'the existential experience of terror, the intensity' (no date). As Stefan Reinecke makes clear, in the example of 'RAF pop', 'what the RAF was, what it wanted and what it did is relegated to the background. The gesture counts, not the content' (2002). And as Jörg Schneider has pointed out, the majority of people wearing 'Prada-Meinhof' slogan T-shirts 'tended to know what Prada was rather than Meinhof' (2003).

Released before the debate on the glamorising potential of the RAF myth had been fully re-ignited, the cluster of post-Wall terrorism films mentioned above touch on the question of myth, most notably in the case of *Baader*, but are ultimately more concerned with the need to resolve the lingering political questions surrounding the RAF. However, it is the most recent film to have emerged from this cinematic RAF revival, Edel's *The Baader Meinhof Complex*, which has positioned itself most explicitly as a direct intervention on debates over identity, memory and myth.

Just prior to its release *The Baader Meinhof Complex* took the cover of *Spiegel*, which ran the bold headline 'a film destroys the RAF myth' beneath a quotation of the film's closing line, as spoken by Brigitte Mohnhaupt (Nadja Uhl) – 'You never knew them. Stop seeing them as they never were.'[3] In light of this claim, the film was promoted more broadly as *the* crucial intervention on the topic of the RAF in the pages of the current-affairs magazine; in what was as much an effusive marketing pamphlet as an essay-length review, Dirk Kurbjuweit heralded the film's arrival as a revelation, proclaiming that 'it will change the debate on German terrorism' (2008: 42). According to Kurbjuweit, the film's relevance and status as a corrective to *Mythos-RAF* was rooted in a representational strategy which, in recent years, has come to define the impact of Germany's most successful producer and screenwriter, Bernd Eichinger, who died suddenly in January 2011.

Although *The Baader Meinhof Complex* was directed by Uli Edel, in the numerous column inches that the film provoked it is Eichinger who is credited as the authorial driving force behind the film. *The Baader Meinhof Complex* falls into the category of the 'history film' insofar as its narrative 'is indexical to a *referential* past, measurable against the memorialised knowledge of a particular event or person[s] and audiovisual recordings and accounts of them' (Drake 2003: 187).

In this vein, the film continues what we might term the 'Eichinger effect' first seen in *Downfall* (*Der Untergang*, Oliver Hirschbiegel, 2004), that is, a representational strategy rooted in an obsession with (hyper-) verisimilitude. Variations on the line 'We have made everything as authentic as possible' were frequently to be heard from Eichinger in the many interviews that accompanied the film's timely release, just a year after the thirtieth anniversary of the German Autumn (Schmitz 2008). From costume and make-up to the choice of locations, props and the recreation of explosions, the film's *mise-en-scène* depicts the politically turbulent late 1960s and 1970s with an exacting attention to detail, not least in the mimetic recreation of the most potent, symbolic moments associated with the RAF and Germany's broader experience of the period remembered in the present as '1968', many of which have long since become indexical cornerstones in the nation's collective memory of events.

On the basis of this loud claim to historical accuracy, Kurbjuweit, who frequently replicates Eichinger's own position, seeks to diminish the film's actual status as a mediated representation of the past:

> The first important decision was taken by Eichinger. He wanted a realistic film, not a work of art, no attempt to build its own tension arc, no attempt to contrive its own identificatory figures as was the case with Schlöndorff and Petzold – somehow nice terrorists [sic]. Eichinger wants to show the people as they presumably were and threads the events together in a sober manner. He is creating less a work of art than a body of history. Illustrated history. (2008: 45)

If, for a moment, we are to take this bold appraisal at face value, then the hyper-realism brings with it claims of a detached historical chronicle and rigorous impartiality, which lends Edel and Eichinger's film a factual documentary quality and seemingly sidesteps the highly problematic relationship between popular film and its function as an 'authentic' memory text. Such concerns will be addressed throughout this chapter, but following Kurbjuweit's line of argument for a moment longer, earlier films such as *The Legend of Rita* and *The State I Am In*, therefore, become failed reckonings with the RAF because they offer unashamedly biased artistic interpretations, which, he goes on to allege, reprogramme the facts, or 'truth' of the referential past:

> All of these films look at their protagonists with an assured sympathy. For Schlöndorff and Petzold they are not so much perpetrators as sufferers. Roth's Baader is a cool hound, chic. These films, by all means successes

in themselves as works of art, have supported the leftist discourse: they create tolerable images for unbearable events. It is a discourse which willingly cuts out the monstrosity of the deeds and grumbles about the motives of the perpetrators. (2008: 45)

For Kurbjuweit such films blur the line between perpetrator and victim in support of the 'leftist discourse', which he defines through its sympathy towards the RAF's *Faschismusvorwurf* ('charge of fascism') against the Federal Republic. Thus, by approaching West German terrorism as 'a tortured form of *Vergangenheitsbewältigung* – a symptom of Germany's difficulty in confronting and working through its Nazi past' (Varon 2004: 15), Kurbjuweit accuses filmmakers of mitigating the atrocity of the RAF's crimes. By focusing on *why* the RAF might have been motivated to throw bombs, yet seldom creating scenes which depict the horrors of the group's violent excess, it is charged that filmmakers have tended to treat the RAF as a sympathetic resistance movement rather than a violent terrorist organisation.

Thus, according to Kurbjuweit, we have been left with a situation whereby 'to date there have been a great many words on the RAF but we still don't have the most important images, and those are the images of the deeds' (2008: 47). Accordingly, the question of *what*, and not *why* forms the representational core of Eichinger's project, a fact attested to by the film's producer in interview: 'the people reveal themselves through the deeds they commit [...]. Crucial is that they do it, not why' (quoted in Kurbjuweit 2008: 47). Thus, under the guise of an impartial historical chronicle with a veracious claim to reality (accordingly, several promotional posters for the film suggest this is 'the true story of the Red Army Faction'), *The Baader Meinhof Complex* positions itself as a corrective to the alleged cinematic reprogramming of the group in the support of myth.

But of course *The Baader Meinhof Complex* is still a verisimilitudinous representation, even if an exacting one, and one which, in terms of aesthetics, marketing and distribution, holds mainstream aspirations. Despite attempts to elide its status as a work of art the film is nonetheless a cinematic imitation of a referential past and so subject to enduring questions about 'the nature of popular film and its function as an approbate or "authentic" memory text' (Grainge 2003: 4) which cannot be and indeed were not ignored by Germany's cultural commentators.[4] The praise heaped on the film by *Der Spiegel* (perhaps unsurprising given that Aust had served as the magazine's editor-in-chief between 1994 and the year of the film's release) was far from unanimous: for its many detractors, the film's lack of analytical and critical distance from its visceral, mimetic recreation of the RAF's deeds was considered to undermine claims for it as a crucial intervention, resulting in a 'failed RAF film' (Huber 2008). Far from seeing *The Baader Meinhof Complex* as a corrective to entrenched cultural myths, in most quarters of the print media the film was considered to serve the inverse of its intended function. Perhaps the loudest voice in this regard was Eckhard Fuhr of *Die Welt*, for whom the film 'fuels the myth of the "war" between the state and its revolutionary opponents because it relates this war without hesitation in the pattern of the action-cinema' (2008). In this regard, and reflecting the broader theme of this volume, for Daniel Kothenschulte *The Baader Meinhof Complex* is a politically and aesthetically conservative 'consensus film about a truly polarised topic', from a producer who 'has worked for a long time on a reorientation of German film politics' (2009).

In the rest of this chapter I wish to explore the ways in which *The Baader Meinhof Complex* presents the RAF as history. In so doing, I will examine the nature of this representation and its implications for the RAF myth debate outlined above, arguing that *The Baader Meinhof Complex* might actually represent the latest thrill ride in the RAF playground, to return to Kraushaar's terminology, thus accomplishing little more than the reproduction of terror(ism) in terms which the film otherwise ostensibly wants to challenge. Moreover, I suggest that this same strategy might also represent a step backwards in the polarised debate on urban terrorism.

THE 'PRADA-MEINHOF' COMPLEX

The Baader Meinhof Complex presents itself as an image-based chronicle of the period between 1967 and 1977 and, as such, exhibits a fascination with the iconic photographs of this period, both in terms of '1968' and the terrorism that followed in its wake. For example, the famous static photograph depicting student demonstrator Benno Ohnesorg bleeding to death next to a black Volkswagen Beetle is brought to life, as it were. Everything is fastidiously recreated (from the car's number plate, to the positioning of the players in the scene) in the form of 'living photographs' for Eichinger's 'illustrated history'. This careful adherence to the photographic truth of its chosen referent allows Eichinger's film to latch on to Germany's collective image-memory of events, thus bolstering its own claim to authenticity. In case the spectator is left in any doubt that such moments correspond to an actual known event, the film reminds us at several key junctures: at precisely the moment when the death of Ohnesorg comes closest to aligning with its photographic referent we see the flash from a journalist's camera – the source of the original image. Moreover, in this split second any distinction between the historical referent and its filmic reproduction collapses because the film also short-circuits temporal distance, presenting a moment captured on 2 June 1967 as, paradoxically, a moment that could have 'originated' from the diegesis of the film. In effect, *The Baader Meinhof Complex* burns itself onto the past, referring to, yet ultimately overwriting the photographic record with its own 'truth' for the media generation. This forceful requisition of documented images from Germany's pool of collective memories points to the problematic issue of authenticity alluded to above because, as Stefan Schmitz suggests, it also 'produces a form of short-circuit in the brain, which now believes that everything else took place in exactly the way that Aust, Eichinger and Edel present it' (2008). A close examination of Eichinger and Edel's cinematic representation of the RAF's terrorism will form the focus of the rest of this section.

The film was celebrated by *Der Spiegel* as a milestone in the production of images surrounding the RAF, but for Jan Schulz-Ojala it represents little more than an 'image grinder', which chews through its referent at the breakneck pace befitting a Hollywood 'politthriller' with little regard for analysis (2008). Echoing this stance, and resonating with Rentschler's pessimistic view of the shift away from a rarefied European tradition of filmmaking in the pursuit of a consensual mainstream aesthetic, Stefan Schmitz maintains of Eichinger's film that 'the rules of the dream factory count, not those of the ivory tower', thus leaving the cinemagoer with an action-packed 'knees-up through ten years of post-war West German history' (2008), the turbulent nature of which seem to refute Kurbjuweit and Eichinger's claim of a 'sober' treatment. Moreover, I would argue that the film's thrilling aesthetic does more to accentuate than diminish the 'intensity' of terror, which, as we have seen above, has informed youth-led conceptions of the RAF in the new millennium. Through its exploration of images of the RAF, *The Baader Meinhof Complex* can be read as stressing the intangible attributes of Kraushaar's 'ideology of adventure', which have lost little of their allure for a younger generation.

Useful to such a reading is the impact of the film's music, not least because, as Carol Flinn reminds us, 'the track becomes not only a harmonious complement but an integral inseparable part of the picture as well' (1992: 46). The original music for *The Baader Meinhof Complex* by Peter Hinderthür and Florian Tessloff owes a clear debt of inspiration to John Powell's score for the Hollywood films that comprise the *Bourne Trilogy*.[5] Set in a world of US political intrigue and clandestine conspiracies, Doug Liman's *The Bourne Identity* (2002) and Paul Greengrass's sequels (*The Bourne Supremacy*, 2004; *The Bourne Ultimatum*, 2007) are gripping Hollywood 'politthrillers', touted upon their release as more realistic takes on the then gadget-driven James Bond franchise. Although the *Bourne Trilogy* 'embraces an ethos that's at odds with the no pain, no gain, no brain mind-set that characterises too many such flicks' it still offers 'no shortage of pop pleasure', as Manohla Dargis of the *New York Times* suggests (2007). Powell's orchestration for the *Bourne Trilogy* certainly activates musical conventions for the suspense and enthrallment associated with the popular pleasures of mainstream cinema. Not only do the musical similarities between the *Bourne Trilogy* and *The Baader Meinhof Complex* create an intertextual association which links the latter to the action-film genre in the minds of spectators, Hinderthür and Tessloff's score speaks with Edel and Eichinger's images. As Flinn also notes with regard to the function of film music, 'Picture and track are so closely fused together that each one functions through the other. There is no separation of *I see* in the image and *I hear* on the track. Instead, there is the *I feel, I experience*, through the grand total of picture and track combined' (1992: 46).

Not only does this affective image–track combination stand as a refusal to Kurbjuweit's claim that *The Baader Meinhof Complex* is anything but a work of 'art', it also points to one of the contradictions within the film's representational strategy, namely the belief that the images, which pay fastidious attention to the horror of the RAF's deeds, do all of the talking. Although the film dwells on *what* rather than *why* in a bid to deny the RAF a glamour potential, the allegedly ascetic focus on images of egregious deeds is nonetheless infected by the terse orchestration of the rhythm-driven score, which stresses the tension and thriller potential contained in its visual partner. Flinn's contention that there is no separation of image and track is underlined by the very titling of the tracks in the film, which are namesakes for the historical moments represented visually: 'Shah Visit to Berlin' ('Schahbesuch'); 'Dutschke Assassination' ('Dutschke Attentat'); 'Bank Hold-up' ('Banküberfälle'); 'Arresting Ensslin' ('Ensslin Verhaftung'), to name but a few.

In the example of 'Bank Hold-up' the frenetic camera-work alone actually does little to deny an action-driven frenzy of terrorist activity, but the music that accompanies the scene conspires further against the sobering claim otherwise made for the images. The heavy use of rhythmic percussion – itself a convention of Hollywood genre cinema's signalling of suspense to an audience – dominates this musical cue, working in combination with the orchestral strings and hints of brass to build further layers of tension that work in conjunction with the visual information. There is no melody or musical through-line to speak of but rather a succession of syncopated, accented motivic fragments which gradually rise in pitch. Indeed, the ever-increasing height of pitch throughout the scene reflects and signals the ever-increasing height of tension to the spectator as the robbery races towards its climax. We are left with an affective totality which corresponds to Flinn's notion of '*I feel, I experience*', whereby the combination of image and track compels an immediate emotional response from the spectator, a response that is above all driven by the intensity and undeniable thrill at the core of this 'anti-capitalist' operation which might aid the glamorisation of the illegal.[6]

Figure 7.1: Along for the ride with Baader.

There are also further question marks over the visual information held in the frame. In order to present the protagonists of the German Autumn 'as they presumably were' necessitates presenting Andreas Baader in all of his boldness. Such a strategy would seem dangerous, however, because although, on the face of it, the RAF's self-appointed leader was little more than a misogynistic bully and petty criminal, it was also his frivolous bravado that saw him elevated to the status of a pop icon at the turn of the millennium. Although the film presents us with a mimetic reconstruction of the cold-blooded deeds that he sanctioned in the name of the RAF's collective project, it does little to distance us from the intangible yet seductive aura of audacious 'coolness' that accompanied them, and which informs his star potential. This appeal is particularly evident during the indoctrination of a soon-to-be crucial member of the RAF's second generation, Peter-Jürgen Boock (Vinzenz Kiefer), whom Baader first encounters in the bath with his lover Ensslin. During the encounter Baader's volatile yet charismatic personality is on full display. He feigns anger over the situation before handing the intimidated yet equally impressed Boock his leather jacket (a potent symbol of his anti-establishment credentials), inviting him to join the rest of the group as they head out to steal more cars. On the one hand this scene serves to illustrate the hold that Baader and his comrades were capable of exerting over impressionable young outsiders, but as the scene develops it also threatens to capture its audience in the same way. To the tune of *My Generation*, which acts here as a metonym for the youthful counter-cultural rebelliousness of 'the sixties', Boock rides with Baader along a deserted autobahn in one of the newly stolen cars, flanked by other members of the group. The self-appointed urban guerrillas tear along the urban highway, swapping lanes at high speed and passing cigarettes between cars before Baader ups the ante by producing a handgun, which he and Boock fire freely from the window of the car at the road signs marking the approach to Darmstadt. This sequence, which is initiated by Baader's declaration 'Let's have some fun', proves to be an intoxicating assault on the senses for the now liberated Boock.

However, the spectator is also invited to share directly in the exhilaration that the sequence provides: through the use of shot/reverse-shot between Baader and Boock, the cinema audience is positioned as a third passenger along for the ride. Moreover, this technique sutures us to both characters' points of view, but in different ways. When we see what Baader sees, the camera pulls back slightly,

Figure 7.2: Terrorism as a sexy adventure?

almost assuming a backseat position which allows us to share in Boock's sense of exhilaration, but when the reverse shot assumes Boock's perspective the camera moves forward so that we assume his position in the passenger seat. Thus when Baader, who is afforded a more extreme close-up, turns to his passenger and declares 'open fire' with a deviant grin he is, in effect, talking to us as well, inviting the spectator to join in the game before the scene eventually cuts to the colourless setting of the newly founded Federal Criminal Police Bureau (*Bundeskriminalamt*, BKA) charged with hunting down Baader and his gang. For Edel, the film shows the terrorism of the RAF for 'what it was – a ghastly bloodbath and dead end' (*Der Spiegel* 2008). However, the filmmakers' decision to present images without commentary or critical distance frequently allows the seductive aura of the Baader-Meinhof generation of terrorists to dominate the frame, thus fuelling the sense of excitement and adventure which informs popular ideas of the RAF in the new millennium. As Fuhr suggests, this 'quixotic troop' inevitably 'appears more colourful, livelier and so ultimately more likable than the valiant policemen and officials, many times over' (2008).

Part of this appeal is undoubtedly derived from the filmmakers' decision to cast a veritable 'who's who' of the German star system in the leading roles, rather than unknowns. Johanna Wokalek leads the roster of highly sexualised female terrorists in the film, exuding sex appeal in her role as Ensslin, not least when she first meets Boock in the bath, which leads in large part to Michael Althen's categorisation of the film as a 'polit-porno' (2008: 33). Moreover, the spectator is not just presented with the character of Andreas Baader but rather Moritz Bleibtreu *as* Andreas Baader, reminding us of Edgar Morin's contention that 'the star determines the many characters of his films; he incarnates himself in them and transcends them' (2005: 27). Bleibtreu's off-screen star persona cannot be easily divorced from his diegetic portrayal of Baader, and so functions as a cultural 'sign' which adds an extratextual layer of meaning to a performance in a film that is aimed at a young, largely mainstream audience.[7] After early screen roles in films which took youth and violence as their topics, Bleibtreu achieved widespread fame as the loveable rogue Mani in Tom Tykwer's international hit *Run, Lola Run* (*Lola rennt*, 1998), and, just prior to *The Baader Meinhof Complex*, took the leading role in Hans Weingartner's *Free Rainer* (*Free Rainer: Dein Fernseher lügt*, 2007), a spiritual sequel to *The Edukators* (*Die fetten Jahre sind vorbei*, 2004) that advances the director's anti-capitalist critique of the Berlin Republic from his previous film. Bleibtreu's earlier, most recognisable roles, therefore also have the potential to bring an added layer of intertextual association to his inhabitation of Baader, namely as a rebellious (anti) hero who challenges the ideological hegemony but in a charismatic and so ultimately likeable way. To have cast unknowns in the lead roles might have lessened the 'infection' of the character by the star, but as it stands, Bleibtreu's performance carries with it the potential to assuage the negative association with blind brutality which the filmmakers claim they otherwise wanted to expose: this union of a star of Germany's silver screen and the terrorist underground, both of whom are already pop-cultural icons, creates a powerful 'composite creature' (Morin 2005: 29) which might inadvertently function as a figurehead for Kraushaar's conception of an 'ideology of adventure'.

Following the deaths at Stammheim, Brigitte Mohnhaupt (Nadja Uhl, recognisable from her turn in Schlöndorff's terrorism film *The Legend of Rita*) offers a verbal disclaimer of sorts; in the last line of dialogue spoken in the film, she suggests to her shocked comrades that the apparent murder of Baader, Ensslin and Jan Carl Raspe was in fact a self-determined act of suicide. As we saw at the start of this chapter it was this line that was seized upon as the chief signifier of the film's myth-crushing potential, but an odd disparity in the film's representational strategy, which I will now explore, would seem further to undermine this intention. Throughout the course of its running time *The Baader Meinhof Complex* exhibits a fascination with a hyper-mimetic rendering of the violence that coloured the German Autumn, most of which is achieved through digital manipulation of the filmed image. When the wife of Federal Judge Wolfgang Buddenberg falls victim to the car bomb intended for her husband, the camera is able to remain in the vehicle, even as the initial explosion violently jerks her head backwards and instantaneously consumes her body. And during the attempted assassination of Rudi Dutschke the spectator is witness to each bullet entering its victim, one of which causes a short, sharp jet of blood to spray over the screen. In both cases, the use of digital technologies 'allow the spectator to have a more intimate relation with the image than is possible in reality' (Manovich 2001: 185), suturing the spectator into the flow of historical events with a potent immediacy, as if they were there. But given the film's obsession with depicting the intricate nature of how those on both sides of the conflict were injured or killed, the apparent immunity afforded to the Stammheim deaths is a salient omission. If the film's conviction is that the Stammheim deaths were clearly myth-building suicides and not state-sanctioned murders, why does the film not show them happen, particularly when the logic that informs the rest of the film demands absolute representation? This omission undermines Mohnhaupt's insistence of self-determined suicides and allows room for doubt over what happened between 11.00 p.m. and 7.41 a.m. on the night of 18 October 1977, which should be anathema to Edel and Eichinger's desired aim of showing the RAF as a bloodstained terrorist organisation rather than a mythic resistance movement as, it is claimed, other filmmakers have tended to treat that generation of terrorists.

Here it is useful to turn briefly to Petzold's *The State I Am In*. Despite Kurbjuweit's claims to the contrary, I would argue that Petzold's film offers a far more decisive antidote to the RAF myth,[8] confronting its audience with a truly sobering aesthetic strategy which drains the potential for terrorist chic from the screen in favour of stressing the numbing banality of life in the terrorist underground. Although the extent of Hans (Richy Müller) and Clara's (Barbara Auer) past crimes remain unclear, the film makes no attempt to apologise for their project, focusing instead on its destructive reality for their long-suffering daughter Jeanne (Julia Hummer). Indeed, for Jeanne, her parents' terrorism is anything but a source of excitement, emerging instead as a suffocating anachronism which corresponds to the director's mission statement for the film: 'no re-mythologisation' (quoted in Althen and Rebhandl 2002). By emphasising a destructive atmosphere of paranoia, exhaustion and decay that denies any sense of dissident heroism, *The State I Am In* circumvents prevailing clichés which have proved a rich source for pop exploitation.

AN OLD CONSENSUS FOR A NEW GENERATION

Another recent film to deal with Germany's legacy of urban terrorism is documentary filmmaker Andres Veiel's *Black Box Germany*, a progressive dual biography released in 2001 which allows a RAF perpetrator (Wolfgang Grams) and a RAF victim (Alfred Herrhausen) to share the frame in a filmic bid to transcend the entrenched ideological battlelines of the 1970s that have otherwise dominated the cultural memory of the RAF.[9] Key to Veiel's determination to move the debate on urban terrorism forward is the need to give a voice to the RAF's targets, with the director averring that 'one cannot speak about the RAF without leaving room for the victims' (see Schäfer 2001). The issue of the longstanding victim/perpetrator dichotomy became a further cause of concern within the domestic reception of *The Baader Meinhof Complex*, a film which, by its own admission, focuses on the terrorists and their deeds.

For Michael Buback, Eichinger's recreation of the historical era that saw his father (Federal Prosecutor Siegfried Buback) murdered in the name of the RAF's aims 'is a perpetrator film during which one has to take pains, at least at the beginning of the film, not to be drawn in by these young people who are so clever, engaged and beautiful' (quoted in Hollstein 2008). The widow of murdered banker Jürgen Ponto also expressed her dissatisfaction with the film's account of events, challenging the representation as a falsification of true history because it separated her from her husband at the moment of his death. In a somewhat audacious retort, Eichinger suggested that 'had our research revealed to us that Frau Ponto was forced to watch her husband's death at close quarters, we would, of course, have filmed it that way. It would have actually – and I realise this will sound cynical – heightened the dramatics of the film' (Sto 2008). Buback's appraisal of *The Baader Meinhof Complex* as a 'perpetrator film' is linked to his further criticism that 'the opponents of the terrorists remain vague. One doesn't know whether they were murdered as people, or rather in terms of their function' (Hollstein 2008). In this way, and unlike *The State I Am In* and *Black Box Germany*, which although they deal with the past are, foremost, films about the present, *The Baader Meinhof Complex* enters the debate as an anachronistic step back in time within the broader landscape of filmic engagements with urban terrorism. It is a film about the past which is also trapped in the polarised mindset of that past. By adopting the perspective of the terrorists without passing comment, the film recreates the RAF's view of its victims as faceless 'character masks' deprived of their humanity. We hardly hear from, nor do we learn anything about, Hanns-Martin Schleyer, who, like the other victims of terrorism in the film, is reduced to an object of the RAF's violence.

Although we are invited to share more closely in the perspective of the terrorists, it is interesting that both Eichinger's aims for the film and Kurbjuweit's review pull the representation of the terrorists back into the terms of engagement which characterised the immediate reactions to the German Autumn. Kurbjuweit's disavowal of the earlier films he feels 'grumble' about the role played by the fascist past and its legacy in provoking the terrorism of the RAF echoes the standpoint of West Germany's political centre during the 1970s, which dismissed any connection between 1945 and 1977 (whether it came directly from the RAF or the group's sympathisers) as an example of its opponents' alleged disconnection from reality. Eichinger's determination that the spectator need only be presented with the visual fact of the RAF's actions without the need for a detailed exploration of the motivation behind them stands at odds with the viewpoint offered by Horst Herold (Bruno Ganz), the head of the BKA charged with the responsibility of bringing Baader and his followers to justice. Herold speaks to his assistant (Heino Ferch) of the pragmatic need to understand the RAF's rationalisation of its conduct in order to capture the terrorists at large and prevent a further escalation of violence, but the filmmakers fail to heed the warning contained in the diegesis of their own film. In a moment of unintended intertextual and historical irony, the Hitler and Speer of Eichinger's earlier war epic *Downfall* are the only figures who give a clear voice to the importance of attempting to understand the RAF's linking of the horrors of the fascist past to the conduct of the Federal Republic in the present, which is otherwise minimised in the film in favour of stressing the international dimension of the terrorists' project. Thus for all of the claims to a crucial intervention in the debate on urban terrorism, *The Baader Meinhof Complex* emerges as a regressive relic of the reactionary ideological impasse which characterised the polarised thinking on the RAF into the 1990s, reviving, even if unwittingly, the ideological battlelines of the 1970s which other filmmakers had been working to deconstruct.

CONCLUSION: THE AUTHENTICITY COMPLEX

Alison Landsberg has coined the term 'prosthetic memory' to describe the ways in which the mass media (particularly through the affective power of popular film) can enable people to experience as memories that which they did not actually live through. As she elaborates,

> In the process that I am describing, the person does not simply apprehend a historical narrative but takes on a more personal, deeply felt memory of a past event through which he or she did not live. The resulting prosthetic memory has the ability to shape that person's subjectivity and politics. (2004: 2)

Landsberg argues for the utopian potential of prosthetic memories which, as outlined in more detail in the introduction to this volume, might generate a positive, empathetic understanding 'precisely by encouraging people to feel connected to, while recognizing the alterity of, the "other"' (2004: 9). But there are also concerns which accompany this highly affective 'experiential relationship' to the past. As Robert Burgoyne notes, 'the production and dissemination of memories that are defined not by organic, individual experience but by simulation and re-enactment are potentially dangerous', not least because they 'pos[e] the threat of alienation and revisionism' (2003: 224). In either case, given the increasing power of the media to construct our sense of the past, we are left with a situation whereby, as Philip Drake argues, 'mediated memories have become increasingly important to how we articulate ourselves and our tastes in the present' (2003: 198). If, as suggested above, the bored youth of the Berlin Republic already have a taste for the vicarious excitement that the terrorist legacy can provide, then the status of *The Baader Meinhof Complex* as a visceral, experiential memory of this past takes on a sharpened poignancy. Schulz-Ojala (2008) comments that, 'whoever remembers those times doesn't need this cranked-up flipbook' of the German Autumn, but then the film is not aimed at those with a personal recollection of its historical referent. The intended negative association with terrorist excess for a younger generation might easily be lost because the film allows too much room for the power of the RAF as an existential symbol of 'rebellion', 'provocation' and 'authenticity' to dominate the frame, a dominance which also frustrates the potential for a positive empathetic understanding of the terrorists' victims, who remain unexplored, and so predominantly invisible throughout the film.

In the view of commentator Frank Schirrmacher, *The Baader Meinhof Complex* 'is neither a documentary nor a history film. The whole thing has something of a parallel universe about it, and so the power to set its own time, and possibly the power to put the whole RAF reception on a new basis' (2008). Schirrmacher's assessment here resonates with Burgoyne's view that 'electronic or audio-visual "lieux de memoire" (sites of memory) have created a kind of second order memory system that is fast becoming a second order reality' (2003: 225). The 'reality' which Edel and Eichinger's project creates is just that – a second-order reality that is closer in tone to the parallel universe of the RAF offered across the pages of *Tussi Deluxe*. Less an 'illustrated history', which as Burgoyne reminds us is 'traditionally conceived as impersonal, the realm of public events that have occurred outside the archive of personal experience' (2003: 225), *The Baader Meinhof Complex* sutures its audience into a visceral second-order memory of the terrorist past and its thrilling potential that works against the film's stated aim of deglamorising the RAF.

For Kothenschulte, the Oscar nomination for *The Baader Meinhof Complex* was a milestone, albeit a lamentable one: 'perhaps we have finally reached the point where German cinema is no longer identified with its art tradition, but rather its commercial mainstream' (2009). Through its use of stars and a commodified global aesthetic the film exhibits a strong mainstream orientation which might actually provide 'new' raw material for the youth's alleged adventure lust and nostalgic celebration of Baader and his comrades. While Kothenschulte's comments about German cinema in the new millennium as a whole are, as this volume chiefly argues, somewhat premature, more comprehensive filmic reckonings with the legacy of the RAF are to be found elsewhere. Whether the perspectives they provide can be heard over the mainstream might of Edel and Eichinger's text, however, is another question.

NOTES

1 As Thomas Elsaesser has noted, as early as the Christmas of 1977 'the German government declared [...] its confidence that the 'terrorist threat' was over and public life in the Federal republic could return to "normal"' (2007: 51).

2 See also for more information and a scan of one of the double pages devoted by the magazine to the 'RAF fashion'. At the time of writing *Tussi Deluxe* has long since been discontinued.

3 English translation taken from the subtitles to the Momentum Pictures DVD release of *The Baader Meinhof Complex* (2009).

4 Even Eichinger's verbose claims for the film in this regard were tempered by a somewhat incongruous aside, which contradicted his outright disavowal of dramaturgical interpretation: 'sometimes one has to diverge from the reality to do justice to the truth' (quoted in Schmitz 2008).

5 For a particularly clear indication of the similarities compare, for example, the track 'Assets and targets', available on the original motion picture soundtrack to accompany *The Bourne Ultimatum*, with 'Bank Hold-up' from *The Baader Meinhof Complex* and its accompanying soundtrack.

6 My thanks go to Ian Sapiro of the School of Music at the University of Leeds for his discussion on the technical aspects of film music.

7 Edel stated in interview that he made *The Baader Meinhof Complex* for his 20- and 21-year-old sons (see Buchner 2008).

8 For a more detailed discussion of the film, see Homewood 2006.

9 Writing in 1997, Friedrich Christian Delius suggested that 'despite all the articles, books, records and films the topic "1977" is still burdened by the aura of a taboo'. The taboo that Delius refers to centred on the apparent prohibition on discussing the terrorist legacy in anything other than polarised terms that otherwise divided the players neatly into a perpetrator/victim dichotomy (Delius 2003: 61).

Chapter 8

The absent Heimat: Hans-Christian Schmid's *Requiem* (2006)

David Clarke

Erich Rentschler's often-cited broadside against a particular kind of German filmmaking in the 1990s, the so-called cinema of consensus discussed in the introduction to this volume, mentions Hans-Christian Schmid's film *23* (1998) as an honourable exception to the trend towards relationship comedies 'focus[ing] on identity crises which are in fact pseudo-crises, for they have no depth of despair, no true suffering, no real joy' (2000: 263). Rentschler attributes to Schmid's film, based on the life of the hacker Karl Koch, who committed suicide in 1989, 'a desire to fathom the psychic and social makeup of today's young Germans' (2000: 275). Rentschler's praise for *23* is also motivated by a general nostalgia for the representation of young people in the critical Young German Cinema of the 1960s and the New German Cinema of the 1970s and 1980s. In films such as Alexander Kluge's *Yesterday Girl* (*Abschied von Gestern*, 1966) or Wim Wenders's *Wrong Move* (*Falsche Bewegung*, 1975), for example, the inability of young people to find a place for themselves in West German society is portrayed as symptomatic of the bankruptcy of the values on which that society was founded, so that the failure of such figures to assimilate becomes a lesson for the viewer in the failings of the postwar Federal Republic. In comparison, the romantic comedies of the 1990s which Rentschler criticises do not seek to show problems which cannot be resolved within the existing social, political and economic status quo.

If we take Schmid's output as a director and (often) scriptwriter for his own films as a whole, however, we can see a tension between what might be broadly termed a socially critical cinema, which shows the hostility of the prevailing social order to young people and their needs, and one that is more 'consensual' in Rentschler's terms. With the exception of Schmid's most recent film *Storm* (*Sturm*, 2009), set in the Yugoslavian conflict of the 1990s, and his *Distant Lights* (*Lichter*, 2003), all of the director's fiction films have focused on coming-of-age stories, depicting adolescents or young adults in the process of establishing an identity independent of the family sphere. His first feature film for theatre release, *It's a Jungle Out There* (*Nach Fünf im Urwald*, 1995), is a tale of fairly mild rebellion, where a teenager, frustrated with the comfortable but claustrophobic world of her parents, goes on a night-time adventure in the big city, accompanied by the shy boy-next-door. This film ends with reconciliation and a better understanding on all sides, but there is certainly no youthful challenge to the fundamental values of the protagonist's bourgeois parents. Much the same can be said about *Crazy* (2000), Schmid's adaptation of the bestselling novel of the same name by teenage author Benjamin Lebert. This story of a young outsider trying to fit in at a boarding school catering largely to the disturbed or rebellious children of the wealthy is not uncritical of the parental generation, which, as in *It's a Jungle Out There*, is too preoccupied with its own domestic problems to recognise the needs of its offspring. However, the central focus of the narrative is the protagonist Benny's search for acceptance within his peer group and his quest to lose his virginity. Although both of these projects are accompanied by a good deal of angst for Benny, and although the film does not end with the suggestion that all of his problems have been resolved, the message is essentially upbeat: Benny will succeed in finding his own identity and place in the world, in spite of, but crucially not in opposition to, his parents.

The tone of *23* and *Requiem* (2006), the latter of which will be the central focus of this chapter, is markedly different. Again, inter-generational conflict is central to the narratives, which in both instances are based on the facts of real cases. Both films end with the madness and death of their protagonists, which can be read as indicative of their failure, in contradistinction to their counterparts in *It's a Jungle Out There* and *Crazy*, to establish a stable sense of self outside the family sphere. In *23*, the life and death of Koch, the rebellious son of a conservative West German newspaper editor growing up in the 1980s, is seen as a failed attempt to make sense of the world after the early death of his hated father. He becomes increasingly obsessed with the so-called Illuminati, an alleged secret society beloved of conspiracy theorists. Schmid's film suggests that Koch's fight against the Illuminati, who supposedly control the political and economic life of the Western world, is a substitute for his rebellion against his now dead father. Koch proves himself incapable of establishing a meaningful sense of the world and his own relation to it which is not reliant on the support of a seemingly overwhelming paternal order. In this sense, the film does not share the essentially consensual tone of other Schmid films like *It's a Jungle Out There* and *Crazy*, in which the protagonists are able to move towards a stable sense of self while leaving parental authority intact. In *Requiem* too, as the following analysis will demonstrate, the protagonist is unable to establish a sense of identity for herself outside the sphere of a family which, while oppressive, is apparently the only source of meaning in an otherwise threateningly meaningless world.

ANNELIESE MICHEL, EMILY ROSE AND MICHAELA KLINGLER

The case of Anneliese Michel, which caused a considerable scandal in Germany in the mid-1970s, is well documented. Anneliese, it is generally accepted, suffered from a form of epilepsy which produced hallucinations and, eventually, psychotic episodes. These were interpreted by Anneliese, who came from a conservative Catholic family, and by those close to her, as manifestations of a demonic possession. Over a prolonged period in her home town of Klingenberg in Lower Bavaria, she underwent a series of exorcisms, performed by Catholic priests. Eventually Anneliese was refusing to eat, which meant that she was not strong enough to withstand the physical strain of the ritual. After her death, her parents and one of the priests involved were put on trial for negligent homicide. For those who believe that Anneliese was possessed by demons, and who visit the shrine at her former home, the young woman died to atone for the sins of Germans and to return them to the Catholic faith (Beier and Neumann 2005).

Schmid's film is not the first to deal with Anneliese Michel's fate. Scott Derrickson's US film *The Exorcism of Emily Rose* (2005) relocates the Klingenberg case to the American Midwest, creating a hybrid of horror film and courtroom drama. Told in retrospect within the framework of the trial against the exorcist, renamed Father Moore, Emily's story includes horrific experiences of possession and exorcism scenes reminiscent of William Friedkin's classic *The Exorcist* (1973). Like Friedkin's film, *The Exorcism of Emily Rose* casts the events depicted as a proof of the existence of the supernatural, proof which leads doubting or agnostic figures back towards belief. Whereas Father Karras in *The Exorcist* is a priest losing his faith who becomes convinced of the existence of God and the Devil through his encounter with the possessed Regan MacNeil, in *Emily Rose* it is an ambitious lawyer, Erin Bruner, who begins to question her agnosticism when, during the trial, she experiences demonic influences in her own life.

Requiem is not a direct response to the success of Derrickson's film: Schmid's project, on which the director had been working on and off for around a decade, was already well underway when *Emily Rose* was released (Beier 2006). However, a brief comparison with the American version of Anneliese Michel's story does highlight key elements of Schmid's approach. In terms of narrative, Schmid concentrates on the experiences of Michaela Klingler, the renamed Anneliese, including those not directly related to her illness, rather than using the 'possessed' woman as a mere catalyst for the religious debate which Derrickson's film rehearses through the courtroom drama. In Derrickson's film the audience learns very little at first hand about Emily Rose before her possession, and her parents are only sketched in as simple, God-fearing folk who loved their daughter. In Schmid's film, however, the constellation provided by Michaela, her sympathetic, indulgent father, and her rather more strict mother is clearly at the centre of the narrative.

In terms of the aesthetic strategies employed by the two films, Schmid's approach differs from Derrickson's in its refusal to make use of special effects. In *Emily Rose*, these tend to make the demonic forces believable to the audience, whereas in *Requiem* these phenomena could just as easily be the products of Michaela's own mental illness. A further stylistic difference which should be noted is Schmid's decision to maintain the original Lower Bavaria setting of the story and to visually recreate the Federal Republic of the 1970s. In the following section, I will explore the possible consequences of this decision to locate the story in a specific social and historical context, rather than placing the events in the more general and abstract frame of the battle between faith and rationality in the modern world, which is the general tenor of *Emily Rose*.

MICHAELA KLINGLER AND THE 1970s: REQUIEM AS A 'BIOPIC'

Not only has Schmid retained the original setting for the story of Anneliese/Michaela, he has also made use of a *mise-en-scène* which clearly seeks to recreate the period in which the real events in Klingenberg took place: the mid-1970s in provincial West Germany are evoked through costume and décor, which are dominated by muted tones, and through the film's use of diegetic and non-diegetic music from the period. Furthermore, the director and his cinematographer Bogumil Godfrejow have chosen to photograph the film using a 16 mm camera, the footage from which has been blown up for the final 35 mm print. This technical decision clearly has consequences for the way the film is shot, since the many interior scenes are predominantly photographed using a hand-held camera, which often gives the film the feel of a fly-on-the-wall documentary; but beyond this, Schmid states that the process of enlarging the original 16 mm footage helps to give the final print 'a noticeable and positive grain, which we felt was something characteristic of a lot of films of the 1970s' (Gabrero 2006). This recreation of the look of the period raises, I would argue, the question of how we should read Michaela's relationship to her times.

In the German context, Schmid's recreation of the 1970s in particular might suggest some commentary on those events which Protestant theologian Uwe Wolff attempts to link to the Anneliese Michel case (1999: 156 and 250), and which, since German unification, have continued to provoke public debate and inspire works of literature and films (Berendse and Cornils 2008; Palfreyman 2006): namely, the radicalisation of youth culture during the student movement of the late 1960s and the subsequent turn to violence among some young leftists in the 1970s. In an interview published as part of the press pack for the German release for the film, Schmid seems to suggest the validity of making such connections between Michaela's actions and those of the radical left in this period, pointing out that she is 'a peer of [the RAF terrorists] Gudrun Ensslin and Holger Meins' (Anon. 2005). A number of the film's German reviewers have followed the director in this reading, interpreting Michaela's story as a 'little aftershock' of the 'violent eruptions' elsewhere in German society at the time (Krekeler 2006), or suggesting that Michaela is torn between the conservative world of her provincial home and the revolutionary atmosphere at her university (Buß 2006). In this sense, *Requiem* could, like Friedkin's

Exorcist in the US context, be read as a metaphor for the more general intergenerational conflict in the 1960s and 1970s.

The potential of the historical setting of the film to provide a key to its interpretation seems, however, to be limited. Whereas *The Exorcist* situates the possession of the adolescent Regan in the context of youthful rebellion in the wider culture, showing her actress mother taking part in a film about student unrest, for example (Kermode 1998: 27), *Requiem* makes no explicit reference to political events or social change in the 1970s. The university which Michaela attends is also plainly not in the grip of radical fervour: we see no demonstrations, radical posters or political meetings.

The limited scope of the narrative, which focuses on Michaela's relationships to only two other figures outside the family home, also throws open to question the validity of a historically contextualised reading of the film which would seek to interpret *Requiem* as a commentary on a particular period in West German history. Although Schmid has stated that his story could only have taken place 'at this time and in this place,' he also relativises the historical specificity of the film by pointing out that, in other times and in other places, Michaela would have faced other obstacles, suggesting that his interest lies more in the way the character deals with those obstacles than with their historically determined nature (Soyez 2006). As he goes on to claim here and in other interviews, his central interest was in the situation within Michaela's family:

> *Requiem* places a greater emphasis on the story of the family than on the exorcism. Because it is about the people. Or about the structure that the individual finds herself in. About not being able to break away from her mother and about the illness that Michaela has in the film. (Soyez 2006; cf. Gabrero 2006; Behrens 2006)

While we should not necessarily take the director's own interpretation as the key to understanding *Requiem*, this statement of intent clearly runs counter to the potential function of the period detail, namely to situate the events in a particular historical context which, implicitly, the film might seek to understand and explore.

These difficulties in attributing a meaning to the film's historical setting are those which are more generally associated with the genre of the biographical film or 'biopic', that is to say a film based on the life of a historical character. Schmid seeks to distance himself somewhat from the conventions of this genre by stating in the intertitle at the beginning of the film that it is only 'based on' true events, and by changing the names of those involved. Nevertheless, *Requiem* displays the same ambiguity in relation to its presentation of history which film scholars have regarded as a feature of the biopic in general. As Robert Rosenstone, a defender of the biopic, points out, by choosing a particular historical life to narrate, a biographer, whether working in film or on the page, implicitly 'make[s] the case that individuals are either at the centre of the historical process – or are worthy of studying as exemplars of lives, actions, and individual value systems we either admire or dislike' (2006: 90). Clearly, Michaela Klingler is not 'at the centre of the historical process', but she certainly has been read as somehow exemplary of a particular set of values held by a group at a certain point in history, which the audience is invited to judge in their historical context. In this sense, Michaela could be seen as a private figure who is nevertheless presented, as William Gwynn puts it, as a kind of 'synecdoche' for a collective historical experience, that is to say a part of a society which stands for its whole at a particular moment (2006: 109). At the same time, however, as my comments above also suggest, *Requiem* might equally be understood as sharing in that dehistoricising tendency of the biopic to 'emphasise individual causality – detached from other factors – as an explanatory model for the world' (Custon 1992: 178), seeing only individual cases of fortune or misfortune without questioning the social conditions which make those cases possible.

REQUIEM AND THE HEIMAT TRADITION

Schmid's *Requiem* appears to position itself, perhaps rather awkwardly, between the stance of a critical biopic, which seeks to come to terms with a particular period in German history through the fate of one figure, and that of an intimate family drama focusing on the causality of an individual life, which, beyond period detail, does not seek to say anything substantial about German society at the time the action takes place. What I would like to suggest in the rest of this chapter is that it is possible to move beyond this interpretative *impasse* by reading the film in relation to a particular tradition of German cinema, namely that of the *Heimatfilm* ('homeland film'). However, I want to argue that Schmid's film is not merely a continuation of the *Heimatfilm* tradition or a reworking of the anti-*Heimatfilm* developed by the New German

Cinema, but rather an invocation of Heimat motifs which actually points to the dissolution of Heimat in the traditional sense.

Heimat as a topos, that is to say the rural or mountain location as a site of tradition, can already be observed in early German cinema, but the period most associated with *Heimatfilm* is undoubtedly the Adenauer era of the 1950s in the Federal Republic, when hundreds of films telling Heimat stories set in a rural 'ultra-conservative never-never-land' came onto the West German film market (Boa and Palfreyman 2000: 98).

However, as Manuela Fiedler points out, the idyllic worlds portrayed in the *Heimatfilm* do not entirely obscure all social conflict and change (1997: 42). Rather, they have a conciliatory approach to dealing with such conflict and change, which provides a sense of continuity and stability, for example by incorporating elements of modernisation in 'a sentimental reconciliation with tradition' (Palfreyman 2000: 32).

A key element in the *Heimatfilm*, that provides a link to Schmid's *Requiem* is the prominence of the relationship of the rural *Heimat* location to the outside world. Although that outside world is not necessarily represented, it is an important factor in the *Heimatfilm's* negotiation with change and is made present either through the arrival of outsiders or through natives who have been away from the Heimat. At its most conservative, as in Veit Harlan's 1942 Heimat melodrama *The Golden City* (*Die goldene Stadt*) or Luis Trenker's *The Prodigal Son* (*Der verlorene Sohn*, 1934), for example, those who turn their backs on their place of origin are punished, but the 1950s films frequently introduce characters who bring with them from the outside knowledge of modern ways which can be integrated into the Heimat to ensure its survival. At the same time, the Heimat can be a place of healing, or a 'therapeutic' space as Johannes von Moltke puts it, for traumatised outsiders who choose to make their homes there (2005: 39).

In the late 1960s and early 1970s, filmmakers of the New German Cinema attempted to reclaim the Heimat topos for their own critical purposes. In films such as Peter Fleischmann's *Hunting Scenes from Lower Bavaria* (*Jagdszenen aus Niederbayern*, 1969) or Rainer Werner Fassbinder's *Katzelmacher* (1969), the provincial setting is no longer portrayed as a space of continuity, community and reassuring tradition, but rather as oppressive and intolerant, maintaining its sense of identity and cohesion only through the exclusion of those who cannot conform to its rigid norms (Boa and Palfreyman 2000: 102–15; Fiedler 1997: 46–58).

Seen in the context of this specifically German film culture, the story told in Schmid's *Requiem* clearly sets up a series of generic expectations rooted in the Heimat tradition. Like many *Heimatfilm* figures, Michaela leaves her rural home in order to experience the wider world and to gain her independence, but, having seen life beyond the Heimat, eventually returns and is reintegrated into the rural community. As I will show below, however, although the world beyond the Heimat proves to be less than satisfactory in a number of key respects, this return to the rural milieu also serves to highlight the evacuation of many of the traditional features of the Heimat, which is now, in effect, absent. The behaviour of Michaela's family in agreeing to her exorcism, in which Michaela colludes, can be read here as an attempt to reinstate a limited, impoverished form of Heimat, which has ceased to exist in the traditional sense. Consequently, it can be argued, *Requiem* is not only a requiem, or act of mourning, for Michaela, but for the Heimat that is now lost.

The key relationship in Michaela's life is that with her mother, who is also the figure most concerned that Michaela will become estranged from her origins if she leaves home. This concern is framed in terms of her fears about Michaela's epilepsy, which barely mask her deeper-rooted fear of her daughter's independence. For example, in a key scene during Michaela's visit home at Christmas, her mother puts the trendy new clothes Michaela has bought in Tübingen, which are actually fairly modest, into the dustbin. The connotations of this action in relation to Michaela's sexuality, which her mother clearly fears, are

Figure 8.1: 'Don't dress like a tramp!': Michaela is confronted by her mother.

obvious, and it is this nuance which the American English subtitles on the current DVD release underline: here Michaela's mother accuses her of walking around dressed 'like a tramp'. However, in the original German, Michaela's mother actually accuses her of dressing 'wie ein Flüchtlingskind' (like a refugee child), making specific reference to the post-World War Two refugees who arrived by their millions in West Germany from the east, and who were often met with suspicion and hostility. Here, then, the mother's fear of her daughter's sexual identity and growing independence is mixed with a fear that Michaela will soon be an outsider who does not belong in the Heimat.

It is important to note, however, that this potential loss of belonging is now chiefly formulated in relation to the family unit and not to the wider rural community. In the same exchange, Michaela's mother reminds her pointedly that she is a 'a Klingler', identifying her primarily with the family name, rather than with the place where the family lives; and it becomes increasingly clear that the family lives a relatively isolated existence within a rural setting which no longer provides a broader sense of belonging and community. *Heimatfilm*, even in its critical mode in late 1960s and early 1970s, tends to engage with the rural community as a whole, showing a cross-section of different classes and professions, with the anti-*Heimatfilm* seeking to show that community as inherently oppressive. In Schmid's film, however, this wider community is simply absent. We see the Klingler family home, but few other common Heimat locations associated with the experience of community, such as a village square or an inn. In fact, the only communal activities which the family partakes in are Catholic church services and pilgrimages, but here too the rest of the participants remain anonymous. The few journeys which the family undertakes, with the exception of the bus pilgrimage to an Italian shrine, are by car, so that the viewer has the impression that the rural milieu, like every other part of West German society by the mid-1970s, is becoming increasingly mobile. This mobility is accompanied, however, by that sense of detachment (and ultimately alienation) which, as Peter Bickle notes, the myth of Heimat sought to overcome in the face of modernisation (2004: 17).

Schmid also simultaneously invokes and subverts the Heimat aesthetic by setting key scenes in the rural landscape, while at the same time refusing to offer it up for the audience's aesthetic pleasure. In the *Heimatfilm* of the 1950s, the act of looking at the Heimat landscape and the appreciation of its beauty often has the function of cementing relationships, especially male–female romances, through a

Figure 8.2: Hanna and Michaela survey the Heimat landscape.

shared identification with the beauty of nature. Here, however, the landscape is relegated to an empty backdrop which resists any such attempt at identification. In the opening scene of the film, for example, we see Michaela climbing a hill to a chapel, where she prays to be admitted to university. Although the viewer does get brief glimpses of the wider landscape, for instance through the chapel door as she enters, Schmid chooses to let the hand-held camera focus tightly on Michaela herself, often in a close shot, so that the landscape is for the most part excluded from view. What we do see of it reveals a dull and muted colour scheme, achieved with the use of colour filters, rather than the vibrant display favoured by the *Heimatfilm*. Similarly, when photographing the car journeys in the film, the camera pans across an empty, almost barren landscape, dominated by brown and green tones. Here the *Heimat* landscape becomes one of alienation and failed identification. For example, in the film's penultimate scene, Michaela's friend Hanna, who is from the same rural community, tries to convince her to return to Tübingen as they climb to the top of a hill and survey the Heimat. Here Schmid chooses to shoot the conversation almost entirely from behind the two young women and to leave the landscape itself as a blurred and grey backdrop to their conversation. We do not share their gaze over the panoramic view, and their inability to communicate, despite the fact that they are both natives of the Heimat which lies before them, suggests that it has lost its integrative force.

In the absence of the Heimat's power to integrate through the community or a shared relationship to the natural landscape, only religion and the family remain as a source of identity for Michaela. In Tübingen, where she attends university, she does manage to make a friend in Hanna and begins a relationship with Stefan. Also, at one point the film even suggests that the city might become the site of a new sense of self and community for Michaela, as the usual *Heimatfilm* sequence of enjoyment in the spectacle of the rural landscape is replaced with a montage of images of Michaela wandering around a picturesque Tübingen with Hanna and Stefan. However, Michaela's experience of university is primarily one of isolation, which she mitigates to some extent through her contact with her two friends, and the pressure to succeed, which is apparently increased by the debilitating effects both of her illness and her medication (at one point we see her throw her pills down the sink as she tries to complete an essay). What we do not see is what Reinhard Mohr has claimed as a typical experience for Michaela's generation, who he describes as the seventy-eighters: no group of like-minded co-generationalists provides a kind of 'replacement family' in which Michaela can escape from the psychological deformations for which the traditional family and community were often made responsible (1992: 51).

Michaela's attempts to find such a 'replacement family' outside her home are undermined by the apparent lack of any shared set of values among those she encounters in Tübingen. This is a particularly important factor given that religion and the family are inextricably intertwined for Michaela, primarily around the figure of the mother. Religious observance in fact becomes a substitute for communication between mother and daughter, for example in the scene where, after going to university against her mother's wishes, Michaela is given a rosary by her in the hope that it will protect Michaela from the dangers of the outside world. When Michaela, recognising the concerns which motivate the gift, attempts to speak to her mother, she turns away saying, 'Enough! Stop it! Please!' As German psychiatrist and author Tilmann Moser suggests in his reckoning with his own religious upbringing, first published in the year of Anneliese Michel's death, religious faith functions here as the only source of a sense of belonging within the family and as a replacement for genuine familial communication (1976: 30 and 61).

In contradistinction to this familial world, Michaela's first experience of university life brings home to her the secularisation of the society she encounters outside the family home. When she enters her first lecture late, the professor asks her what she believes in, to which she replies simply, 'In God.' This answer is met with hilarity among her fellow students, and her best friend Hanna is also routinely dismissive of her faith. At the same time, neither Hanna nor the other students, as their professor quickly points out, seem to have any alternative set of beliefs to set against Michaela's religion. Not only is the political unrest of the 1970s entirely absent from Schmid's portrayal of university life, the alternative value system which the Left sought to set against that of the mainstream of postwar German society is absent here too, so that the student movement of the late 1960s appears not to have achieved the 'socio-cultural refounding' of the Federal Republic which some commentators have claimed for it in retrospect (Koenen 2007: 23); rather, it has left a vacuum. Therefore, although the religious community represented by the family may be oppressive, the alternative world of the city and the university does not appear to offer a framework of meaning or a coherent set of values which could form the basis for Michaela's sense of belonging and identity. Indeed, the costs of the secular university milieu's distance towards established value systems are demonstrated in the figure of Hanna, who is portrayed, at least at the beginning of the film, as directionless and unsure of her place in the world.

Viewed in this context, Michaela has much in common with Father Borchert, who persuades both Michaela's own priest, Father Landauer, and the family that Michaela's mental difficulties are the result of a possession by demons. He is a figure also clearly troubled by the 'Godlessness' of the world and who sees in Michaela a person who is, as he says, equally sensitive to this. Even more so than Michaela, he is shown as an isolated figure. When Michaela travels to see him after an attack she suffers on Christmas Eve, we see him seated in a bleak room in a village where, as he himself points out, 'not even 50 souls' joined the Christmas Eve mass. His desire to persuade her that she is being tested by God, like (the fictional) St Catherine of Biasca whom she so admires, is implicitly linked to his own desire to reassure himself of God's existence in a world in which religion is relied upon, if at all, as a kind of 'insurance policy against bad times', as he puts it. Eventually, he is able, with Michaela and her family, to construct a separate world of belief that isolates them from the rest of society, while as the same time giving meaning to their experiences.

Michaela is not only a helpless victim of this process. The brain scan she receives, for instance, in a scene which recalls the juxtaposition of supernatural events with equally horrific modern medical procedures in *The Exorcist*, is shown to be alienating and traumatic, and Michaela eventually makes a conscious decision to turn her back on scientific approaches to her condition. More important, however, is the framework which her particular version of Catholic religion provides her with to make sense of her ecstatic and hallucinatory experiences. The youth culture which Michaela encounters at university is only capable of containing and giving meaning to these in a limited fashion, for instance in the two sequences in the film when Michaela dances to rock music. In the first, for example, after she has kissed Stefan for the first time, Schmid uses the colour of the disco lights to create a psychedelic visual effect, which hints at Michaela's state of mind; in the second, when she seems to have lost control of herself entirely, she dances in an uncharacteristic red dress, a colour suggesting both sensuality and excess, but also with links to sin in Catholic symbolism and, of course, to Satan. On the one hand, these moments, in which Michaela engages with the youth culture of the 1970s, would seem to suggest a desire for those intense and transgressive experiences which Michael Rutschky diagnoses as a typical feature of the alternative culture of that decade, through which young people hoped to escape what were perceived as the deadening effects of life in mainstream West German society (1980: 97). However, Michaela is driven to give a meaning to these moments of hallucination which re-establishes her connection with her family, thus moving against this broader societal trend.

The key scene of Michaela's reintegration into the family takes place in the domestic and maternal space of the family kitchen. Significantly, Michaela's screams and abuse, the symptoms of her alleged possession, drive out her father, who initially believes that she should be treated in a hospital according to the principles of modern science. Michaela threatens to do more damage to the family crockery unless he starts to pray, suggesting that she is in fact the one who pushes her parents into an acceptance of the supernatural origin of her illness. Rather than be committed to a mental hospital and placed at the mercy of modern psychiatry, which might cure, but would fail to give meaning to her illness, Michaela chooses to stay within the family home and allow her condition to take its place within her parents' belief system. Crucially, it is the mother who, as representative of both religion and the family, makes the decision finally to accept this preferred interpretation of Michaela's situation. As Elizabeth Boa and Rachel Palfreyman have noted, the Heimat is often configured as a maternal space (2000: 183–84); yet here it is the limited domestic sphere associated with the mother, not the wider Heimat community, which provides a refuge from effects of modernisation which Michaela encounters.

By the end of the film, when Hanna visits Michaela and takes her for a walk into the countryside, in the sequence already discussed, she has attained a sense of peace, but also, and more importantly, a sense of the meaningfulness of her situation within the framework offered by her family's religion: 'I'm suffering for the greater good, for a higher purpose,' she tells Hanna. Schmid ends his film with a slow zoom onto Michaela's contented face as she is driven back to her parents' home by Hanna to meet her death. There is significant irony in this final image, after which the audience is informed by way of an intertitle that Michaela dies as a result of the exorcism. Although the audience can see that Michaela is deluded, there is no denying that she is also at peace, so it is not easy to dismiss her actions out of hand. As I have argued, Schmid places significant emphasis on Michaela having chosen this way of dealing with her experiences, and it is clear that this path has its own psychological rewards. She is no longer in the alienating, secularised and disorienting world of modernity beyond the Heimat, but can believe that she has been reintegrated into the Heimat's meaning-giving structures. However, it is undeniable that the version of the Heimat presented by Schmid is a significantly impoverished one compared with the idylls of the *Heimatfilm* in the 1950s. It is only within the limited domestic sphere that the effects of modernity can be held at bay and that community and identity can be maintained at the cost of becoming cut off from the outside world. The Heimat as traditionally understood has disappeared, to be replaced by private spaces in which private rituals of belonging are performed.

CONCLUSION: THE AMBIGUITY OF CONSENSUS

Eric Rentschler's critique of the 'cinema of consensus' attacks films which offer no challenge to the prevailing social and political values of the post-unification Federal Republic, but concentrate rather on the harmless trivialities of life within that social and political status quo. My reading of Hans-Christian Schmid's *Requiem* in relation to the Heimat tradition shows, however, that this film engages with the notion of consensus in quite a different way. *Requiem* addresses the consequences of modernisation in Western societies in a fashion which raises the film above a specific critique of the 1970s. Just as in the *Heimatfilm*, Schmid examines the consequences of modernisation which threaten progressively to wear away at the individual's sense of community, shared values and common identity. However, instead of providing a neat incorporation of modernity into the eternal values of the Heimat, as is typical of the *Heimatfilm* of the Adenauer era, *Requiem* portrays the desire to reinstate its meaning-giving certainties as potentially dangerous and self-destructive. This desire becomes dangerous, Schmid's film asserts, when that broader community once represented by the (always idealised) notion of Heimat has atomised in the face of continuing modernisation. When there is no longer any Heimat community into which one could retreat from the modern world, Schmid's film suggests, the tendency to seek refuge in private fanaticism as a poor echo of that experience can lead to disastrous consequences. It is in this context that we can perhaps understand the director's own suggestion that Michaela might be compared to today's suicide bombers:

> The consensus in Michaela's family was finally that she was a martyr and that this gave meaning to an otherwise meaningless world. That is frightening and surprising. Today there are young people who go so far in their faith that they blow up a bus full of people with 10 kilos of explosive in their luggage. (Behrens 2006)

The act of self-destructive violence becomes, so Schmid implies, the price which the subject regards as worth paying in order to re-establish a sense of meaning founded in a set of communal beliefs, and in opposition to the uncertainties of a modernity characterised by a 'crisis of value' (Orr 1993: 7). In this sense, Schmid's film reflects on wider processes which can certainly be observed in the provincial 1970s West Germany of Michaela's home, but which continue to resonate with contemporary concerns both within and beyond Germany. As Zygmunt Baumann suggests, for example, in our contemporary world, in which all meaning-giving systems are increasingly subject to doubt, the 'lust for community' based on 'a shared idea' can, paradoxically, become even more powerful (1991: 245–46). Michaela, I would argue, provides a good example of this phenomenon.

In conclusion, a reading of Hans-Christian Schmid's film *Requiem* in relation to the *Heimatfilm* tradition reveals not only the film's rootedness in a specifically German film culture, but also its more widely relevant consideration of the desire for consensus, community and shared meaning in the face of those aspects of modernity which undermine these values. At the same time, Schmid demonstrates how the overriding desire for such consensus can lead to a self-destructive isolation from the rest of society and the challenges which that society poses to the certainty of belief.

Chapter 9

Play for today: situationist protests and uncanny encounters in Hans Weingartner's *The Edukators* (2004)

Rachel Palfreyman

Hans Weingartner's film *The Edukators* (*Die fetten Jahre sind vorbei*) of 2004 is one of a number of films that, from the vantage point of post-unification Germany, reflect on the actions and concerns of the 1968 generation, as well as on their political legacy for the Berlin Republic. As such, it might be seen as having something in common with films which address 1970s West German terrorism more overtly in a turn towards 'Westalgie' identified at the turn of the century (Fischer et al. 2000: 284; see also Plowman 2003). Films such as Volker Schlöndorff's *The Legend of Rita* (*Die Stille nach dem Schuss*, 2000) and Christian Petzold's *The State I Am In* (*Die innere Sicherheit*, 2000) presented fictional accounts of a Red Army Faction (RAF) remnant in the Berlin Republic. Other films, such as Andres Veiel's *Black Box Germany* (*Black Box BRD*, 2001), Christopher Roth's *Baader* (2002) and Uli Edel's *The Baader Meinhof Complex* (*Der Baader Meinhof Komplex*, 2008) had some basis in the documented history of the RAF in the 1970s and 1980s, though they varied quite wildly in range from documentary to more or less fictionalised treatments. In the context of the formal disbanding of the RAF at the end of the 1990s and the release of some former RAF members, such films constitute a reckoning with the old Federal Republic, with some of them in particular trying to understand the historical chains of violence that appeared to characterise the postwar democracy and keep successive generations seemingly trapped in a compulsion to repeat the violence committed by their parents, albeit in reaction against the perceived authoritarianism of previous generations. A recurrent preoccupation in the cinematic responses to West German terrorism is the origin of the RAF's violence. In many of the films, from the earliest responses to West German terrorism through to films of the current century, such violence emerges from a psychological dialectic that looks towards the historical vanishing point of National Socialism (see Homewood 2006 and 2008; Palfreyman 2006).

In common with many of the films on this subject, *The Edukators* presents the key historical conflict in the Federal Republic of Germany as a family or generational clash. However, there are some significant differences in the way this generational quarrel is staged. *The Edukators* leaves aside both the violence of the 1960s and 1970s, and indeed the origins of that violence, but rather interrogates the values of 1968. It also engages with a different aspect of the counter-cultural activism of May 1968, offering a situationist response to what Guy Debord identified in 1967 as the 'spectacular' society of late capitalism (2009). Established in 1957, the Situationist International was a grouping of European avant-garde artists and thinkers influenced by Dada and surrealism. Ultimately, however, they rejected both. After Dada, art no longer seemed to offer a path to revolution: the situationists felt that any work of art could be 'recuperated', or turned back to the advantage of capitalist society, made a product, as it were, regardless of its maker's revolutionary intent (Gray 1998: 1–6). Situationist ideas are underpinned by a critical reading of capitalism rooted in Marxist philosophy. For the situationists, alienation was not restricted to labour relations, but the commodification that Marx identified had spread out to encompass all aspects of life (Plant 1992: 11–12). This state of affairs was what the situationists referred to as 'the spectacle': the whole of society was a kind of 'one-way transmission of experience [...] a form of communication to which one side, the audience, can never reply; a culture based on the reduction of almost everyone to a state of abject non-creativity, of receptivity, passivity and isolation' (Gray 1998: 6). According to Debord, however, the spectacle contains within itself the origins of its own destruction (1957: 36–37) and will decay from within given the right kind of revolutionary action: the creation of 'situations', which freely construct (rather than passively receive) everyday life; *détournement*, or subversive turning of the spectacle; *dérive*, or playful psychogeographic drifting to subvert the designed environment and create new encounters and routes that follow unconscious desire (Knabb 2006: 178; Plant 1992: 58–59).

Their Marxist underpinnings notwithstanding, the situationists were not at all sympathetic to the 'bureaucrats' of Politburo communism (see the telegrams sent to the Politburos of China and the Soviet Union, Knabb 2006: 437–38). Their political activism was marked by a 'pleasure-seeking libertarianism' (Plant 1992: 1) and as such they sought to fuse poetic and playful impulses with political activism and insight to move towards a revolutionary 'transformation of everyday life from a realm of bland consumption to free creation' (Plant 1992: 5). Given the capacity of the spectacle to recuperate attempted rebellions for its own ends, however, the construction of situations which will bring about the destruction of the spectacle is fraught with difficulty. In Weingartner's film, the post-millennial situationist Jan struggles to manage the balance between art and politics needed to achieve a truly creative revolution against the spectacle.

In a very broad sense, Weingartner tests the validity of the ideas and values of the 1960s in the new German republic which seeks to understand its new identity via an examination of the past, but which is also deeply preoccupied with a critical understanding of its capitalist imperialism in an age of globalisation. The family conflict modelled in the film suggests a reckoning with the past, a quest structured as a 'vertical', historical argument between two generations (and hinting, too, at still older generations). In this case there is a distinct generational reversal, in that the younger characters are the ones who are the first to rehearse arguments from the 1960s as 'new situationists', with Hardenberg (Burghart Klaußner) seemingly representing the establishment. When Hardenberg counters with his own reminiscences about his communard days and SDS (Socialist German Student Union) connections, his position as their 'father' takes on a political symbolism. In addition, 'sibling' conflict within the younger generation presents a 'horizontal', synchronous examination of Germany as a thoroughly decadent manifestation of late capitalism. As such, *The Edukators* could scarcely be seen as continuing the tendency towards the bland and trivial alluded to by Rentschler (2000: 263–64), for all its direct and deliberate targeting of a young audience, its use of popular German star Daniel Brühl in a leading role, and studiedly cool touches like the use of the Jeff Buckley version of the Leonard Cohen song 'Hallelujah'. Indeed, it is an overtly political film which seeks to find new ways of interrogating, but also encouraging, a critical stance against capitalism and globalisation. The situationist ideas and practices of the 1950s and 1960s, with their focus on spectacle, separation and the experience of everyday life as a commodified representation, are thoroughly prescient when applied to the postmodernity of post-unification Germany, so that Weingartner's film is not just a reappraisal of German history, but offers a blueprint for a new situationist response to the suffocation of the spectacle.

The Edukators is the story of anti-capitalist protesters whose protest goes wrong when they are forced to kidnap the victim of a supposedly non-violent 'happening'. It is a generically hybrid film which might be described as a love triangle, a *Heimatfilm*, a heist film, a family melodrama, a mountain film, or an anti-capitalist fable. The film's interaction with generic traditions and presentation of narrative meaning is structured as fundamentally unstable and undecidable. The Heimat locale is sandwiched between scenes of a contemporary urban Germany and, bookended by scenes of police in full combat gear at the beginning and end of the film, functions as a kind of dream sequence, or an imagined idyll of German culture where the conflict of the two groups can be examined away from the pressures of urban society (perhaps disingenuously suggesting that class and generational division are an effect of the city). The Heimat intermezzo flickers between the resolution of a love triangle, the reconciliation of two conflicted generations, and the exploration of a shared set of values rooted in the comradely political struggle of 1968. Shots of the communal straw sleeping area in the mountain hut recall the scene in *The White Hell of Piz Palü* (*Die weisse Hölle vom Piz Palü*, 1929) where Maria (Leni Riefenstahl) ends up between her husband Hans (Ernst Petersen) and Dr Johannes Krafft (Gustav Diessl) on her honeymoon, but also suggest a politically motivated communal living, reprised at the end of the film when Jan (Brühl), Peter (Stipe Erceg) and Jule (Julia Jentsch) share a hotel bed. Large parts of the film are more like a heist movie, however, or even a city symphony with the scenes of Jan and Jule watching the urban round from balconies and rooftops. And the family structures evoked throughout suggest that the film could be seen as a kind of terrorist family melodrama in the tradition of *Marianne and Juliane* (*Die bleierne Zeit*, 1981) or *The State I Am In*.

The film also screened with two different endings, or rather with additional material in the version released in Germany, something which has caused much viewer comment, despite Weingartner's suggestion that the two endings amount to more or less the same thing.[1] The German release has a sequence showing the smartly dressed educators taking Hardenberg's yacht as part of Jan's long-held dream to sabotage European television satellites. In international distribution, the film ends with the police forcing their way into the empty flat, and Jan, Peter and Jule waking up apparently in a Spanish hotel. The reason given for this discrepancy is that the final sequence was not finished when the film was screened at Cannes, and having already signed international distribution agreements Weingartner did not want to force distributors to take the film with a different ending. However the two endings came about, the situation has emphasised the degree of ambiguity about the film's narrative resolution. It is possible to read the ending in a number of different ways, with even the note 'some people never change' somewhat ambiguous.[2] It appears to suggest that the educators always knew that Hardenberg would call the police, despite his promise not to, however one could argue that the note suggests Hardenberg has not changed from his days as a radical, and that he is in collusion with them to attack the satellite, having in the end retained his radical sensibility. This sort of reading seems more likely when the final scene on the yacht is included – have they stolen it? How did they know where it was moored? Has Hardenberg turned sympathiser by telling them where the yacht is and giving them his keys and papers for use in their sabotage attack? Was the police raid on the flat merely designed to maintain Hardenberg's credibility? The various ways that viewers have interpreted the endings of the film are not all equally plausible, but it is true that much in the film is left unresolved, most of which hinges on the careful concealment of what Hardenberg really thinks, and indeed does – key narrative moments in the film are not shown. The centre of the film's ambiguous representation of Germany's political morality is Hardenberg. The true identity and moral position of the co-opted '68 generation remains mysterious.

Although a love triangle appears to be at the heart of the film, key relationships are construed implicitly or explicitly as family relationships between a 'parental' generation and a rebellious younger generation, and at the same time as sibling conflicts and rivalries. Indeed, though one could read the film as pitting a representative of the respectable bourgeoisie against young outsiders who are against everything their society stands for, there is a surprising emphasis on morality throughout the film, which emerges as a crucial and problematic preoccupation of the younger characters. The conflicted parties concede and re-conquer the moral high ground with a pulsating regularity throughout the film, which itself flickers through a series of different genres and narrative patterns. Inversion and oscillation ripple through the film, which far from providing a fixed and stable assessment of contemporary Germany leaves questions largely open and for the most part unanswered – though there is a clear dialectical shift (clearer in the German version than in the international edit) on the part of the younger characters away from their previous activist habits to a new synthesis of collective and individual, of poetic prank and political strike.

Weingartner's film is thus emblematic of a kind of undecidable conflict over the moral soul of the new Germany. It engages with the history of the Federal Republic, and indeed with German film history, remaining ambiguous about the conflict between these generations, but presenting the encounter between them as enormously significant. There is virtually no explicit reference to National Socialism, but as I argue elsewhere the film is fantastically preoccupied with guilt and morality throughout, suggesting that echoes of past conflict are still relevant to today's struggles, especially in Jule's need to pay years of penance for an old misdemeanour (2010: 159). Nevertheless, the struggle for the dominant ideals of the Federal Republic is fought out without the explicit involvement of an older 'grandparental' generation. Instead the crucial conflict is fought out between a co-opted '68 generation and a somewhat uncertain younger generation, confident in their cause, but unsure of how to resist assimilation by capitalism, as well as unsettled by the speed with which they veer towards violence and sacrifice the purity of their ideals to save themselves. A degree of disquiet over the danger of 'recuperation' by state and capital is one of a number of points of comparison with situationist aesthetics and thinking.

If any, the younger generation is the one to become violent, so rather than young innocent lives blighted by the transgressions of their parents, as in Petzold's *The State I Am In*, here a parental figure is in danger from a younger generation, and the origins of the younger figures' violence are exposed as desperate and self-serving; there is some gesture in the film's structure towards examining their motives, and there are some hints at first that the younger generation is rational as well as radical, but ultimately we see that chance and desire guide their actions rather than a convincing ideology and considered strategy. Nevertheless, the film suggests that the clean wit and rationality of the educators' original strategy must be complicated by desire, aggression and a stronger political impulse. In eventually reuniting politics and art they arrive at a different mode of situationist protest, one which might yield a more productive and startling 'situation' rather than just a sterile 'happening', which might be ripe for recuperation by the establishment. Jan, Peter and Jule eventually carry out a much more ambitious attack on the great symbol of the spectacle: television. Indeed the film warns throughout and in a host of different ways of the danger of co-option by the capitalist establishment, a recurrent preoccupation of the Situationist International (Plant 1992: 75–110; Gray 1998: 6). Thus the values of the 1968 generation, now of parental age, are threatened more by recuperation and bourgeois conformity than by a betrayal in violence.

The Edukators shows guilt and responsibility for the ills of German society as something passed back and forth between the generations. Yet the reflection on the West German past and German present that it offers does not seek to blame the past for the problems of the present. Indeed guilt is treated somewhat satirically as a false and problematic basis for self-understanding and self-knowledge. Nor is the past glamorised in a way that has caused disquiet in recent years in Germany.[3] Weingartner does not appear interested in the apportioning of blame and polarised oppositions that have characterised some of the recent debates. Instead, the film presents a thoroughly ambiguous encounter between two postwar generations which suggests that reflection on the ideals and activism of 1968 might yet be of crucial importance in developing a sharper and more critical understanding of the current problems of German society. This discussion will explore Weingartner's reflection on 1968 and its legacy, looking both at the development of the younger generation's quasi-situationist critique of German capitalism, and the way in which this is then altered somewhat by an ambiguous encounter with an enigmatic 1968 figure. Weingartner's engagement with 1968 and desire to make political films clearly suggest that his film could certainly be seen as part of a wider trend in more recent German cinema to revive interest in 1960s and 1970s West German political culture and focus more or less directly on West German terrorism (see the introduction to this volume). In some respects, however, The Edukators represents something of a departure from some of the other related films, in that Weingartner is interested primarily in 1968 as a repository of ideas and ideals, rather than an indulgent bourgeois slide into violence (however much such violence is explained). Such a focus marks the film as having a somewhat different attitude to its critical reckoning with German society. The relative absence of violence allows a less polarised, and potentially more critical, reading of society. It remains unclear whether the film manages itself to avoid the recuperation it repeatedly warns against; it is in any case suggested in *The Edukators* that an overly developed fear of capitalist assimilation might be detrimental to political activism.

THE NEW SITUATIONISTS: DIRTY PLAY AND AN ATTACK ON THE SPECTACLE

The first section of the film shows the three protagonists trying to find modes of political activism appropriate to their times, in the face of the perceived apathy of the 'Generation X' (Schnibben 1994: 58), or 'Berlin Generation' (Bude 2001) and the seemingly all-conquering ability of capitalism to assimilate opposition. Political questions and conflicts are presented deliberately, even ostentatiously, on an individual scale. It is true that Jule engages with traditional collective campaigning, such as demonstrations and leafleting, but ultimately she finds these public efforts against capitalism 'totally pointless' and confesses to Jan that she cannot find anything she wants to believe in. The state manages to control such officially sanctioned irritations, and the protesters do not succeed in disrupting consumerism or commerce. In demonstrating the ineffectiveness of Jule's activism, an image of German society as clearly dominated by what the situationists referred to as the spectacle is presented. Indeed, the first section of the film in Berlin implies that the kind of social analysis that Guy Debord and Raoul Vaneigem put forward in the 1960s is still highly relevant in the post-millennium German capital. The issue facing the German population is clearly not so much material deprivation, but an isolation and commodification that dominate every sphere of life. Leisure and culture are experienced as commodities to be bought, so that access to all these aspects of life involves further participation in the capitalist relations that exist in the workplace. Quite in line with Debord's and Vaneigem's analysis, Jan's reading of society in *The Edukators* suggests that there is no unalienated private sphere beyond the exploitation of work; all life is entirely commodified and almost every effort to find fulfilment in the society of the spectacle actually involves sustaining exploitative capitalist relations – the entire purpose of production is consumption (Plant 1992: 10–13). The whole of society comprises the distorted reality of alienated consumption, but presents itself as a natural and unquestionable phenomenon: thus, according to Debord, the world has 'receded into a representation' (2009: 24) 'in which the appearance of real life is maintained in order to conceal the reality of its absence' (Plant 1992: 10). The society of the spectacle Debord writes of is strikingly close to the post-millennial German society depicted in *The Edukators*, notwithstanding Jan's more contemporary image of the spectacle as the 'matrix' of the Wachowski brothers' 1999 film: every kind of expression, pleasure and experience can only be achieved by consuming, and so one lives as a spectator, at one remove from what might be deemed reality. 'It is not just that the relationship to commodities is plain to see – commodities are now *all* there is to see: the world we see is the world of the commodity' (Debord in Plant 1992: 12). The spectacle is therefore the '*materialisation* of ideology', it is ubiquitous and appears natural and complete, so as apparently to compensate for the alienation inherent in everyday life (Debord 2009: 138).

In *The Edukators*, the society of the spectacle is invoked in a number of ways. The demonstration at a sports shop highlights one of the paradigmatic symbols of commodity branding in the globalised world: the Nike swoosh and the other sportswear brands, which have come under particular scrutiny in the climate of such bestsellers of anti-globalisation as *No Logo* (Klein 2000). A current symbol of exploitation in the developing world, almost as the Vietnam War was in the 1960s, branded sports shoes epitomise the empty, insatiable desires of consumers and the ideology of the spectacle. At another social level, commodification and spectacle are encapsulated by the precise presentation of food in the high-end restaurant where Jule works and from which she is eventually sacked. The sculptural placement of food on the plate, the precise choreography of cutlery and the correct glass for the correct liqueur are satirised as spectacular rituals, a commodification of bourgeois lifestyle that masks exploitation 'below stairs' in a comparable manner to the sports shop's presentation of branded shoes.

In addition, there are numerous references to television as a paradigmatic example of the workings of the spectacle. Television functions as a technological sedative, partly responsible for maintaining the population in a state of commodified isolation; it is not in the least surprising that the eventual protest 'situation' that the educators pursue is a pan-European attack on television satellites. There is no discussion of cinema as forming part of the spectacle which forms the basis of the film's social critique; the ambiguity over characters' benign or malign influence and the tensions in the narrative between *détournement* and recuperation appear thus to extend to the film itself and its own role in both encouraging resistance to the spectacle and forming part of a commodified and 'spectacular' representation of life.

Debord's society of the spectacle is the stage where 'the commodity has succeeded in *totally* colonising social life' (2009: 38). In *The Edukators*, the reach of the commodification of life is shown when Jan breathes from an oxygen concentrator apparatus rather than breathing the air that is all around him. The sale of 'better' air, to someone like Jan, who has clear and critical social insights, demonstrates the all-conquering commodification of the society of the spectacle. It is a curious sequence: Jan attempts to breathe another air in his consumption of oxygen. But even as he is trying to escape the environment that surrounds him in some sense, he is caught up in an act of apparently gratuitous commodification. In addition, for those moments he exists at one remove from the atmosphere that is 'freely' around him, creating a separation between environments. In his consumption of oxygen concentrated by a machine, Jan seems to enact the situationist view of 'the world of everyone's separation, estrangement and nonparticipation' (Canjuers and Debord 1960: 390). Jan is an apparently unwilling spectator, or perhaps audience, for Peter and Jule having sex in the next room, and as he retreats to his oxygen mask and loud

Figure 9.1: Jan breathes the air of commodification and separation.

music, Jan's analysis and observation of the world appear to propel him into rituals that are precariously positioned between critique and resigned submission to the isolation, separation and fragmentation of the spectacle.

Indeed such is the all-pervasive nature of the society of the spectacle that although situationist analysis focuses on the exploited proletariat, it is difficult to see space outside the alienation of the spectacle for any class. Weingartner's film suggests that the bourgeoisie does not escape alienation either, but is also dominated by the spectacle, and subject to the same ideological suffocation both within and beyond the sphere of work and production: society offers only an unrelieved consumption that no class escapes. Once a student communard, the wealthy bourgeois Hardenberg describes the process of slowly becoming entangled in property and aspiration, and claims a yearning for a less commodified existence. The power of the spectacle to co-opt, or recuperate every possible disruption and rebellion is thus made repeatedly clear in both generations. Jule's useless demonstrations, which even she appears to find boring, almost seem to resemble an advertising promotion for the shop: 'dissent is turned into a spectacle of its own, and rebels become spectators of their own rebellion, consuming the life in which they want to participate, and slotting into a seductive and glamorous role in which they can have no real effect' (Plant 1992: 69). Hardenberg was apparently in the top echelons of student activists in 1968, but has been easily recruited to an utterly commodified bourgeois lifestyle.

The spectacle, then, is ubiquitous and appears all-conquering, and where opposition emerges this too can be recuperated: 'even the most hostile action can be made to reproduce the alienation of the whole' (Plant 1992: 69). The power of the spectacle to recuperate does not, however, go unanswered. In Raoul Vaneigem's social analysis the spectacle reaches a 'saturation point', where everyday reality might burst out (1994: 135). With the spectacle potentially wobbling under its own weight, situationists looked in particular to the aesthetic and political energy of Dada to find ways of expressing dissent. They termed their satirical revision of consumer spectacle *détournement*. An act of subversion, the playful turning of consumerism and spectacle back on itself, *détournement* is a 'reclamation of lost meaning' (Plant 1992: 86) which takes elements of the spectacle and redirects them, or reverses them, subverting their meaning. The famous comic strips which were subverted to replace love stories and superhero adventures with political slogans and propaganda are classic examples of *détournement* (see Gray 1998: 14, 59, 86). The line between *détournement* and recuperation is a fine one indeed, as acts of dissent cannot emerge from a space of analysis untainted by the spectacle, but are internal to the dominant society of the spectacle (Plant 1992: 75). Indeed, 'the most radical of gestures is [...] vulnerable to integration, and expressions of dissent are often deliberately fostered as political safety-valves' (Plant 1992: 75.) Nor can the two impulses necessarily be seen as opposites, as in the case of the proverbial Che Guevara T-shirt marketed in the decades since the 1960s. Jan is critical of such a commodified recuperation, but it would be naïve to suppose that the original image from the 1960s was an 'authentic' revolutionary intervention – it was always already a product of the society and political discourses it sought to undermine (Plant 1992: 110). The very proximity of the two apparently opposite impulses, the impossibility of absenting oneself from dominant discourses and the sense that all political acts of subversion and dissent are vulnerable to being themselves turned, or recuperated, by the spectacle become recurrent preoccupations in *The Edukators* and are replicated in the film-spectacle itself, with its doubled ending, its flickering between genres and repeated transfers and transactions between two generations, who are now opposed, now allied, now innocent victims, now guilty perpetrators.

In their political activism, Jan and Peter attempt to avoid the kind of conventional political activism which Jule engages in, and which appears so easily recuperated, not to mention lacking the joy, play and pleasure essential to the situationist project. Accordingly, they engage in a secret individual campaign which draws on situationist models in a poetic, carnivalesque protest. They target individuals, disrupting the peace and security of their homes to try and unsettle the sense of confident triumph of the haute-bourgeoisie in the allegedly post-ideological era. But situationist tactics are not their only inspiration: Robin Hood is invoked as the two engage in a kind of fabulous thrill-seeking invasion of the villas of the wealthy. Their outlaw behaviour is conducted according to a strict moral code designed to ensure the purity and beauty of their intervention. Their brand of protest functions as the hip installation of guerrilla *auteurs*, something that it feels churlish to describe as crime. The theory is that they will not be dismissed as mere common-or-garden criminals,

Figure 9.2: Jan and Peter's original quasi-situationist protest: a
precise installation.

and their message will unsettle and destabilise the certainties of the
wealthy from within. But the clean precision of their artistic homage
to situationist protest, and their adherence to a sexual morality rooted
in an older spectacle, the Church, lays them wide open to recuperation
by dominant cultures.

In line with their aestheticised disavowal of the sheer disorder of
common crime, the rearrangements of the accoutrements of haute-
bourgeois lifestyle are precise and ordered: precarious pyramids, careful
diamonds of Russian dolls, resembling nothing so much as the precision
placement of cutlery and glasses in the posh restaurant where Jule is
a waitress, or indeed the delicate positioning of food on the plate.
Striking at the home, the heart of the bourgeois value system, they
hope to undermine the poise of the decadently wealthy and attack
the foundations of a value system they purport to despise. But there is
no 'dirty protest', no destructiveness as such, the shiny acquisitions
remain sparkling and are, as Jule later comments, more striking and
beautiful than before in their deranged, defamiliarised state. Indeed,
her outsider's view of the scene stages it as a spectacle and the film
spectator cannot but connect it with a reified art industry that Debord
and the situationists felt was at best an ambiguous social force, at worst
a comfort and support to bourgeois capitalism (see Plant 1992: 177–83
on the art strike of the early 1990s).

At the same time their moral code gives them a self-bestowed legitimacy, but it is a legitimacy that is only sustainable if they can maintain the rigour of their code, which has elements of a kind of courtly chivalry about it, including the chaste refusal to actually steal anything. Jan is like a warrior priest, skilled and courageous, earnestly preaching and fanatical about his cause, punishing Peter like a wayward acolyte when he finds that he has broken the code by stealing a watch. However, Jan's courtly code disintegrates when his monastic devotion is swept aside in a sexual betrayal of his brother-warrior.

The love triangle recalls the mountain films *The Holy Mountain* (*Der heilige Berg*, 1926) and *The White Hell of Piz Palü* in which rivalry over a woman leads to disaster. Jule functions as a disturbing force between the young men, and precipitates the shattering of all their moral codes. At times she is a virtuous victim, a kind of Cinderella or damsel in distress, showing solidarity towards a colleague in trouble, and destined for a decade of drudgery and servitude through one moment's mistake. (She was sued for an enormous sum after driving – uninsured – into a top-of-the-range Mercedes.) She is also, however, shown as drunk and vengeful, and in this state her 'victimhood' explodes the neat procedures and controlled excitement of Jan's educational measures. Jan breaks the rules of the brotherhood by taking her out in their van instead of Peter, and she insists on targeting her creditor, so that the educational measures are not just individual, but personal. Her dangerous spontaneity (something also valued by the situationists see Vaneigem 1994: 194–96), ignoring all the educators' carefully established procedures, results in a highly risky and messy attack. Not content with the gallery-style installation of the house contents, she smashes wine bottles, drinks champagne and persuades Jan to throw the leather settee into the swimming pool, which is also where Jan and Jule kiss, betraying their comrade. Jule instinctively grasps the situationist desire for a carnival which does not shy away from destruction, pleasure and desire. Her dirtier and more aggressive revenge on the man whose legal action keeps her in thrall to a large debt impels all three into an unplanned kidnapping with no obvious endgame, but ultimately it is this action which forces Jan finally to reappraise his cultural happenings and engage in a braver and more incisive political action.

Even before the botched action against Hardenberg, Jan's developing relationship with Jule appears to change his view of political strategy. The slogan 'every heart is a revolutionary cell' daubed defiantly on the wall of Jule's flat recalls the political graffiti of the situationists, such as the famous 'Ne travaillez jamais' ('Never work') and is an act of messy rebellion, as well as one that alludes to the situationist understanding of love, passion and desire as having a revolutionary power (see Vaneigem 1994: 26), something that the monastic Jan has apparently lacked up to this point. Jule rejects the landlord's financial hold over her by refusing to try and regain her deposit. This prefigures her eventual messy vengeance against Hardenberg, so in one sense, she might appear to be a new acolyte of Jan's, learning from him a new political consciousness. Certainly he does 'teach' her in a rather earnest manner. But ultimately, in this film of reversals and recuperations, it is Jan who learns and changes through his contact with Jule. Ruled by accurate maps, plans and diagrams, which are emphasised in close-up in the credits and at a number of points throughout the film, Jan learns from Jule spontaneity and recklessness. He had already observed to Peter that their activism lacked a wider political context and needed to move up a level, but it is with Jule that he moves beyond nocturnal surveillance of an individual villa to a vantage point where the two of them look out over the great city streets. Her lack of control takes him metaphorically off the map (indeed, she trips Hardenberg's burglar alarm which Jan's study of plans and diagrams was supposed to prevent) and propels him into an uncharted crisis. There are faint hints of the revolutionary 'drift', or *dérive*, of the situationists, where individuals or groups let go of their normal activities and stroll or drift through urban spaces allowing chance to draw them into encounters that render visible the psychogeographic contours of the city (Debord 1958: 62–63).

Despite Jan's efforts, established in the opening section of the film to adhere to a firm, indeed rather rigid, moral framework to provide legitimation for his playful/self-righteous 'education' of individual bourgeois, such rigidity is never allowed to persist in the film. Quite in keeping with the uncertainty of *détournement* and recuperation, the film flickers between positions that appear opposed, but are perhaps closer than they first appear. For example, the educators are presented as sympathetic characters, but it is not easy for spectators to settle into unequivocal judgements. Or spectators make judgements which are quite wildly polarised. The characters are by turn morally irreproachable and dreadfully culpable. Jule's 'victimhood' in being saddled with an old debt is itself quite ambiguous. Certainly, the punishment does not fit the crime; nevertheless, an accident while driving uninsured is not quite worthy of the moral outrage that ensues, something that is ironised in the film when her debt is compared to the debt of developing countries, with all the attendant hints at problematic comparison of suffering that this entails.

In addition, the caricatures of the bourgeois restaurant diners fussing icily over the correct glass for a liqueur, or the harassment of a homeless person without a tram ticket by zealous inspectors are pantomime sketches or clichés, so that even as we enjoy hissing and booing at the villains, we are aware that this critique of society is also an entertaining caricature, making a spectacle of the spectacle. Jan, Peter and Jule themselves seem to flip-flop between rejecting bourgeois morality and actually aspiring to it. Jule wants to live 'wild and free', but has been forced by her debt to aspire to a bourgeois career, something Jan deplores. However, Jan's guilty feelings about betraying his friend over Jule demonstrate a strong attachment to a rather conventional morality, which Hardenberg is able to exploit. And Jan's insistence on his moral code, his careful preparations, his discipline and his minimisation, but acceptance, of risk suggest that he might do rather well in the world he disavows.

The to-ing and fro-ing over culpability continues throughout the film, with Hardenberg the aggressor becoming a victim, and the young educators guilty of abduction, though all the while Hardenberg is playing them and sometimes seems more in control than they do. Such uncertainties and inversions particularly characterise the time the two opposed generations spend together in the mountains. Even in this apparently antagonistic confrontation, it is not easy to pin them down to particular roles or positions. In the Heimat setting – a spectacle of its own – and bound by the kidnapping, they start to function as a group, sliding between a group of student housemates and a family. Whose turn is it to pay for wine and dope? Whose turn is it to cook and go shopping? Hardenberg easily slips into the role of Jan's father when the two of them are seen in the village, and shows a convincing 'fatherly' concern towards Jule.

Hardenberg expresses sympathy for their ideals while always deploring what they have done (they themselves of course also deplore it – they just don't know how to end it). He reveals his past as a fully paid-up sixty-eighter (or spins a yarn to this effect) and suggests that the young educators have much in common with the 1968 generation's desire for social and political revolution. For his part, Jan establishes his situationist position in a stinging attack on

Hardenberg; it is as if a ghost from Hardenberg's past is confronting him with the very discourse of 1968:

> I have news for you, executive. The system is overheated. We're just the start. Your time is almost up [...] Mental illness is on the increase. There are more and more serial killers, shattered souls, senseless violence. You won't be able to sedate them forever with game shows and shopping!

Jan's words in this sequence recall the rhetoric of the situationists in the late 1960s: 'SHAKE IN YOUR SHOES BUREAUCRATS' (Knabb 2006: 437), or Vaneigem's 'You Won't Fuck With Us Much Longer!' (1994: 271).

The Edukators stands in a long tradition of construing the tensions and struggles of German terrorism in familial terms, and in common with films like *The German Sisters, The State I Am In* and *Black Box Germany* suggests that past generations' political struggles and sins cast a long shadow over younger generations. In this case, the difficulty of establishing a separate identity as a revolutionary youth movement discussed by Jan and Jule is borne out in the mutual acknowledgement of the two generations, as they seem to peer into a dirty mirror at each other. They exchange positions throughout the film, from bearing moral authority through victimhood, to an uncomfortable perpetration, to a contrived and sceptical reconciliation and finally an attempt to regain their original conflictedness. As Jan comments earlier, it has become more difficult to rebel, because everything has been done before, and because the symbols of the earlier revolution have been drained of meaning in the process of becoming co-opted by capitalism as a commercial product. Their separateness is in any case difficult to maintain in a situation which emphasises kinship, the kinship of the mountains. Finally, they all bed down together, Alpine refuge-style, in the one sleeping area in the hut. The image flits between one of a family group and a kind of Heimat commune.

In the same way, the relationships between the characters and their eventual need to forgive betrayal have the character of a family bond, albeit one that on the surface is a rejection of nuclear monogamy. The struggle between Jan and Peter is like a conflict between siblings, where the brotherly bond remains ultimately stronger than their other relationships and can eventually accommodate the wild woman. One might even read the friends' eventual mutual acceptance of Jan and Jule's betrayal as a kind of 'gift' or even 'sacrifice-gift' between the friends, which confounds social rules. Possibilities of subverting bourgeois exchange and rediscovering ideas of the gift which have no place in a society based on rational exchange, but have 're-emerged in values such as hospitality, friendship, and love' were an important aspect of situationist thinking, and were seen as a key distinction from the consumerist economy of the spectacle (Vaneigem 1994: 79).[4] This is not to suggest anything as banal or reductive as Peter making a 'gift' of Jule to Jan, which sounds rather closer to bourgeois notions of exchange. What is crucial in *The Edukators* is Jule's own vital role in breaking the two couples (Jan and Peter on the one hand, Peter and Jule on the other) and forming a fluent friendship between the three based on gift and sacrifice, operating beyond social convention and rational exchange. According to Vaneigem, 'the pleasure of giving clearly marks the frontier between the world of calculation and the world of exuberance, of festivity' (1994: 76). The eventual accommodation between the three friends leaves them still sharing a bed in their Spanish hotel and downplays the romantic narrative between Jan and Jule, emphasising instead the comradely friendship and sexual freedom evoked by Hardenberg in his tales of the 1960s. A rejection of petit-bourgeois sexual mores is implied, at the same time arguably allowing Jule, the disruptive female element, into the sanctity of male friendship.

While *The Edukators* is marked by structural, narrative and generic ambiguities throughout, there are two important developments in the film that emerge as crucial to the success and integrity of the younger generation of political activists. Firstly, the male-bonded warrior priests are disturbed in their monastic dyad by a wild woman, who disrupts the clinical protests and forces a re-evaluation of Jan's code of honour and pedantic morality. He himself knows that he needs to develop political activism on a grander scale, with an eye to the wider political context, and he claims to disapprove of bourgeois morality. But his prank activism betrays an attachment to the morality he disavows, and seems ripe for recuperation. Jule's introduction of a messy, reckless element to their pristine installations sexualises their protest and gives their political activism a stronger spirit of carnival and festivity. Her disorderly behaviour leads all three of them to a fuller and more effective understanding of the situationist project.

Jule is also the catalyst for the second key development, the encounter with the 1968 generation, through which Jan, Peter and Jule learn that what counts is not an individualised chic protest or a rigid adherence to a code that gives them the moral high ground, but the ambition and scope to strike against a mass institution with a reach and influence far beyond a few wealthy individuals. All this takes place regardless of Hardenberg's motivation and true position. He is thoroughly co-opted and recuperated to the society of the spectacle from his former position as communard and social revolutionary. But even so, the dialogue with the 1968 generation yields a number of important insights that strengthen the younger characters' political resolve and desire to develop their situationist-inspired activism on a grander public scale. The recuperated figure of Hardenberg voices some of the 'best ideas' that Jan earlier tells Jule 'always survive'; he functions as a reminder to them not to be paralysed by the thought that rebellion has all been done before, or a fear that political protest could become a profitable product bolstering the capitalist economy. Hardenberg seems to show them how to be more ambitious and more pragmatic in their activism.

Weingartner's film remains very deliberately and thoroughly open in its critical assessment of Germany. Hardenberg is sarcastic when he asks Jan whether he sees himself as some sort of saviour of Germany, but Weingartner's post-unification Germany does seem in need of saving. It is not at all clear where answers might lie: the motivation of the '68 generation is treated with scepticism and remains completely unresolved. However, the film does emphasise the importance of the encounter between that generation and a contemporary slacker generation of anti-capitalist protesters, even if it is a hypothetical encounter, an imaginary meeting taking place in the middle of a *Heimatfilm*. The 1968 generation, in the figure of Hardenberg, is presented as inscrutable and dubious, and the absolute lack of flashback or corroboration to his story means that he is not glamorised, but shown entirely in terms of what he has become, so in that sense the problematic allure of 1968 is not indulged in here, as it is in other films. However, it does not seem true to say that 1968 is not mythologised – Hardenberg is like the sphinx, posing riddles, 'what was I and how did I get like this?' or 'can ideals of justice be pursued with force?' the answer to which might be a passage or gateway forwards. Or perhaps he is an oracle in the classical tradition: one which will never give a straight answer to a straight question. Political questions and preoccupations in both generations are thus left woven into a rather open texture, but the introduction of a disruptive female element to the warrior-priest model and the encounter with an enigmatic voice of 1968 are presented as crucial in shaping a greater social ambition, even if the 1968 generation are themselves neither especially admirable nor even easily readable. For all the aesthetic élan of the earlier protests, these ultimately emerge as pedantically planned and somewhat trapped in a conventional morality. However, Jan's quest for a situationist social revolution is given a forceful if unlikely push by the carnivalesque festivities of Jule's messy and angry protest, the unplanned excursion off the city plan into the rural Heimat, and the encounter with the mysterious fallen angel of 1968.

NOTES

1 For further discussion see 'Outsider Inbox', Outsider, 6, http://outsider. lu/?q=node/40#04 accessed 25 March 2010.
2 See internet reviews and discussions on sites such as the Internet Movie Database, http://www.imdb.com/title/tt0408777/usercomments?start=0, last accessed 6 April 2010.
3 The controversial RAF exhibition which eventually opened under the title 'Vorstellung des Terrors: Rote Armee Fraktion' (Representations of Terror: the Red Army Faction) was originally planned to have the title 'Mythos RAF' (The Myth of the RAF). Public funding was withdrawn after protests by relatives of victims of the RAF, and there was widespread disquiet at the representation of the RAF in *The Baader Meinhof Complex* as sexy icons of youth culture. (See Chris Homewood's discussion of *The Baader Meinhof Complex* in this volume.)
4 One of the key journals of the situationists was entitled *Potlatch*, a reference to the practice of sacrifice-gift prevalent in native North American cultures. The *potlatch*, which involves extravagant gift-giving without a clear exchange, presents something of a challenge to capitalist notions of economy and was indeed banned in the nineteenth century in Canada and the USA.

Chapter 10

German *Autoren* dialogue with Hollywood? Refunctioning the horror genre in Christian Petzold's *Yella* (2007)

Jaimey Fisher

> I have the feeling that I make films in the cemetery of genre cinema, from the remainders that are still there for the taking.

Christian Petzold (2008)

In weighing the legacy of Fassbinder on German cinema, Michael Sicinski argues that the true heir to Fassbinder's project in contemporary film is not so much Oskar Roehler, who has openly and approvingly cited Fassbinder in films like *Agnes and His Brothers* (*Agnes und seine Brüder*, 2004), but rather Christian Petzold (2009: 6–7). This might seem surprising given that Petzold does not tend to mention Fassbinder when discussing influences on his work; in fact, he seems to prefer to cite French and especially Hollywood filmmakers (2008). Of course that kind of citation, respect and even adoration is itself very Fassbinderian, and it is the nature of these citations that I would like to consider here as we contemplate the new directions and politics of contemporary German cinema. I want to explore the character of precisely this commonality between Fassbinder and Petzold, namely his approving, even adoring, citation of Hollywood genre cinema and his political use of such genres. These two directors are probably the most critically celebrated narrative filmmakers of their generations, and this particular confluence of the popular and political arises from their engagement with, and variation on, Hollywood genre films.[1] The politicisation of existing genres, I would like to suggest, raises intriguing questions about art and auteurist cinema and their relationship to popular, especially Hollywood, genres. A number of important European auteurist filmmakers have explored and, as I shall term it, refunctioned the mechanisms and subtexts of Hollywood genres for their own purposes. Such an argument should be regarded as a piece, albeit a modest one, of the current, broader-based effort (Elsaesser 2005; Cooke 2007b) to reconceptualise European art versus Hollywood cinema – considered, all too often, as opposing, even binaristic poles – and to rethink them as mutually dependent and constitutive parts of a wider system of world cinema (something to which Fassbinder's work also pointed).

Yella follows the struggles of its eponymous protagonist, a young woman from the former East Germany, to find work. Yella plans to leave behind her small home town of Wittenberge for Hannover in the former West, where she has managed to secure a position at an aerospace company (Alpha Wings). On her way to her first day at work, however, viewers learn of her estranged husband, Ben, who insists that she let him drive her to the train and then drives them both off a bridge in a (attempted?) murder/suicide. Yella apparently escapes the sinking Range Rover, climbs out of the river, and manages to get to her job, only to learn that the firm is bankrupt and her position gone. At the hotel where she is staying, she meets a private-equity analyst, Philipp, who hires her as a freelance assistant and with whom she has a subsequent affair. All seems to be going well until Philipp loses his job because he has been embezzling money from his firm; Yella pressures one of their would-be clients for extra capital to fund one last scheme of Philipp's. Instead of succumbing to this pressure, the client drowns himself behind his house in water that quickly becomes the river at the beginning of the film, returning viewers suddenly to the plunge of Ben's Range Rover off the bridge. As viewers watch a close repetition of the sinking sports-utility vehicle and then Yella on the river bank, they realise that she died in the accident and that most of the plot has been imagined and/or fantasised by her, her final thoughts before she expired in the first few moments of the film.

Although largely functioning as an 'art film' in its festival premiere and then in its distribution channels, both nationally and internationally, *Yella* works with Hollywood genre in intriguing ways. Hollywood genre films have tended to be contrasted with so-called art cinema in film-studies scholarship. For critics writing in the 1970s and 1980s, like David Bordwell (1986) and Steve Neale (2002), the question was how to describe the formal as well as institutional differences between Hollywood cinema and art cinema, even if, as Bordwell has observed, art cinema can be seen to operate as its own, separate genre (1986). By art cinema, I mean films, as described by Bordwell and other scholars (Grant 2007), that are marketed to niche, usually art-house audiences and that generally operate at a distance, or at least a feigned one, from Hollywood style and narrative. Art versus Hollywood or mainstream cinema were the binaries as traditionally drawn, and although there have been recent efforts (for instance in Bergfelder, Carter and Göktürk 2002) to move away from such a dichotomy, it is also worth noting that, perhaps particularly in German studies, this distinction has retained considerable critical force, not least in Eric Rentschler's influential critique of a 1990s 'cinema of consensus' (2000), which this volume takes as its point of departure. Rentschler's now often-cited critique of popular and presumably genre cinema also offers a simultaneous paean to the art cinema of the 1970s (260–77). Rentschler's piece thus ends up revisiting the conventional dichotomy between art and popular cinema without elaborating how some of that art cinema has quite often deployed certain cinemas of generic consensus.

Petzold himself, when asked by Marco Abel in an interview in *Cineaste* about this criticism of a 1990s cinema of consensus, disputes these kinds of distinctions between art and popular cinema, a symptomatic response, I am arguing, for his cinema. Abel asks Petzold what he thinks about Volker Schlöndorff's and Rentschler's criticisms of 1990s popular cinema, particularly about Schlöndorff's assertion that German directors need more film theory, and Petzold responds to these criticisms revealingly:

I'm not sure about this. I don't think we will improve filmmaking in Germany by offering more film theory seminars. We were in need of instructors who could think cinema rather than divide it into neat, teachable categories [...] and the German *Autorenkino* is at least partially to blame for this. They participated in this pigeonholing – art house over here, mainstream over there, nonstars vs. stars, etc. Those who participated in divvying up cinema this way were the death of cinema [...] by the end of the 1980s we had two kinds of cinema: the miserable cinema of literature and an escapist, lowbrow cinema, which wanted to be the opposite of this literary cinema. And before you knew it someone like Dominik Graf, for whose attempt at making intelligent genre films I have the utmost respect, found himself in an incredibly lonesome position. (2008)

Petzold explains the dead-end dichotomy into which German *Autorenkino* ran itself, and addresses the criticisms of 1990s genre cinema by questioning the familiar, even reified contrast between art and genre cinema. His response to criticisms of 1990s genre cinema is a respect, and I shall argue, yearning for 'intelligent genre film', even if it leaves one – presumably himself and as well as Graf – in a lonely position.

NEW DIRECTIONS IN GENRE? ART-CINEMA DIRECTORS AS CONSUMERS OF GENRE CINEMA

In the recent analysis of new directions in German cinema there has been the tendency, as in Rentschler's framing concept of a cinema of consensus, to re-establish the conventional dichotomy of art versus popular cinema. For example, in the critical reassessment of German cinema since 2000 critics have tended to contrast the recent aesthetic and political ambitions of German cinema with the German genre cinema of the 1990s that went before, amending Rentschler's distinctions historically but not so much critically (for further discussion, see Fisher and Prager, 2010 as well as Cooke and Homewood's introduction to this volume). Certainly, Petzold is among those directors who has pushed German cinema in an aesthetically innovative and challenging direction, but one of the more noteworthy aspects of his cinema is how he insists on working with Hollywood cinema – indeed, as was the case with Fassbinder, what is perhaps most remarkable about Petzold's art cinema is not its antagonism to Hollywood genre cinema, but the homage it pays to it.

Petzold himself has consistently emphasised how important genre cinema is to him and to his films. Certainly genre films are, as with Fassbinder before him (1971: 9–13), something about which Petzold thinks and something that he admires: both filmmakers have emphasised how they are avid, if canny, consumers of genre films. As early as *The State I Am In* (*Die innere Sicherheit*, 2000), for instance, Petzold recounts how his teacher and collaborator Farocki called his script a 'late western' (2001). Then, by way of explaining the peripatetic family in that film – a rather non-western element – Petzold (2001) recalls how he originally conceived of the story upon watching Kathryn Bigelow's horror film *Near Dark* (1987). After seeing Bigelow's movie,

189

he wrote a script about a vampire family that drifted around the world unattached and unmoored – the undead provided the model for his widely celebrated depiction of a terrorist family (see also Homewood 2006). Even more remarkably, in the *Cineaste* interview cited above, when asked about his aesthetic 'sternness' (a question that would seem to invite arch European art-cinema attitude), Petzold revealingly responds that his watching American genre films was always very important for him:

> When I was eighteen I saw John Carpenter's *Halloween* (1978). That was a major filmic event for me, which left its mark on me to this day. It's a film with mental, subjective images, as well as objective ones; their alternation creates the sensation of horror. You never really know whether what is on screen is objective or subjective. And sometimes the possessor of the gaze suddenly steps into what appears as a point of view shot, thus appearing as an object, not subject, in front of the camera. This comes as a shock every time anew. I think this really formed me. Hitchcock does this frequently as well. (2008)

I do not think we should be so much shocked by an art-cinema director's citing of Hollywood genre cinema as a formative cinematic experience and as a continuing influence. Rather, we ought to investigate how important such genre films and genres themselves are to these filmmakers' consumption of cinema, and their thinking through cinema. This thinking through genres transpires not only in their own (auto)biographies, nor merely in their assessments of cinema history, but also in their confronting the representational challenges and aesthetic decisions occasioned by filmmaking.

Such aesthetic decisions come up in other interviews Petzold has given about his style. In an interview with the *Tageszeitung*, Petzold talks about often preferring music to explanatory speeches in his stagings, about favouring a character's musically scored reticence over expository dialogue. Anyone familiar with his films will understand this representational strategy as one of his trademark auteurist touches, from *The State I Am In* to *Jerichow* (2009), in which characters' silence and inscrutability seem to predominate in many key scenes and sequences – they frequently inhabit what Petzold (2002) underscores as a *Schwebezustand* (abeyance). Indeed, such moments of sustained silence, of existential abeyance, seem to be one of those crucial moments of openness, of art-cinema ambiguity, running through his oeuvre, one that would tie his work to that of directors like Antonioni.[2] But, in response to a question about this relative lack of dialogue and preference for openness rather than closed and/ or complete exposition, Petzold (2002) answers that this kind of silence is precisely what he most appreciates in westerns, and then recounts how he saw and admired it in films like *Winchester 73* (1950), which for him contrast starkly to most German television films.

YELLA AND THE AUTEURIST REFUNCTIONING OF HORROR

Despite Petzold's appreciation of genre films – and his emphatic attribution of inspiration and influence to them – it is likewise important to acknowledge that his films are auteurist works as well, that is, films that highlight the individual perspective and approach of the filmmaker behind the film and go beyond the mere parameters of the genre.[3] But this auteurism need not be seen as a return to, or even dated residue of, the high-art cinema of the late 1960s and 1970s and need not be, I am arguing, contrasted to the works' generic aspects. Instead, we would do well to rethink the notion of *auteur* for this particular historical moment, to refigure the *auteur* within, rather than against, the systems of world and often genre cinemas. Amidst recent studies of cinema that emphasise popular cinema, genre film and the star system, some have argued, like Mary Wood, that the *auteur* persists even as art cinema, as it was known in the 1960s and 1970s, fades (2007: 28). Certainly the reception of Petzold's films also underscores some of these late or revised *Autorenkino* aspects. The films straddle, in a way reminiscent of many of Fassbinder's mid- and late-career films, genre and auteurism and do so, I would emphasise, politically. What is interesting in both directors' films of this sort is not the essentially generic characteristics – ferreting out, for example, what exactly in *Yella* qualifies it as a horror film – but rather the way these directors refunction (to use a Brechtian term and concept) the genre in an auteurist mode and why such refunctionalisations occur.[4]

This focus on genre recontextualisation and refunctionalisation within specific texts illuminates how these genres circulate but also mutate transnationally. Beyond merely underscoring how Hollywood cinema is important around the globe and even for auteurist directors, such an analysis allows for an investigation of the specific parameters of such refunctionalisations, including contextual and historical specificity as directors redeploy globally circulating genres. And it is these refunctionalisations of globally circulating genres that are at work in some of Germany's most successful art cinema, not least because in these variations one can find the political refunctionalisation of generally apolitical genres. Such a line of questioning would not so much trace how *auteurs* reinvent the cinema system *sui generis*, nor would it seek to unmask covert genre elements, but rather to investigate how *auteurs* work with (if not merely within) genre and deploy generic conventions for their own ends. Such generic refunctionalisation, I would like to unfold, combines moments of alternating proximity and distance to the genre.

Petzold's approving citation of Kathryn Bigelow's *Near Dark* and John Carpenter's *Halloween* is telling. While filmmakers Fassbinder and Almodóvar are best known for working with melodrama (Thau 2007), with Petzold's most admired cycle of films, those of the so-called *Ghost Trilogy* (*The State I Am In*, *Ghosts* [*Gespenster*], 2005 and *Yella*), it is the horror genre that seems most pertinent to probe. But how exactly does this kind of auteurist refunctioning transpire? How do the alternating moments of proximity and distance to the genre function? Petzold (2007) has said, even while acknowledging the debt of *Yella* to Herk Harvey's 1962 *Carnival of Souls*, that it required the confluence of horror with reading Marc Augé (1995) on non-places and seeing Farocki's film on private equity for him to realise his film. That said, many of *Yella*'s basic parameters indeed seem to engage with, or at least echo, constitutive aspects of the horror genre. In their influential analyses of horror films, Carol Clover (1992) and Linda Williams (2003) have underscored how horror functions as a 'body genre', one that spectacularises extreme bodily sensations. Williams emphasises, on the one hand, how horror films tend to depict a woman's body in the convulsive throes of terror (parallel to her model of pornography's depiction of the female body in the throes of ecstasy) (2003: 142–44). On the other hand, these kinds of representations and their subsequent sensations, Williams argues, in turn address themselves directly to the body of the viewer (2003: 145–46).

The first 12 minutes of *Yella* seem to build on these conventions surrounding the woman's body in the horror film, transcending, one should observe, the familiar deployment of the woman's body in New German Cinema.[5] Many directors of the New German Cinema, including Alexander Kluge, Volker Schlöndorff and the Fassbinder of the *FRG Trilogy* (*BRD Trilogie*, 1979–81) phase, put female characters at the centre of their plots in order to allegorise postwar Germany. But Petzold would seem to foreground women protagonists more for genre reasons than as any kind of homage to the New German Cinema. In the context of the horror genre, a long line of scholars (Neale 1980: 61; Jancovich 2002) has emphasised the centrality for the genre of a male-gendered monster who attacks a woman whose body is sexualised by the context that produces both the monster and the assault on the woman's body (very much the small-town, oversexed milieu of *Halloween*). The opening of *Yella* would seem proximate to these genre conventions: the film begins on a train, in a compartment with medium shots of Yella's body as she changes her clothes. While the film foregrounds her (semi-naked) body immediately, subjugating her to the familiar gaze of the camera, she would seem to control her person and economic future: she is, apparently, changing her clothes for her own (economic) purposes. But after she arrives in what viewers learn is her hometown, the camera suddenly cuts to an unanticipated, hand-held point-of-view shot of someone watching her from afar. It is a deliberate point-of-view shot from a male predator's perspective, one that is familiar in its gendering and its threat from the earliest horror films that offer the uncanny POV of the monster stalking its prey. This kind of sudden predator's POV occurs at key moments in the two horror films that Petzold cites above, in both *Halloween* and *Carnival of Souls*, and is often seen as one of the key technical markers of the genre (Jancovich 2002: 5). A few minutes later, after her estranged husband Ben insists on taking Yella to the train so she can depart Wittenberge for Hannover and her new job and life, he attacks her on a detour from the station, decrying how she went to Hannover to show off her pretty legs, get a new job, leave him behind. His attempt to kill them both follows in short order.

While *Yella* invokes these familiar horror scenarios and techniques and thereby veers closely to the genre in the film's first 12 minutes, the film then distances itself from these kinds of sensation almost entirely. The sensational aspects of horror are invoked but then departed from in favour of the subdued, peripatetic wanderings of Yella and then her new lover and employer Philipp. Williams (2003) writes that what brackets these body genres off from more accepted genres is their excessive proximity to the body, the lack of critical distance, but this is precisely where Petzold then aims: a horror film with a critical distance about what produced the horror, a horror film refunctioned to unfold primarily by the bright light of day in business meetings and hotel lobbies. In a way reminiscent of Fassbinder's hot

Figure 10.1: Ben's POV shot on Yella's arrival back home.

and then suddenly cold melodramas, Petzold seems to refunction the horror film by draining it of its sensationalist extremes, to distance it from the genre while invoking it, to make a ghost of the horror genre itself. This invocation and then sublation of generic aspects underscore what he says in the opening epithet: he is making films in the cemetery of genre, with its remnants and scraps, which he deliberately refashions and refunctions.

This draining of the horror genre's standard bodily sensations mimics precisely what the film implies about affect in the context of contemporary capitalism, and in so doing points to the key political dimension of the film. *Yella* seems to deploy a body genre, one usually reliant upon and frolicking in bodily sensations and extreme affect, to show how contemporary society undercuts precisely those sensations. More precisely, contemporary capitalism denatures and recolonises bodily sensation and desire, something that *Yella* tracks very closely, as her amorous desire, sexual experience and imagination itself become inextricably intertwined with and obscured by her career plans: for the most pointed if not poignant example, her fantasy replaces her husband – the failed blue-collar worker turned entrepreneur – with a scheming private-equity analyst and negotiator. Amidst these distortions of fantasy by capitalism, the film seems to move into a register of coldness about and detachment from her surroundings, such as when Yella hears the distant, distracting rustling of water in the midst of a meeting and then increasingly towards the end of the film. Thus, even as the film distances itself from bodily sensations and extremities, Petzold is nonetheless able to create such uncanny and eerie moments by refunctioning assorted remnants and scraps of the horror genre, remnants and scraps more subtle than convulsions of terror, namely its cognitive effects. As it tracks how bodily sensation and desire are lost to the subject, *Yella* refunctions and recontextualises horror's cognitive effects on viewers to realise its particular brand of auteurist-horror.

In his work on 'art-horror' – the deliberate creation of fear and disgust by literature, painting and film – Noël Carroll (1990) elaborates the core of horror beyond its often-cited affective phenomena; instead, he emphasises how this sort of art achieves its affective responses with calculated cognitive effects. Distinguishing art-horror from 'naturally' occurring horror, Carroll (1990: 31) emphasises not so much (or only) bodily sensations and affective extremes, but rather how these artworks offer a 'set of instructions' to guide viewers' or readers' responses. Horror films, for example, deliberately control the status of viewer knowledge and deliberately manipulate viewer curiosity and plot disclosure over the course of the narrative. Many genres, including thrillers, rely on a relative lack of viewer knowledge, and then dogged curiosity, to drive their plots forward, but Carroll suggests that horror films are unique because they offer scenarios – and often rather grotesque creatures – that adamantly defy our cognitive classificatory schemes. The cognitive challenges posed by confusing scenarios and comprehension-bending creatures are precisely what generates fascination and curiosity along with fear, with the former elements crucial to explaining the persisting yet perplexing popularity of the genre (Carroll 1990: 32–33). Such cognitive challenges, it seems to me, are precisely what Petzold references in his 'formative' experience of seeing Carpenter's *Halloween*: his interest in the cognitive effects and confusion of horror, the deliberate manipulation of subjective and more objective shots to confuse the viewer about what is 'real' and what subjective, about what is our own and what others', about what is to be feared and what not.

Such cognitive effects are perhaps the most important horror aspect of the sub-genre of horror by which *Yella* has been directly influenced, namely works like Harvey's *Carnival of Souls* that are based on Ambrose Bierce's short story 'An Occurrence at Owl Creek Bridge'. In a recent refinement of this cognitive approach to horror, Aviva Briefel (2009) analyses works influenced by Bierce's short story, including both *Carnival of Souls* and *The Sixth Sense* (1999, which Petzold also cites, 2008), although she seems unaware of *Yella*. Briefel argues that a 'spectral incognisance' marks these scenarios in which the protagonists die at some early point in the story, but, along with the viewers, only realise that they are dead much later in the plot. When they realise they have been dead for most of the narrative, both they and the viewers are invited to revisit the plot up to that point, to refigure it in light of this sudden and surprising disclosure. In these narratives, death becomes an uncanny but also intellectual experience, one of deliberate clue finding, rather than a sudden or searing experience of terror and then nothingness (Briefel 2009: 97–98). In this way, these films based on the Bierce story are a sub-genre of horror that emphasise some of the cognitive elements of horror of the sort that Noël Carroll foregrounds.

A central aspect of the cognitive operations of these films' spectral incognisance is, Briefel argues, their particular mechanisms of empathy and identification (2009: 99). Because viewers are led to empathise, even identify, with a character who they belatedly learn has been dead throughout, they review the plot before its ultimate conclusion to search for narrative clues to this surprising, cognitively challenging fact – in some ways, this search back over the plot is the narrative conclusion, one beyond the regular linear form of narrative. In this regard, the trick of these horror narratives functions for viewers as a kind of *fort/da* (gone/there), or perhaps *da/fort*, with death, to evoke the Freudian game of a child's mastering the mother's absence by throwing away a toy and then retrieving it, thereby rehearsing control over and eventually overcoming anxiety at the mother's departure. Here, in the horror genre's play with death and dying, viewers are drawn unawares uncomfortably close to identification with death (the *da*); but upon realising the character is and has been dead, viewers draw away rapidly from the protagonist in a more detached search for narrative clues, a narrative act that distances itself from the absorbing linearity of mainstream Hollywood narratives (the *fort*). This mechanism subverts the progressive linearity of such narratives and the kind of progress they imply.

It is in these mechanisms that one can perhaps most appreciate Petzold's refunctionalisation of horror in *Yella*, in which the film, with its sudden disclosure but also uncanny clues throughout, distances viewers from their initial identification with Yella. The film's cognitive game – its own 'set of instructions' – drives viewers towards reflection on the traces of her death to be found in the labour and love set amidst the Hannover expo grounds, the industrial park that mixes economy and leisure, underscoring the broader themes of the film, and in particular Petzold's political project. The filmmaker has said that the 'the "cinema of identification" gets on [his] nerves,' so he made a film in which the 'degree of identification is lower than usual' (2008). I would emphasise how he has developed a character and located her in a plot and setting in which horror's cognitive, rather than empathetic-emotional, mechanisms move into the foreground to transform the standard identification of mainstream narrative film. As viewers reconsider the plot elements for clues to her early death, they reclassify many of the plot's more peculiar or cognitively challenging moments as subjective: what seemed to be objective plot points now emerge as deformed figures of her imagination, maimed by capitalism's molecular recasting of subjects. Horror's cognitive confusion about the subjective versus the objective creates very particular audience effects that serve to undercut identification, creating critical distance from the seemingly realist milieu and inviting self-reflection about the mechanisms of the artwork in creating such effects.

A brief comparison of two scenes from *Carnival of Souls* and *Yella* bring such mechanisms into starker relief while also registering the differences between the horror cult classic and Petzold's auteurist recasting of it. Briefel outlines how at some late moment in the narrative, the already-dead protagonist is frequently led to revisit the film's earlier events and realise that something has been amiss (namely, their understandable but misguided confidence in their status as living). *Carnival of Souls* offers such a scene when an increasingly confused Mary is taken in by a doctor, who brings her to his office and reviews various elements of the plot with her. She revisits the sequence of narrative events up until that point, revisits it not only for the doctor, but also so that viewers can review what has been uncannily, eerily happening to her. The good doctor then helpfully glosses these events, reflectively listening, in order to hint to viewers that they have been offered the necessary plot clues about her early but unrecognised demise. The doctor, in this helpful and paternalistic approach, recalls the authority figures of earlier horror films, in which some socially vested figure such as a doctor, a scientist or a police officer helps overcome the monster and guide the protagonist through the troubled cognitive waters of the horror disturbance.

Even as it nods to Harvey's *Carnival*, however, *Yella* studiously avoids any such stabilising figure and any such clarifying scene: there is no authority figure at all, no vestige from an earlier social moment who can offer comfort to the protagonist in the throes not so much of terror but of cognitive confusion. While Philipp might seem to serve such a function at first, his own business plans begin to weigh on, rather than help, Yella.[6] At *Yella*'s conclusion, characters inexplicably start to ignore Yella entirely, suddenly radicalising her occasional detachment from her surroundings, for instance when she spills and breaks a glass of water and hears the rustling of water, neither of which register for her interlocutors. At the end, even Philipp, without forewarning, ignores her presence, consigning her to the realm of the dead. The film then abruptly cuts back to her sitting in a taxi (here at 81 minutes, but first encountered at 23 minutes into the film) and then cuts even further back to her sitting in Ben's Range Rover (first encountered at 12 minutes into the film), circling backward through the plot. The film ends with ambiguity about her awareness of her status as dead even as viewers realise, due to the ever-clearer circularity of plot, that they should rethink and reconsider its apparent linear progression.

When, at the film's conclusion, Yella is suddenly left inscrutably sobbing in the cab that circles narratively back to the opening minutes' Range Rover, she might be crying because she realises she is dead or because she realises the awful circularity and destructiveness of capitalism, its 'creative destruction' of everyone around her. The circularity of capitalism's creative-destructive mechanisms is precisely what the film conveys: Ben's firm has been bankrupted and he left unemployed; the Hannover firm that hired Yella is bankrupt before she gets there and leaves her unemployed; and then, climactically yet repetitively, Philipp – her apparent hero-saviour – is also left unemployed, which triggers Yella's own inadvertent killing of an innocent from whom she tries to extort money. The very ambiguity of the crying drives home Petzold's message of the destructive force of capitalism: alongside the premature and late-realised death of the protagonist there is capitalism's circularity, repetition and destruction of linear progress. This recognition of circularity, the detachment from character and identification with narrative form itself, is what this horror plot brings to Petzold's refunctionalised horror film. The mechanisms with which it reaches this recognition – undercutting identification, compelling a revisitation and reanalysis of what seemed to be an objectively verifiable set of events, forcing a subsequent process of self-reflection on both the narrative and the character within it – underscore how the film achieves a level of quasi-modernist contemplation. But revealingly, *Yella* arrives at these mechanisms of distance, self-reflection and ambiguity via a manipulation, or re-functioning, of the cognitive scraps and remnants of a popular genre.

CONCLUSION: WOMEN AT THE WHEEL, OR THE 'FINAL
GIRL' IN THE LATE-CAPITALIST AUTOMOBILE

The cognitive challenges and confusion of horror become the cognitive challenges and confusion of capitalism – this is the core of Petzold's generic engagement in *Yella*, one that goes far in explaining the film's operations as well as, I hope, underscoring how a German *auteur* (one not named Fassbinder) takes up and transforms Hollywood genre in his cinema. This homologous linkage between popular genre and art-cinema film, largely via narrative and viewer knowledge, constitute what Rick Altman has termed the 'syntax' of the horror genre, or the way in which a genre puts together its various building blocks (2003: 27–41). Altman contrasts the syntax of a genre to its 'semantics' – that is, its particular *mise-en-scène*, its spaces, costumes, actors – and it is the semantics of his quasi-horror film with which Petzold deliberately re-sets the genre in the late-capitalist landscape of Hannover, amidst anonymous hotels and contemporary meeting rooms, rather than in small-town middle America. Even here in the semantics, however, Petzold negotiates a certain nearness and distance to the horror genre, in the project of refunctioning and refashioning it for his own purposes. To conclude, I want briefly to return to what seems, on the face of it, the clearest semantic link to horror, the use of a sympathetic female protagonist, and link it to another of Petzold's apparently auteurist touches, the automobile, to emphasise how Petzold engages with the horror genre, not because he is a down-the-line genre filmmaker, but rather because he is a canny reader of genre film who appropriates and refashions elements of the genre for his own art-cinema purposes.

Petzold's critique of the 'cinema of identification' cited above actually comes in his response to Marco Abel's question about why he so often uses women protagonists in his films, probably most conspicuously in *Yella*. Petzold suggests that he uses women protagonists in part to make sure that he himself does not over-identify with his own protagonists, which corresponds to, as he recounts above, his overall project of avoiding the 'annoying' cinema of identification. Petzold's use of women protagonists to explore the post-*Wende* social milieu, however, provides another example of his formative engagement with American genre films. In discussing his use of female protagonists, it is not so much the direct influence of New German Cinema that influences his decisions but rather his reading of genre films and the lasting impression they have made on him and his filmmaking:

> when I started making films in [the former East Germany] [...], I discovered the mythological location of so many German legends – the river landscapes [sic], etc. – as a place abandoned by the women who used to live there. All the women gone: this was the first moment when I thought, this is movement, this is an image, and I can make a film about this! Then I watched Fritz Lang's *The Blue Gardenia* (1953), for I was always curious about these women who, in the 1930s in the US, live together in large urban environments, working as phone operators or in department stores, who are nineteen, twenty years old, and who all came from the country, from Arizona, Texas, Montana, who now sit in bars and become protagonists in gangster stories, who are there to find millionaires. And I thought: where did all the girls from the former East Germany go? Which dreams do they have? What kind of fortune hunters are they? Then I read a lot about Irish women. And when you watch John Ford films, you notice how women always seem to sit in the front of stagecoaches. Of course it is the men on whom the films focus – they fight, shoot, scream – but it is the women who are the real agents of movement. One always has the feeling that it is the women who leave because there is no place for them anymore, no riches, no one who can take care of them. And this was the starting point for *Yella*: we narrate the topic of reunification as a story about a woman who is looking for fortune. (2008)

In this passage, Petzold is answering Abel's question about the relevance of the *Wende* to his recent films, but it is once again telling that Petzold quickly transitions from German particularity (observations he made while shooting in the former GDR) to genre films, all be they films from important directors (Fritz Lang, John Ford). While the use of women protagonists for such films is clearly part of their generic aspect, and Petzold takes as his point of departure these moving women seeking their fortunes, he also simultaneously refunctions this element to highlight his particular reading of genre films and their specific social aspects: the semantic shift to western Germany becomes the frontier for Yella as an ambitious, upwardly mobile woman. Once again, his relationship to genre, to its scraps and remnants, offers him the materials for his own approach to filmmaking as well as analysis of the contemporary social situation.

From the first scene to the last, *Yella* is indeed a woman on the move seeking her fortune, both vocational and emotional. Although he does not mention the horror films that influenced him in this context, it is worth noting that both *Carnival of Souls* and *Halloween* feature female protagonists who, as socially transgressive individuals, serve as transitional figures for their cinematic and spatial milieus. In *Carnival of Souls*, Mary has, like Yella, moved to a new city for a job and is left to navigate a series of occupational and social situations as an unattached, independent woman in a context geared to exploiting them. *Halloween* is symptomatic of another kind of transgression, that of what Carol Clover (1992: 35–39) has called the 'final girl', she who survives those murdered, not least because of her ability to assume a male position in the narrative as strong (even while shrieking) and attacking (even while screaming). Although this gender negotiation

Figure 10.2: *Carnival of Souls* (1962): 'May I just sit here?'

was an echo of 1970s feminism, the 'final girl' ended up often reduced to a more masculine woman. In both films – in a way to which Petzold would likely be sensitised, given the above passage – women assume a different narrative position because of their transgression of conventional gender stereotypes, their ambiguous negotiations of conventionally masculine roles (*Carnival*'s Mary travelling for a job and consistently rejecting men, *Halloween*'s Laurie attacking the psychotic killer). Yella, too, in her extorting money from Dr Gunthen and then causing his untimely, watery death, seems to have assumed, even usurped, narrative positions held initially by Ben and Philipp respectively.

Petzold mentions that the presence of women in the front of the stagecoaches – riding shotgun – struck him in the westerns of John Ford, and it is telling that both *Carnival*'s Mary and Yella have emphatic relationships to the contemporary stagecoach, the automobile. In her reading of spectral incognisance in *The Sixth Sense*, Briefel locates its horror effects, the circularity and the unending nature of the unrecognised death in a scenario that narrates driving: automobile driving becomes a metaphor for the external life and circular narrative that produce it (2009: 99). In both the *Carnival of Souls* and in *The Hitchhiker* (1960) – the *Twilight Zone* version of the Bierce story – the protagonists go on apparently living after they have actually been killed in car crashes, and in *Carnival of Souls* in particular Mary continues to have a somewhat complicated, tortured relationship to the mammoth car she drives around Salt Lake City to take up her new job. Her slow realisation of her early death comes closest when she goes to have her car repaired and is suspended, in a kind of *Schwebezustand*, mid-air, literally going nowhere.

In all these narratives, the fateful drive opens up time into a seemingly eternal present, only to be cut abruptly short at the end of the film by the realisation of the much earlier, vehicular death. Petzold retains the image of a woman in an automobile as a metaphor of social transformation while refashioning its generic semantics for Germany's contemporary capitalism: in Mercedes taxis in which businessmen sexually proposition employees, in Audi estates that serve as a business platform, and in dilapidated Range Rovers that suddenly plunge twice, like Farquar in Bierce's 'Owl Creek Bridge' or Mary in Harvey's *Carnival of Souls*, off the bridge. With the many automobiles of *Yella*, Petzold registers one of his most conspicuous auteurist touches, but he is, as I have aimed to demonstrate above, deliberately refunctioning a popular genre in its syntax and semantics, much as Fassbinder did. Although more consistently taking up horror rather than melodrama, Petzold's work highlights the European *auteur*'s thoroughgoing engagement with globally circulating genres, genres that Petzold refunctions for his own purposes, but genres that also underscore the global flows into which cinema, and its *auteurs*, have always already been interwoven.

Notes

1 Although Fatih Akin is certainly also critically acclaimed, Petzold has actually won more awards from German film critics: for example, four of his last six films have won Best Film from the Association of German Film Critics (2000, 2004, 2007, 2009).

2 Bordwell suggests that ambiguity is a key textual strategy of 1970s art cinema (1986: 209).

3 As Bordwell points out, the *auteur* serves as a 'textual force who communicates (what is the film saying?) and "who" expresses (what is the artist's personal vision?). Lacking indefinable stars and a familiar genre, the art cinema uses the concept of authorship to unify the text' (Bordwell 1979: 62).

4 I have in mind here the way in which Brecht refunctioned, for instance, tragedy in *Mann ist Mann*. See Lyons 1994.

5 Johannes von Moltke discusses this New German Cinema phenomenon within the framework of contemporary cinema (von Moltke 2010: 157–85).

6 In this sense, Philipp seems more akin to *Halloween*'s reworking of the convention of a helpful social authority, with its emphatically ineffectual doctor, than to the earlier horror films, including *Carnival of Souls*, with its stock social-authority figures like a doctor or policeman who assists the main character with his or her horror problem.

Chapter 11

'A sharpening of our regard': realism, affect and the redistribution of the sensible in Valeska Grisebach's *Longing* (2006)

Marco Abel

Realism represents the attempt to establish contact with reality in some manner, to consider reality valuable enough to narrate it [...]. An attempt to make visible the everyday, to remember it. Even if one does not understand it. A sharpening of our regard, as it were.

Valeska Grisebach (2007a: 79–80)

THE 'BERLIN SCHOOL' AS COUNTER-CINEMA

One of the most interesting aspects of German film production in the third millennium has been what filmmaker Christoph Hochhäusler suggestively describes as an 'incursion of reality' into German film (quoted in Rohnke 2006). In coining this phrase, the director of four critically praised films, *This Very Moment* (*Milchwald*, 2003) and *Low Profile* (*Falscher Bekenner*, 2005), *The City Below* (*Unter dir die Stadt*, 2010) and *One Minute of Darkness* (*Eine Minute Dunkel*, 2011), offers us a framework through which we might assess the accomplishments of a number of directors associated with the contemporary German filmmaking movement known as the Berlin School, of which Hochhäusler is one of the key directors together with about a dozen others including Christian Petzold, Angela Schanelec, Thomas Arslan, Ulrich Köhler, Maren Ade and Valeska Grisebach.[1] Beyond serving as a useful descriptive claim, however, Hochhäusler's phrase implies that the films he has in mind are not merely different from but aesthetically and politically *opposed* to the majority of films the German film industry funds and promotes today.

Indeed, the sense that the directors of the Berlin School are engaged in the production of what I think may best be conceptualised as a *counter-cinema* is further strengthened by Christian Petzold's recent claim that the German film industry actually hates the Berlin School.[2] Perhaps no better evidence exists for the validity of Petzold's assessment than 'Das Schmollen der Autisten' ('The pouting of the autistic'), a brief essay by the president of the German Film Academy, Günter Rohrbach (2007),[3] in which he decries German film critics as autistic because of their alleged tendency to dismiss German film productions that end up finding a substantial theatre-going audience, such as Tom Tykwer's *Perfume: Story of a Murderer* (*Das Parfum: Die Geschichte eines Mörders*, 2006),[4] while lavishing critical praise on smaller-scale films that regularly vanish at the box office, as was true for Valeska Grisebach's second feature, *Longing* (*Sehnsucht*, 2006). However, in the end Rohrbach's polemic is much less an attack on German film critics and their apparent penchant for supporting films that do not have considerable marketing budgets at their disposal (with which to inform the public of their existence) than an ideologically motivated put-down of those filmmakers to whom some of the better-known German film critics occasionally lend their support – especially those directors associated with the Berlin School. What is ultimately at stake in Rohrbach's essay is not the fact that German film critics send their readers into the wrong films but the very right to define what German national cinema is or should be – the very *Hoheitsrecht* ('sovereign right') to delineate the contours of how Germany represents itself through the medium of its cinema.[5]

What ultimately bothers Rohrbach (and the establishment for whom he speaks) about the Berlin School is that it has been greeted with considerable enthusiasm *outside Germany*, for this attention lavished upon a group of filmmakers who collectively have made barely more than forty features to date directs attention away from those films by which the 'official' Germany is all too eager to have itself represented: to wit, the remarkable Academy Awards success German films have recently enjoyed. We might call these productions 'state films' (in the sense that Deleuze and Guattari (1987: 376) posit Kant and Hegel as state philosophers who endow philosophy with a normative, juridical role): films that afford the country's official culture the chance to carefully mould its image abroad, implicitly (if not explicitly) insisting on its right to be treated as just another 'normal' country by virtue of the fact that it eagerly promotes at home and abroad cinematic self-representations that allegedly confront its citizens in an honest manner with the horrors of the country's totalitarian past. Or, evoking Eric Rentschler's perspicacious 'cinema of consensus' coinage, these 'state films' give voice to the very consensus view desired by 'official' German culture and its functionaries such as Rohrbach.

Although I would strongly counsel against any wholesale application of Rentschler's term to a film-historical context that he did not initially set out to describe and evaluate, it stands to reason that in many respects the 'cinema of consensus' diagnosed by the influential Harvard film historian has managed to transform itself from a commercially successful yet critically disreputable cinema into a formula for producing films that have become 'respectable' cultural productions while maintaining their commercial punch. Whereas the original cinema of consensus films were incapable of garnering glory for Germany abroad, the desire for consensus Rentschler locates in them has now found considerably more successful forms of expression in a series of history films that work like a charm at the Academy Awards.[6] These films cater to an audience that can find in them both confirmation of its own preconceived notions about Germany ('the Nazis!'; 'the Stasi!') and the comforting, even feel-good perception that this people has finally managed to shed its totalitarian past and join the community of 'normal' nations.

It is this particular *perception* of Germany that constitutes the real issue at stake in Rohrbach's essay; for what these 'state films' are in the process of achieving is what Jacques Rancière (2004) describes in terms of a 'distribution of the sensible', or what in our case we would have to call a *re*distribution of the sensible. For the French philosopher, aesthetics (the realm of the sensible) is not opposed to politics but rather immanent to it: aesthetics directly exerts a force on the level of politics rather than merely mediating the 'proper' realm of the political through representations thereof, as is usually claimed. Aesthetics – the mode through which the world becomes sensible and perceptible to and for us (the word for 'perception' in ancient Greek was 'aistheton', from which we derive 'aesthetics') – directly enacts a political force by framing and reframing for subjects what they can and cannot sense and perceive. Differently put, the political force inherent to the aesthetic distribution of the sensible is precisely a force that directly acts on reality because it acts on our sensations and perceptions; it affects, to use the phrase I chose for the translation of this essay's epigraph, our *regard* for reality.

If we can agree that Rohrbach and the industry he represents are indeed worried exactly about this affectively charged relation between aesthetics – here, the cinema – and reality, then we can also begin to understand why Rohrbach's real target is the Berlin School and why he singled out Grisebach's seemingly completely apolitical and commercially unsuccessful film *Longing* as a major focus for his scathing critique of German film critics: we might say that *Longing* marks the eruption into speech of those (in this case the Berlin School at large) who otherwise find themselves merely spoken for, if not altogether ignored and frequently silenced. Judging from the film's critical reception, this eruption into discourse facilitated by *Longing* is itself defined by the film's particular mode of encounter with (German) reality – an aesthetic mode of encounter that simultaneously invokes the register of representational realism and its attendant truth claims and affectively intensifies this register to such a degree that our *perception* of the reality (and truth) it seemingly represents is put at stake. In so doing it offers a counter-program to the aesthetics of the 'state films', contesting their representational claims, not by dialectically arguing against them on the level of content but by mobilising a different mode of rendering reality sensible; as a result, *Longing* invites its viewers to reassess the 'state films'' self-serving, consensus-driven representational claims (to 'normality') precisely by virtue of the fact that the plane of the sensible itself is being affected – altered, reconfigured, redistributed – by the eruption into speech that Grisebach's unassuming film performatively marks.

LONGING'S AFFECTIVE INTENSIFICATION OF REALISM

The 82-minute-long *Longing* is Grisebach's follow-up to her even shorter debut film, *My Star* (*Mein Stern*, 2001). Both films were shot with non-professional actors whom Grisebach recruited on the streets of Brandenburg and Berlin respectively. What immediately stands out in both films is that they are not content-driven. Like *My Star*, *Longing* is unlikely to strike viewers as narratively complex – something to which the film's epilogue playfully attests when a young girl *appears* to recount to a group of friends the very story we have just watched.[7] Having studied at the Film Academy in Vienna with directors such as Michael Haneke and Ulrich Seidl, Grisebach describes her aesthetic approach to her stories and characters in terms of practising 'radical observation' (Geppert 2002), the purpose of which is to foreground the *being* of the characters rather than their playing. This radical observation manifests itself in how her camera remains rigorously phlegmatic in both of her films, a characteristic her cinematography has in common with many other Berlin School films but perhaps with none more so than Köhler's *Bungalow* (2002), in which we follow a teenager on the cusp of adulthood whose phlegmatic affect is rendered palpable by the film's often static *mise-en-scène*.

But this cinematic phlegmatism on the part of Grisebach's camera is not an index of her lack of interest in her protagonists. It is, rather, precisely the aesthetic device that ensures that her films sidestep the aesthetic and ethical, indeed political, traps of voyeuristic social reporting. According to one critic, what differentiates *My Star*, and in my view *Longing* as well, from just such social reporting that implicitly or explicitly insists on teaching a bourgeois audience something about a class with whom they have otherwise little to do is 'the positioning of the camera, which never condescends and never violates people's private sphere. At no time does the film expose; Valeska Grisebach and her film team never know something better' (Rall 2002: 38). Grisebach encounters her subject matter immanently, heeding the being of her protagonists, who enact the fictional story based on a script but bring to it their own *being* – that is, their life experiences, ideas and affects. Grisebach allows all of this to manifest itself in her films by creating the conditions for the camera to be receptive to this reality, its chance occurrences, and the forces that produce and thus affect the characters. In short, the aesthetic approach Grisebach exhibits in her films is precisely an attempt to render visible the everyday – that which she herself may actually not understand, or in any case understand in ways that differ from the understanding exhibited by her characters; it is an attempt to find ways of sharpening her and *our* regard of and for the reality we witness on screen, a reality filtered, and thus rendered affectively sensible, for us through the specific *stylistic* means by which Grisebach transforms pro-filmic reality into the reality of an aesthetic experience that cannot be reduced to the old chestnuts of 'authenticity' or 'documentary'.

Consider, for example, the film's opening sequence of scenes that begins with what appears to be a car accident and a rescue mission. This event subsequently triggers both a public and private discursive response, and it is precisely in the transition from one to the other that the film subtly reworks the very aesthetic assumptions and attendant perceptual habits that frame for us *how* we respond to the events on screen. Before we even see anything, we hear the sound of a car approaching and coming to a stop. Then we are exposed to an extreme close-up of a man frantically moving about, breathing heavily as he asks someone off screen, 'Do you hear me?' The ensuing wide shot reveals a first-aider trying to save a man who, as we subsequently learn, must have driven his car head-on into a tree. As children approach the scene, a series of wide shots reveal a rural environment, suggesting that this event carries the force of the extraordinary in what must otherwise be rather ordinary lives spent in the countryside somewhere in former East Germany.

The overall pacing and shot selection of this opening sequence seems firmly rooted in a documentary-realist tradition, affording the audience the sense of being in the middle of the action. The sensation of documentary immediacy is likely further enhanced for viewers because of the unknown faces and bodies we see on screen. Though we may not be aware that none of the people we see are professional actors – that is, 'real' people cast in a fiction film – the combination of the freshness of their faces and their 'being' on screen, their presence, if you will, intensifies the very effect of documentary immediacy that the cinematographic and sound choices already suggest to us.

The next scene, however, forces us to reassess our likely perception of the event with which *Longing* began. As we eavesdrop on a number of firemen discussing the event, we discover that the accident was actually a suicide attempt. Foreshadowing the film's epilogue, the firemen, like the children later on, reveal their varying attitudes towards the event in a bewildered yet compassionate manner, while Markus (Andreas Müller) silently listens. As Dell (2006) astutely points out, for the villagers the 'accident is first a medial phenomenon, the glue that holds the village community together through the very process of talking about it. [...] The accident affords the opportunity to examine what is fixed, to interrogate that which is taken for granted, to take a stand.' What the film introduces here, then, is the question of storytelling and through it that of perception – our regard of and for reality – itself. In so doing, *Longing* contradicts its initial documentary-style aesthetic, which affectively framed our perception of the event through its *in medias res* immediacy in a manner that it now explicitly foregrounds as problematic. As we find ourselves confronted with a series of storytellers who collectively tell and reflect on an event, as well as a listener on screen who, like the audience in the theatre or at home, intently listens and reflects the reflection itself, we are prodded to call into question our likely initial response to the opening sequence, which we were prone to assess within the framework of documentary or representational realism – an aesthetic lens that trades on the notion of 'authenticity' and thus 'truth'. What initially seemed to be a genuine accident the film now reveals as an intentional act – a suicide.

At a minimum we will have to come to terms with the fact that even if what we had initially witnessed on screen functioned on the aesthetic level of documentary-realism, this level is no guarantor of transparency: what we see is not necessarily what we get. As a result, the film sets in motion the very demand Grisebach has of the cinema, of realism, namely to sharpen our regard of reality by affecting our perception of it. It is as if the film here challenged viewers to suspend their tried and tested viewing habits, their habits of perception – habits, as it turns out, that are misleading, not least because such habits, as necessary as they may be to cope with everyday life, are dependent on and expressive of a range of clichés that we tend to harbour about reality. An aesthetically induced sharpening of our regard of reality amounts to an intensification of our care for it, enacting an ethics of response-ability that suspends, however tentatively and momentarily, the very perceptive habits formed by the repetitive articulation of an aesthetic of representational realism characteristic of 'state films'. Such an aesthetic is primarily invested in delimiting the field of the sensible and thus in reducing perception to the logic of recognition – the affirmative re-cognition of that with which we are (or are assumed to be) already familiar: perception as the recognition of reality as cliché, if you will.

But what is a cliché? In Deleuze's words,

> A cliché is a sensory-motor image of the thing. As Bergson says, we do not perceive the thing or the image in its entirety, we always perceive less of it, we perceive only what we are interested in perceiving, or rather what it is in our interest to perceive, by virtue of our economic interests, ideological beliefs and psychological demands. We therefore normally perceive only clichés. (1989: 20)

This mode of perception, with which we were seemingly being invited to approach *Longing*, is, however, disrupted by Grisebach's subtle shift of aesthetic registers. At the moment when the film intensifies the logic of the apparently realistic telling of a story to the degree that the *process* of telling itself is foregrounded more than what the tale represents, 'our sensory-motor schemata jam or break', as Deleuze would have it, and 'a different type of image [appears]: a pure optical-sound image, the whole image without metaphor, brings out the thing in itself, literally' (1989: 20). There are numerous moments when such pure optical-sound images break through the seemingly representational-realist surface of the film's aesthetic, and they are almost always marked by a hard optical and sound cut that startles our perception precisely by virtue of its affective contrast with regard to the sensations produced by the otherwise nearly invisible cuts of Grisebach's editor, Bettina Böhler. These hard cuts occur precisely at those moments when the film's documentary-realist tone is pushed to an extreme. It is through these cuts that the film performatively accomplishes a transformation in our perception. Obtaining an entirely different affective quality, these moments affect *our* perception of the reality to which we are exposed, indeed *how* we perceive it: from a perception of a reality re-presented to a perception of the reality of this representation itself. The film is structured around an entire series of such moments, which taken together obtain a serial rhythm that functions as the film's mechanism through which it redistributes that which we can sense or perceive.

The first such moment occurs when Grisebach cuts from the fire station to a very long shot of Markus standing by a lake at dusk, with his wife Ella (Ilka Welz) gradually approaching. The camera is perfectly still and holds the shot for forty seconds. With the diegetic sound emphasising the rural setting, we observe the couple from a considerable distance in a perfectly framed shot as they eventually embrace each other. The shot's astonishing length and its perfectly centred composition cannot help but call attention to itself: unlike prior shots that were firmly anchored in documentary aesthetics, this shot is akin to a *tableau vivant*. It is as if we were beholding a painting, as if we were now looking at mediated rather than 'real' reality. What the film had just accomplished on the discursive level it now reiterates in purely cinematic fashion; yet it is precisely this iterative process that imbues this seemingly 'mediated' moment with its own reality and affective force – a force that we sense *before* it appears to us as the

Figure 11.1: Ella and Markus by the lake.

mediation – that is representation – of something else. As we are invited by this long interval of narrative standstill, even breakdown, leisurely to behold the *mise-en-scène* in ways that might call to mind André Bazin's writings on realism, we are affectively induced to shift our perception of the film's aesthetic programme from one firmly rooted in a documentary-realist tradition to one suddenly bordering on the melodramatic. Crucially, however, the scene's sheer intensity is rendered affectively sensible even though it holds the couple at a considerable distance from our gaze; refusing to allow the actors to represent their characters' emotions (no method acting here), the film, through what the director describes as the film's 'alternation of nearness and distance' (2007b), through its sudden shift in aesthetic register from the immediacy of the documentary-realist to the mediacy of the *malerisch*-melodramatic, directly acts upon our nervous system and effects in and for us a perceptive readjustment – a redistribution – of what we are sensing.[8]

The film is filled with examples of such radical affective shifts. I am thinking here, for example, of the hard sound cut that links the silence dominating a beautifully composed *malerisch tableau vivant* of the couple lying in tight embrace on their marital bed and the sudden incursion of raw reality in the form of the sound of a saw that begins one of the many scenes in which the film can be said to function as a document of bodies at work, relying here as elsewhere on a simple and subtle use of shot/reverse-shot, often framed in medium-close to extreme close-ups, which help to emphasise affectively a sense of immediacy, or being-there-ness, for the viewer. And later on in the film, after the onset of Markus's affair with the waitress Rose (Anett Dornbusch), harsh cuts link a sequence of scenes. First, Markus and Ella are dancing with each other at their local village's annual bonfire. As their dancing gets more intimate, with the couple closely embracing, a sudden cut occurs to a close-up of them having sex. It is the film's most explicit scene; the directness with which the camera depicts their naked bodies in the act of lovemaking clearly contributes to the intensity of this moment, which is further aided by the direct sound of their breathing.

And then another harsh cut violently reframes our perception once more, as the camera now depicts Markus, alone, standing outside in the early morning. With the camera closely behind him, he wanders around as diegetic sound captures the chirping of birds and trees swaying in the wind. Eventually a shot over his shoulders points to the lake, at which he stares. The length of this scene, characterised by the pastoral quietness, once more transforms the register of documentary-realism that framed our ability to respond to the previous scene so that through a continuation of the realist register the very same morphs into the *malerisch*-melodramatic evoking German Romanticism, calling attention to the haunted beauty of its composition. As if desiring to make sure we are really receptive to the shifts of aesthetic registers and thus to the sensations to which it exposes us, the film suddenly interrupts the *malerisch* mood once again with a startling sound cut linking the absolute quietness dominating the image to the metallic sounds made by Markus climbing a ladder to fix a silo pipe, perhaps an hour later, perhaps days, weeks, or even months.[9]

However, though *affectively* this repetitive dynamic is characterised by the scenes' difference from each other, both the *tableaux vivants* and the documentary-realist shot/reverse-shot sequences exhibit Grisebach's expressed desire to push the act of observing her characters to a radical extreme. That is to say, the melodramatic *tableaux vivants* are not the dialectical opposite of the realist shot/reverse-shot sequences. Rather, the dynamic linkage of these two aesthetic modalities results in an intensification of the act of observing itself – of regarding the reality at which she points her camera and sound-recording devices; the result is that *Longing* posits these cinematic registers as two equally artificial inflections of, and attitudes towards, reality, rather than presenting either as the means by which the film allows us to take comfort in the belief that what we see is really what we get. Grisebach herself calls this aesthetic dynamic – which is responsible for effecting in the viewer a redistribution of what is sensed, of the perception of reality, indeed of our perception of *how* we (are made to) perceive reality – 'colloquial':

> The film's way of telling the story was supposed to appear colloquial, ordinary, sketched in static and moving takes, in between tableau-like images that emphasise the common, model-like nature of the situation. [...] Time and again it was about the interaction of nearness and distance. The severe frame as resistance to the 'documentary'. (2007b)

The colloquial quality of her shots (she likens it to the language of contemporary American literature, which to her is 'so laconic, abbreviated, so colloquial' [2006]), juxtaposed with the *tableaux vivants*, amounts to a film aesthetic that puts into question both our assumptions about representational realism/documentary and artificial melodrama. It is precisely the subtle back and forth that affects our perception of what we see and hear on screen as well as how we might think about our perceptions of the real in general.

The Utopia of Sehn-sucht[10]

The two aesthetic modalities of representational realism and *malerisch tableaux vivants* function on the same sliding scale of a cinematic process of approaching pro-filmic reality that time and again marks itself as being *productive* of our perception of the reality of representation rather than claiming for itself the deceptive status of a truthful representation of a reality. And it is just this properly cinematic aspect of *Longing* that marks it as a political film: it cinematically *refuses* the implicit and explicit truth claims inherent to the aesthetic of documentary or representational realism to delimit the realm of the sensible, the perceptible, as one defined by the pleasures of recognition. The film does not instil in the viewer the self-serving sensation of knowing familiarity with the world as it really 'is', as the aesthetics of 'state films' tend to do; nor does *Longing* place viewers in the voyeuristic position of the social rumour monger. Instead of falling into the trap of accepting these aesthetic modalities as the proper lens through which to encounter reality, *Longing* directly works on our senses so that they are forced to readjust themselves, to modulate their degree of receptivity. The film solicits our capacity to *see again*, to enact our *regard* for reality in ways that make the latter worth remembering even though we do not necessarily understand what we are performatively made to remember in the act of regarding the reality of the filmic representation. In short, the politics of *Longing* – and I have suggested elsewhere that this is one of the keys to the filmmaking of the Berlin School in general – is precisely that it effects a transformation in and of the viewer (see Abel 2008). This transformation occurs as a result of the film acting directly upon our nervous system without taking a detour through the mediating logic of representational realism that tends to territorialise our perceptions and sensations of reality on the level of truth claims and a self-servingly defined 'proper' morality, always already validated in advance by virtue of the state-sanctioned distribution of the sensible.

Such transformation is, of course, what the film itself dramatises within its diegesis and for which it finds time and again cinematic means of expression. It not only demonstrates how the protagonists themselves are transformed but also affectively instils such transformative effects in the viewer. There is perhaps no better example of this than the daring cut that elliptically transforms Markus from being immersed in a moment of drunken melodramatic sentiment to one of

Figure 11.2: Markus 'feeling it'.

soberly awakening to a new reality that he is not yet capable of understanding. On his weekend retreat with his fire brigade, Markus, like his colleagues, gradually gets drunk. Suddenly, Grisebach cuts forward in time, revealing Markus in the act of dancing all by himself, with his eyes closed tight and his head leaning sideways. Oblivious to his environment, he is completely absorbed by the melodramatic sentiments expressed by Robbie Williams's, 'Feel' (2002). As the British singer croons that he wants 'to feel real love'; that he has 'got too much life running through [his] veins going to waste'; and that although he does not want to die he is not too 'keen on living either', the camera follows Markus's every move for about two minutes, shot in intimate medium and extreme close-ups. Grisebach holds this scene far beyond the length that would seem justified by its content. As viewers, we understand early on in the scene that Markus is drunkenly 'feeling it'. But before long *we* begin to feel slightly embarrassed, even awkward at watching him give himself over so intensely to the moment, to the corny lyrics, which, so we sense, say everything he cannot bring himself to say, or, perhaps, admit: that there is indeed too much life running through his veins going to waste. Our sensation of embarrassment at the sight of a grown man dancing in this way is triggered simultaneously by and in stark contrast to the sheer sincerity with which the film's Romeo comports himself. Our sensation of embarrassment is not endorsed by the film, which throughout pursues a rigorously a-judgmental stance towards its characters and their actions, absolutely refusing to cater to any consensus-driven sense of morality characteristic of both the original 'cinema of consensus' films diagnosed by Rentschler and the 'state films' promoted by Rohrbach today. Rather, this sensation is an effect of the instantaneous transformation our perception is forced to undergo. Precisely as a result of the film's refusal to judge Markus as embarrassing does the realm of what is sensible for us get readjusted. We find ourselves confronted with sensations to which we want to respond by having recourse to our habituated, comforting representationalist concepts, which we sense, however, have no purchase on the very forces triggering our sensations in the first place.

And the longer the scene continues the more our concern shifts away from the level of content – *what* we see – and to our very ability to respond to the affective forces impinging upon our nervous system: the sheer intensity of Markus's emotions is rendered affectively sensible for us. And what this affective intensity marks for us, on our bodies, is precisely that aspect of the titular notion that exceeds its determination by a specific object. What the film manages to induce in us – precisely because it does not merely communicate its protagonist's experience on a content level (through, say, dialogue) but actually renders it sensible through *how* the cinematography stages Markus's affective transformation – is a force immanent to the emotion of *Sehn-sucht* that exceeds its emotional, subject-centred content and gets to its affective, non-object driven, utopian quality. The scene ever more intensely affects us with the *reality* of the sensation of *Sehn-sucht* itself, not its object-cause (i.e., the object 'for' which one might long) but the logic of this sensation itself: what we feel, so to speak, is our own yearning *for the intensity of the state of addiction*, not addiction 'to' something but just addiction in and of itself, the state of being addicted – of living life to such an intense degree that it pushes through the everyday sphere into an elsewhere, which though thoroughly rooted in the material here and now is also utopian precisely because it is not yet in existence, or rather obtains existence only in this moment, performatively.

And at just this moment of maximum affective intensity – at its most intense rendering of the sensation of utopia – the film deploys another harsh cut, moving us to a different space, time and affective state, with Markus gradually coming to consciousness in a bed that turns out to be that of Rose, the waitress we had previously only cursorily noticed as she served and danced with the firemen; here the 'realism removes itself from the melodramatic and fairytale-like and opposes it with an unwieldy rawness as a mode of resistance' (Grisebach 2007b). The immediacy yet hesitancy and tenderness of the way Grisebach renders the 'morning after' reminds us once more of the 'reality, the "not-staged", atmospheric, which withdraws from the realm of the melodramatic, makes it banal in a good way' (Grisebach 2007b). From here on the main plot develops more or less in line with the story recounted by the girl in the film's epilogue.

By finding ways of affecting our sense perceptions, the film forces us to re-see our world, not because the film provides us with a metaphor or allegory that suggests to us that what we see on screen represents our lives, or the lives of people we might know, but rather because the film accesses our perceptive apparatus on the pre-singular, pre-subjective level, thus directly intervening in how we perceive, rather than 'what' we perceive. By affecting *how* we perceive, the film effects a redistribution of the sensible in and for us: relations and possibilities, indeed potentials that had not been sensible before, do now obtain the force of actuality for us, become sensible and in so doing demand a response from us, the content and quality of which, of course, is itself not determined by this affectively generated act of redistribution.

But the fact that this transformation is imbued with a utopian quality does not mean this utopianism is easy to sustain. For one, of course, the love-triangle reaches a breaking point with Rose's accident. But even before that we can observe the immanent limits of the very utopian potential actualised by Grisebach's aesthetic encounter with reality. For although Markus has indeed undergone an affective transformation, he is still not able to communicate it on a discursive level. Whether with Ella or Rose, the communication of their feelings continues to rely on the most banal and clichéd of statements ('I love you so'; 'I long so much for you'; 'You are so beautiful' etc.), just as Williams's song is, for all its success, nothing but an amalgamation of clichéd sentiments typical of catchy pop songs. And the tonal quality of their enunciation marks theses sentences not so much as dialogues but as stand-alone illocutions, as if the speakers do not know how to communicate with each other, not least because they actually have no pre-existing framework through which to turn the intensity of their feelings for each other into discourse. It is as if they do not know how to verbalise their emotions to each other, as if their feelings exceeded words, which is ultimately why the words they do speak are uttered rather flatly and are, in terms of their content, reminiscent of the very clichés that television, movies and pop songs endlessly recycle.

That is, what we sense here is precisely the insufficiency of *these* words – but not of words in general. *Longing* does not trade in some prelapsarian mysticism, nor does it embrace the logic of Heidegger's jargon of authenticity rooted in the realm of metaphysical Being. Instead, it is the very realist quality of much of the film that constantly serves to remind us of the *materialist* aspect of people's emotions, feelings and ultimately their affects – that which is material through and through and must be insisted on as preceding the subjective territorialisation of individual feelings. Even though these characters are at a loss for words that might 'really' express what is entirely new to them, they do not reconcile themselves to the impossibility of finding words, nor do they flee into some mystical realm, but instead they *test* out how it sounds to verbalise these emotions with all the earnestness they can muster, as if they felt that there are still nuances within the very clichés that can be wrested away from them and re-activated, used anew, with a force that is qualitatively different from that communicated by the sheer content of these clichéd utterances.

CONCLUSION

Bert Rebhandl (2006) has argued that *Longing* presents us with a 'realism of desire', that is an articulation of the reality of desire, rather than a representation of the object of desire that the characters are governed by and can never obtain. In short, *Longing* exhibits a *realism of affect*, rendering sensible the affective forces that immanently reside within subjects and manifest themselves as *Sehn-sucht* – a yearning for the affective sensation of yearning itself, rather than a longing for something in particular. And it is this insistence on taking seriously this logic of *Sehn-sucht* that is ultimately expressive of Grisebach's aesthetic undertaking, her *political* intervention in post-unification Germany and German cinema. For the film's inflection of '*Sehnsucht*' as *Sehn-sucht* is precisely expressive of a different attitude towards reality, an attitude that does not satisfy itself with re-presenting what has already been shown many times, or with depicting from a superior point of view the insufficiencies of the lives of others. It is an attitude that is generous towards life – one that, as Grisebach puts it, starts with the impetus that reality is worth being taken seriously, being valued, and being remembered. Precisely because she values reality she is pushed to remember, and in doing so alter, it; and the desire to affect such change through cinematic means that can be said to be in line with much of what Bazin once wrote about a different filmic environment is precisely the outcome of finding value in reality itself, for if this were not the case it is hard to see why one would want to change it.

Valuing reality – and the resulting urge to sharpen our regard of and for reality – finally necessitates the film's ending. Rather than considering the epilogue an error, as one otherwise sympathetic critic does (Suchsland 2006a), I see it as the film's final and perhaps most explicit dramatisation of its larger ethical and political logic. Rather than reintroducing order into disorder and thus affording the viewer the very comfort we tend to receive from the 'cinema of consensus', the final challenge issued by the girl – guess with whom he is now living? – is precisely a challenge that, if we are not attentive, pushes us to make the same 'error' that the film has laboured hard to move us away from, namely to reduce life to the level of object-hood, of content. Reminiscent of Sirkian endings that provide the most clichéd resolutions possible after having revealed why such resolutions are precisely impossible, *Longing* teases us with the possibility of gaining comfort through obtaining a potential solution by ultimately challenging us to choose, to decide: Rose or Ella? But it strikes me that the point of the film's epilogue is not a matter of choosing at all. For to choose a solution and thus to affirm one's power to do so would be precisely to practice a mode of perception that the film has rigorously challenged: namely a choice based on the assumption that the girl's story is a truthful re-presentation of the tale we just witnessed. But just as the film itself repeatedly blocked our inclination to respond to it on the level of representational realism, so the storytelling at the end reiterates once more that storytelling primarily serves an affective rather than a truth-telling function: it participates in the distribution of the sensible rather than in the state function of representing.

That the girl's story is in line with the film's aesthetic challenge is marked by the fact that her story actually does not perfectly match what it allegedly represents in the key of reality and truth. In fact, the entire rhetorical exigency of the film's epilogue should make us question its representational function and, indeed, its 'nature'. After all, if the girl were really to tell a true story about the very events we have just witnessed then we would have to ask what the purpose of doing so is, given that her immediate *diegetic* audience – the other children – clearly come from the same village or area and surely would be as familiar with the story as she is, thus making it not only unnecessary for her to tell it but indeed illogical in the way the film presents her act of storytelling as one that presents novelty *to her listeners*. Rather than reinstituting order by explaining to us what happened after the film cuts away from the aftermath of Markus's own suicide attempt, the film's epilogue is *Longing*'s most extreme dramatisation of its redistribution of the sensible, for what we witness here, in the most explicit way possible, is precisely an eruption of those into speech who are otherwise at best spoken for and generally simply ignored. The girl's story – and her interlocutors' responses – do not constitute a representation of what we already know but an intervention on the level of reality itself. Here, the children are neither represented by others nor represent something else but mark their eruption into discourse, into being counted, however momentarily.

Grisebach accomplishes the sharpening of our regard by affective means, rather than by the logic of representation. Of course, we can play the guessing game the girl invites us to play – but it is a *children's* game. What matters to the children, as the entire scene clearly demonstrates, is *the game itself* rather than the outcome, the act of talking – of fabulating – rather than any particular content. What matters, in the end, is their playful experimentation with the very means of perceiving the world, as such experimentation introduces novelty to their realm of experience rather than providing an exercise in truth-telling and -finding susceptible to final judgment. This is why the camera abruptly cuts away and shows the children walk in the distance, leaving us unsure of whether or not the girl revealed the answer to her guessing game. What counts is the act of imagining, and thus producing, reality – of redistributing the sensible – rather than depicting pre-existing reality itself. In this, Grisebach's filmic philosophy might strike us as old-fashioned ('the power of the imagination'), but such an assessment would have to ignore the very a-subjective or pre-subjective logic of affect through which the film works on its viewers. And the institutional response given to the film suggests that this logic cannot easily be folded into the economic desires of the industry and, moreover, seems to threaten the self-proclaimed *Hoheitsrecht* to define what constitutes German national cinema today. For such a small-scale film this is by no means a small accomplishment.

NOTES

1 For an in-depth discussion of the Berlin School see Abel (2008).
2 'We are terribly isolated in the [German] film industry. I choose my words carefully when saying that we were hated in a profound manner' (quoted in Mandelbaum 2009). See also Vahabzadeh (2009), in which Petzold's statement first appeared in German on the day of the German Film Prize award ceremony hosted by the German Film Academy.
3 The German Film Academy, founded in 2003 and opposed by many of the Berlin School directors, desires to be the German pendant to the Academy of Motion Picture Arts and Sciences.

4 Whereas, according to www.ffa.de, *Perfume* attracted more than 5.5 million theatrical viewers, *Longing* petered out at 25,000, a number fairly representative for most Berlin School films other than Christian Petzold's films and Maren Ade's *Everyone Else* (*Alle Anderen*, 2009).

5 For an elaboration of this argument, see Abel (forthcoming).

6 And while these films are no blockbusters abroad, they are the most successful German films in the international marketplace.

7 In various promotional interviews, Grisebach revealed one of the sources for the film's main story. In the DVD booklet, the director informs us that the impressions she gained from the roughly two hundred interviews she conducted with people in rural Brandenburg on the subject of longing began in her mind to combine with a story she was told in a French village about a bricklayer.

8 '*Malerisch*' is an art-historical term meaning 'painterly' introduced by Swiss art historian Heinrich Wölfflin; formally, *malerisch* paintings are very much the opposite of photo-realism.

9 One of the characteristics of the film's hard cuts is that they effect temporal gaps that frequently leave obscure how what precedes such cuts temporally relates to what succeeds them. These narrative ellipses not only create space for the chance immanent to reality as well as the reality of chance to incur into the film's *mise-en-scène* but also imbue the film with a timeless quality that Grisebach strived to achieve (see 2007b) in order to prevent her film from becoming little more than sensationalist social reporting vociferously declaring the 'state of Germany in 2006'.

10 The German '*Sehnsucht*' – a composite of the verb '*sehnen*' and the noun '*Sucht*' – literally means 'the addiction to longing'.

Chapter 12

Too late for love? The cinema of Andreas Dresen on *Cloud 9* (2008)

Laura G. McGee

If cinema has the task of exploring the issues of life, then being old should also be in the movies.

One should never be too sure in life. Not even after thirty years of marriage.

Andreas Dresen (2008b; 2008c)

The population of Germany is aging rapidly. According to data from the German Federal Office for Statistics, people over the age of 65 already make up 20 per cent of the population of nearly 82 million. Even with continued immigration, the low birth rate and rising life expectancy mean that by 2050, the percentage of individuals over the age of 65 is expected to reach 33 per cent of a total population of 69 million.[1] The demographic trend to an aging society in Germany has substantial social, political, economic and cultural implications, not least of all for cinema. This chapter explores the reasons why senior citizens have been underrepresented on the silver screen, and whether the *Seniorenfilm* (senior citizens' film) will likely replace the beloved genre of the *Kinderfilm* (children's film). It argues that the 'geriatric romance' (Johnson 2007: 57) *Cloud 9* (*Wolke 9*) is not simply an aged version of the 1990s relationship comedies decried in Eric Rentschler's essay on the 'cinema of consensus'. According to Rentschler, the protagonists of such comedies – 'attractive, successful and around thirty – run up against the reality principle and confront the responsibilities of the adult world. [...] These films focus on identity crises which are in fact pseudo-crises for they have no depth of despair, no true suffering, no real joy.' Rentschler further expresses the concern that these comedies, for which German cinema had become known in the 1990s, did not travel well, because they were 'out of touch with the world at large and the larger world' (2000: 262–63). In *Cloud 9*, Andreas Dresen sheds light on a serious aspect of contemporary German society that has been largely invisible in cinema, that of love and sex among older people (defined as 60-plus). This chapter examines studies of media representations of older people, as well as post-millennial films about love between older people in order to show the unique contribution of Dresen's film. Finally, it is suggested here that while aspects of Dresen's film seem radical compared to images of the elderly in cinema to date (e.g. the physicality of the aged bodies or the spontaneity of the female protagonist), given recent developments in cinemagoing trends in Germany, *Cloud 9* is quite possibly at the forefront of a shift in cinematic representations of aging.

APPROPRIATED BODIES

Aging is a phenomenon heavily imbued with cultural meaning. Its representation in cinema has been studied by cultural historians, film-studies specialists and gerontologists; thus a crossing of national and disciplinary boundaries serves this discussion. The representation of aging in cinema is both the product of prevailing discourses on aging in society (time-bound and culture-bound), as well as a narrative imposed on the body to serve economic interests. In a study of love and the aging male in early-twentieth-century film, F.M. Hodges finds that cinematographic presentations of geriatric male sexuality faithfully adhere to the medical dogma of the day. The cinematic downfalls and deaths of Immanuel Rath in *The Blue Angel* (*Der blaue Engel*, Josef von Sternberg,1930) and Gustav von Aschenbach in *Death in Venice* (*Morte a Venezia*, Luchino Visconti, 1971) made sense to audiences because they confirmed popular expectations about the penalties of passion and desire among aging males (2003: 20–21). Heather Addison cites age theorist Margaret Morganroth Gullette in noting that aging and the perception of it are a product of culture rather than merely an objective physical process (2005: 32). In Gullette's analysis, youth has been associated with fun, sexuality, intensity and hope, all of which become precious commodities that are threatened as midlife approaches (1997: 5–6). Addison shows that in the wake of mechanisation in the industrial age, manufacturers and advertisers sought consumers to absorb the 'excess' goods that could now be generated. Breeding continual dissatisfaction and envy prompted young adult consumers to buy products purported to maintain their state of youthful attractiveness (2005: 34). What better means to preserve the images of youthfulness – even beyond death – than the film productions of Hollywood, which freeze for eternity the images of youthful beauty? In Foucault's terms then, 'the political investment of the body is bound up [...] with its economic use' (1977: 25–26). Young bodies sell products that allegedly hold off the advance of time, or at least the appearance of it.

If young bodies are imbued with value for economic ends, what is the value of old bodies? Should they appear at all – and to what end? Gerontologist Robert Yahnke finds a didactic use for fourteen international films he selected, because they present 'models of successful aging'. His conclusion:

> A primary task for elders is to serve as mentors and guides, to assist in key transitions in the lives of others, and to affirm and uplift others in the process. Finally, old age is viewed as a time of stability and serenity. The old have arrived at a place of wholeness and resolution, and their character and identity are complemented by their valued place in the community. (2005: 74–75)

Yahnke appropriates examples of senior citizens with normative behaviours for teaching purposes. However, this too utilises aging as a kind of commodity. Writing on 'Aging and the scandal of anachronism', Mary Russo argues *against* conforming to normative ideas of age-appropriate behaviour for, as she puts it, 'acting one's age, in a certain sense, can be understood as a caution against risk-taking [...] until finally, acting one's age means to die' (1999: 27). Not acting one's age, as Russo points out, 'is not only inappropriate but dangerous, exposing the female subject, especially, to ridicule, contempt, pity, and scorn – the scandal of anachronism' (1999: 21). Russo sees such a risk as worthwhile, however, for 'not taking the risk means matching cultural expectations of decrepitude and death' (see Chivers 2006: 213). In *Cloud 9*, it is precisely this 'scandal of anachronism' that motivates Inge's adult daughter to implore her to keep her affair secret.

The silver screen has not been kind to the elderly. Largely absent or appearing as secondary characters, older people tend to be negatively valued, with women faring more poorly than men. David Thomson laments that the film business seems to have dropped older people from their stories, depriving viewers of film narratives of 'people as they become most experienced, most sympathetic and most amusing'. Instead, 'there has been a tendency to suggest that "old-timers" are bitter, grumpy, cantankerous and narrow' (2006). Alonso Duralde observes that 'most characters born before WWII get shoved into one of several shallow senior-citizen categories: doddering, mentorish, frisky or profane' in contrast to the wide variety of characters older people may have in reality (2009). When older characters do appear, men are able to 'move into their 50s and 60s and still be viewed as engaging and sexually attractive stars', as Patrick McCormick suggests in his analysis of Hollywood, an analysis that may be loosely applied to the German context (2001: 46). As examples he cites Sean Connery, Clint Eastwood, Paul Newman and others. Women of the same age, however, have been largely unable to get past the 'wrinkle ceiling' (2001: 47). A substantial study of 100 top-grossing motion pictures from the 1940s to the 1980s found that older female characters are under-represented compared to society at large and more negatively portrayed (Bazzini et al 1997: 531). 'As compared to males, older females were perceived as less friendly, less intelligent, less good, possessing less wealth, and being less attractive' (1997: 541). Whereas men may be perceived to improve with age (accruing wisdom or intellectual competence), women have been taught that the basis for esteem and power is beauty. Thus advancing years will inevitably bring decline, powerlessness and invisibility.

Studies of the German media landscape find that older people are often stereotyped in ways that render them powerless, sexless, or not to be taken seriously. Hanns Flueren, Marion Klein and Heidrun Redetzki-Rodermann's survey of the daily soaps in Germany determined that figures of 60 and older are stereotyped into four categories: the altruist (always there for others, selfless), the professional (white collar, vital, male), those who won't leave the stage (self-centred, manipulative) and the authoritarian (the patriarch) (2002: 24–25). According to the same article, realities of aging are obscured, and viewers could get the impression that following youth there comes a never-ending adulthood. It found that age is constructed and valued from a distinctly male perspective, and that older women are completely accepted only when they make themselves useful to the younger generation (2002: 26). An examination of images of older people in both German- and English-language cinema published in *Film-dienst* determined that more older men than women appear as central figures in feature films (Koebner 2006). Older men who do appear may be terribly lonely and feel useless (*About Schmidt*, Alexander Payne, 2002), be pitiable as they pursue unrequited love for a younger woman (*Nelly and Monsieur Arnaud*, Claude Sautet, 1995), or may rise out of their passivity in a last-ditch effort to leave a legacy (*Ikiru*, Akira Kurosawa, 1952 or *Million Dollar Baby*, Clint Eastwood, 2004). The same article is not optimistic about the portrayal of older women: uninteresting men can become interesting due to their age; they then possess the ability to listen, to consider carefully, to teach and to learn from their own mistakes; feature films seldom grant this capacity to older women (Koebner 2006: 39). The only redeeming female senior citizen Koebner identifies is the British hobby detective Miss Marple, who gains authority and therefore competence because she is connoted asexually due to her age.

Geriatric Romance: the Last Taboo

Do older people fall deeply or suddenly in love – even in the movies? And if so, what does it look like? A little known DEFA production *Age Can't Protect You from Love* (*Alter schützt vor Liebe nicht*, 1989) was directed by Achim Hübner and premiered on 25 February 1990. Its title is a variation on the German proverb 'Alter schützt vor Torheit nicht', which equates in English to 'No fool like an old fool'. The film's brief plot summary suggests that an older person who falls in love can hardly be taken seriously: 'A freshly-minted pensioner falls so heavily in love that it takes his children's breath away. Amusing comedy about a lusty senior citizen' (*Lexikon des internationalen Films* 2000/2001). Apparently, love among older people provides good material for a comedy and appears ridiculous to the younger generation, who are supposed to have the monopoly on love and sex.

In the first decade of the third millennium there are new developments in the direction of a broader representation of the lives of senior citizens on the silver screen. Marion Siegel asserts that a genre such as the 'senior citizens' film' does not exist, since films featuring older people vary so widely in theme and approach (2009). This makes sense, as senior citizens will live another two to three decades after reaching their sixties, several times the period of childhood, in which 'children's films' may have appeal. A quick survey of 14 feature films about older people gives a sense of trends in North American and European cinema. A number of outstanding films since 2000 feature individuals, couples or families grappling with the devastating effects of advancing Alzheimer's, among them *Iris* (Richard Eyre, 2001, UK/USA), *My Father* (*Mein Vater*, Andreas Kleinert, 2003, Germany), *Away from Her* (Sarah Polley, 2006, Canada), and *The Savages* (Tamara Jenkins, 2007, USA). Quite a few comedies have appeared, many of which find their humour in groups of older people who embark on new projects, show outstanding talent, or defy stereotypes of physical decline and associated asexuality. These tend to be upbeat and empowering as older people combine forces and create a productive community with a common goal. Among these are: *Calendar Girls* (Nigel Cole, 2003, UK/USA), *Late Bloomers* (*Die Herbstzeitlosen*, Bettina Oberli, 2006, Switzerland), *Young at Heart* (Stephen Walker, 2007, UK), *Mid-August Lunch* (*Pranzo di Ferragosto*, Gianni Di Gregorio, 2008, Italy) and *Dinosaurier* (Leander Haußmann, 2009, Germany), a remake of the prizewinning *Lina Braake* (Bernhard Sinkel, 1975, Germany). Romantic features often combine genres, for instance American director Nancy Meyers's two romantic comedies, *Something's Gotta Give* (2003, USA) and *It's Complicated* (2009, USA). *Cherry Blossoms – Hanami* (*Kirschblüten Hanami*, Doris Dörrie, 2008, Germany) and *Cloud 9* combine elements of romance and drama, and Dresen's *Whisky with Vodka* (*Whisky mit Wodka*, 2009, Germany) – in typical Dresen style – is both comic and tragic. It is notable that six of the 14 American and European productions mentioned here were directed by women and present strong-minded older women as their heroines.

Romance plays an important role in seven of the 14 films. In *Iris* and *Away from Her*, the loss through Alzheimer's of mental capacities lead to the unwanted end of a long-term loving relationship while both parties are still alive. Nancy Meyers's two comedies poke fun at philandering and superficial older men who prefer young flesh but who come to their senses in the end and return to the smart, witty, wise and sexy women closer to their own age. In *Cherry Blossoms – Hanami*, a man journeys to the place his recently deceased wife always wanted to go in order to know her better and make peace with his memory of her. Both Dresen's films mentioned in this section, *Cloud 9* and *Whisky with Vodka*, feature an older protagonist in a kind of love triangle. Of all the films discussed here, both European and North American, *Cloud 9* stands out in its treatment of the lives of older people. Dresen portrays love, including sex and sexuality, among older people with a kind of brutal honesty that foregrounds the ambivalence of lived realities in contemporary society, a trademark of his storytelling in films even on very different topics. An introduction to Dresen and his films helps set the context for a closer examination of *Cloud 9*.

ANDREAS DRESEN

Andreas Dresen stands out as one of the last (youngest) directors to train in the former East Germany and subsequently to launch a successful career in the unified Germany. In the decade since his breakthrough film *Night Shapes* (*Nachtgestalten*, 1999), Dresen's films have achieved a very positive audience share, with *Summer in Berlin* (*Sommer vorm Balkon*, 2006) reaching nearly a million viewers, and *Cloud 9* garnering a respectable 480,000 since it won the 'Coup de Coeur' ('Heart throb') audience prize at its premiere in Cannes. For the sake of comparison, Fatih Akin's much-heralded *Head-On* (*Gegen die Wand*, 2004) was seen by nearly 780,000 viewers; Hans-Christian Schmid's *Distant Lights* (*Lichter*, 2003) brought 157,000 viewers into the cinemas. Dresen's films appeal because they are entertaining, and are complex because they combine tragic and comic elements in a way that invites reflection, while also offering what Eric Rentschler and other critics found missing in the relationship comedies of the 1990s – an engagement with 'the "large" topics and hot issues, the messy complications of post-wall reality, themes like right-wing radicalism, chronic unemployment, or the uneasy integration of the former GDR into the Federal Republic' (2000: 262).

Dresen came to filmmaking at a very early age. Born in Gera in 1963, he is the son of actress Barbara Bachmann and theatre director Adolf Dresen. He grew up in Schwerin, and by his own account spent many hours as a child in the theatre cantina waiting for his mother, or at home by himself playing puppet theatre. He made his first films as a teenager and took them on a tour of campgrounds in the former East, on what he and his friends nicknamed their 'DREFA Sommertour'.[2] His application to study film at the Academy for Film and Television 'Konrad Wolf' in Potsdam-Babelsberg was rejected – not uncommon

– but he was accepted on the second round, and began studies in 1986. That year a new rector was named to the Academy, Lothar Bisky (more recently associated with the political leadership of the Left Party in Germany). Bisky helped enable the production of critical student films. Dresen's socialisation and training as a filmmaker occurred at a time when there was an increasing desire to show the problems of individuals within society and the problems caused by societal structures, and this has remained a trait of Dresen's film production. Had Bisky not been at the helm of the film school, and had a shift to greater liberalisation not occurred in cultural politics in the late phase of the GDR, students like Dresen and his classmate Andreas Kleinert (director of *My Father*, mentioned above) might very well have been exmatriculated.[3] Like all future feature-film directors in the GDR, Dresen received training in documentary filmmaking, and it provided him with a skill he has utilised both in that genre and in lending his feature films a Dogme-like aesthetic, giving the appearance that the *mise-en-scène* is authentic, rather than constructed.[4] This is effective in *Cloud 9*. With regard to content, even his early student films demonstrate a keen eye for showing human problems in society. An excellent early example is *What Everyone Has to Do* (*Was jeder muss...*, 1988), about a young man completing his military service far away from his wife and new baby. Dresen was offered his diploma after the oral defence for *Short Cut to Istanbul* (*So schnell geht es nach Istanbul*, 1990), but preferred to postpone his graduation so that he could make his first full-length feature film under the auspices of the Academy. That debut was *Silent Country* (*Stilles Land*, 1992), one of the first German films to portray the East German experience of the end of the GDR. *Silent Country* and Dresen's student shorts have been issued on DVD with English subtitles, as have almost all of his features. After a number of productions for television, many with socially critical themes, Dresen made his entrance into cinema production with the risky project *Night Shapes*, nearly seven years in the works. Since then, Dresen has put out almost a film a year, some of them developed through lengthy research and revisions, as *Night Shapes* was, others based on a spontaneous decision about a good script, for example Wolfgang Kohlhaase's *Summer in Berlin*, and still others developed from a concept by a pared-down team working intensively and collaboratively over a period of a few months, for instance *Grill Point* (*Halbe Treppe*, 2002) or *Cloud 9*.

Dresen has said that his collaboration with the same crew and some of the same actors over time facilitates his creative work and makes the risk-taking of films such as *Cloud 9* easier. As creator of a diverse film oeuvre, Dresen has availed himself not of a single, identifiable aesthetic or approach, but has experimented according to subject matter, over a series of films in a progressively collaborative manner that contributes to a particularly edgy, realistic effect often dubbed 'authentic' by reviewers and critics, a simplification Dresen himself rejects.[5] Dresen shares with Fassbinder and other critical filmmakers a desire to point to problems and to encourage reflection and change through cinema. Dresen's films question a diversity of societal structures – less their intent than their actual practice – calling the viewer's attention to his or her own complacency, habits and everyday assumptions. The films do not offer black-and-white scenarios or easy solutions, but rather often ask more questions than they answer. Dresen locates many of his films in the territory he comes from, but the issues he takes up transcend borders – homelessness and the search for love in *Night Shapes*, unemployment and urban blight as well as the experience of women in traditionally male domains in *The Policewoman* (*Die Polizistin*, 2000), political engagement in *Vote for Henryk!* (*Herr Wichmann*, 2003), fear in modern capitalist society in *Willenbrock* (2004), coping with long-term unemployment in *Summer in Berlin*, and love in an aging society in *Cloud 9* – to name many (but not all) of Dresen's films. It becomes apparent that Dresen's films of the 1990s and beyond take up a variety of serious topics.

Several Dresen films before and after *Cloud 9* feature older characters, and along with them some of the challenges and opportunities that aging brings. Dresen cast Christel Peters (1916–2009) for no less than four films, each time representing a different aspect of aging. In *Changing Skins* (*Raus aus der Haut*, 1997), she is the wise and spirited grandmother who intervenes in the kidnapping staged by her granddaughter and granddaughter's boyfriend of their school principal. Because of her life experience and her fearlessness, she commands authority from more than one generation in the film, and her actions help resolve its central conflict. In *Night Shapes*, she is seen very early in the film as a frail, elderly lady whose shopping bags are knocked from her hands by a fleeing thief. She is an indirect victim of crime, and in the busy train station no one heeds her verbal protests. A helpless figure in the tough urban environment, she is almost invisible. She is seen again later as a frail and somewhat isolated resident in a high-rise apartment. In *The Policewoman*, the character she plays suffers from dementia. When the film's protagonist

Anne encounters her, she has wandered once again from the understaffed facility where she lives onto the central reservation of a busy highway. The police can do little more than return her to where she belongs, as they have done many times before. The problem is chronic, and no one is able to effect change. They can only maintain a dysfunctional status quo. In *Summer in Berlin*, Christel Peters plays a feisty, sometimes difficult, older woman – by then she was about ninety – who receives home care from Nike, one of the film's two main characters. She loves to have Nike read her romantic novels, a task for which Nike is not being paid, and for which she receives a scolding from the woman's daughter (played by Dresen's mother, actress Barbara Bachmann). Soon after, the old woman dies quite suddenly while trying to play her accordion. *Whisky with Vodka* presents the story of an aging film star named Otto Kullberg (Henry Hübchen) whose chronic alcohol abuse motivates the production company of his current film project to bring in a younger double, with whom all scenes are filmed a second time. Confronted with the fact that he is so easily replaceable, Otto must pull himself together in an effort to beat out the competition. While he succeeds in completing the film, he remains in many ways an incorrigibly selfish character who has not changed fundamentally at the film's end. He may have performed better than the double assigned to his character when it comes to drinking and carousing, but he has not been victorious over the passage of time, nor over opportunities missed in the past. He remains in many ways a lonely old man. Whereas Otto resists change, Inge in *Cloud 9* embraces change, but must live with the unanticipated consequences.

LOVE AND SEX IN CLOUD 9

In January 2007 Dresen approached his long-time friend and producer Peter Rommel with the idea of making a film about love in old age. This idea had been with him since he saw an exhibit in the 1980s of images of older people photographed naked in their home environments. He had found it odd at first, and then quite natural. A further inspiration was a 1997 short film by Belgian friend Piet Eekman, *My Grandmother's Men* (*Die Männer meiner Oma*, 1997), in which Eekman interviewed his then 78-year-old grandmother about the men in her life. In the film, and also on the DVD of *Cloud 9*, she talks with surprisingly little inhibition about her experiences with men and with sex. Dresen felt that although human beings are living longer, older people are conspicuously absent from film and television portrayals. According to Dresen, the stories that do exist fail to acknowledge that love and sex are a serious part of senior citizens' lives: 'All you find are watered-down stories in which the old folks are allowed to fall in love again in a cute, lukewarm manner. But they are not granted true passion, a racing pulse, sex' (*Wolke 9* Press material 2008: 9). Dresen found that while one can read a great amount about older people and even about older people and sex, there are few images of older people of this kind in cinema (2008a).

Dresen wanted to fill this gap by filming a love story from the point of view of a woman, and using the improvisational method that was so productive with *Grill Point*. The team was to be as small as possible to facilitate the development of dialogues collaboratively, and so that the particularly intimate sex scenes could be filmed more easily. With just the idea for the story in its basic form, he identified potential cast and crew members who agreed to film with him later that spring in Berlin. Despite the controversial topic and the lack of a script, Dresen's friend and producer Peter Rommel found funding for the project, and Senator Film guaranteed distribution even before the film was made, a far cry from Dresen's lengthy struggle to find a distributor for *Night Shapes* less than ten years before. Dresen developed the story for *Cloud 9* collaboratively with dramaturg Cooky Ziesche, scriptwriter Laila Stieler, and editor Jörg Hauschild. They established a plot and ending for the film. The biographies of the characters were then developed in greater detail with the cast, so that each actor had a basis to motivate the actions and dialogue of his/her character. The real work on the film began with the establishment of Ursula Werner, Horst Rehberg and Horst Westphal to play three primary characters. Actress Ursula Werner (born 1943), a member of the ensemble at the Maxim Gorki Theatre in Berlin, plays Inge in the film's main role. Ursula Werner had minor roles in two previous Dresen films: in *The Policewoman* and *Willenbrock*. Her husband Werner is played by Horst Rehberg (born 1937), a long-time theatre actor in Schwerin and Cottbus, who also had a role in Dresen's *Police Call 110: The Exchange* (*Polizeiruf 110: Der Tausch*, 1996). The man with whom she has a relationship is Karl, played by Horst Westphal (born 1929), an experienced actor with a long career on stages in Berlin, Dresden,

Schwerin and Weimar to his credit, as well as diverse television and film appearances, among them in Dresen's *Train in the Distance* (*Zug in die Ferne*, 1990) and *Silent Country*. Inge's grown daughter Petra is played by Steffi Kühnert, a theatre and cinema actress who has had roles in numerous German films, among them Dresen's *Grill Point*. Filming occurred in the Treptow district of Berlin and outside the city from mid-May to early July 2007.

Inge is in her late sixties, retired, and living with Werner, her husband of thirty years, in their Treptow apartment. She sews occasionally to supplement her retirement income and, it appears, to keep busy. She sings in a choir and has a close relationship with her daughter. Her husband Werner is a retired school teacher and train fanatic who rides the train because he enjoys it, not because he is going anywhere. The motif of train riding as a simple pleasure rather than to get somewhere different becomes a metaphor for Werner's view of their relationship. Werner and Inge are most often seen in interior shots at home, except when they are riding the train. Even the shots in the train carriage show Werner and Inge separated by glass and steel from nature rushing by. While Werner is happy to live this way, Inge seems to feel isolated, even trapped. On one such ride she cries. Werner's train riding is in essence a circular, or stationary movement, like the rotation of the vinyl LPs on which he listens to recordings of locomotives from the GDR. There is no trajectory from one place to another, little or no forward movement, but rather a satisfaction with the present moment, and to a certain degree a nostalgic orientation. Their life together is comfortable, steady and not without tenderness and sex. However, Inge and Werner are in fact going somewhere. The routines of daily life and of caring for the aging body (Inge helps Werner with simple physical exercises to help maintain his strength; she shampoos his hair in a bathtub scene, as one might typically do for a child), suggesting an inevitable physical and mental decline and a narrowing of life's possibilities that will eventually end in death. While in many ways positively weighted, the figure of Werner is also associated with fear of this decline and death, as indicated in a scene with his own father in a nursing home, where Inge feeds Werner's father strawberries one by one, again as if he were a child. On leaving, Werner says to Inge, 'If I ever end up like that, you can take me into the forest and shoot me.' When Inge discovers in Karl a kind of opposition to her current life, she risks Russo's 'scandal of anachronism' (1999). As she puts it to Werner during an argument,

Figure 12.1: Werner likes to ride the train. Inge begins to cry.

she just wanted to fall in love one more time (implication: before she dies).

Leaving her apartment on a warm, sunny afternoon, Inge walks swiftly along a pavement. The highly sexualised image of large amounts of swirling, floating poplar pollen that fill the air like large snowflakes, an occurrence that lasts only briefly late each spring in Berlin, set the stage for what is about to take place. Inge delivers a pair of altered trousers to the apartment of a man named Karl, whom she apparently hardly knows. There is a sudden intimacy as he tries on altered trousers in his living room, and within minutes they are having sex on the floor. The room is so flooded by bright daylight that parts of the image seem overexposed, adding to an association of newness, even awkwardness and discomfort with the scene. The association of bright natural light with Inge's relationship to Karl continues throughout the film. The interiors of Karl's apartment are lighter than Inge and Werner's. The brightness of scenes associated with Karl or with Inge and Karl together suggest that Dresen wishes to shed light on the subject of love and sex between older people to place a positive association on this otherwise taboo topic. The brightness further represents Inge's optimism and her openness to something new. After being with Karl, we see her looking at herself in the mirror naked, as if discovering anew the sexual being that she is. Sex between Inge and Karl is full of tenderness, passion and even laughter. Having met Karl, Inge begins to see Werner in a different light. Opposing worlds collide.

Figure 12.2: Inge delivers trousers. The pollen of poplar trees fills the air.

Werner is a train rider. Karl is a cyclist. Werner goes along for the ride, just to watch the scenery fly by. Karl pedals hard to get somewhere. And he wants to feel and smell the world around him while doing it. Inge feels attracted to this life force, and despite her efforts to convince herself that 'Riding the train can be nice too', her husband Werner fades increasingly into Karl's shadow.

Unable and unwilling to keep her strong feelings to herself, Inge tells her daughter Petra about Karl, and subsequently confesses her affair to her husband Werner against Petra's advice. The drama of these events is heightened through omissions to the dialogue made in cutting and montage. On an afternoon when Inge and Petra talk in a café, the viewer can imagine what Inge has said as Petra reacts with 'Oh! Really!?' The conversation that follows is rendered not through shot/reverse-shot of mother and daughter conversing, but instead the camera shows Inge's face as she expresses first her euphoria, then her longing for Karl, and finally as she panics about the implications. The very tight cutting as Inge speaks adds tempo to the avalanche of emotions when she finally expresses what she has never before put into words. Petra encourages Inge to enjoy her affair, but advises her not to say a word to Werner. Inge, however, finds it impossible to continue to lie to Werner. The scene in which she finally tells Werner is similarly pared-down, beginning not with her words, but with his: 'Could you repeat that?' The camera focuses not on her, but on him, his eyes wide with disbelief. Werner is angry. 'Have you lost your marbles?' he yells at her. The hand-held camera stays close, nearly between the two as they spar in the kitchen. In this film, the camera's emphasis on close shots of faces is characteristic of the entire film, compelling the viewer to follow Inge – and Karl and Werner – through a range of experiences and emotions from elation to rage to despair. Inge is a strong female figure who makes an extremely difficult decision that has consequences.

MORE 'SILVER SEX' ON THE WAY

With *Cloud 9*, Andreas Dresen breaks new ground in the portrayal of the lives of older people in cinema. *Cloud 9* is neither a romantic comedy nor a tragic story of Alzheimer's, as are many films featuring older people even in this millennium. Instead, it offers a serious treatment of love, of passion and of sex among older people. The pared-down approach to plot and dialogue, as well as the close-up shots of faces draw viewers into the emotions stirred in Inge by her late-in-life love affair. Inge is alternately 'on cloud nine' due to her feelings for Karl and devastated by the loss of the comfortable intimacy she had with Werner in their thirty-year marriage. For older people, 'falling in love' may or may not have age-specific implications. With this film, Dresen suggests it does. In any case, *Cloud 9* has called much attention to a neglected aspect of the lives of a growing demographic in Germany. According to Vera Bamler, in her article 'Sexualität im Alter – (k)ein Problem?' (2009: 5), the sex lives of older people are more strongly represented in the media since *Cloud 9*. For psychotherapist Kirsten von Sydow, this is at least in part due to the fact that the '68 generation is reaching senior-citizen status. Von Sydow is cited as saying that today's 60- to 70-year-olds are more self-determined and make higher demands on the quality of partnerships, relationships and sexuality than did the previous generation (Siegel 2008). The 2008 publication of the German-language translation of sex expert Ruth Westheimer's book *Dr. Ruth's Sex After 50* made a splash across German popular media, and brought this topic further into public awareness.[6] Even as life expectancy continues to rise, the life span for women remains ahead of men's, leaving more time and more disposable income in the hands of women. According to Thane Peterson in *Businessweek* magazine, this is likely to have implications for the box office (2003). While box-office attendance was down overall in Germany according to a 2004 report, it was up for the over-fifty age group (Bennett and Taylor 2004: 56). It is likely that realistic, dynamic and differentiated portrayals of the lives of senior citizens on the silver screen will continue to grow. Dresen's *Cloud 9* is part of a strong first step in that direction.

NOTES

My sincere thanks to Brittany Duncan, Derek Dunkelberger, Sean Kinder, Brooke Shafar, Spencer Walters and Rialda Zukic for lively discussions, feedback and/or assistance with research as this manuscript took shape.

1 An interactive population pyramid shows percentages based on the '12. koordinierte Bevölkerungsberechnung': http://www.destatis.de/bevoelkerungspyramide.
2 This word play combines 'DEFA' (the film production company for all films in East Germany) with 'Dresen'.
3 Lothar Bisky describes his time as Rector at the Academy for Film and Television 'Konrad Wolf' in Potsdam-Babelsberg in Chapter 7 of his autobiography (Bisky 2005: 131–56).
4 'Dogme' refers to the Dogme Manifesto (1995) of Danish filmmakers Lars von Trier and Thomas Vinterberg, which is very purist in its call for the use only of objects and light found on site in making a film, rather than the construction of these.
5 While Dresen's films have repeatedly been described as having or showing 'authenticity', he himself distances himself from the idea. He has often stated that all films, even Dogme films are a created product. See Hallberg and Wewerka 2001 or Abel 2009.
6 On 22 October 2008, Westheimer appeared on the Johannes B. Kerner show. She discussed her book and Dresen's *Cloud 9*.

Chapter 13

'Seeing everything with different eyes': the diasporic optic of Fatih Akin's *Head-On* (2004)

Daniela Berghahn

When in his seminal article 'From New German Cinema to the post-wall cinema of consensus' (2000) Eric Rentschler mourns the demise of the West German *Autorenkino* and with it the loss of a critical edge, political commitment and artistic innovation in contemporary German cinema, he could not have reckoned with the invigorating creative force of the Young Turks, which was yet to establish itself. German-Turkish directors Thomas Arslan and Fatih Akin are mentioned almost as an afterthought at the very end of Rentschler's essay and referred to as the 'pliers of a liminal cinema' that surveys the 'multicultural realities of a post-Wall community' (2000: 275). At the turn of the millennium it would have required some farsightedness to predict that the revival of German cinema would be in no small measure due to German-Turkish filmmakers, above all, star director Fatih Akin. After a promising start with his feature-film début *Short Sharp Shock* (*Kurz und schmerzlos*, 1998), a ghetto-centric gangster movie aesthetically modelled on *Mean Streets* (1973) by the Italian-American director Martin Scorsese and sharing a number of similarities with Matthieu Kassovitz's *Hate* (*La Haine*, 1995), his breakthrough came with the critically acclaimed *Head-On* (*Gegen die Wand*, 2004), the first German film in 18 years (after Reinhard Hauff's *Stammheim*) to win the Golden Bear at the International Film Festival in Berlin. At the time, the jury's decision was interpreted as a political signal that reflected a change of attitude towards a 'migrant cinema, which has depicted Germany for more than 20 years as the immigration country it refuses to be' (Nicodemus 2004a). The press celebrated the 'Turkish renewal of German cinema' (Nicodemus 2004a), thereby explicitly acknowledging the impact which second-generation German-Turkish filmmakers such as Akin and Arslan and less prominent directors such as Ayşe Polat, Züli Aladağ and Sülbiye Günar have had on German film culture.

Of course, the cinematic portrayal of migrants in German cinema is nothing new, but dates back to the late 1970s, when the New German Cinema's celebrated *auteurs* made films about Turks and other immigrant communities in Germany. Films like Rainer Werner Fassbinder's *Ali: Fear Eats the Soul* (*Angst essen Seele auf,* 1974), Helma Sanders-Brahms's *Shirin's Wedding* (*Shirins Hochzeit,* 1976), Werner Schroeter's *Palermo or Wolfburg* (*Palermo oder Wolfburg,* 1980) and subsequent films made by German director Hark Bohm (*Yasemin,* 1988) and Turkish director Tevfik Başer (*Forty Square Metres of Germany* [*40 Quadratmeter Deutschland*], (1986); *Farewell to a False Paradise* [*Abschied vom falschen Paradies*], (1989) are pessimistic narratives about the marginalisation of migrants and the victimisation of Turkish women. Except for Fassbinder's highly stylised art-house film, these cinematic texts stand in the tradition of the social-problem film, relying on a 'heavy dose of documentary realism to bring to public attention a variety of social concerns' (Fenner 2006: 23). The first phase of German-Turkish cinema is dominated by narratives which perpetuate predictable binary oppositions such as 'urban/ rural, oriental/occidental, native/other, hegemonic/subaltern, oppressor /victim' and seek to arouse the viewer's 'sense of moral indignation and compassion' (Fenner 2006: 24–25). While this trend still continues in a number of films made by second-generation German-Turkish filmmakers, on the whole the coming-of-age of the next generation of directors initiated a shift from miserabilist social dramas to a cinema that offers a more differentiated picture of the Turkish diasporic community. By and large their films depict hyphenated identities not as a precarious state of the in-between but instead as a source of mutual cultural enrichment.

Most of the Young Turks were either born in or came to Germany at a very young age. 'Home' for these filmmakers tends to be Hamburg or Berlin, rather than Ankara or Istanbul. A significant number of films made by second-generation German-Turkish directors engage with issues of identity and belonging, but there are also some that cannot be categorised as migrant or diasporic cinema because they eschew what Kobena Mercer has called 'the burden of representation'

(1990). The Young Turks refuse to be the spokespeople for their ethnic constituency, and want the freedom to choose themes not related to their migratory background. Mennan Yapo's *Soundless* (*Lautlos*, 2004) is a thriller about an assassin that emulates the French *cinéma du look*; Bülent Akinci's *Running on Empty* (*Der Lebensversicherer*, 2006) and Thomas Arslan's *Vacation* (*Ferien*, 2007) feature the existential conflicts of German protagonists. Still, the majority of hyphenated-identity directors play an important role as cultural brokers, and their status within German and Turkish cultures often rests on them being mediators of marginality and alterity. As Graham Huggan argues in *The Postcolonial Exotic: Marketing the margins*, cultural and ethnic otherness has become part of a 'booming "alterity industry"' in which 'marginality [has become] a valuable intellectual commodity' (2001: vii–viii). Fatih Akin, whom Nezih Erdoğan characterises as a 'skilful strategist, complicit in the construction of an intriguing media image that sparks debates and controversies which go far beyond the themes and quality of his films' (2009: 27), is certainly making the most of this market opportunity, deploying strategies of 'self-othering' in the successful attempt to shift his films out of the ethnic niche – to which much of German-Turkish cinema was hitherto relegated – into the mainstream.

This chapter explores how the interstitial position which Fatih Akin occupies as a diasporic Turkish filmmaker is inscribed in his films, in particular his greatest commercial and critical success *Head-On*. Drawing on recent theoretical debates about 'transnational' and 'migrant and diasporic' cinema, it seeks to identify a number of distinctive thematic concerns and aesthetic strategies employed by Akin which make this film a textbook example of contemporary diasporic cinema in Europe.

DEFINING MIGRANT AND DIASPORIC CINEMA

The growing attention that has recently been paid to the work of film directors with a migratory background, both in the context of German and other national cinemas, goes hand in hand with a general shift from national to transnational film studies. In the era of globalisation, hitherto prevalent critical approaches probing the relationship between the cinemas of particular nation-states and national identity no longer corresponds straightforwardly with the reality of film production and circulation. Much of contemporary

European cinema is transnational in respect of its multinational or pan-European sources of funding, its transnationally mobile crew and its target audiences. In comparison with global Hollywood, however, diasporic cinema tends to be more limited in its address, targeting primarily specific national audiences, diasporic collectivities dispersed across several countries or continents, as well as cosmopolitan cinephiles with an interest in world cinema.

Migrant and diasporic cinema challenges the concept of national cinema and 'the national' inasmuch as it articulates and constructs migrant and diasporic identities which transcend the boundaries of the nation-state. It is a particular type of transnational cinema that resists the homogenising effect of globalisation, foregrounding instead issues of cultural and ethnic diversity. It is concerned with the collective memory or the postmemory (Hirsch 1997) of the migratory experience, which has had a profound impact on the cultural identity and the aesthetic sensibilities of migrant and diasporic filmmakers. While migrant filmmakers are first-generation immigrants who have themselves experienced migration,[1] diasporic filmmakers are second- or subsequent-generation immigrants, either born and/or raised in the destination country. They have no personal recollection of migration and often little familiarity with their parents' country of origin. They access their families' histories of migration and dispersal through oral history, family photos and home videos. Occasionally the boundaries between the two are blurred, given that many filmmakers migrated at a very young age. Moreover, in order to avoid an essentialising understanding of migrant and diasporic cinema, based on the filmmakers' biology or biography, it is imperative to open up the concept by including films borne out of the cross-pollination occurring in the 'diaspora space' (Brah 1996: 209) made by filmmakers who articulate a prosthetic memory (Landsberg 2003) of migration and diaspora but who themselves belong to the majority culture (see Berghahn and Sternberg, 2010).

Migrant and diasporic cinema is characterised by a distinctive aesthetic approach, which reflects the 'diasporic optic' (Moorti 2003) of its creators. Inscribed in migrant and diasporic cinema is a particular 'way of seeing [...which] underscores the interstice, the spaces that are and fall between the cracks of the national and the transnational as well as other social formations' (Moorti 2003: 359). Diasporic aesthetics reflect a 'subject position that lays claim to and negotiates between multiple affiliations [...and that] seeks to reveal [a] desire for multiple homes through specific representational strategies' (Moorti 2003: 359). Consequently, migrant and diasporic cinema is aesthetically hybrid, juxtaposing and fusing stylistic templates, generic conventions, narrative and musical traditions, languages and performance styles from more than one (film) culture.

Born out of the experience of displacement, migrant and diasporic cinema is characterised by a heightened sense of mobility. The dominance of transitional and liminal spaces signals that this particular type of transnational cinema is concerned with identities in flux. A predilection for claustrophobic interiors (especially in early German-Turkish cinema) and locations on the peripheries of global cities (e.g. the *banlieue* in Maghrebi-French cinema) underscores the social marginalisation experienced by many migrant and diasporic subjects. As a cinema that originates from marginalised collectivities that are negotiating their place in the social fabric of hegemonic host societies, migrant and diasporic cinema is centrally concerned with identity politics and the 'other'. It probes difference along the multiple coordinates of race, colour, ethnicity, nationality, gender, religion, generation, class and sexuality. Its strategic agenda is the relocation of the margins to the centre, the valorisation and, ultimately, 'the redemption of the marginal' (Stam 2003: 35).

FATIH AKIN: HEIGHTENED MOBILITY, CONTESTED BELONGING

Born in Hamburg-Altona to Turkish parents in 1973, Fatih Akin began his career in the film industry as an actor. But as he got tired of playing the stereotypical Turk, he turned to scriptwriting with the intention of developing less clichéd roles for himself. When Akin pitched the screenplay for *Short Sharp Shock* to Wüste Film Productions, producer Ralph Schwingel discovered the aspiring scriptwriter's talent and suggested that, rather than playing the Turk Gabriel in the film, he try his hand at directing (Schwingel 2007). During the next few years, Akin and Schwingel worked together on the road movie *In July* (*Im Juli*, 2000) and on *Solino* (2002), the story of an Italian immigrant family in Duisburg.[2] In 2004, Akin founded his own film-production company, Corazón International, which co-produced *Head-On*, as well as Akin's subsequent films: the musical documentary *Crossing the Bridge: The Sound of Istanbul* (2005), *The Edge of Heaven* (*Auf der anderen Seite*, 2007) and *Soul Kitchen* (2009).

At the beginning of his career, Akin referred to himself as a German filmmaker (Mitchell 2006), cited the films of Martin Scorsese and John Cassavetes as his chief inspiration, and downplayed his Turkish background. But with the surprise success of the German-Turkish co-production *Head-On*, this changed and the hyphenated-identity director publicly pronounced his dual allegiance to Germany and Turkey: 'I have dual German and Turkish citizenship. I consider myself as a German director [...]. But my personality is split in two – and I still don't know whether I am a Turk or a German' (Akin 2004). In the Turkish press, Akin was reported to have said in 2005, 'I am a gypsy in Hamburg and a dervish in Istanbul [...] My home is Hamburg but I am also the spicy voice of Istanbul. And I love spicy food. I need spice to feel alive' (cited in Erdoğan 2009: 34). As Nezih Erdoğan outlines in 'Star director as symptom: reflections on the reception of Fatih Akin in the Turkish media' (2009), the German-Turkish filmmaker has been at the centre of hotly contested media debates in Turkey, which, on the one hand, claim the prodigal Turkish son for their own national (film) culture while, on the other hand, criticising him for refusing to do military service in Turkey.

Since Akin has embraced his Turkish roots with pride, he has embarked on a mission that seeks to reposition Turkey and Turkish culture in the shifting geographies of the new Europe. For example, the musical documentary *Crossing the Bridge: The Sound of Istanbul* makes much of the suspension bridge across the Bosporus which connects Europe and Asia, the Occident and the Orient, and to which the film title alludes. The trope of the bridge, frequently invoked to underscore the idea of two 'ostensibly discrete cultures, religions and civilizations' (Adelson 2005: 6), is the film's central conceit, and is used by Akin to highlight Turkey's important strategic position. At the beginning of the film, its narrative voice Alexander Hacke of the German experimental band Einstürzende Neubauten comments: '72 nations have crossed this bridge', thus proposing that Turkey is by no means on the periphery of Europe, but instead occupies a central position in international relations and cultural exchange.

In fact, the majority of Akin's films seem to suggest that all paths lead to Istanbul, with their transnationally mobile protagonists embarking on journeys of various kinds that take them to Turkey. *In July* is an exuberant road movie that takes its protagonist Daniel (Moritz Bleibtreu) away from his dull and secure existence as a schoolteacher in Hamburg across the Balkans to Istanbul in pursuit of the elusive Melek (Idil Üner), a Turkish woman with whom he falls in love at the beginning of the film. The film is replete with border crossings, chance encounters en route, and culminates in the protagonist's decision not to return to Germany but to continue his travels towards eastern Turkey. In an ironic cameo appearance, Akin inserts himself into the film's diegesis, playing the dim-witted border official at the makeshift Romanian-Hungarian border who performs an impromptu wedding for Daniel and his travel companion Juli. As Rob Burns notes in his discussion of the film, 'just as the border-guard demonstrates how easily seemingly impermeable boundaries can be effaced' when, after the wedding, 'he does not allow Daniel simply to duck under the barrier but insists on having it removed from his path – so, too, the director conceives his film as a whole as dismantling obstacles to transnational understanding' (2009: 24).

Similarly, the six main characters of the multi-strand narrative of Akin's *The Edge of Heaven* move back and forth between Turkey and Germany – and end up in Turkey, regardless of their national origins. Clearly, home has become a negotiable and relative concept. Nejat (Baki Davrak), a professor of German literature and son of a Turkish 'guestworker', travels from Bremen to Istanbul in search of Ayten (Nurgül Yesilçay), a Turkish political activist, in order to inform her of her mother's accidental death at the hands of his father. Meanwhile the beautiful and fiery Ayten has fled to Germany to seek political asylum, but is deported and imprisoned upon her return to Turkey. Her German friend and lover Lotte (Patrycia Ziolkowska) follows her to Turkey, hoping to secure her release from prison, but is accidentally shot dead in the backstreets of Istanbul. Nejat's father, Ali (Tuncel Kurtiz), is also sent back to Turkey after completing his prison sentence in Germany. Lotte's mother (Hanna Schygulla) comes to Istanbul in order to retrace the last steps of her daughter and to accomplish Lotte's mission, the liberation of Ayten. Nejat relinquishes his professorship at a German university, takes over a German bookshop in Istanbul and stays in Turkey for good. The film's final scene shows him on the shores of the Black Sea, where he is awaiting his father's return from a fishing trip.

The protagonists' intersecting itineraries between Turkey and Germany seem to suggest that the two countries have moved closer together in the age of transnational mobility – and perhaps not just in terms of geography. Akin's films draw attention to the interweaving of Turkish and German cultures. For example, by casting Hanna Schygulla, Rainer Werner Fassbinder's muse and one of the most prominent screen icons of New German Cinema, and Tuncel Kurtiz, best known in the West for his collaboration with the late director Yılmaz Güney, Akin intended to bring together 'two living film legends [...] who wrote film history' (Akin 2008). By paying homage to Turkish and German film histories, he acknowledges the impact of both upon his own creative sensibilities.

Yet this form of intertextuality is only one of numerous devices through which Akin draws attention to the 'other within', thereby problematising the notion of difference and the designation of Turkey as Europe's 'other'. On the level of narrative, for example, *The Edge of Heaven* frequently links difference and commonality (Burns 2009: 18). The accidental killing of the Turkish prostitute Yeter (Nursel Köse) in the film's first chapter corresponds to the accidental killing of the German student Lotte in the second; Ali's imprisonment in Germany is mirrored by Ayten's in Turkey; Yeter's coffin is unloaded from an aeroplane at Atatürk airport, while Lotte's coffin is loaded onto what looks like the same aeroplane, which will take her body back to Germany.

More interestingly, perhaps, is the process of appropriating the 'other' in terms of cinematic, musical and narrative traditions. Nowhere is Akin's aesthetic strategy of creolising appropriation, the intermeshing of Turkish and German cinematic and musical traditions, more apparent than in the melodramatic love story *Head-On*.

The Diasporic Optic of Head-On

Head-On is the story of a dark and destructive passion which unexpectedly develops between 20-year-old Sibel (Sibel Kekilli) and 44-year-old Cahit (Birol Ünel), both of Turkish origin and living in Hamburg. They meet in a clinic after having attempted suicide: Sibel by slitting her wrists, Cahit by driving head-on against a brick wall with his car (hence the film's German title, *Gegen die Wand*). The beautiful and highly promiscuous Sibel proposes a marriage of convenience to the cocaine-sniffing Cahit because she hopes to escape from her family's vigilant efforts to protect her honour through an alibi marriage. 'I want to live, Cahit. I want to live, I want to dance, I want to fuck. And not just with one guy. Do you understand!?' she explains to Cahit, before smashing a beer bottle and slitting her wrists with it. The drop-out Cahit appears to be the ideal husband in such a set-up, since he has nothing to lose and is likely to give Sibel the freedom she desires, while his Turkish background will make him acceptable in the eyes of her parents.

The traditional Turkish wedding is a sham, and Sibel spends the wedding night with another man. However, all is well until Sibel and Cahit fall in love with each other, an unforeseen change in the couple's relationship marked by Sibel cooking a traditional Turkish meal for her husband – her mother's recipe, as she stresses. That night, Cahit accidentally kills Nico, one of Sibel's lovers. Cahit is sentenced to several years in prison and Sibel flees to Istanbul in order to escape her brother's retribution for the shame she has brought upon the family. There, she gradually succumbs to the same self-destructive impulse that determined Cahit's actions in Hamburg: she drinks heavily, starts taking opium, gets raped and provokes a group of thugs to beat her up and nearly kill her. But she survives. Several years later, Cahit is released from prison and tracks her down in Istanbul. When the two meet again, they are both reformed characters: Cahit no longer looks like a tramp, and sticks to water rather than alcohol. Sibel has traded the role of *femme fatale* for that of mother. She has a four-year-old daughter, lives with her boyfriend, presumably the girl's father, and

Figure 13.1: Sibel and Cahit staging a traditional Turkish wedding.

wears androgynous clothes and a short-cropped boyish hairstyle. Even though she agrees to a few nights of clandestine passion with Cahit in a hotel in Istanbul, she ultimately decides that her future lies with her family. The film's penultimate scene shows Cahit embark alone on his onward journey to Mersin. Mersin, though not his home town as such, is his family's place of origin, and therefore seems to offer Cahit, a second-generation Turkish immigrant and German citizen, the opportunity to reclaim his Turkish identity. Cahit's journey to his parents' Heimat is but one of many instances of what could be interpreted as itineraries of reverse migration in Akin's oeuvre.[3] As I have argued elsewhere (2006a), such home-seeking journeys do not only put an end to the protagonists' hyper-mobile restlessness but also hail the promise of their redemption.

Not only is the plot of *Head-On* a far cry from the predictable conflicts and ethnic stereotypes of the first wave of German-Turkish cinema, Akin's prizewinning film also represents a new departure in terms of the hybrid aesthetic strategies he employs to tell this melodramatic love story. The film music ranges from popular Turkish songs such as 'Dönmeyen yıllar', performed by the famous *Arabesk* singer Orhan Gencebay, and Sezen Aksu's 'Yine mi Çiçek' to international hits such as 'I Feel You' by Depeche Mode and tracks by German avant-garde and new-wave artists Alexander Hacke ('Tract') and Mona Mur ('Snake' and 'Into your Eyes'). This seemingly eclectic mix of roughly forty songs reflects the multiple cultural affiliations of the director and of his protagonists, Sibel and Cahit. But it does more than just that. 'The soundtrack is the heart of *Head-On*,' writes Andreas Busche (2004). The music determines the film's narrative structure, underscores the characters' feelings and frames of mind and serves as a running commentary. For example, the lyrics of Wendy René's soulful number 'After Laughter (Comes Tears)', which we hear as a radiantly smiling Sibel buys a gingerbread heart with 'I love you' written on it for Cahit, anticipates the disastrous turn which Cahit and Sibel's *amour fou* will take in the very next scene when Cahit kills Sibel's lover with a fatal blow.

Nowhere is the significance of music more apparent than in the six musical interludes which frame and interrupt the linear narrative of *Head-On*. The film's opening scene shows a musical ensemble, consisting of six men dressed in black tie and one woman in a long vibrant red dress, performing against the picturesque backdrop of the Golden Horn and the Süleyman Mosque in Istanbul. The six musicians, who are symmetrically arranged with the female singer at the centre, sit on chairs on a stage made up of layered Turkish rugs, facing directly into the camera. This tableau, reminiscent of a clichéd picture-postcard impression of Istanbul, is repeated five more times with some minor modifications. The static and repetitive nature of the musical interludes introduces an element of stasis, interrupting the narrative flow and contrasting with the protagonists' mobility and search for identity and belonging.

The Roma clarinettist Selim Sesler and his ensemble accompany Idil Üner, a German-Turkish actress and familiar face from numerous recent films, who sings mournfully about the pain of unrequited love. The poetic lyrics of the first song, 'Saniye'm', express the suffering of a man whose love for Saniye, with her long floating hair, remains unanswered. Other songs follow, similar in mood and tone. The lyrics of the film's final ballad, 'Su karsiki dagda bir fener yanar', which sets in as Cahit realises that Sibel will not join him on the bus to Mersin, vocalise Cahit's silent despair: 'Over there on the mountain a beacon is burning, falcons fly over its shimmering light. Have all those who love and who have lost their lovers lost their senses like me? I am

Figure 13.2: Musical interludes against a clichéd picture-postcard impression of Istanbul.

infinitely sad. May my enemies go blind. I have lost my mind. May the mountains rejoice in my stead.' The archaic nature imagery invoked here to describe the pain of lost love creates an incongruous juxtaposition with the ugly urban setting of Istanbul bus station and the grey concrete bridge across the intersection of the motorway which marks Cahit's point of departure and final separation from Sibel. This apparent incongruity extends to the protagonists: two damaged, self-destructive individuals whose feelings of desire and despair are elevated by these poetic ballads about unrequited love.

While, on the one hand, the musical interludes underscore the protagonists' emotions, fulfilling a similar function to the non-diegetic mood music in classical Hollywood melodrama, on the other hand, the on-screen appearance of the musical ensemble precludes precisely the affective response in the audience normally triggered by the musical scores of melodrama. In fact, the musical interludes and the epic narrative of the lyrics have been variously compared to the chorus of a Greek tragedy, the distanciation devices of Brecht's epic theatre, and even 'the aesthetic of switches and inserts [...] described by Lalitha Gopalan with reference to Bollywood as a *Cinema of Interruptions*' (Göktürk, 2010: 221). Rather than inviting the audience's emotional identification, the musical interludes draw attention to the staging of the melodrama.

Akin plays with and subverts the conventions of melodrama further when, at the end of the sixth musical interlude, the musicians rise from the chairs on which they have been sitting and bow, signalling that their performance is over. Through this simple gesture, the ontological status of the entire film and its relation to the orchestral interludes is questioned: 'Has the audience watched a film with orchestral interludes, or a concert with cinematic inserts?' asks Deniz Göktürk in 'Sound bridges: transnational mobility as ironic melodrama' (2010). Is the film's entire narrative merely an illustration, or rather an updated version of the fateful love rendered in the traditional songs?

The problems arising in the attempt to assign an unambiguous meaning to the musical intervals are largely due to the fact that the sources of Fatih Akin's artistic inspirations are difficult to trace. He is 'tapping into a warehouse of cultural images' (Moorti 2003: 359) taken from classical Greek, German, Turkish and possibly even Indian high culture and/or popular culture, taking a mix-and-match approach, thereby creating an innovative representational grammar 'that seeks to capture the dislocation, disruption and ambivalence that characterizes' (Moorti 2003: 359) his protagonists' lives – and, arguably, his own: in Hamburg, Fatih Akin revealed in an interview, 'I no longer have the eye for telling stories [...] But in Turkey I have the feeling that I'm seeing everything with different eyes' (Akin, Beier and Matussek 2007).

Although Akin declares that his Hamburg home has become all too familiar to nourish his creativity and imagination, pitting it against the invigorating force of Turkey, coded as the foreign and exotic other, his films tell a different story. Their most distinctive aesthetic strategy is what Moorti theorises under the concept of the 'diasporic optic'. She compares it to a 'sideways look' (2003: 360) that does not endeavour to reproduce home in the diaspora by 'superimposing images of home and abroad, past and present, on each other'. Instead, the diasporic optic reconstitutes home 'in several locales simultaneously [...] it centres on the affect and desire to produce home as a tenuous fragile web of relations [...] shared affiliations and longings' (Moorti 2003: 360). By drawing on the epistemes and cultural codes of more than one culture simultaneously, it probes existing representational practices and invites multiple decoding positions, which depend on the culturally specific knowledge of the audience.

Thus, in the attempt to make sense of the rich intertexuality of *Head-On*, a German audience is likely to tap into a warehouse of cultural connotations significantly different from those associated with Turkish or German-Turkish audiences. German cinephiles are likely to place *Head-On* in 'the genealogy of Sirk-Fassbinder melodrama into which Akin is inscribing himself' (Elsaesser 2008). While the German-born Hollywood *émigré* Detlef Sierck/Douglas Sirk subverted the conventions of classical Hollywood melodrama in numerous ways, Fassbinder inflected the generic conventions further when he gave Sirkian melodrama a distinctly Brechtian twist. According to Fassbinder, Brechtian distanciation techniques invite the audience to witness emotions and to reflect upon them, but forestalls emotional identification. Fassbinder wanted to go further than that by letting his audience 'feel *and* think': 'I want to give the spectator the emotions along with the possibility of reflecting on and analysing what he is feeling,' he stated in a much-quoted interview with *Cineaste* in 1977. Just as much as Fassbinder denied his indebtedness to Brechtian aesthetics, arguably, as Gerd Gemünden suggests, to highlight his 'own originality and creativity' (1994: 59), Fatih Akin denies the influence of Fassbinder upon his oeuvre – yet film critics and scholars do not seem to tire of tracing the affinities between these two prolific German *auteurs* (see Akin, Beier and Matussek 2007; Handling 2007; Elsaesser 2008). Both rely on melodrama to reach large audiences, and both inflect this popular genre through their own distinctive signatures. Both infuse melodrama with a high degree of artificiality, be it static tableaux, multiple framing devices and a Sirkian camp use of colour in the case of Fassbinder's *Ali: Fear Eats the Soul*, or the similarly static tableaux of the musical interludes, which look like deliberately corny picture postcards from Istanbul, or the architectonic symmetry of mirror-image scenes, through which Cahit's and Sibel's lives are connected. For example, in the Hamburg-based part of the film, Cahit dances, suffused in red light with blood streaming down his arms in a bar, while in the Istanbul-based part of the film, Sibel dances under the influence of drugs and alcohol with a red spotlight illuminating her face, while the other guests stare at her, bewildered.[4] The semicircle of patrons in the bar, fixing their eyes upon Sibel's trance-like dance, is also reminiscent of the scene in Fassbinder's *Ali: Fear Eats the Soul* in which the female bartender and guests are staring at Ali and Emmi on the dancefloor. Here, too, the onlookers' incredulous gaze signifies social marginalisation or exclusion.

Turkish audiences are likely to see things differently. Rather than placing Akin's film in the tradition of Sirk's and Fassbinder's melodrama, they will associate it with Yeşilçam, Turkey's popular cinema, which flourished during the 1960s and 1970s. Yeşilçam (lit. 'green pine'), named after the street in Istanbul's Beyoglu district, where the film studios, production companies and agencies were based, is the Turkish equivalent of classical Hollywood cinema. According to Savas Arslan, Yeşilçam modifies and translates Western, in particular Hollywood, cinema 'by putting it into the vernacular, transforming it into a local product, by openly pirating scripts, themes and footage from Hollywood and European films' (2009: 85). This 'Turkified' genre cinema is characterised by a melodramatic modality (Arslan 2009: 85), predictable binary oppositions such as rural–urban, poor–rich and decadent–honourable, which reflect in simplified terms the social and economic conditions of Turkish society at the time. Whereas melodramatic love stories of the 1960s usually end happily, Yeşilçam melodrama of the 1970s and 1980s often ends with broken hearts and lives torn apart, reflecting the mood of the times, when the hope for the modernisation of Turkish society gradually began to fade as unemployment and other major social problems loomed large.

The 1970s are also known as the golden age of *Arabesk* music and film. As Martin Stokes outlines in his study *The Arabesk Debate* (1992), *Arabesk* was originally a type of music associated with the labour migrants who moved from rural south-east Turkey to Istanbul and other urban centres, where most of them settled in *gecekondus*, squatter towns, on the urban periphery. But soon Turkish *Arabesk* developed into a more encompassing social and cultural phenomenon of rapid urbanisation. It also had a significant impact on the film industry. Famous *Arabesk* singers, including Orhan Gencebay, Ferdi Tayfur, İbrahim Tatlıses, Müslüm Gürses along with the child singer Kücük Emrah, starred in *Arabesk* films which revolved around intense emotions such as *'hüsran'* (disappointment, sorrow), *'özlem'* (yearning, longing), *'kara sevda'* (melancholy) and *'hasret'* (longing, ardent desire) (Stokes 1992: 145–49).[5] The initial migration to the city, the disintegration of the family, the sense of deracination, alienation and solitude in the urban environment bring about the protagonists' 'emotional malaise whose description occupies most of the *Arabesk* lyric texts' (Stokes 1992: 144). In the big city, traditional codes of honour clash with modern morality, resulting in the protagonists' moral conflicts and their social and psychological decline. Love is depicted as an all-powerful force from which there is no escape. 'Love and fate are inexorably intertwined. Without love, the protagonist has no fate. Put another way, the fate of the protagonist is to love, and this love is the cause of his self-destruction' (Stokes 1992: 156). The ill-fated lovers of *Arabesk* films drown their sorrow in alcohol and are condemned to endure their fate passively.

Akin's *Head-On* is clearly indebted to the *Arabesk* tradition, as has been noted by, among others, the German-Turkish writer Feridun Zaimoğlu. Too numerous are the correspondences to be overlooked: the pivotal role played by music; dislocated, ill-fated lovers, who numb their *kara sevda* with alcohol and drugs, who slit their wrists, crush glass with their bare hands and whose despair culminates in attempted suicide. Zaimoğlu explains Sibel and Cahit's multiple acts of self-mutilation as a distinctly Oriental way of dealing with ecstasy and agony: Orientals publicly flagellate themselves as an act of penitence, until blood is streaming down their backs, while ecstatic fans, from the poor urban periphery, express their idolisation of a pop star by cutting themselves in public with razor blades (Zaimoğlu 2002). But Akin modifies the narrative paradigm of *Arabesk* film, empowering his protagonists in the end to determine their own destiny rather than passively succumbing to the destructive powers of an ill-fated love. This idea is, once again, emphasised by music: 'Life's what you make it', the film's final song programmatically states as the credits roll.

The hybrid aesthetics of *Head-On* are a treasure trove, or possibly a Pandora's Box, inviting audiences, critics and scholars to decipher this multicultural web of references. Thus, Zaimoğlu also places *Head-On* in the context of German Romanticism, praising it as a 'grandiose love epic [that] revives German Romanticism' (2002), while Deniz Göktürk considers the Turkish film *Cholera Street* (*Agir Roman*, Mustafa Altioklar, 1997) to be 'a major source of inspiration (Göktürk 2010: 224). After all, Akin provides an explicit clue to this particular film: before Sibel slits her wrists in the bathroom of her and Cahit's Hamburg flat, she puts on a CD with the title 'Agir Roman', as a close-up of the CD label shows. Turkish viewers will immediately recognise the film music from *Cholera Street*, which adds an additional interpretative dimension to *Head-On*. Yet audiences not familiar with Turkish cinema are likely to miss this particular reference, as well as the numerous other ones to Turkish popular culture.

Thus, watching one and the same film across borders results in different decodings, the result of the diasporic optic inscribed in *Head-On* itself. When Zaimoğlu asked Akin in an interview whether one needs a '*Türkenbonus*' ('bonus of being Turkish') in order to understand his film, the director replied that one can see the film from three different vantage points, a German-German one, a German-Turkish one and a Turkish-Turkish one. In *Head-On*, he tried to reconcile these different perspectives, aiming for the largest common denominator (Akin and Zaimoğlu n.d.).

CONCLUSION

What, then, does Fatih Akin bring to contemporary German (as well as Turkish) cinema that makes him such a powerful and distinctive creative force? Why is his *Love, Death and the Devil Trilogy*,[6] of which *Head-On* is the first and *The Edge of Heaven* the second part, frequently compared to Fassbinder's *FRG Trilogy* (*BRD Trilogie*, 1979–81) and the tradition of politically *engagé* cinema which, at the turn of the new millennium, Eric Rentschler feared was lost forever? Arguably with the exception of his contribution to the omnibus film *Germany 09: 13 Short*

Films about the State of the Nation (*Deutschland 09: 13 kurze Filme zur Lage der Nation*, 2009) modelled on the New German Cinema omnibus film *Germany in Autumn* (*Deuschland im Herbst*, 1978), Akin is not a political filmmaker as such – nor was Fassbinder, for that matter. Both attempt to marry the popular with the political, and both are more interested in the politics of representation than in politics as such, at least in their films. Therefore, much of the media discourse on Akin's contribution to the ongoing debates about multiculturalism, integration, *Leitkultur* and Turkey's accession to Europe centres on his star persona: he is a *Vorzeige Deutschtürke*, that is a role-model German-Turk whom both the Turkish community in Germany and in Turkey, as well as German advocates of a liberal multicultural Germany are eager to enlist as their ambassador. As the Green Party parliamentarian Özcan Mutlu commented shortly after *Head-On* won the Golden Bear, 'When I come to think of it, I am sure that with Fatih Akin's success, a new era for us Turks here in Germany has begun' (quoted in Lau 2004). But Akin's high media profile should not distract from his achievements as a filmmaker: by problematising the notion of difference and by rewriting the master narrative of the German nation 'by and from the margins' (Moorti 2003: 371), Akin has turned a new page in German film history. In that sense, Akin's films are anything but a cinema of consensus, nor are they in stylistic terms. Akin's diasporic imaginary is, perhaps, best summarised in the words of a much more famous diasporian, Salman Rushdie, who pronounced migration and the ensuing process of hybridisation as the chief sources of innovation in contemporary culture: 'Mélange, hotchpotch, a bit of this and a bit of that is how newness enters the world. It is the great possibility that mass migration gives the world [...] change-by-fusion, change-by-conjoining. It is the love song to our mongrel selves' (1991: 394).

Notes

The quotation 'Seeing everything with different eyes' is taken from Akin, Beier and Mattusek 2007. This chapter has evolved out of a larger research project, funded by the AHRC under the Diasporas, Migration and Identities Programme, on Migrant and Diasporic Cinema in Contemporary Europe (www.migrant cinema.net), which I led between 2006 and 2008. Some of the material in this article has been previously published in Berghahn (2009) and Berghahn and Sternberg (2010).

1   It is perhaps worth noting that the majority of migrant and diasporic films across Europe are made by diasporic rather than migrant filmmakers, presumably because first-generation immigrants are too absorbed by the economic struggle of establishing themselves and finding a livelihood in the host country. In the German-Turkish context, most films about first-generation immigrants were made by German directors.

2   For a discussion of *Solino* see Berghahn 2006a; for the reception of *Solino* in Germany and Italy, see Schwingel 2007; for a discussion of *In July* see Burns 2009.

3   In the documentary *When I Am Thinking of Germany: We Have Forgotten to Return (Denk ich an Deutschland: Wir haben vergessen zurückzukehren,* 2001) Akin undertakes a similar journey, exploring his family's history of migration and re-migration and visiting his father's place of origin on the Black Sea coast. *Short Sharp Shock, Solino* and *The Edge of Heaven* all culminate in homebound journeys.

4   For insightful discussions of similar mirror-image scenes, see Burns 2009: 16–17 and Göktürk (2010).

5   I am indebted to Açya Tunç, who has kindly shared her knowledge of the *Arabesk* tradition in Turkish music and film and its relationship to Yeşilçam melodrama with me.

6   Akin refers to the title of this trilogy in an interview with Zaimoğlu (Akin and Zaimoğlu n.d).

Chapter 14

No place like Heimat: mediaspaces and moving landscapes in Edgar Reitz's *Heimat 3* (2004)

Alasdair King

What was once a film in a movie theatre, then a fragment of broadcast television, is now a kernel of psychical representations, a fleeting association of discrete elements: [...] The more the film is distanced in memory, the more the binding effect of the narrative is loosened. The sequence breaks apart. The fragments go adrift and enter into new combinations, more or less transitory, in the eddies of memory: memories of other films, and memories of real events.

Burgin (2004: 67)[1]

PROLOGUE

It is almost halfway into the final episode of Edgar Reitz's six-part film series, *Heimat 3: A Chronicle of Endings and Beginnings* (*Heimat 3: Chronik einer Zeitenwende*, 2004) that one of the most disorienting sequences of this concluding production in the *Heimat* trilogy occurs. In some ways, this could be the *mise-en-abyme* of *Heimat 3*. Hermann, Reitz's central character in both *The Second Heimat: Chronicle of a Generation* (*Die zweite Heimat: Chronik einer Jugend*, 1992) and *Heimat 3*, has packed up his Munich apartment – 'the old stories are packed away in boxes' – thereby giving up finally and definitively his alternative 'home', the approximate English translation for the extraordinarily emotive German concept of Heimat, which implicitly evokes a sense of one's community, of one's roots, as well as the specific place where one lives. In so doing, he has committed fully to the main house he has built up with his partner, Clarissa, on the banks of the Rhine, very near the Hunsrück village of Schabbach, his childhood home, and thus Hermann seals his reintegration into the physical space of the Heimat. We accompany Hermann as he drives north-west across Germany, from Munich, up the crowded *Autobahn*, busy with traffic transporting goods across Europe and with tourists driving long distances to holiday destinations. An extreme close-up, a shot rarely used in this film series, picks out the anxiety on Hermann's face as he concentrates on the immediate physical dangers posed by these increased and disturbing trans-European flows of goods and people – he almost collides with a huge transporter as he joins the *Autobahn*. His voiceover – again, a technique used sparingly in *Heimat 3* – underscores the heightened significance of this journey itself, and also of the scope it allows Hermann for interiority, for self-reflection, as he outlines a cartography of south-west Germany and of the countries and regions beyond the horizon in each direction. There then follows a series of five inserts, each held for several seconds with a static camera, of extreme long-shot landscape images of the Hunsrück countryside. Their composition registers familiar Reitz images, too, the line of telegraph poles stretching into the distance, like the narrow country lanes, and the rolled bales of hay, freezing time in their stillness, while also suggesting that these landscapes are connected spatially and temporally to greater and wider worlds of social interaction. The inserts are followed by a cut to a long shot of Hermann, now in the

Figure 14.1: Hermann in front of the Pro-Winz Kino.

main street of the town, as he moves towards a low-angle camera, which pans to follow his walk down the street and towards the local camera shop and photographer's studio. As *Heimat 3* utilises a shot/reverse-shot to establish Hermann looking at the shop and subsequently at the framed photos in its window, the camera, now in front of the shop and looking at Hermann in medium shot, captures in the background the local cinema, the Pro-Winz Kino (in reality, based in Simmern). As the camera tracks backwards and to the side, for no more than five seconds, it holds in frame behind Hermann's head a large film poster which advertises a two-part screening of Edgar Reitz's *Heimat*, the blue poster displaying prominently a black-and-white still of the central character, Maria Simon, in fact Hermann's mother.

Just how is this disorienting image to be read?[2] On one level, the presence of the poster is thoroughly self-reflexive, drawing attention from within the otherwise consistent diegesis to its constructed nature, acting to break the frame, even for a few seconds, of the narrative based on Hermann's journey and perspective. But while this self-reflexive act is not necessarily at odds with the mode of the *Heimat* trilogy itself, given the complexity particularly of the first *Heimat* film series (*Heimat: A German Chronicle* [*Heimat: eine deutsche Chronik*], 1984) (see Wickham 1991: 35–45), it is out of keeping with the more basic 'mimetic realism' that has characterised *Heimat 3* in its earlier episodes. What the presence of the *Heimat* poster within the diegesis does point to, above everything else, is that *Heimat 3*, in textual terms, must be seen directly in relation to *Heimat*, and not as a completely self-contained work that merely follows the first in Reitz's trilogy. In this sense, *Heimat 3* exists in a simultaneous and not simply sequential relationship to the first *Heimat* film series.

INTRODUCTION

How does *Heimat 3* fit into the framework we are considering, that of the 'cinema of consensus'? Overall, *Heimat 3* has not been particularly well received, and what consensus there may be seems to suggest that it is a missed opportunity, and certainly carries little of the aesthetic complexity or cultural consequence which marked out the reception of Reitz's original *Heimat* series. As one of the signatories of the Oberhausen Manifesto in 1962, which helped to provide the impetus for far-reaching changes in West German cinema culture that precipitated the emergence of the New German Cinema of the 1970s and 1980s, Reitz's long career has seen him set himself firmly against the increasing demands for a commercial entertainment cinema in Germany. His auteurist credentials are impeccable, reinforced in interview after interview, and his bitterness about negotiations and compromises with various funding bodies underline his stubborn refusal to adopt a pragmatic approach to contemporary cinema and to cede to the pressure to make mainstream narrative cinema along the lines suggested by existing Hollywood models. The aesthetic complexity of his original *Heimat* film series also aligned his filmmaking with other key directors of the New German Cinema, such as Rainer Werner Fassbinder, Alexander Kluge and Helma Sanders-Brahms, who over the same period at the beginning of the 1980s were committed to the interrogation of images of German history, 'in the hope of refining memories and catalysing changes', as Eric Rentschler puts it (2000: 264). The lukewarm reaction, outlined below, of some critics to *Heimat 3* might suggest a move by Reitz towards 'consensus', towards the aesthetic mainstream and away from his earlier commitment to the provision of a more critical assessment of the state of Germany, a move of considerable importance given the turbulent social and political experiences of the German population in the decade following unification. In the light of this, I would like to look at the critical reception of the film, as a short introduction, then talk about two aspects arising from Reitz's film, first the frameworks in which we may be viewing it, its mediaspaces, and second its attempts to construct Heimat spaces, its local landscapes. In so doing, it may be argued that even if *Heimat 3* is not in itself as consistently rewarding and critically challenging as Reitz's first *Heimat*, it may be richer than has been assumed, and is certainly a complex media event that raises some significant questions about cinema, the moving image and a sense of belonging in contemporary Germany.

Edgar Reitz's *Heimat 3* was first shown at the Venice Film Festival in September 2004, where it was screened over three afternoons. It completed Reitz's monumental trilogy of works on the changing nature of provincial life in the twentieth century initiated with the release of the much-discussed *Heimat* in 1984, an exploration of modernisation within the particular spaces of the Hunsrück region in western Germany where Reitz originated. With the (shortened) televising and subsequent DVD release of *Heimat 3* splitting the chronicle into six episodes (which constituted a running time of almost twelve hours), Reitz returned to the Hunsrück to address the changing German landscape over the decade between the fall of the Wall and the millennium celebrations. *Heimat 3* premiered in Germany in the Hunsrück, at the Pro-Winz Kino (the cinema's name suggests a pun celebrating both the provincial and the world of small things more generally) on 25 September 2004, and at the Urania Kino Berlin at the beginning of October, before staggered screenings at 17 regional cinemas in Germany between October and early December, followed by its television broadcast on ARD between 15 and 29 December.[3] Given the turbulent events chronicled in *Heimat 3*, and the ongoing discussions throughout that period concerning the unified Germany's national identity, it is significant that in comparison to the enormous reaction to the initial *Heimat* film series, response to the final part of the trilogy was relatively muted in Germany, triggering little public or academic debate, and only fleeting interest from cultural commentators in the *feuilletons*. However, the viewing figures for the shortened television version – the cuts in running time were bitterly contested by Reitz and his supporters, and actually removed some of the most complex material – were seen as high enough for the film to be considered a success by the television companies which had invested heavily, ARD and SWR.[4]

This contrasted with the comparatively disappointing audience attendance for the Venice Film Festival screening, which numbered barely one hundred and fifty diehard loyalists by the final afternoon, and which left one film critic asking whether what had changed since the original *Heimat* was down to Reitz losing his touch, perhaps falling into the trivialising mode of narrative favoured by television soap operas, or whether in fact the audience in Germany itself had changed and no longer wished to view the aging of characters like Hermann and Clarissa, with whom it had previously so identified (Schulz-Ojala 2004). The reception of the screening of Reitz's new film in the German press was generally lukewarm: Katja Nicodemus of *Die Zeit* described *Heimat 3* as 'disappointing. Sometimes even embarrassing', suggesting that Reitz was no longer able to capture the changing moods of Germany or to register the impact of the historical events successfully, concluding that '*Heimat*, that most ambitious of German television projects, began as the account of an epoch and is ending as a soap opera' (2004b). Nicodemus's disappointment with the screening at Venice was echoed by several other commentators (see Nord; 2004 and Althen 2004). However, when *Heimat 3* was screened in Germany three weeks later, the response was more positive, with Peter W. Jansen concluding that *Heimat 3* was a fitting conclusion to a trilogy which had become the 'apotheosis of European cinema' (2004). Eckhard Fuhr argued that the early negative reaction ('There had been talk of a plummet into the aesthetics of the television soap opera') to *Heimat 3* in Venice ought to take into account that although the film started awkwardly it picked up and ended strongly, concluding 'a magnificent epic of the century' (2004b). Writing in the *FAZ*, Hans-Dieter Seidel made particular reference to the effectiveness of *Heimat 3* as a film series through the filter of his own recollected viewing experience of the first *Heimat* back in the summer of 1984, during which he, and by extension the audience, had felt the creation of an authentic new world on screen into which they were drawn, identifying affectively with both Schabbach as a place and with the stories of the characters (2004). While it seems that, for many critics, precisely this deeply affective viewing experience was lacking in their initial responses to seeing *Heimat 3*, the remembered viewing of the initial *Heimat* might still form the intertextual viewing frame, the 'remembered film', when viewing *Heimat 3*. This is a key part of the viewing framework brought to these filmed scenes, along with, for so many Germans, an awareness of having recently lived through these key events. Indeed, Hermann's re-entry into the village life of Schabbach and his rediscovery of spaces and objects was registered particularly by Seidel, who noted the degree to which the audience members would be sharing his emotions at confronting the familiar after so many years away (2004). Klaudia Brunst noted that 'To an even greater degree than previously, *Heimat 3* will have to be measured against the individual memories of the audience' (2004). Brunst's point is acute, as Reitz's new series both registered so many well-known recent events, thus participating in the revisiting and reweaving of the tapestry of memories discussed by Germans, as well as reinhabiting sites and continuing stories familiar from the previous two *Heimat* works.

MEDIASPACE

In terms of the early critical reception of the film, it is significant that several commentators touch on two issues that raise questions about both the contextual and the formal aspects of Reitz's film. One concerns the viewing framework within which audiences might encounter *Heimat 3*, and the other concerns the narrative mode utilised by Reitz to chronicle the events of the decade following the fall of the Wall. Of course, *Heimat 3* is linked temporally far more closely to the historical and public events that structure its wider world than was the case with the initial *Heimat*. The original film was made and broadcast with a substantial distance of over sixty years between then and the starting point of the narrative; with *Heimat 3*, the events featured all belong to the very recent past, and have been heavily represented and discussed through all forms of media, and so specific demands are made on the 'media literacy' and direct memories of the viewing audience. Also, *Heimat 3* enters into a German environment already shaped by familiarity with the overwhelming success of the first *Heimat*, which substantially influenced cultural debate on German history, the provincial, and national identity in the 1980s and after.[5] This is not so much a question of having to prove its merits as a sequel, but has far more to do with the way in which Reitz's first film series had reshaped fundamentally perceptions of locale, landscape and belonging in the Federal Republic and beyond. Contemporary understanding of place and identity, then, for the viewing audience of *Heimat 3* had been shaped already through the media phenomenon created in the wake of the huge viewing figures for the original *Heimat*. *Heimat* had, in this sense, not merely registered the processes of local and national self-understanding as one of its key themes, but had participated in fostering a sense of national (and transnational, given its popularity outside Germany) community through the widespread shared viewing experience of its episodes on television, particularly, and in the ensuing debates.

The constructed village of Schabbach, a composite with features borrowed from at least a dozen neighbouring Hunsrück villages, Hermann's birthplace and the centre of the first film series, assumed very firm physical contours established not through a genuine singular geographical history, but through the narrative ability of Reitz's film team and also through the extra-filmic media discussions of the series. In this way, *Heimat 3* might be understood as participating in this ongoing process of creating and reconstructing a mediated locale in the form of 'Schabbach', a very specific meeting point of media representations and of physical geography. As Nick Couldry and Anna McCarthy have written recently, 'as electronic media increasingly saturate our everyday spaces with images of other places and other (imagined or real) orders of space, it is ever more difficult to tell a story of social space without also telling a story of media, and vice versa' (2004: 1).[6] Couldry and McCarthy adopt the concept of 'mediaspace' to denote the interrelations between media practices and spatial constructions, which they define as 'a dialectical concept, encompassing both the kinds of spaces created by media, and the effects that existing spatial arrangements have on media forms as they materialize in everyday life' (2004: 1–2). With the success of the original *Heimat* series and the rise in tourism to the Hunsrück based on the desire to experience physically the landscape and sites utilised to construct the fictional village of Schabbach by Reitz and his team, this region has become a pertinent example of the concept of the 'mediaspace' envisaged by Couldry and McCarthy, whose concept also allows for the building up of a virtual, physically separate set of participants or contributors into a more solid 'imagined' community, which at various times may also join together physically and understands itself as a specific body. These are processes in which the *Heimat* trilogy itself can be seen to participate, given the longstanding websites devoted to the three film series, internet fora and real-world meetings in the Hunsrück and other locations.[7]

The actual Hunsrück space has been transformed in part by the media event of the *Heimat* series, which has affected materially how that space is perceived, experienced, remembered. Not only are there virtual spaces, particularly the very detailed and informative fansites and pages on the *Heimat* trilogy, but also physical space has been altered through Reitz tourism. In the cemetery in Sargenroth, a village south of Simmern, it was noted that there were graves in place for the fictional deceased – Maria and Paul Simon, Eduard and Lucie – from the first *Heimat* film series, with those of Anton and Ernst joining them after the filming of *Heimat 3*. The graves were only distinguished as fake resting places through small stickers acknowledging their part in the film production, but they were not immediately removed after filming, not least because of the desire to accommodate *Heimat* tourists once again (see Fritz 2004). The Hunsrück tourist agency, Hunsrück-Touristik GmbH, produced a brochure about places relating to Reitz's film in the region, and set up guided bus tours and Rhine trips to tie in with the geography featured in the series.[8] A *Heimat* tourist trip taking in 20 of the most prominent *Heimat* locations was led by local resident Eva-Marie Schneider, who had played Marie-Goot in the first film series. The tourist route set up to build on Reitz's success embraced the *Gasthof* run by Rudi Molz and his wife, where visitors could ask to see a photo album from filming, while the Hunsrück museum in Simmern had an exhibition of props from *Heimat 3*.[9] These familiar Hunsrück locations thus became part of a clear 'media pilgrimage' which exploited the huge popular success of Reitz's first *Heimat* series.[10]

Schabbach as 'mediaspace' notwithstanding, *Heimat 3* also enters into a very different media environment from that which embraced Reitz's first Schabbach project. It is, in significant ways, an environment already informed and knowledgeable about the consumption of *Heimat* as a media text. In ways, it could be argued that *Heimat 3* plays with this state of affairs and with the audience's possible prior knowledge of the earlier 'remembered' film, to draw on Victor Burgin's concept.[11] There are a number of parallel scenes in *Heimat 3* which pick up on or echo visually earlier key sequences, not least in Episode 6. So *Heimat 3* might be said to operate as a text that works as a palimpsest, and through which the viewer can see shifts between the two productions. It is in this palimpsest relation, or even in a version of pastiche of *Heimat* that *Heimat 3* becomes a more complex piece of filmmaking. In his discussion of the 2002 Todd Haynes film *Far From Heaven*, which deliberately echoes the narrative tensions and aesthetic forms of the classic 1950s Sirkian melodramas, and Fassbinder's Sirkian *Ali: Fear Eats the Soul* (*Angst Essen Seele auf*, 1974), Richard Dyer suggests that Haynes's film works as a form of pastiche in its sustained imitation of key elements of these earlier films, in attitude, look, and *mise-en-scène* chiefly, rendering the film's relationship particularly to Sirk as one of 'extreme closeness with elements of discrepancy and slight distortion, very like but not quite' (2007: 175).[12] Dyer argues that '*Far From Heaven*'s pastiche thus simultaneously in its likeness enables us in imagination to feel with the 1950s in the terms of the 1950s while in its not-quite-likeness conveying the epistemological difficulty of such imagining' (2007: 177). This 'epistemological difficulty', a 'not-quite-likeness', is an element that comes to mind in viewing the complex final episode of *Heimat 3*, with its revisiting of several key elements from the final episode of the first *Heimat*. While this is not to suggest that *Heimat 3* should be seen as a pastiche of Reitz's original 1984 film, the viewing of *Heimat 3* in 2004 and after must be considered as taking place to a significant extent through an interpretive framework and image bank which features above all memories of viewing the first *Heimat*. Reitz clearly plays with this in his construction of elements of *Heimat 3*, and particularly in the concluding episode, where the chronological and relatively simple narrative linearity is disrupted by a number of more complex visual and verbal layerings. The viewing experience of *Heimat 3*, in places deliberately, given Reitz's imitative construction of scenes, requires that the audience brings both its recent experiences of the events of German unification and after to hold in place as the narrative progresses, but also, and in complex ways, that the audience works through the experience of both watching *Heimat* and drawing on that viewing in debates around the construction of German national identity.

A second formal question concerns the narrative mode utilised. One clear and repeated criticism in the German press was that Reitz's *Heimat 3* failed to achieve the aesthetic heights of the previous parts of the trilogy because of its close adherence to the conventions of the soap opera. Although Reitz's first *Heimat* series, with its intense focus on the relationships and rhythms of everyday life across several generations of the Simon family, did work with the kind of material that might be the focus of a soap opera, Reitz's narrative forms made his first series quite distinct. His use, for example, of amateur actors, authentic biographical material, changes in film stock, irregular-lengthed and self-contained episodes all suggested, in Rachel Palfreyman's view, a complex and aesthetically rich work comprised of an 'illegitimate' mix of genres and a main mode of 'estranged naturalism' rather than the 'mimetic realism' typically associated with the soap opera (2000: 126–28). *Heimat 3*, at first glance, and certainly in the earlier episodes, does seem to offer viewers the kind of 'mimetic realism' that Reitz clearly tried to avoid in his first *Heimat* film. This is not helped in the version broadcast on German television, with its regular screening slot and strictly cut 90-minute episodes, the cuts having taken away some of the less 'mimetic' sequences. In her review of *Heimat 3*, Barbara Knorpp raises the question that Reitz deliberately draws more extensively on soap-opera conventions as a way of subverting audience expectation. She argues that *Heimat 3* is 'lighter, at times even shallow, and overdramatic' and that it utilises the 'melodramatic form of television drama' to a much higher degree than *Heimat*, with its intense and contemplative focus on the slow rituals of everyday life. She views this as a deliberate strategy on the part of the director: 'By deliberately appropriating popular fiction and soap opera Reitz brings in questions of taste, aesthetics and the conventions of the European art house cinema' (2007: 128). In this way, Reitz is able to subvert audience expectations instead of repeating familiar forms of narration, a move which continues, rather than moves away from, the aesthetic self-reflexivity more characteristic of the New German Cinema than later commercial and consensual German filmmaking, but to what effect? Arguably, given the bleak ending sequence, the soap-opera conventions of understanding family life are undermined, unable to contain the reality of aging, and of facing the future. The ultimate failure of the soap-opera conventions to prove themselves adequate to the registration of social and historical change over the decade following German unification allows the audience the opportunity to revisit the earlier episodes of *Heimat 3* in the knowledge that, like the overwhelming euphoria which initially greeted the rapid dismantling of the Berlin Wall and which turned sour later in the decade, a little critical distance and analytical sobriety is a useful corrective.

In this respect, Reitz's *Heimat 3* aligns itself more firmly with the tenets of the New German Cinema film traditions than might initially be supposed, and moves Reitz a considerable distance from the films that mark out the 'cinema of consensus' of the 1990s and beyond. There are places in *Heimat 3* where formally Reitz uses different modes of filmmaking that disrupt the 'mimetic realism' critics associated with soap operas. In terms of embedding *Heimat 3* explicitly in the world of technologically reproduced visual imagery – and here it is hard not to think of the key use of photographs in structuring the narrative and methods of recounting past episodes used in *Heimat*, as well as the visits to the cinema made by Maria and Pauline – little use is made of film clips or of other visual images until the final episode. The photograph of the Molzes, juxtaposed with the ironic poster celebrating the screening of *Heimat*, are rare returns to the use of layered visual material found in *Heimat*, and arguably achieve a heightened significance because of this. The cinema, as building, as institution, as artform, like the photograph of the Molzes, achieves a preservative function, a time-Heimat in a Germany that seems to offer no spatial refuge. In terms of operating as a self-reflexive media text, there appears to be less complexity in *Heimat 3* than was the case with the first *Heimat* film series,[13] the third series chronicling events in the decade following unification in often quite mundane fashion. However, there are moments when this tone is disrupted and when it could be argued that Reitz situates his narrative in a broader world of media images and texts and invites the viewer to be more active in making sense of sequences. As Hermann and Clarissa are in the hotel room celebrating their reunion, the images of events at the Wall outside are playing on the television screen in the room. The footage used draws on Jürgen Böttcher's award-winning documentary, *The Wall* (*Die Mauer*, 1990), produced by the documentary division of DEFA, and already a significant part of the German image-memory of the initial fall of the Wall. The euphoria of the Berliners sitting on the Wall and attempting to dismantle it piece by piece is matched by the private joy of Hermann and Clarissa. Viewers watching *Heimat 3* after its release in 2004 already bring to the viewing of these layered documentary scenes, and by extension also perhaps the union of the two protagonists, the knowledge that the euphoria was shortlived and that the decade saw a sobering reassessment of the tasks of unification on every level, and a growing disillusionment with the process as it was experienced by many Germans.[14]

LOCAL LANDSCAPES

Heimat 3 participates in the ongoing construction of Schabbach as an extratextual mediaspace, while also utilising a number of local spaces in its textual narrative. In the period following German unification, one of Reitz's central concerns is whether Heimat can still be considered a spatial category. Of course, the *Heimatfilm* itself must be seen as a profoundly spatial genre with its emphasis on the construction of territories, borders, inclusions and exclusions at specific historical moments.[15] In a period of such turbulent change in terms of flows of capital and people, this stage of Germany's modernity may, Reitz seems to propose, have made much more difficult a sense of geographical belonging. In his early sketches for *Heimat 3*, Reitz was adamant that although Hermann had returned to Schabbach, ostensibly making it once again the 'centre of the world' that it had been through most of the first *Heimat* series, the defining sense of place, of a spatial repository of shared experiences which Schabbach had offered to its inhabitants previously, could no longer be assumed in the late twentieth century. The reasons for this could be found less in any great changes internal to the provincial village (which is represented across the trilogy not as an untouched and timeless rural idyll, but explicitly, and increasingly in *Heimat 3*, as a meeting point of various flows: economic, technological, migratory), but more in the expanded dimensions of everyday life experienced by the main protagonists. Hermann and Clarissa, principally, but also many other key characters, are seen as typically in transit in a space which now assumes continental and even global physical (as well as virtual) dimensions. The key spaces which initially mark out this nomadic and deracinated couple's inhabitation of German territory clearly belong to the order of sites which Marc Augé has termed the 'non-places' of 'supermodernity' (see 1995: 75–115),[16] the sites in the contemporary globalised world of transit, travel and economic transactions such as the airport lounge, the motorway, the cash machine and the out-of-town supermarket, as opposed to the more organically rooted places of village or town life, the places of belonging which fall within the traditions of Heimat thinking. We first meet Hermann and Clarissa as a couple in the hotel lobby, one of these key non-places, and the symptomatic space of atomised modernity according to Kracauer's famous essay (see 1995: 173–85).[17] Reitz's purpose, following Kracauer's line on the significance of the hotel lobby as a counterpoint to the experience of Heimat, is to accompany Hermann and Clarissa in their quest to move from the hotel lobby and to attempt to construct a new (or regained) Heimat constituted by shared time as much as space.

The direction of *Heimat 3* is of an initial movement by Hermann and Clarissa away from the constant global transit they associate with professional accomplishment, and towards a new, constructed, home-as-Heimat. The big unification project for them becomes the renovation of a derelict villa situated high above the Rhine; the house occupies a very deliberate borderline position where the Hunsrück, the space connected to Hermann's childhood, looks out towards the Rhine, that is to say, the point at which the Hunsrück most clearly is connected to the flows of the wider world. The Rhine is not only a significant river in German myth and national cultural self-understanding, but economically it connects western Germany to the rest of Europe and beyond. It also encompasses quite deliberately, according to Reitz, the noise and pollution of contemporary social exchange.

As in the previous two *Heimat* series, a house comes to take up a symbolic position as a partial version of the Heimat.[18] Hermann does not return directly to occupy the Simon house of the first *Heimat*, which has been restored and which appears to be now closer to an empty museum piece than a dwelling.[19] The Günderrode house operates as a metaphor for a possible construction of Heimat, standing in symbolically for a joint east–west German building project, placed on a highly mythic and romanticised location above the Rhine near the Lorelei rock.[20] However, the question arises about the representation of a possible Heimat in the third film. The Günderrode house is scarcely an organic space like the Simon house in the first *Heimat*, and takes on an ambiguous, even uncanny, aura.[21] Is there indeed any spatial refuge in *Heimat 3*?

Ernst lives in isolation, chained into his farmhouse. Anton's doomed patriarchal house falls apart amid jealousies and tensions. Even Lulu's flat in Cologne is depicted as a chaotic space, full up and claustrophobic, broken into by her well-intentioned but intrusive father and her neighbours. Utopian spaces are particularly hard to find, although there are brief glimpses of aspects of belonging and community in temporary events in specific places, such as for the musicians, Hermann and Clarissa, on stage, or for Anton and his fellow Schabbachers at the football stadium. Even the Molz inn, which takes on a communal centrality arguably occupied in *Heimat* by the kitchen of the Simon household – with its 'centripetal pull', and dominated by Maria Simon, Hermann's mother – becomes a place of sadness and loss after Rudi Molz's sudden death.[22] That space is never as significant as the Simon kitchen had once been, in any case, and is not visited again by the camera; instead, Rudi and his wife occupy the screen as images, in the framed photograph, and as the ghostly figure in Hermann's dream in the final episode.

The 'centripetal pull' in *Heimat 3* takes place less around the village of Schabbach, which in the first *Heimat* exerted its effects across generations of relatively settled families; where it is felt in *Heimat 3* it takes a broader form, operating at a national level. A renewed sense of *German* identity is exhibited by geographically mobile sets of characters and their families who travel, somewhat arbitrarily in the narrative, to Schabbach to begin new lives or to take up work after unification. The movement of the ethnic Germans and their families returning from Russia and the lands of the former Soviet Union, as well as migration within the unified Germany, primarily from east to west, allows for an assumption that the specifics of the local exert less of a pull here than does the more general sense of national belonging through 'blood ties' and the economic pressure to be mobile to find employment. The woes of Clarissa's mother, whose sense of identity is still characterised by her self-representation as a 'migrant' and who after decades still struggles to throw off her sense of not belonging in western Germany, do however suggest that achieving a sense of Heimat in Schabbach may prove hard for the new arrivals. Reitz's exploration of new identities in contemporary Germany is still worryingly conservative in its focus on ethnic Germans and their sense of 'blood ties', when so little attention is paid to the increasingly multicultural nature of the newly unified Federal Republic. There are few non-white faces to be seen in *Heimat 3*, exceptions including the African-American families leaving the local US military base and the African-American wife of Clarissa's son, who has migrated to the United States, and whose marriage ceremony, in a contemporary echo of the celebrated '*Fernehe*' ('long-distance marriage') scene from the first *Heimat*, is mediated by communications technology. There is strikingly little interest in exploring, within this contemporary questioning of the nature of Heimat, the general tensions between Heimat and 'Fremde', its other, the foreign world beyond its confines, that came to the fore in *Heimat*, and in particular the longstanding question of the identity, cultural, political, social and religious, of the highly significant waves of Turkish migration to Germany is conspicuously not addressed.[23]

Heimat seems an elusive category at the local level. The only spatial refuges for the central characters are more typically short-lived literal lines of flight, voyages above the ground, often vertical rather than horizontal, but in each case these spatial trajectories are temporary, ending in death. Ernst's plane allows him the mobility and distance from the network of social relations that he finds so inhibiting, until he realises his longing for an heir. His flight ends with his crash into the Lorelei rock, filmed ambiguously so that the audience cannot be certain whether this is a form of suicide or a tragic accident. His love of flying is echoed in the fascination of the young Matko with all kinds of technology, not least the small motorcycle he uses to move around the countryside as he pleases. Matko's attachment to a homing pigeon prefigures his desire to be free, like Ernst, to rise above the hostile treatment he receives from his contemporaries. His interest in Ernst's plane and experiences as a pilot suggest a possible line of flight, which again culminates in a tragic death as, caught up in a battle about inheritance and family ties, he climbs the Lorelei rock and throws himself off, arms outstretched, mimicing a pose he had held earlier in the episode when being driven fast in Hartmut's car. Vertical journeys are also significant in the thrilling bungee jump taken by Lulu and her partner, Lutz. Again, this brief trajectory away from economic and familial demands and the pressures of the ground is temporary and will be ended irrevocably by Lutz's death in a banal traffic accident.

Heimat 3 proposes that there are few enduring utopian Heimat spaces remaining: the local landscapes around the Hunsrück offer little lasting solace, the constructed space of the house rarely lives up to its idyllic setting, Germany's mythical landmarks, the Rhine, the Lorelei rock, are deathly spots, and points of national and political communion and identity, like the Brandenburg Gate, are experienced in mediated fashion, by way of the television screen. Individual lines of flight end in death or a blank screen. In *Heimat*, as Johannes von Moltke has argued, various communications and transport technologies linked up Schabbach within a wider national and international network, making the Heimat always an open rather than a fully closed space, and a location subject to both centripetal and centrifugal forces. The role of technology in mediating this linked relationship between the local and the wider world was crucial for Reitz throughout *Heimat*. Far from being perceived as only damaging to a sense of Heimat, new technologies were represented by Reitz often in positive ways and associated with sympathetic characters like Eduard as they served to reinforce and foster community (von Moltke 2005: 218). In *Heimat 3*, there is less optimism regarding more recent technological developments. The characters who are most involved with the latest developments in computing and communications include Clarissa's son, Arnold, whom we encounter initially as a student. He has to face courtroom charges after hacking into the security system of a bank, to the puzzlement of Clarissa's mother, who cannot understand that he

Figure 14.2: Lulu immobile against the glass screen.

could have committed a serious offence without leaving the house, thus introducing to the Heimat the dimensions of virtual places and cyberspace, although these are only noted in passing. We subsequently encounter Clarissa's son by way of filmed footage of his wedding in the United States noted above.

A second character who becomes involved with the most recent technology is the amiable east German electrician, Tillman, who marries a local woman he meets while working on the Günderrode house. She inherits a local electrical goods shop, which gives Tillman contact with the newest goods. He updates Hermann's computer and brings Clarissa an early mobile phone, but again the role of this newest technology is never treated with the depth accorded to earlier technological innovations in *Heimat*. The growth in communications technology and in computing, and the emergence of virtual spaces, appears to be of only marginal interest to Reitz as he charts the recent history of Germany and the difficulties in establishing a spatial identity based on a sense of Heimat. If, as von Moltke argues of the first film series, 'the "mediation" of home through the history of the media is one of the stories that Reitz's film tells quite explicitly, reflexively, and with as much fascination as nostalgia', then this is treated less extensively in the chronicle of contemporary German life that Reitz sets out in *Heimat 3* (2005: 219). The technology prioritised in *Heimat 3* is mostly connected to transport, not least in the fetishisation of cars, which offer an atomised rather than collective experience.[24]

In conclusion, if the Heimat is no longer locatable in spatial terms as a 'local landscape', it may still resonate as a 'mediaspace', a construct of a specific place and its mediated experience, bringing a temporary community of viewers, or fans, together at a specific time. *Heimat 3* suggests that the sense of community, belonging and collectivity that is traditionally associated with the geographical Heimat may reside, in the contemporary moment, as much in the attachment to a constructed 'mediaspace' as to the local landscape. Heimat may have become something which resides in a collective viewing experience, across internet sites, for example, in the associated fan culture and audience reaction, and thus short-lived, temporary and mobile, rather than anchored in a fixed geographical space. The positive collective viewing experiences at the Schabbach football stadium and while watching the 1990 World Cup in *Heimat 3* also help to support this possibility. Overall, there is an element of cultural pessimism in Reitz's third film series about the ongoing possibility of a contemporary spatial Heimat, reinforced by the final image of the static, almost-frozen face of Lulu caught through the pane of glass, tears forming and running down her cheek.

Caught against this screen, Lulu's spatial immobility and sense of despair suggest that the Günderrode house, and by extension Schabbach, offer her little real sense of belonging. Even if the aesthetic strategies used by Reitz in *Heimat 3* are no longer as consistently innovative as in the first two instalments of his *Heimat* trilogy, the concluding film series underscores the difficulties of creating a sense of community within the borders of the film itself and is sceptical about the opportunities for consensus in the present. If Reitz's filmmaking no longer constructs spatial refuges for its key characters, then perhaps we must look for temporary moments of belonging in the director's trilogy, and look towards the possibility of Heimat cinema redeeming moments in time for us, creating a Heimat of time-images.[25]

NOTES

1   Similarly, Tom Conley, drawing on Christian Metz but close here to Burgin's idea of the 'remembered film', argues that 'in cinema, the spectator's consciousness produces an imaginary space that taps into the memory of other films. Cinema awakens feelings whose origins are not easily located' (2006: 292).

2   It could be read in light-hearted manner, especially as Hermann has his face turned away from it during this sequence, as a brief nod to the cult status of the *Heimat* phenomenon, an acknowledgement of its own popularity both locally and beyond Germany, and hence a salute to its long-term fans. In part, too, the poster advertising the cinema screening of the first *Heimat* might be seen as a gesture by Reitz which attempts to underscore the cinematic rather than televisual claims of his whole enterprise, at a time when he had had to make extensive compromises with the TV companies who had offered the financial backing necessary for *Heimat 3* to get off the ground at all.

3   On the dates of the film screenings in Germany, see Seidel 2004. The DVD release in the UK claims to run to 761 minutes; Reitz complained that the TV release in Germany, on ARD at the end of December 2004, was cut to six 90-minute episodes.

4   It was broadcast at prime time (8.15p.m.) on the first channel across the Christmas period, and averaged 2.87 million viewers per episode, a market

share of around 9 per cent. The first episode on 15 December 2004 was watched by 3.8 million, a market share of 12.3 per cent, significant in ARD's battle for overall market share with RTL.

5   It was estimated that 25 million west German viewers, or over 50 per cent of the potential German audience, had watched at least one of the episodes screened on ARD, and an average audience of nine million had watched each episode. Discussing the impact that Reitz's film had created in the Federal Republic, Anton Kaes suggested that both the film, and its reception, should be considered an 'emanation – and agent – of a collective longing for identity' (1989: 183).

6   Couldry and McCarthy define five levels of mediaspace, including two that are particularly pertinent to the *Heimat* trilogy in terms of its status as a film series, and so as a media text. This concentrates on the textual and also production side, at the expense of a full engagement with consumption, which is beyond the scope of this essay. Level 1 involves media images and representations of specific spaces, local, global and national, and so has the most immediate resonance for the *Heimat* trilogy as a textual phenomenon, with its construction out of recognisable and existing local elements the village of Schabbach. Level 2, significantly, focuses on how these images and representations are circulated, flow across space, and – of great interest here – how they reconfigure social space (2004: 5–6).

7   See, for example, www.*Heimat*123.de and www.*Heimat*123.net.

8   See www.*Heimat*123.de/heimtour.htm for details of the Hunsrück tours.

9   The first *Heimat* was filmed in over forty places, which increased with *Heimat 3*. Schneider commented that many local people enjoyed their involvement in the making of the *Heimat* trilogy, and that the production had changed their lives. The attempts to preserve the sites set up in *Heimat* and *Heimat 3* continued with discussions about converting the Günderrode house itself into a *Heimat* museum and café. The house was originally in Seibertsheim, built in 1780, and rebuilt on the banks of the Rhine near Oberwesel for *Heimat 3*. See Fritz 2004.

10 On the wider significance of visiting media sites, see Nick Couldry on the phenomenon of 'media pilgrimages': 'Media pilgrimages are specifically journeys to points with significance in media narratives' (2003: 76).

11 Talking of chains of associations triggered by remembering sequences from films, Victor Burgin writes, '[b]ut associations lead not only to roots in personal history. In selectively incorporating fragments from the image environment they also branch out to weave private and public into a unitary network of meanings. [...] Our forgotten answers to distant questions may reverberate down history to shatter remembered films. But what concerns us most is what we make from the fragments' (2004: 72).

12 Dyer writes that '*Far From Heaven* is highly palimpsestic, layered over at least three previous films, each of which shows through' (2007: 174).

13 If in its mode of address, *Heimat* managed to exceed the boundaries of the soap opera in its chronicling of everyday life in Schabbach, one of the ways it managed to encourage a more active engagement with its sequences was through its thematic concern with charting the impact of media technologies and with its highly reflexive stance towards questions of representation (see Wickham 1991).

14 In similar fashion, it could be proposed that Reitz utilises the viewing audience's awareness of how unification was represented in German cinema at the beginning of the 1990s. As Martin Brady argues, the tone of the earlier episodes of *Heimat 3* borrows from both reunification romances, such as Rudolf Thome's *Love at First Sight* (*Liebe auf den ersten Blick*, 1991) in its portrayal of a romantic affair standing as allegory for the processes of political unification, and the slapstick humour and stock characters which appeared in unification comedies such as Detlev Buck's *No More Mr Nice Guy* (*Wir können auch anders*, 1993) (2005: 57–58). In addition, the extensive coverage of the family watching the World Cup in Italy, 1990, parallels the famous ending of Fassbinder's *The Marriage of Maria Braun* (*Die Ehe der Maria Braun*, 1979).

15 See King 2003: 130–47. On the history and key generic concerns of the *Heimatfilm*, see von Moltke 2005: particularly 1–18 and 21–35.

16 Other key spaces for Hermann and Clarissa in this film include Augé's airport lounge, but also the expensive car, the train or taxi, the concert hall, the recording studio and the post-concert reception, all of which parallel Augé's topographies of 'supermodernity'. However, although Hermann and Clarissa are initially often presented in these non-places, they do offer some complexity, as motorway journeys in cars, and petrol stations, service areas, airports, car interiors and train carriages all host key conversations and encounters, for Hermann, Clarissa, and characters like Ernst and Matko particularly.

17 According to Kracauer, the hotel lobby's architecture frames the emptiness and void at the heart of modern urban life; the hotel visitors have no sense of Heimat and are, memorably, 'guests in space'. This essay, originally intended as part of a book-length study of the detective novel that Kracauer worked on between 1922 and 1925, draws heavily on Georg Simmel's urban sociological writings, and shares Simmel's concerns about the estranging power of architectural space in the modern city. Hermann and Clarissa are also at this moment *guests in time*, as their own personal joy at this chance encounter is solipsistic ('This is all just for us') and not enacted as part of the larger historical events occurring around them – for it is directly outside the lobby of Berlin's Hotel Kempinski that Germany is in the process of becoming

a unified homeland. Again, the Kempinski is hardly an innocent choice of reunion, as it is a site of considerable historical interest itself in that city's development, and so arguably a 'place' rather than a 'non-place' in Augé's terms.

18 In the first *Heimat*, the Simon house with its adjacent smithy came to be the heart of family life, the 'centre of the world' ('Mitte der Welt'), staging its series of encounters and departures, and dominated by the matriarchal figure of Maria Simon, Hermann's mother. The Simon house seemed to belong organically to Schabbach spatially and also temporally, as it claimed to have been home to the Simons across generations. In *Die zweite Heimat*, Hermann's new life in Munich finally seems to establish itself on a firm footing when he becomes part of the entourage of students that meets up in the villa they name 'der Fuchsbau' (the fox's den), the site of a number of affairs, arguments and creative experiments.

19 The idea of the house or home as Heimat is significant here too. As David Morley has argued, debates around the concept of the home and those surrounding Heimat have tended not to be conducted in any related way. Citing Eric Hobsbawm's point that home is essentially private, whereas Heimat is by definition collective, David Morley has attempted to conceive these two categories as being in close relation with one another in the contemporary moment, not least because of the huge growth in media technologies, which often link up the private sphere with the much wider sense of the public world beyond. See Morley 2000: 3–4.

20 See Johannes von Moltke's argument that Schabbach in *Heimat* operated as a metonym, rather than as a metaphor, connected as it was to the wider world (2005: 224–25).

21 As Anthony Vidler has noted, there is a long history of the haunted house being employed as the spatial registration of the phenomenon of the uncanny. Hermann and Clarissa's creative abilities are both compromised in that setting, with Clarissa particularly affected and falling seriously ill. Her fate could be compared to that of the beautiful and gifted daughter in E.T.A. Hoffmann's famous short story, 'Councillor Krespel' ('Rat Krespel'), who lives in the strange house built in the woods by her father, and is trapped in the house, despite being, in Vidler's words, 'blest with an uncannily harmonious singing voice, [...] Unable to sing lest she die of the effort' (1992: 29ff).

22 On the importance of both centripetal and centrifugal forces to the construction of space and place in Reitz's first *Heimat*, see von Moltke 2005: 216–18.

23 For a discussion of the issue of the concept of a German national Heimat after 1989, which includes all ethnic Germans linked through 'blood ties' while excluding non-white German citizens, see Morley 2000: 33.

24 One critic has suggested that the frequent appearances of BMWs in *Heimat 3* owed much to BMW's status as 'official sponsor' (Seidel 2004). Even when the driver is not alone in a car, communication between the characters is rare. *Heimat 3* typically stages significant discussions in transit in railway carriages. For an interesting reading of the car as non-place, and on the attempts by drivers to overcome this, see Bull 2004.

25 For a more detailed investigation of Reitz's idea of the time-Heimat, see King 2011.

BIBLIOGRAPHY

Aaron, Michele 2007, *Spectatorship: The power of looking on*, Wallflower, London.

Abel, Marco 2008, 'Intensifying life: the cinema of the "Berlin School"', *Cineaste* 33/4, http://cineaste.com/articles/the-berlin-school.htm.

— 2009, '"There is no authenticity in the cinema!": an interview with Andreas Dresen', *Senses of Cinema* 50, http://www.sensesofcinema.com/2009/50/andreas-dresen-interview.

— forthcoming, '22 January 2007: the establishment strikes out against the "Berlin School"', in Jennifer Kapczynski and Michael Richardson (eds), *A New History of German Cinema*, Camden House, Rochester, NY.

Addison, Heather 2005, 'Transcending time: Jean Harlow and Hollywood's Narrative of Decline', *Journal of Film and Video* 57/4, pp. 32–46.

Adelson, Leslie 2005, *The Turkish Turn in Contemporary German Literature: Towards a New Critical Grammar of Migration*, Palgrave Macmillan, Basingstoke and New York.

Adorno, Theodor W. 1977, 'The essay as form', in Shierry Weber Nicholsen (trans.), *Notes to Literature*, vol. I, Columbia University Press, New York, pp. 3–23.

— 1981 (1949), 'Cultural criticism and society', in Samuel and Shierry Weber (trans.), *Prisms*, MIT Press, Cambridge, MA, pp. 17–34.

Akin, Fatih 2004, 'Das Zornige gehört auch zu mir: Fatih Akin über seinen preisgekrönten Film *Gegen die Wand*', *epd Film* 4, www.epd.de/1stgate epd/thementexte2/19191_28985.htm.

Akin, Fatih, Lars-Olav Beier and Matthias Matussek 2007, 'From Istanbul to New York', *Spiegel* online, 28 September, http://www.spiegel.de/international/zeitgeist/0,1518,508521,00.html.

Akin, Fatih and Feridun Zaimoğlu n.d., 'Interview mit Fatih Akin', DVD bonus material of *Gegen die Wand*, Universal Pictures Germany Inc.

Akin, Monique 2008, *Fatih Akin – Tagebuch eines Filmreisenden. Ein Film von Monique Akin*, bonus material special edition of *Auf der anderen Seite*. Pandora Film.

Althen, Michael 2004, 'Aus weiter Ferne, so nah', *Frankfurter Allgemeine Zeitung*, 3 September.

— 2008, 'Die Sache mit der Hummersuppe', *Frankfurter Allgemeine*, 24 September.

Althen, Michael and Bernt Rebhandl 2002, 'Wie das Politbüro die Verhältnisse im deutschen Film zum Tanzen brachte' (Interview with Christian Petzold and Harun Farocki), *Frankfurter Allgemeine*, 23 May.

Altman, Rick 2003, 'A semantic/syntactic approach to film genre', in Barry Keith Grant (ed.), *Film Genre Reader*, vol. III, University of Texas, Austin, pp. 27–41.

Andreas (sic) 2001, *Karl-May-RAF*, http://www.salonrouge.de/raf-pop.htm.

Anon. 2005, 'Interview mit Hans-Christian Schmid and Bernd Lange', http://www.requiem-der-film.de/downloads/interview_schmid_lange.pdf.

Anon. 2006, '*Das Leben der Anderen* production notes', http://thecia.com.au/reviews/l/images/lives-of-others-das-leben-der-anderen-production-notes.rtf.

Ansen, David 2005, 'Trapped in a vipers' nest: a spellbinding look at Hitler's days in the bunker', *Newsweek*, 21 February.

— 2007, 'A Waking Nightmare: Sex, spies und audiotape in corrupt East Germany', *Newsweek*, 12 February.

Archibald, David 2008, 'An interview with Stefan Ruzowitsky', *Cineaste* (web-only), http://www.cineaste.com/articles/the-counterfeiters.htm.

Arendt, Hannah 1963, *Eichmann in Jerusalem: A report on the banality of evil*, Viking, New York.

— 1993, *Besuch in Deutschland – Die Nachwirkungen des Naziregimes* (1950), Rotbuch, Berlin.

Arndt, Stefan 2003, 'Das vergessene Jahr', in Michael Töteberg (ed.), *Good Bye Lenin!*, Schwarzkopf und Schwarzkopf, Berlin, pp. 136–47.

Arslan, Savas 2009, 'The new cinema of Turkey', in Daniela Berghahn (ed.), *New Cinemas*, special issue, 'Turkish-German Dialogues on Screen', 7/1, pp. 83–97.

Augé, Marc 1995, *Non-places: Introduction to an anthropology of supermodernity*, John Howe (trans.), Verso, London.

Bamler, Vera 2009, 'Sexualität im Alter – (k)ein Problem?', in *Frühlingsgefühle im Herbst des Lebens – Liebe Erotik, Sexualität im Alter und ihr Einfluss auf Betreuungsbeziehungen*, 15. Salzburger Diakonie-Dialoge, pp. 5–10.

Bathrick, David 1995, *The Powers of Speech: The politics of culture in the GDR*, University of Nebraska, Lincoln.

— 2007, 'Whose hi/story is it? The US reception of *Downfall*,' Rachel Leah Magshamrain and David Bathrick (trans.), *New German Critique* 102/34/3, pp. 1–16.

Bauer, Katja 2007, 'Die feine Grenzlinie auf dem Weg zum Verra', *Stuttgarter Zeitung*, 27 February.

Baumann, Zygmunt 1991, *Modernity and Ambivalence*, Polity Press, Oxford.

Bazzini, D. G., W. D. McIntosh, S. M. Smith, S. Cook, and C. Harris 1997, 'The aging women in popular film: underrepresented, unattractive, unfriendly, and unintelligent', *Sex Roles*, 36, pp.531–43.

Behrens, Volker 2006, '"Mein Glaube sieht anders aus": Regisseur Hans-Christian Schmid über Kirche, Aberglauben und Exorzismus', *Hamburger Abendblatt*, 4 March, p.7.

Beier, Lars-Olav 2006, 'Die neuen Heimatfilme', *Der Spiegel* 6, p.146.

Beier, Lars-Olav and Conny Neumann 2005, 'Gruß aus dem Jenseits', *Der Spiegel* 47, p.147.

— 2007, 'On the Oscar campaign trail', *Spiegel* online, 23 February, http://www.spiegel.de/international/spiegel/0,1518,466450,00.html.

Bennett, Ray and Joel Taylor 2004, 'Aging auds give German b.o. hope', *Hollywood Reporter* 386/8, p.56.

Berendse, Gerrit-Jan and Ingo Cornils 2008, 'Introduction: the long shadow of terrorism', in Berendse and Cornils (eds), *Baader-Meinhof Returns: History and cultural memory of left-wing terrorism*, Rodopi, Amsterdam, pp.9–20.

Bergfelder, Tim 2005, *International Adventures: Popular German cinema and European co-productions in the 1960s*, Berghahn, Oxford and New York.

Bergfelder, Tim, Erica Carter and Deniz Göktürk 2002, 'Introduction', in Bergfelder, Carter and Göktürk (eds), *The German Cinema Book*, BFI, London, pp.1–12.

Berghahn, Daniela 2006a, 'No place like home? Or impossible homecomings in the films of Fatih Akin', *New Cinemas* 4/3, pp.141–57.

— 2006b, 'Post-1990 screen memories: how East and West German cinema remembers the Third Reich and the Holocaust', *German Life and Letters* 59, pp.294–308.

— 2009, 'Introduction: Turkish-German dialogues on screen', in Berghahn (ed.), *New Cinemas*, special issue, 'Turkish-German Dialogues on Screen', 7/1, pp.3–9.

— 2010, 'Diasporas, film and cinema', in Kim Knott and Seán McLoughlin (eds), *Diasporas: Concepts, identities, intersections*, Zed Books, London, pp.12–49.

Berghahn, Daniela and Claudia Sternberg 2010, 'Locating migrant and diasporic cinema', in Berghahn and Sternberg (eds), *European Cinema in Motion: Migrant and diasporic film in contemporary Europe*, Palgrave, Basingstoke.

Bickle, Peter 2004, *Heimat: A critical theory of the German idea of homeland*, Boydell & Brewer, Rochester, NY.

Bischoff, Willi (ed.) 2005, *Filmri:ss – Studien über den Film 'Der Untergang'*, Unrast, Münster.

Bisky, Lothar 2005, *So viele Träume*, Berlin, Rowohlt.

Boa, Elizabeth and Rachel Palfreyman 2000, *Heimat: A German Dream: Regional loyalties and national identity in German culture 1890–1990*, OUP, Oxford.

Bordwell, David 1979, 'The art cinema as a mode of film practice', *Film Criticism* 4/1, pp. 56–64.

— 1986, *Narration in Fiction Film*, University of Wisconsin, Madison.

Boyd, William 2005, 'Decline and fall,' *Guardian*, 19 March.

Boym, Svetlana 2001, *The Future of Nostalgia*, Basic Books, New York.

Bradshaw, Peter 2007 '*The Lives of Others*', *Guardian*, 13 April.

Brady, Martin 2005, '*Heimat 3*', review, *Sight and Sound* 15/5, pp. 57–58; 15/6, pp. 58–60.

Brah, Avtar 1996, *Cartographies of Diaspora: Contesting identities*, Routledge, London and New York.

Breinersdorfer, Fred 2006 (ed.), *Sophie Scholl: Die letzten Tage*, Frankfurt am Main, Fischer.

Breinersdorfer, Fred and Marc Rothemund 2006, 'Inspiration durch Fakten: Bemerkungen zum Konzept des Films', in Breinersdorfer (ed.), *Sophie Scholl: Die letzten Tage*, Frankfurt am Main, Fischer, pp. 316–30.

Briefel, Aviva 2009, 'What some ghosts don't know: spectral incognizance and the horror film', *Narrative* 17/1 (January), pp. 95–108.

Brunst, Klaudia 2004, 'Wiedervereinigung – made im Hunsrück', *Berliner Zeitung*, 2 October.

Buch, Esteban 2003, *Beethoven's Ninth: A political history*, Richard Miller (trans.), University of Chicago Press, Chicago.

Buch, Hans Christoph 1999, 'Schönen Gruß von Charlie Chaplin', *Tagesspiegel*, 9 November.

Buchner, Kathrin 2008, 'Der Baader Meinhof Komplex: Das sagen Jugendliche zum RAF-Film', *Stern.de*, http://www.stern.de/unterhaltung/film/640818.html.

Bude, Heinz 2001, *Generation Berlin*, Merve, Berlin.

Bull, Michael 2004, 'To each their own bubble: mobile spaces of sound in the city', in Nick Couldry and Anna McCarthy (eds), *Mediaspace: Place, scale and culture in a media age*, Routledge, Abingdon and New York, pp. 275–93.

Burger, Adolf 2007 (1983), *Des Teufels Werkstatt: Die größte Geldfälscheraktion der Weltgeschichte*, Elizabeth Sandmann, Munich.

— 2009, *The Devil's Workshop: A memoir of the Nazi counterfeiting operation*, Frontline Books, London.

Bürger, Peter 1972, Theorie der Avantgarde, Suhrkamp, Frankfurt am Main.

Burgin, Victor 2004, *The Remembered Film*, Reaktion, London.

Burgoyne, Robert 2003, 'Memory, history and digital imagery in contemporary film', in Paul Grainge (ed.), *Memory and Popular Film*, Manchester University Press, Manchester and New York, pp. 220–36.

Burns, Rob 2009, 'On the streets and on the road: identity in transit in Turkish German travelogues on screen', in Daniela Berghahn (ed.), *New Cinemas*, special issue, 'Turkish-German Dialogues on Screen', 7/1, pp. 11–26.

Busche, Andreas 2004, 'Punk oder türkische Folklore? Fatih Akins Film *Gegen die Wand* rückt gegen alle kulturellen Zuschreibungen an', *Die Zeit*, 11 March, http://www.zeit.de/2004/12/Gegen_die_Wand.

Buschkämper, Timo 2007, 'Nicht auf KZ-Opfer reduzieren', interview with Stefan Ruzowitzky, *Filmreporter.de*, 1 April, http://www.filmreporter.de/stars/interview/723;Nicht-auf-KZ-Opfer-reduzieren.

Buß, Christian 2006, 'Gott schweigt', *Spiegel* online, 2 March, http://www.spiegel.de/kultur/kino/0,1518,403930,00.html.

Byg, Barton 1995, *Landscapes of Resistance: The German films of Danièle Huillet and Jean-Marie Straub*, University of California Press, Berkeley.

Canjuers, Pierre and Guy Debord 1960, 'Preliminaries toward defining a unitary revolutionary program', in Ken Knabb (trans. and ed.) 2006, *Situationist International Anthology*, revised and expanded edition, Bureau of Public Secrets, Berkeley, pp. 387–93.

Carroll, Noël 1990, *The Philosophy of Horror or Paradoxes of the Heart*, Routledge, London.

Chaudhuri, Shohini 2006, *Feminist Film Theorists*, Routledge, London.

Chaussy, Ulrich 2006, 'Biographische Notizen', in Fred Breinersdorfer (ed.), *Sophie Scholl: Die letzten Tage*, Frankfurt am Main, Fischer, pp. 85–158.

Cheon, Hyun Soon 2007, *Intermedialität von Text und Bild bei Alexander Kluge: zur Korrespondenz von Früher Neuzeit und Moderne*, Königshausen & Neumann, Würzburg.

Chivers, Sally 2006, 'Baby Jane grew up: the dramatic intersection of age with disability', *Canadian Review of American Studies* 36, pp. 211–27.

Clover, Carol 1992, *Man, Women, and Chain Saws: Gender in the modern horror film*, Princeton University Press, Princeton.

Cohen, Roger 2000, 'Music at site of Nazi camp ignites protest', *New York Times*, 6 May, http://www.nytimes.com/2000/05/06/arts/music-at-site-of-nazi-camp-ignites-protest.html.

Collins, Andrew 2007, '*The Lives Of Others*', *The Film Programme*, BBC Radio 4, first broadcast 13 April.

Conley, Tom 2006, 'Landscape and perception: on Anthony Mann', in Martin Lefevbre (ed.), *Landscape and Film*, Routledge, New York and Abingdon, pp. 291–313.

Conrad, Vera 2004 (ed.), *Der Untergang: Materialien für den Unterricht*, Clever! Verlag, Munich.

Cooke, Paul 2004, 'Ostalgie's not what it used to be: the German television GDR craze of 2003', *German Politics & Society* 4/22, pp. 14–24.

— 2005, *Representing East Germany Since Unification: From colonization to nostalgia*, Berg, Oxford.

— 2006, 'Abnormal consensus: the new internationalism of German Cinema', in Stuart Taberner and Paul Cooke (eds), *German Culture, Politics, and*

Literature into the Twenty-First Century: Beyond normalization, Camden House, Rochester, pp.223–37.

— 2007, '*Der Untergang* (2004): victims, perpetrators and the continuing fascination of fascism,' in Helmut Schmitz (ed.), *A Nation of Victims? Representations of German wartime suffering from 1945 to the present*, Rodopi, Amsterdam/New York, pp.247–61.

— 2007, 'Introduction', in Cooke (ed.), *World Cinema's 'Dialogues' with Hollywood*, Palgrave, New York, pp.1–16.

Cooke, Paul and Andrew Plowman 2003 (eds), *German Writers and the Politics of Culture: Dealing with the Stasi*, Palgrave, Basingstoke.

Couldry, Nick 2003, *Media Rituals: A critical approach*, Routledge, London.

Couldry, Nick and Anna McCarthy 2004 (eds), *Mediaspace: Place, scale and culture in a media age*, Routledge, Abingdon and New York.

Custon, George F. 1992, *Bio/Pics: How Hollywood constructed public history*, Rutgers University Press, New Brunswick.

Dargis, Manohla 2007, '*The Bourne Ultimatum* (2007): still searching, but with darker eyes', *New York Times*, 3 August.

Debord, Guy 1957, 'Report on the construction of situations and on the international situationist tendency's conditions of organization and action', in Ken Knabb (trans. and ed.) 2006, *Situationist International Anthology*, revised and expanded edition, Bureau of Public Secrets, Berkeley, pp.25–43.

— 1958, 'Theory of the dérive', in Ken Knabb (trans. and ed.) 2006, *Situationist International Anthology*, revised and expanded edition, Bureau of Public Secrets, Berkeley, pp.62–66.

— 2009, *Society of the Spectacle*, Ken Knabb (trans.), Soul Bay Press, Eastbourne, first published 1967.

Deleuze, Gilles 1989, *Cinema 2: The time-image*, Hugh Tomlinson (trans.), University of Minneapolis, Minneapolis.

Deleuze, Gilles and Félix Guattari 1987, *A Thousand Plateaus: Capitalism and schizophrenia*, Brian Massumi (trans.), University of Minnesota Press, Minneapolis.

Delius, Friedrich Christian 2003, *Warum ich schon immer recht hatte und andere Irrtümer: Ein Leitfaden für deutsches Denken*, Rowohlt, Berlin.

Dell, Matthias 2006, 'Ums Ganze', *Der Freitag*, 8 September, http://www.freitag.de/2006/36/06361302.php.

Denby, David 2005, '*Downfall*', *New Yorker*, 21 February.

d'Orves, Nicolas d'Estienne 2008, 'Nouvelle vague Allemande', *Le Figaro*, 18 January.

Drake, Philip 2003, '"Mortgaged to music": new retro movies in 1990s Hollywood cinema', in Paul Grainge (ed.), *Memory and Popular Film*, Manchester University Press, Manchester and New York, pp.183–201.

Dresen, Andreas 2008a, interview on the *Wolke 9* DVD, Senator Home Entertainment.

— 2008b, 'Schwimmen Sie nackt, das ist viel besser', interview with Christiane Peitz and Esther Kogelbloom, *Tagesspiegel*, 31 August.

— 2008c, 'Sex im Alter ist schöner, ungenierter', interview with Felix von Boehm and Ingmar Bertram, *Frankfurter Rundschau*, 2 September.

— 2009, interview, *Senses of Cinema* 50, http://www.sensesofcinema.com/2009/50/andreas-dresen-interview.

Drilo, Coco (sic) 2001, *Das RAF-Mode-Phantom*, http://www.salonrouge.de/raf-hype2.htm.

Duralde, Alonso 2009, 'Old folks rarely find a good home onscreen', *Today*, 26 May, http://today.msnbs.msn.com/id/30945270/.

Dyer, Richard 2007, *Pastiche*, Routledge, Abingdon and New York.

Ehrlicher, Gerhard 2006, 'Die Realität war eine andere', *Frankfurter Allgemeine Zeitung*, 21 June.

Eichinger, Bernd 2004a, 'Daher kommen wir: Der Regisseur Oliver Hirschbiegel über seinen Film *Der Untergang*', interview with Anke Westphal, *Berliner Zeitung*, 11 September.

— 2004b, interview, http://www.der-untergang.de.

Eisenstein, Sergei 1977, 'A dialectic approach to film form', in Jay Leyda (ed. and trans.), *Film Form: Essays in Film Theory*, Harcourt, Brace & Janovich, New York, pp. 45–63.

Elley, Derek 2005, '*Downfall – Der Untergang*', *Variety*, 15 February.

Elsaesser, Thomas 1989, *New German Cinema: A history*, BFI Books, London.

— 1996, 'Subject positions, speaking positions: from *Holocaust, Our Hitler*, and *Heimat* to *Shoah* and *Schindler's List*', in Vivian Sobchack (ed.), *The Persistence of History: Cinema, television, and the modern event*, Routledge, New York and London, pp. 145–83.

— 2002, 'New German Cinema and history: the case of Alexander Kluge', in Tim Bergfelder, Erica Carter and Deniz Göktürk (eds), *The German Cinema Book*, BFI, London, pp. 182–91.

— 2005, *European Cinema: Face to face with Hollywood*, University of Amsterdam Press, Amsterdam.

— 2007, *Terror und Trauma: Zur Gewalt des Vergangenen in der BRD*, Kulturverlag Kadmos, Berlin.

— 2008, 'Ethical calculus: the cross-cultural dilemmas and moral burdens of Fatih Akin's *The Edge of Heaven*', *Film Comment*, May/June, http://www.filmlinc.com/fcm/mj08/heaven.htm.

Emmerich, Wolfgang 1996, *Kleine Literaturgeschichte der DDR: Erweiterte Neuausgabe*, Gustav Kiepenheuer, Leipzig.

Erdoğan, Nezih 2009, 'Star director as symptom: reflections on the reception of Fatih Akin in the Turkish media', in Daniela Berghahn (ed.), *New Cinemas*, special issue, 'Turkish-German Dialogues on Screen', 7/1, pp. 27–38.

Evans, Owen 2010, 'Redeeming the demon?: the legacy of the Stasi in *Das Leben der Anderen*', *Memory Studies*, 3/2, pp. 1–14.

Falck, Marianne 2006, *Filmheft: Das Leben der Anderen*, Bundeszentrale für Politische Bildung, Bonn, http://www.bpb.de/publikationen/OLS9BA,0,0 Das_Leben_der_Anderen.html.

Farmer, James C. 2003, *Opera and the New German Cinema*, PhD dissertation, University of Iowa.

Fassbinder, Rainer Werner 1971,'Imitation of life: Über Douglas Sirk', *Fernsehen und Film* 2 (February), pp. 9–13. Published in English as: Fassbinder, Rainer Werner 1992, 'Imitation of life: on the films of Douglas Sirk', in Michael Töteberg and Leo A. Lensing (eds), *The Anarchy of Imagination*, Johns Hopkins Press, Baltimore, pp. 77–89.

— 1977, 'Interview with Rainer Werner Fassbinder', first published in *Cineaste*, 8/2, http://encarta.msn.com/sidebar_762504310/interview_with_rainer_ werner_ fassbinder.html.

Fenner, Angelica 2006, 'Traversing the screen politics of migration: Xavier Koller's *Journey of Hope*', in Eva Rueschmann (ed.), *Moving Pictures, Migrating Identities*, University of Mississippi Press, Jackson, pp. 28–38.

Fest, Joachim 1973, *Hitler: Eine Biographie*, Propyläen, Berlin.

— 2002, *Der Untergang: Hitler und das Ende des Dritten Reiches*, Alexander Fest Verlag, Berlin. Published in English in 2004, *Inside Hitler's Bunker: The last days of the Third Reich*, Farrar, Straus & Giroux, New York.

Fiedler, Manuela 1997, *Heimat im deutschen Film: Ein Mythos zwischen Regression und Utopie*, Coppi, Alfeld.

Fischer, Arthur, Yvonne Fritzsche, Werner Fuchs-Heinritz and Richard Münchmeier 2000, *Jugend 2000 13: Shell Jugendstudie*, Leske and Budrich, Opladen.

Fisher, Jaimey 2010, 'German historical film as production trend: European heritage cinema and melodrama in *The Lives of Others*', in Jaimey Fisher and Brad Prager (eds), *The Collapse of the Conventional: German film and its politics at the turn of the twenty-first century*, Wayne State University Press, Detroit, pp. 186–215.

Fisher, Jaimey and Brad Prager 2010, 'Introduction', in Fisher and Prager (eds), *The Collapse of the Conventional: German film and its politics at the turn of the twenty-first century*, Wayne State University Press, Detroit, pp. 1–38.

Flinn, Carol 1992, *Strains of Utopia: Gender, nostalgia, and Hollywood film music*, Princeton University Press, Princeton, NJ.

Flueren, Hanns J., Marion Klein and Heidrun Redetzki-Rodermann 2002, 'Das Altersbild der deutschen Daily Soaps', *Medien Praktisch* 1, pp. 23–27.

Forrest, Tara 2007, *The Politics of Imagination: Benjamin, Kracauer, Kluge*, Transcript, Bielefeld.

Foucault, Michel 1977, *Discipline and Punish: Birth of the prison*, Alan Sheridan (trans.), Penguin, London.

| Bibliography |

French, Philip 2005, '*Sophie Scholl: The Final Days*', *Observer*, 30 October.

Friedberg, Anne 2006, *The Virtual Window: From Alberti to Microsoft*, MIT Press, Cambridge, MA and London.

Fritz, Herbert 2004, 'Schnitzeljagd fuer Cineasten', *Frankfurter Rundschau*, 16 October.

Fuhr, Eckhard 2004a, 'Auf Augenhöhe', *Die Welt*, 25 August.

— 2004b, 'Familienbande reissen nicht', *Berliner Morgenpost*, 30 September.

— 2008, 'Terror als Action', *Welt* online, 18 September, www.welt.de/kultur/article2461404/terror-als-Action.html.

Fukuyama, Francis 1992, *The End of History*, Penguin, New York.

Funder, Anna 2007, 'Eyes without a Face', *Sight and Sound* 5/17, pp. 16–20.

Gabrero, Daniel G. 2006, 'Interview with *Requiem* director Hans-Christian Schmid', *Vertigo* 5, http://www.vertigomagazine.co.uk/showarticle.php?sel=bac&siz=1&id=632.

Gallagher, Tag 2009, 'The greatest filmmakers you've never heard of', *Sight and Sound* (December), pp. 38–41.

Gemünden, Gerd 1994, 'Re-fusing Brecht: the cultural politics of Fassbinder's German Hollywood', *New German Critique* 63, special issue on Rainer Werner Fassbinder, pp. 54–75.

Geppert, Anna 2002, 'Das Leben riecht so gut', *Tagesspiegel*, 3 January, http://www.tagesspiegel.de/kultur/art772,1924160.

Gleiberman, Owen 2005, '*Downfall*', *Entertainment Weekly*, 21 February.

Göktürk, Deniz 2010, 'Sound bridges: transnational mobility as ironic melodrama', in Daniela Berghahn and Claudia Sternberg (eds), *European Cinema in Motion: Migrant and diasporic film in contemporary Europe*, Palgrave, Basingstoke, pp. 215–34.

Gorbachev, Mikhail and Daisaku Ikeda 2005, *Moral Lessons of the Twentieth Century: Gorbachev and Ikeda on Buddhism and Communism*, I.B. Tauris, London.

Grainge, Paul 2003, 'Introduction: memory and popular film', in Grainge (ed.), *Memory and Popular Film*, Manchester University Press, Manchester and New York, pp. 1–20.

Grant, Barry Keith 2007, *Film Genres: From iconography to ideology*, Wallflower, London.

Gray, Christopher 1998 (trans. and ed.), *Leaving the Twentieth Century: The incomplete work of the Situationist International*, Rebel Press, London, first published 1974.

Grisebach, Valeska 2006, 'Man stürzt, steht wieder auf und latscht weiter', Interview with Christina Nord, *Taz*, 18 February, http://www.taz.de/index.php?id=archivseite&dig=2006/02/18/a0189.

— 2007a, 'Von hier aus', *Revolver* 16, pp. 74–91.

— 2007b, 'Helden des eigenen Lebens', *Sehnsucht* DVD, Piffl Medien.

Gross, Jane 2008, 'Silver hair on the silver screen', *New York Times*, 31 July, http://newoldage.blogs.nytimes.com/2008/07/31 http://newoldage.blogs.nytimes.com/2008/07/31/silver-hair-on-the-silver-screen.

Gullette, Margaret Morganroth 1997, *Declining to Decline: Cultural combat and the politics of the midlife*, University of Virginia Press, Charlottesville.

Gwynn, William 2006, *Writing History in Film*, Routledge, Abingdon.

Haase, Christine 2006 'Ready for his close-up? Representing Hitler in *Der Untergang/Downfall*, 2004', *Studies in European Cinema* 3/3, pp. 189–99.

— 2007, *When Heimat Meets Hollywood*, Camden House, Rochester, NY.

Habermas, Jürgen 1991, 'Ein nützlicher Maulwurf, der den schönen Rasen zerstört', in *Verleihung des Lessingpreises 1989 an Alexander Kluge: Reden anlässlich der Preisübergabe im Passage-Filmtheater Hamburg am 25. September 1990*, Kulturbehörde, Hamburg, pp. 7–14.

Hagen, Wolfgang and Niklas Luhmann 2004, *Warum haben Sie keinen Fernseher, Herr Luhmann?: letze Gespräche mit Niklas Luhmann, Dirk Baecker, Norbert Bolz, Wolfgang Hagen, Alexander Kluge*, Kadmos, Berlin.

Hake, Sabine 2002, *German National Cinema*, Routledge, London.

— 2007, 'Historisierung der NS-Vergangenheit. *Der Untergang* (2004) zwischen Historienfilm und Eventkino', in Inge Stephan and Alexandra Tacke (eds), *Nach-Bilder des Holocaust*, Martin Kley (trans.), Böhlau, Cologne, pp. 188–218.

Hallberg, Jana and Alexander Wewerka 2001, 'Zwischen Impuls und Korsett. Andreas Dresen im Gespräch', in Jana Hallberg and Alexander Wewerka (eds), *Dogma 95: Zwischen Kontrolle und Chaos*, Alexander Verlag, Berlin, pp. 319–26.

Halle, Randall 2008, *German Film after Germany: Toward a transnational aesthetic*, University of Illinois Press, Urbana and Chicago.

Halle, Randall and Margaret McCarthy 2003, *Light Motives: German popular film in perspective*, Wayne State Press, Detroit.

Handke, Sebastian 2006, 'Die Wanzen sind echt: Kinodebatte über *Das Leben der Anderen*', *Tagesspiegel*, 8 April.

Handling, Piers 2007, '*The Edge of Heaven/Auf der anderen Seite*', http://www.cinema.bg/sff/distribution/eng/movie.php?movieSid=908.

Hansen, Eric 2004, '*Downfall*', *Hollywood Reporter*, 16 September.

Harmsen, Torsten 2006, 'Irgendwie geht's um Stasi: 700 Schüler sehen auf Einladung Klaus Bögers *Das Leben der Anderen*', *Berliner Zeitung*, 4 April.

Henckel von Donnersmarck, Florian 2007, *Das Leben der Anderen: Filmbuch*, Suhrkamp, Frankfurt am Main.

Higson, Andrew 2000, 'The limiting imagination of national cinema', in Mette Hjort and Scott Mckenzie (eds), *Cinema and Nation*, Routledge, London and New York, pp. 63–74.

Hillman, Roger 2005, *Unsettling Scores: German film, music, and ideology*, Indiana, Bloomington.

Hirsch, Marianne 1997, *Family Frames: Photography, narrative and postmemory*, Harvard University Press, Cambridge, MA and London.

Hirte, Ronald 2002, 'Ein Später Held: Sigmund Jähns Flug ins All', in Silke Satjukow and Rainer Gries (eds), *Sozialistische Helden: Einen Kulturgeschichte von Propaganafiguren in Osteuropa und der DDR*, Ch. Links Berlin, pp. 158–73.

Hodges, F. M. 2003, 'The penalties of passion and desire: love and the aging male in early 20th century film,' *The Aging Male* 6, pp. 18–23.

Hodgin, Nick 2004, '*Berlin is in Germany* and *Good Bye, Lenin!* Taking Leave of the GDR?', *Debatte: Review of Contemporary German Affairs* 12/12, pp. 25–46.

— 2011, *Screening the East: Heimat, memory and nostalgia in German film since 1989*, Berghahn Books, Oxford.

Hodgin, Nick and Caroline Pearce 2011, 'Introduction', in Hodgin and Pearce (eds), *The GDR Remembered: Representations of the East German state since 1989*, Camden House, Rochester, NY.

Hollstein, Miriam 2008, 'Buback-Sohn sieht im RAF-Drama einen Täter-Film', *Welt Online*, 20 September, www.welt.de/kultur/article2469200/Buback-Sohn-sieht-imRAF-Drama-einen-Taeter-Film.html.

Homewood, Chris 2006, 'The return of "undead" history: the West German terrorist as vampire and the problem of "normalizing" the past in Margarethe von Trotta's *Die bleierne Zeit* (1981) and Christian Petzold's *Die innere Sicherheit* (2001)', in Stuart Taberner and Paul Cooke (eds), *German Culture, Politics, and Literature into the Twenty-First Century: Beyond normalization*, Camden House, Rochester, NY, pp. 121–35.

— 2008, 'Making invisible memory visible: communicative memory and taboo in Andres Veiel's *Black Box BRD* (2001)', in Gerrit-Jan Berendse and Ingo Cornils (eds), *Baader-Meinhof Returns: History and cultural memory of German left-wing terrorism*, Amsterdam, Rodopi, pp. 231–49.

Huber, Christoph 2008, 'Neu im Kino: Das bleierne Zeitbild', *Die Presse*, 19 September, www.diepresse.com/home/kultur/film/filmkritik/415955/index.do.

Huggan, Graham 2001, *The Postcolonial Exotic: Marketing the margins*, Routledge, London and New York.

Hutcheon, Linda 1994, *Irony's Edge: The theory and politics of irony*, Routledge, London and New York.

James, Nick 2006, 'All Together Now', *Sight & Sound* 16/12, pp. 26–27.

Jancovich, Mark 2002, 'General Introduction', in Jancovich (ed.), *Horror: The film reader*, Routledge, York, pp. 1–20.

Jancovich, Mark, Lucy Faire and Sarah Stubbings 2003, *The Place of the Audience: Cultural Geographies of Film Consumption*, London, BFI.

Jansen, Peter W. 2004, 'Deutschland, blaue Blume: Auf der grossen Leinwand: Edgar Reitz' *Heimat 3* kommt nun nach Berlin', *Tagesspiegel*, 29 September.

Jekubzik, Günter H. (n.d.), 'Wenders Interview', http://www.filmtabs.de/archiv/Personen/Wenders%20in%20Aachen.html.

Jenschonnek, Günter 2006, 'Sehnsucht nach unpolitischen Märchen', *Süddeutsche Zeitung*, 16 May.

Johnson, Brian D. 2007, 'The last taboo: geriatric romance', *Maclean's* 120/2, p.57.

Junge, Traudl with Melissa Müller 2003, *Bis zur letzten Stunde: Hitlers Sekretärin erzählt ihr Leben*, Munich, Claassen Verlag. Published in English as: 2003, *Until the Final Hour: Hitler's last secretary*, London, Weidenfeld & Nicolson.

Kaes, Anton 1989, *From Hitler to Heimat: The return of history as film*, Harvard University Press, Cambridge and London.

— 1992, *From Hitler to Heimat: The return of history as film*, Harvard University Press, Cambridge, MA and London.

Kauffmann, Stanley 2005, 'Last Acts', *New Republic*, 21 February.

Kermode, Mark 1998, *The Exorcist*, revised 2nd edn, BFI, London.

Kershaw, Ian 2004, 'The Human Hitler', *Guardian*, 17 September.

King, Alasdair 2003, 'Placing *Green is the Heath* (1951): spatial politics and emergent West German identity', in Randall Halle and Margaret McCarthy (eds), *Light Motives: German popular film in perspective*, Wayne State University Press, Detroit, pp.130–47.

— 2011, '*Heimat 3*: Edgar Reitz's time machine', in James Skidmore and Gabriele Mueller (eds), *Cinema and Social Change in Germany and Austria*, Wilfrid Laurier University Press, Waterloo.

Klein, Naomi 2000, *No Logo*, Flamingo, London.

Kluge, Alexander 1975, *Gelegenheitsarbeit einer Sklavin: Zur realistischen Methode*, Suhrkamp Verlag, Frankfurt am Main.

— 1980, *Die Patriotin: Text und Bilder,* Zweitausendeins, Frankfurt am Main.

— 1984, 'Schicksal und seine-Gegengeschichten: Zu zwei Textstellen aus Opern', Merkur: deutsche Zeitschrift für europäischces Denken, 38:6 pp.639–50.

— 1991, 'Öffentlichkeit 1990', *Verleihung des Lessingpreises 1989 an Alexander Kluge: Reden anlässlich der Preisübergabe im Passage-Filmtheater Hamburg am 25. September 1990*, Kulturbehörde, Hamburg, pp.15–26.

— 2000a, *Chronik der Gefühle*, Suhrkamp, Frankfurt am Main.

— 2000b, *Facts & Fakes: Fernseh-Nachschriften,*Vorwerk 8, Berlin.

— 2007, *Geschichten vom Kino*, Suhrkamp, Frankfurt am Main.

— 2008, *Nachrichten aus der ideologischen Antike: Eisensteins 'Kapital'*, Absolut Medien, Berlin.

Kluge, Alexander and Christian Schulte 1999, *In Gefahr und grösster Not bringt der Mittelweg den Tod: Texte zu Kino, Film, Politik*, Vorwerk 8, Berlin.

— 2002, *In Gefahr und grösster Not bringt der Mittelweg den Tod: Texte zu Kino, Film, Politik,*Vorwerk 8, Berlin.

Kluge, Alexander and Christopher Pavsek 1996, *Learning Processes with a Deadly Outcome*, Duke University Press, Durham, NC.

Kluge, Alexander and Martin Weinmann 2007a, *Sämtliche Kinofilme*, Zweitausendeins, Frankfurt am Main.

— 2007b, *Neonröhren des Himmels: Filmalbum*, Zweitausendeins, Frankfurt am Main.

Knabb, Ken 2006 (trans. and ed.), *Situationist International Anthology*, revised and expanded edition, Bureau of Public Secrets, Berkeley, CA.

Knörer, Ekkehard 2004, 'Riecht wie Führerbunker', *Jump Cut Magazin*, 22 September.

Knorpp, Barbara 2007, 'Edgar Reitz's *Heimat 3*', *Global Media and Communication* 3/1, pp. 125–28.

Koch, Gertrud 2004, 'Das Nichts für einen Schnauzbart', *Taz*, 30 December.

Koebner, Sascha 2006, 'Oldtimer: Alte Menschen im Film', *Film-dienst* 16, pp. 38–40.

Koenen, Gerd 2007, *Das rote Jahrzehnt: Unsere kleine deutsche Kulturrevolution, 1967–1977*, Fischer, Frankfurt am Main.

Koepnick, Lutz 2002a, 'Reframing the past: heritage cinema and Holocaust in the 1990s', *New German Critique* 87, special issue on Postwall Cinema, pp. 47–82.

— 2002b, *The Dark Mirror: German cinema between Hitler and Hollywood*, University of California Press, Berkeley.

— 2004, '"Amerika gibt's überhaupt nicht!" Notes on the German heritage film', in Agnes C. Mueller (ed.), *German Pop Culture: How American is it?*, University of Michigan Press, Ann Arbor, pp. 191–208.

Körte, Peter 2006, 'Der Unberührende: *Das Leben der anderen* ist der ideale Konsensfilm', *Frankfurter Allgemeine Sonntagzeitung*, 19 March.

Kothenschulte, Daniel 2009, 'Im Guten wie in Bösen; Potzdonner: "Der Baader Meinhof Komplex" ist für den Auslands-Oscar nominiert', *Frankfurter Rundschau*, 23 January.

Kracauer, Siegfried 1995, 'The hotel lobby', in *The Mass Ornament: Weimar Essays*, Harvard University Press, Cambridge.

Kraushaar, Wolfgang 2008, 'Warum die RAF bis heute verklärt wird', *Welt* online, 7 September, www.welt.de/kultur/article2408097/warum-die-RAF-bis-heute-verklaert-wird.html.

Krekeler, Elmar 2006, 'Am Kreuzweg: Hans-Christian Schmid verfilmt nach einem authentischen Fall ein deutsches "Requiem"', *Welt*, 2 March, p. 29.

Kruger (sic), Bernhard 1958, 'I was the world's greatest counterfeiter', interview with Murray Teigh Bloom, *American Weekly*, 8 June, pp. 6–9 and 15 June, pp. 20–23.

Kurbjuweit, Dirk 2008, 'Bilder der Barbarei', *Spiegel* 37.

Landsberg, Alison 2003, 'Prosthetic memory: the ethics and politics of memory in an age of mass culture', in Paul Grainge (ed.), *Memory and Popular Film*, Manchester University Press, Manchester, pp. 144–61.

— 2004, *Prosthetic Memory: The transformation of American remembrance in the age of mass culture*, Columbia University Press, New York.

Landy, Marcia 1997, *Cinematic Uses of the Past*, University of Minnesota Press, Minneapolis.

Lane, A. 2006, 'Evil Touch', *New Yorker*, 27 February.

Langer, Lawrence L. 1991, *Holocaust Testimonies: The ruins of memory*, Yale University Press, New Haven, CT and London.

Langston, Richard 2008, *Visions of Violence: German avant-gardes after Fascism*, Northwestern University Press, Evanston, IL.

Lau, Jörg 2004, 'Die Türken sind da', *Zeit online*, 26 February, http://www.zeit. de/2004/10/T_9frken.

Levi, Primo 1988 (1986), *The Drowned and the Saved*, Raymond Rosenthal (trans.), Vintage, New York.

Lewis, Alison 2003a, 'Reading and writing the Stasi file: on the uses and abuses of the file as (auto)biography', *German Life and Letters* 61, pp. 377–97.

— 2003b *Die Kunst des Verrats: Der Prenzlauer Berg und die Staatssicherheit*, Königshausen und Neumann Verlag, Würzburg.

Lexikon des internationalen Films 2000/2001, Net World Vision, Munich.

Lindenberger, Thomas 2008, 'Stasiploitation – why not? The scriptwriter's historical creativity', *German Studies Review* 31, pp. 557–66.

Lutze, Peter C. 1998, *Alexander Kluge: The last modernist*, Wayne State University Press, Detroit.

Lyons, James K. 1994, '*Mann ist Mann* and the death of tragedy in the 20th Century', *German Quarterly* 67/4 (Autumn), pp. 513–20.

Maischberger, Sandra (1999), 'Sonnenallee – Eine Mauerkomödie: Interview mit Leander Haußmann und Thomas Brussig', in Leander Haußmann (ed.), *Sonnenallee: Das Buch zum Farbfilm*, Berlin, Quadriga, pp. 8–24.

Malkin, Lawrence 2006, *Krueger's Men: The secret Nazi counterfeit plot and the prisoners of Block 19*, Back Bay Books, New York.

Mandelbaum, Jacques 2009, 'Christian Petzold: "Je pèse mes mots en disant qu'on nous a profondément haïs"', *Le Monde*, 22 April, http://www.lemonde.fr/cinema/article/2009/04/21/christian-petzold-je-pese-mes-mots-on-nous-a-profondement-hais_1183418_3476.html.

Manovich, Lev 2001, *The Language of New Media*, MIT Press, Cambridge, MA.

Marktdaten, Filmhitlisten, German Federal Film Board (Filmförderungsanstalt/ FFA), www.ffa.de.

McCormick, Patrick 2001, 'Who's afraid of women in leading roles?', *US Catholic*, June, pp. 46–48.

McCormick, Richard W. and Alison Guenther-Pal 2004, *German Essays on Film*, Continuum, New York.

Mercer, Kobena 1990, 'Black art and the burden of representation', *Third Text* 4/10, pp. 61–78.

Metz, Christian 2000, 'The imaginary signifier', in Robert Stam and Toby Miller (eds), *Film and Theory: An anthology*, Blackwell, Oxford, pp. 408–36.

Michael, Klaus 1995, 'Alternativkultur und Staatssicherheit 1976–1989', in Deutscher Bundestag (ed.), *Materialien der Enquete Kommission, Aufarbeitung von Geschichte und Folgen der SED-Diktatur in Deutschland:* III/3, nomos Verlag, Baden-Baden, pp. 1636–75.

Mitchell, Charles P. 2002, *The Hitler Filmography: Worldwide feature film and television miniseries portrayals, 1940 through 2000*, Mcfarland & Company, Jefferson, NC.

Mitchell, Wendy 2006, 'Going to extremes: Fatih Akin on his German-Turkish love story *Head-On*', http://www.indiewire.com/people/people_050119akin.html.

Möbius, Hanno 1991, *Versuche über den Essayfilm: Filme von Chris Marker, Alexander Kluge, Hartmut Bitomsky, Harun Farocki, Ioris Ivens, Derek Jarman, Johan van der Keuken*, Institute für neuere dt. Literatur, Marburg.

Mohr, Reinhard 1992, *Zaungäste: Die Generation, die nach der Revolte kam*, Fischer, Frankfurt am Main.

Moorti, Sujat 2003, 'Desperately seeking an identity: diasporic cinema and the articulation of transnational kinship', *International Journal of Cultural Studies* 6/3, pp. 355–76.

Morin, Edgar, 2005, *The Stars*, University of Minnesota Press, Minneapolis.

Morley, David 2000, *Home Territories: Media, mobility and identity*, Routledge, London and New York.

Morrison, Richard 2000, 'In this terrible place, an Ode to Joy', *Times*, 9 May, pp. 18–19.

Moser, Tilmann 1976, *Gottesvergiftung*, Suhrkamp, Frankfurt am Main.

Müller, Haro and Jan Mieszkowski 1996, 'Identity, paradox, difference: conceptions of time in the literature of modernity', *MLN* 111/3 (April) pp. 523–32.

Neale, Steve 1980, *Genre*, BFI, London.

— 2002, 'Art Cinema as Institution', in Catherine Fowler (ed.), *The European Cinema Reader*, Routledge, London, pp. 103–21.

Negt, Oskar 1994, *Unbotmässige Zeitgenossen: Annäherungen und Erinnerungen*, Fischer, Frankfurt am Main.

Negt, Oskar and Alexander Kluge 1981, *Geschichte und Eigensinn*, Suhrkamp, Frankfurt am Main.

— 1993, *Deutschland als Produktionsöffentlichkeit*, Suhrkamp, Frankfurt am Main.

— 1997, 'Public sphere and experience: selections', Peter Labanyi (trans.), in Rosalind Krauss et al. (eds), *October: The second decade 1986–96*, MIT Press, Cambridge, MA, pp. 225–47.

Nicodemus, Katja 2004a, 'Ankunft in der Wirklichkeit: Mit Fatih Akins "Gegen die Wand" siegt das das deutsche Kino über die deutschen Träume von einer Leitkultur', *Zeit*, 19 February, http://www.zeit.de/2004/09/ Berlinale-Abschluss.

— 2004b, 'Westdeutsche Provinzler, mit sich selbst beschaeftigt', *Zeit*, 9 September.

No author 2005, '"Ich bin in manchen Dingen nicht hart genug" Wäre er nicht ein guter Bundespräsident geworden? Es sollte nicht sein', *Tagesspiegel*, 17 May, http://tagesspiegel.de/zeitung/Sonntag;art2566, 2088945.

No author 2007, 'Keinen Plan von der DDR', *Spiegel*, 22 November, http:// www.spiegel.de/schulspiegel/0,1518,518913,00.html.

Nord, Cristina 2004, *'Keine Heimat'*, *Tageszeitung*, 10 September.

Nyiszli, Miklos 1993 (1960), *Auschwitz: A doctor's eyewitness account*, Arcade, New York.

Orr, John 1993, *Cinema and Modernity*, Blackwell, Cambridge.

'Outsider Inbox' 2010, *Outsider* 6, http://outsider.lu/?q=node/40#04.

Palfreyman, Rachel 2000, *Edgar Reitz's* Heimat: *Histories, traditions, fictions*, Peter Lang, Oxford.

— 2006, 'The fourth generation: legacies of violence as quest for identity in post-unification terrorism films', in David Clarke (ed.), *German Cinema since Unification*, Continuum, London, pp. 11–42.

— 2010, 'Links and chains: trauma between the generations in the Heimat Mode', in Paul Cooke and Marc Silberman (eds), *Screening War: Perspectives on German Suffering*, Camden House, Rochester, NY, pp. 145–65.

Peitz, Christiane and Esther Kogelbloom, *Tagesspiegel*, 31 August.

Perz, Bertrand 2002, 'Österreich', in Volkhard Knigge and Norbert Frei (eds), *Verbrechen erinnern: Die Auseinandersetzung mit Holocaust und Völkermord*, Beck, Munich, pp. 150–62.

— 2006, *Die KZ-Gedenkstätte Mauthausen: 1945 bis zur Gegenwart*, Studien Verlag, Innsbruck, Vienna and Bolzano.

Peter, Joachim and Thorsten Jungholt 2009, 'Die große Sehnsucht nach der guten, alten DDR', *Welt*, 30 March, http://www.welt.de/politik/article 3472551/Die-grosse-Sehnsucht-nach-der-guten-alten-DDR.html.

Peterson, Thane 2003, 'Aging women: movies' golden oldies', *Businessweek* online, http://www.businessweek.com.

Petzold, Christian 2001, 'Nach dem Schiffbruch', interview with Christiane Peitz, *Tagesspiegel*, 25 January.

— 2002, 'Die Musik muss anschaffen gehen', interview with Christian Buss, *Tageszeitung*, 28 May.

— 2007, 'Wracks mit reicher Geschichte: Der Regisseur Christian Petzold über seinen neuen Film "Yella"', *Stuttgarter Zeitung*, 5 September.

— 2008, 'The cinema of identification gets on my nerves: an interview with Christian Petzold', interview with Marco Abel, *Cineaste* 33/3, http:// www.cineaste.com/articles/an-interview-with-christian-petzold.htm.

— 2009, 'Wiederaufstehung in der Prignitz: Christian Petzold über Seelandschaften und seinen neuen Film "Jerichow"', interview with Peter Uehling, *Berliner Zeitung*, 8 January.

Petzold, Christian and Harun Farocki 2002b, 'Wie das Politbüro die Verhältnisse im deutschen Film zum Tanzen brachte', interview with Michael Althen and Bert Rebhandl, *Frankfurter Allgemeine Zeitung*, 23 May.

Plant, Sadie 1992, *The Most Radical Gesture: The Situationist International in a postmodern age*, Routledge, London.

Plowman, Andrew 2003, 'FRG Identities: Constructing West German identity in The Age of Globalisation', in Stuart Taberner (ed.), *German Literature in the age of globalisation*, University of Birmingham Press, Birmingham, pp. 47–66.

Politycki, Matthias 1998, 'Endlich aufgetaucht: Die 78er Generation', in *Die Farbe der Vokale*, Luchterhand, Munich, pp. 19–22.

Pollmanns, Marion 2006, *Didaktik und Eigensinn zu Alexander Kluges Praxis und Theorie der Vermittlung*, Büchse der Pandora, Wetzlar.

Prager, Brad 2006, 'The haunted screen (again): the historical unconscious of contemporary German thrillers', in Laurel Cohen-Pfister and Dagmar Wienroder-Skinner (eds), *Victims and Perpetrators: 1933–1945 and beyond: (re)presenting the past in post-unification culture*, Walter de Gruyter, Berlin, pp. 296–315.

— 2010, 'Suffering and sympathy in Volker Schlöndorff's *Der neunte Tag* and Dennis Gansel's *NaPolA*', in Paul Cooke and Marc Silberman (eds), *Screening War: Perspectives on German suffering*, Camden House, Rochester, NY, pp. 187–206.

Preusser, Heinz-Peter 2007, 'Eine romantische Synthese und ihr notwendiges Scheitern: Edgar Reitz' filmische Chronik *Heimat 1–3*', *Seminar* 43/2, May.

Radow, Dieter 2007, 'Die innere Wiedervereinigung', *Frankfurter Allgemeine Zeitung*, 12 April.

Rall, Veronika 2002, *Mein Stern*, review, *EPD Film*, January, p. 38.

Rancière, Jacques 2004, *The Politics of Aesthetics*, Gabriel Rockhill (trans.), Continuum, London, pp. 7–45.

Rebhandl, Bert 2006, 'Realismus des Wünschens', *Spiegel*, 7 September, http://www.spiegel.de/kultur/kino/0,1518,435454,00.html.

Rees, Jasper 2005, 'My part in his downfall', *Sunday Times*, 20 March.

Reimer, Robert and Carol Reimer 1992, *Nazi-Retro Film: How German narrative cinema remembers the past*, Twayne, New York.

Reinecke, Stefan 2002, 'Das RAF-Gespenst', *Tageszeitung*, 5 September.

— 2008, 'Der Baader Meinhof Komplex', *EPD Film*, 25 September.

Rentschler, Eric 1996, *The Ministry of Illusion: Nazi cinema and its afterlife*, Harvard University Press, Cambridge, MA.

— 2000, 'From New German Cinema to the post-wall cinema of consensus', in Mette Hjort and Scott Mckenzie (eds), *Cinema and Nation*, Routledge, London and New York, pp. 260–77.

— 2002, 'Postwall prospects: an introduction', *New German Critique* 87, pp. 3–5.

— 2008, 'A cinema of citation: Eric Rentschler on the films of Alexander Kluge', *Artforum International*, 1 September, pp. 1–13.

Rohnke, Cathy 2006, 'The school that isn't one: reflections on the "Berlin School"', http://www.goethe.de/kue/flm/thm/idd/en1932607.htm.

Rohrbach, Günter 2007, 'Das Schmollen der Autisten', *Spiegel*, 22 January, pp. 156–57.

Rosenstone, Robert 2006, *History on Film/Film on History*, Longman, New York.

Rössling, Ingo 2006, 'Film und Diskussion: Enkel von Stasi-Opfer zeigt Flagge', *Die Welt*, 29 March.

Rothberg, Michael 2000, *Traumatic Realism: The demands of Holocaust representation*, University of Minnesota Press, Minneapolis and London.

Rupprecht, Annette Maria 2006, 'Florian Henckel von Donnersmarck: XXL', *German Films Quarterly*, http://www.german-films.de/en/germanfilmsquarterly/ seriesgermandirectors/florianhenckelvondonnersmarck/index.html.

Rushdie, Salman 1991, *Imaginary Homelands: Essays and criticism, 1981–1991* Granta, New York.

Russo, Mary 1999, 'Aging and the scandal of anachronism', in Kathleen Woodward (ed.), *Figuring Age: Women, bodies, generations*, Indiana University Press, Bloomington, pp. 20–33.

Rutschky, Michael 1980, *Erfahrungshunger: Ein Essay über die siebziger Jahre*, Kiepenheur & Witsch, Cologne.

Ruzowitzky, Stefan 2007, 'Kino interview: "Ich mag grosses Gefühlskino"', *Zitty Berlin*, 21 March, http://www.zitty.de/kultur-kino/2146/.

— 2008, 'The director interviews: Stefan Ruzowitzky, *The Counterfeiters*', *Filmmaker*, 22 February, http://filmmakermagazine.com/directorinterviews/ 2008/02/stefan-ruzowitzky-counterfeiters.php.

Sanyal, Debarati 2002, 'A soccer match in Auschwitz: passing culpability in Holocaust criticism', *Representations* 79, pp. 1–27.

Schäfer, Annette 2001, 'Gespräch mit Andres Veiel', *Black Box BRD Official Website,* http://www.black-box-brd.de/interview.html.

Schirrmacher, Frank 2008, 'Diese Frau brauchte mich ganz', *Frankfurter Allgemeinen Sonntagszeitung*, 14 September.

Schlömer, Thomas 2004, 'Der Führer ist der Führer', http://www.filmspiegel. de.filme.untergangder/untergangder_1.php.

Schlöndorff, Volker 2004, 'Volker Schlöndorff: "Das Thema Holocaust darf man nicht Spielberg allein überlassen"', interview with Christian Buss, *Chrismon: Das evangelische Magazin* (August).

Schlüpmann, Heide and Jamie Owen Daniel 1988 '"What is different is good": Women and Femininity in the Films of Alexander Kluge', *October* 46, pp. 129–50.

Schmitz, Stefan 2008, 'Das letzte Gefecht der RAF', *Stern*, 20 November, http://www.stern.de/kultur/film/der-baader-meinhof-komplex-das-letzte-gefecht-der-raf-639429.html.

Schneider, Jörg 2003, 'Die RAF-Inflation: "Wie ie Rote Armee Fraktion", kurz nach ihre Auflösung, zu einem Pop-Phänomen stilisiert wird', *Frankfurter Rundschau*, 31 July.

Schnibben, Cordt 1994, 'Eine heikle Zielgruppe', *Der Spiegel* 38, pp. 58–63.

Scholl, Inge 1979, *Die weiße Rose*, Fischer, Frankfurt am Main.

Schulte, Christian and Winfried Siebers 2002, *Kluges Fernsehen: Alexander Kluges Kulturmagazine*, Suhrkamp, Frankfurt am Main.

Schulz-Ojala, Jan 2004, 'Wiedersehen in Schabbach: Edgar Reitz praesentiert bei den Filmfestspielen Venedig den Abschluss seiner *Heimat*-Trilogie', *Tagesspiegel*, 5 September.

— 2007, 'Willkommen in der Geisterbahn', *Tagesspiegel*.

— 2008, 'Extrem laut und unglaublich fern', *Tagesspiegel*, 18 September.

Schweitzer, Eva 2007, 'Die "Anderen" und Amerika', *Berliner Zeitung*, 21 February.

Schweizerhof, Barbara 2004, 'Der Mann mit dem Schnurrbart', *Freitag*, 10 September.

Schwingel, Ralph 2007, 'Moving Turkish-German cinema into the mainstream: the producer's perspective', conference presentation, 'The Industrial Context of Migrant and Diasporic Cinema in Contemporary Europe', 13 January, http://www.migrantcinema.net/podcasts/.

Scott, A.O. 2005, 'Movie review *Downfall*: the last days of Hitler: raving and ravioli', *New York Times*, 18 February.

Seegers, Lu 2008, 'Das Leben der Anderen oder der "richtige" Erinnerung an die DDR', in Astrid Erll and Stephanie Wodianka (eds), *Film und kulturelle Erinnerung: Plurimediale Konstellationen*, Walter de Gruyter, Berlin, pp. 21–52.

Seibt, Gustav 2004, 'Hitler-Verfilmung *Der Untergang:* Eine unangenehme Person', *Süddeutsche Zeitung*, 9 September.

Seidel, Hans-Dieter 2004, 'Und das hat mit ihren Filmen die Loreley getan: Das schwere Erbe eines deutschen Epos: Wehmuetiger Blick auf *Heimat 3 – Chronik einer Zeitenwende* von Edgar Reitz', *Frankfurter Allgemeine Zeitung*, 1 October.

Sicinski, Michael 2009, 'Once the Wall had tumbled: Christian Petzold's *Jerichow*', *Cinema Scope* 38 (Spring), http://www.cinema-scope.com/cs38/feat_sicinski_jerichow.html.

Siegel, Marion 2008, 'Sex im Alter kein Tabu mehr: Das Liebesleben von Senioren im Fokus der Medien', *Generation 50-Plus*, 3 November, http://generation-50-plus.suite101.de/article.cfm/sex_im_alter_kein_tabu_mehr.

— 2009, 'Senioren im Film: Wie das Alter im Kino thematisiert wird', *Generation 50-Plus*, 12 June, http://generation-50plus.suite101.de/article.cfm/senioren_im_film.

Sinka, Margit 2000, 'Tom Tykwer's *Lola rennt*: a blueprint of millennial Berlin', *Glossen* 11, http://www.dickinson.edu/glossen/heft11/lola.html.

Skidmore, James 2002, 'Intellectualism and emotionalism in Margarethe von Trotta's *Die bleierne Zeit*', *German Studies Review* 25/3, pp. 551–67.

Sombroek, Andreas 2005, *Eine Poetik des Dazwischen: zur Intmedialität und Intertextualität bei Alexander Kluge*, transcript, Bielefeld.

Sontag, Susan 1975, 'Fascinating Fascism', *New York Review of Books*, 6 February.

Sorlin, Pierre 2001, 'How to look at an "historical film"', in Marcia Landy (ed.), *The Historical Film: History and memory in media*, Rutgers University Press, New Brunswick, pp. 25–49.

Soyez, Alexander 2006, 'Der Teufel im Detail: Hans-Christian Schmid über seinen presigekrönten Exorzismus-Film "Requiem"', *Berliner Morgenpost*, 5 March, p. 22.

Spiegel 2008, 'Promiandrang bei der Premiere', 16 September.

Stam, Robert 2003, 'Beyond Third Cinema: the aesthetics of hybridity', in Anthony Guneratne and Wimal Dissanayake (eds), *Rethinking Third Cinema*, Routledge, London and New York, pp. 31–48.

Stanitzek, Georg 1998, 'Autorität im Hypertext: "Der Kommentar ist die Grundform der Texte" (Alexander Kluge)', *Internationales Archiv für Sozialgeschichte der deutschen Literatur* 23/2, pp. 1–46.

Stecher, Thorsten 1999, 'Sexy DDR', *Die Weltwoche*, 18 November.

Stein, Mary Beth 2008, 'Stasi with a Human Face? Ambiguity in *Das Leben der Anderen*', *German Studies Review* 31, pp. 567–79.

Sterritt, David 2005, 'Hitler's fall: a German view', *Christian Science Monitor*, 18 February.

Stilwell, Robynn J. 2007, 'The fantastical gap between diegetic and nondiegetic', in Daniel Goldmark, Lawrence Kramer and Richard Leppert (eds), *Beyond the Soundtrack: Representing music in cinema*, University of California Press, Berkeley, pp. 184–202.

Sto 2008, 'Ponto-Witwe geht gerichtlich gegen RAF-Kinofilm vor', *Spiegel* online, 1 November, www.spiegel.de/kultur/kino/o,1518,587854,00.html.

Stokes, Martin 1992, *The Arabesk Debate: Music and musicians in modern Turkey*, Clarendon Press, Oxford.

Stollmann, Rainer 2005, *Die Entstehung des Schönheitssinns aus dem Eis: Gespräche über Geschichten mit Alexander Kluge*, Kadmos, Berlin.

Stone, Rob 2007, 'Between sunrise and sunset: an elliptical dialogue between American and European Cinema', in Paul Cooke (ed.), *World Cinema's 'Dialogues' with Hollywood*, Palgrave, Basingstoke, pp. 218–87.

Stuhlpfarrer, Karl 2002, 'Österreich', in Volkhard Knigge and Norbert Frei (eds), *Verbrechen erinnern: Die Auseinandersetzung mit Holocaust und Völkermord*, Beck, Munich, pp. 233–52.

Suchsland, Rüdiger 2006a, 'Die Fallen des Lebens', *Artechock Filmmagazin*, http://www.artechock.de/film/text/kritik/s/sehns2.htm.

— 2006b, 'Mundger konsumierbare Vergangenheit', *Teleopolis*, 23 March.

Tabori, George, 1974, *The Cannibals*, Davis-Poynter, London.

Thau, Eric 2007, 'All that melodrama allows: Sirk, Fassbinder, Almodóvar, Haynes', in Paul Cooke (ed.), *World Cinema's 'Dialogues' with Hollywood*, Palgrave, New York, pp. 188–200.

Thomson, David 2006, 'Ten films where the old do not go gentle', *Guardian*, 15 December, http://www.guardian.co.uk/film/filmblog/2006/dec/15/tenfilms wheretheolddonot.

Tilmann, Christina 2007, 'Wer ist Florian Henckel von Donnersmarck', *Tagesspeigel*, 25 February.

Toplin, Robert Brent 2002, *Reel History: In defense of Hollywood*, University of Kansas Press, Lawrence.

Tykwer, Tom 2006, 'New mix new rules', *Sight and Sound* 16/12, pp. 28–31.

Uecker, Matthias 2000, *Anti-Fernsehen? Alexander Kluges Fernsehproduktionen*, Schüren, Marburg.

Vahabzadeh, Susan 2009, 'Was heißt schon Favorit?', *Süddeutsche Zeitung*, 24 April.

Vaneigem, Raoul 1994, *The Revolution of Everyday Life*, Donald Nicholson-Smith, (trans.), 2nd revised edition, Rebel Press, London, first published 1967.

Varon, Jeremy 2004, *Bringing the War Home: The weather underground, the Red Army Faction, and revolutionary violence in the sixties and seventies*, University of California Press, Berkeley.

Vidler, Anthony 1992, *The Architectural Uncanny: Essays in the modern unhomely*, MIT Press, Cambridge, MA.

Vincendeau, Ginette 2000, 'Issues in European cinema', in John Hill and Pamela Church Gibson (eds), *World Cinema: Critical approaches*, OUP, Oxford, pp. 56–65.

von Moltke, Johannes 2002, 'Heimat and history: *Viehjud Levi*', *New German Critique* 87, special issue on Postwall cinema, pp. 83–105.

— 2005, *No Place Like Home: Locations of Heimat in German Cinema*, University of California Press, Berkeley and Los Angeles.

— 2007, 'Sympathy for the devil: cinema, history and the politics of emotion', *New German Critique* 34, pp. 17–43.

— 2010, 'Terrains vagues: landscapes of unification in Oskar Roehler's *No Place to Go*', in Jaimey Fisher and Brad Prager (eds), *The Collapse of the Conventional: German film and its politics at the turn of the twenty-first century*, Wayne State University, Detroit, pp. 157–85.

Weingarten, Susanne 1997, 'Was nun, Jan?', *Spiegel* 12, pp. 216–17.

Weiss, Peter 1965, *The Investigation*, Calder and Boyars, London.

Welter, J. 2005, '*Sophie Scholl: Die letzen Tage*', *Die Zeit*, 14 February.

Wenders, Wim 2004, 'Tja, dann wollen wir mal', *Die Zeit* 44, 21 October.

Werber, Niels (n.d.), *Vom Glück im Kampf: Krieg und Terror in der Popkultur*, http://homepage.ruhr-uni-bochum.de/niels.werber/Antrittsvorlesung.htm.

Wickham, Christopher J. 1991, 'Representation and mediation in Edgar Reitz's *Heimat*', *German Quarterly* 64/1, pp. 35–45.

Wilke, Manfred 2008, 'Fiktion oder erlebte Geschichte? Zur Frage der Glaubwürdigkeit des Films *Das Leben der Anderen*', *German Studies Review* 31, pp. 589–98.

Williams, Linda 2003, 'Film bodies: gender, genre, and excess', in Barry Keith Grant (ed.), *Film Genre Reader*, vol. III, University of Texas, Austin, pp. 141–59.

Wilson, V. 2005, '*Sophie Scholl: The Final Days*', *Sight & Sound* 15/11, p. 80.

Wolff, Uwe 1999, *Das bricht dem Bischof das Kreuz: Die letzte Teufelsaustreibung in Deutschland 1975/1976*, Rowohlt, Reinbek bei Hamburg.

Wolke 9, press material, Senator Film, 2008.

Wood, Mary P. 2007, *Contemporary European Cinema*, Hodder Arnold, London.

Worthmann, Mertin 2001, 'Mit Vorsicht Genießen', *Die Zeit*, 27 September, p. 40.

Yahnke, Robert E. 2005, 'Heroes of their own stories', *Gerontology and Geriatrics Education* 26/1, pp. 57–76.

Zaimoğlu, Feridun 2004, 'Lebenswut, Herzhitze', *Der Tagesspiegel*, 10 March, http://www.tagesspiegel.de/kultur/lebenswut-herzhitze/497810.html.

Zander, Peter 2006, 'Im Ausland wird man immer zuerst auf Nazis angesprochen: Das nervt', *Die Welt*, 21 March.

INDEX

For film titles, see Index of Films on p. 307

| INDEX |